Medieval Callings

Medieval Callings

Edited by

Jacques Le Goff

Translated by Lydia G. Cochrane

The University of Chicago Press

Originally published as *L'uomo medievale,*

THE UNIVERSITY OF CHICAGO PRESS, CHICAGO 60637

Paperback edition 1996
Printed in the United States of America
99 98 97 96 5432

∞ The paper used in this publication meets the minimum requirements of the American National Standard for Information Sciences—Permanence of Paper for Printed Library Materials, ANSI Z39.48-1984.

Library of Congress Cataloging-in-Publication Data

Uomo medievale. English.
Medieval callings / edited by Jacques Le Goff ; translated by Lydia G. Cochrane.
p. cm.
Translation of: L'Uomo medievale.
Includes bibliographical references.
ISBN 0-226-47086-5 (alk. paper)
1. Civilization, Medieval. 2. Occupations—History. 3. Professions—History. I. Le Goff, Jacques, 1924– II. Title.
CB351.U5913 1990
909.07—dc20 89-28998
CIP

Contents

Translator's Note

Avoidance of gender-marked terminology is nearly impossible in general discussion of the Middle Ages, a time when all society—men and women alike—seems to have spoken and written in a language of male dominance. For that reason, but also for fear of misrepresenting the thoughts of some of the authors of these essays—the book was entitled *Medieval Man* in its Italian edition—this translation contains unabashed use of the term "men."

The Middle Ages were also a time in which the spelling of names varied enormously. Nearly all the names that appear in this work have been verified in one reference work or another, and names that do not appear in the index under one element should be searched under the other.

The translator and the University of Chicago Press would like to thank the authors who took the trouble to read the translation of their essays, to respond to queries, and to make corrections and suggestions. The essays originally written in French have been translated from the French, and Piotr Górecki deserves many thanks for a careful comparison of the translation of Bronislaw Geremek's essay with the Polish original.

The University of Chicago Press would like to thank Daniel Bornstein for contributing the supplementary readings that follow the bibliographies provided by the author given at the end of each chapter.

Introduction
Medieval Man

Jacques Le Goff

This presentation of medieval man offers ten profiles written by ten of today's leading medievalists. But did such a man ever exist? Might he be an abstraction remote from historical reality?

The definition of a "human" history—the only history worthy of the name—was given half a century ago by Marc Bloch and Lucien Febvre. It was an inalienable acquisition. But was that "human" history the history of *man* or the history of *men?* Lucien Febvre offered an answer: "Man, the measure of history, its unique measure. Even more, its reason for being." Febvre went on to declare, however:

> Men, the only object of history—of a history that is not interested in who knows what eternal, abstract man, profoundly immutable and perpetually identical to himself, but in men, taken always within the framework of the societies to which they belonged; in men [who were] members of those societies in a clearly defined period in the society's development; men gifted with multiple functions, diverse activities, varied preoccupations and attitudes, all of which mix together, collide, contradict one another, and end up agreeing on a peaceful compromise, a *modus vivendi* that is called Life.[1]

Man and men, men in the society of the Christian West in their principal functions—that is, in their essence, but also in the concrete reality of their social status, their trade, their profession—in the age of a medieval diptych whose first panel shows the prodigious development of Christianity between the year 1000 and the thirteenth century and whose second panel shows that turbid time called the later Middle Ages, when a world of the past in crisis and a new Middle Ages, the Renaissance, whirled in tandem. But also living people in their social situation, with their beliefs and their practices. Such is the subject of this book.

Man or Men?

Most of the authors of these profiles have emphasized diversity in the type of medieval men that they present. Giovanni Miccoli has even preferred to speak of "monks" rather than "the monk." Indeed, there was a world of difference between the monks of Provence (Lérins, Saint-Victor of Marseilles) of the fourth and fifth centuries, who took inspiration from the eastern model of the Fathers of the desert, and the Cluniac monks of the tenth century and beyond; between the Irish monks of the seventh and eighth centuries and the Cistercians of the twelfth century; between St. Benedict and Joachim of Fiore.

1. Lucien Febvre, *Combats pour l'histoire* (Paris: A. Colin, 1953), pp. 103 and 20–21.

Solitude or apostolic mission; manual work or intellectual labor; service of God in prayer and in the liturgical functions or service of Christianity in the military orders of soldier monks that rose out of the crusades; the hermit's life or the cloister: how many options there were! Nonetheless, men of the Middle Ages were conscious of a particular type and a collective personage, the monk; the person who, on an individual or collective basis, separated from the rest of society in order to live in a privileged relationship with God. Or, following one of the many medieval definitions of the monk: *Is qui luget:* "he who weeps," who wept for his own sins and for the sins of humanity and who sought, with a life of prayer, meditation, and penance, to obtain personal salvation and the salvation of all humankind.

Jacques Rossiaud, taking up the problem of the "city-dweller," asks, "What did the beggar and the burgher, the canon and the prostitute"—all city-dwellers—"have in common? Or the inhabitants of Florence and of Montbrison? Or the new townspeople of the first growth of cities and their descendants of the fifteenth-century?" He offers an immediate answer: "They could not possibly have been unaware of one another. They were integrated into the same small, densely populated universe, and it imposed forms of sociability unknown in the village, a specific way of living, daily familiarity with money, and, for some, an obligatory opening onto the world at large." Obviously, the medieval city-dweller existed in contrast to the peasant, a contrast that is much attenuated and totally different today.

From the broad diversity of the female condition in the Middle Ages Christiane Klapisch-Zuber has chosen a direction and a point of view: the woman strictly defined by her position and her functions in the bosom of the family. And Klapisch-Zuber has found, beneath the multiple social levels of families and a slow and often hindered improvement in the status of women during the five centuries with which this volume is concerned, the way was always barred by an underlying medieval ideology that saw woman as a deceitful being, a temptress, the Devil's handmaid, an eternal Eve only partially compensated by Mary, a being who required close surveillance, but who was a necessary evil for the existence and the continuing wellbeing of the family, for procreation, and for the control of one of the major dangers for Christian man, sexuality.

To cite a final example of diversity, Enrico Castelnuovo asks how we can discern—from the twelfth-century goldsmith to the architect, the sculptor, and the designer of Gothic stained-glass windows; from the miniaturist to Giotto—the expression and the awareness of an emerging personage, later to be known as an artist, on the part of both the creative artist himself and the society for which and within which he created.

Medieval Man

But to return to man: did the men of the Middle Ages themselves recognize a reality that one might call "man"? Did they discern, in the heterogeneous society in which they lived, a model that could be adapted to both the king and the beggar, to the monk and the jongleur, to the merchant and the peasant, to rich and poor, and, to speak in terms of gender, to both woman and man?

The answer is certainly affirmative, and it should even be emphasized that few epochs have had a stronger sense than the Western and Christian Middle Ages of the eleventh to the fifteenth centuries of the universal and eternal existence of a human model. In this society dominated by and imbued with religion to its innermost fiber, this model was of course defined religiously and, first and foremost, by the highest expression of religious knowledge, theology. If there was a human type who had no place in the panorama of medieval man it was precisely the profound unbeliever, the person who would later be called a libertine, a freethinker, or an atheist. At least to the thirteenth century and even up to the end of what we choose to call the Middle Ages, we find only an insignificant number of people who denied the existence of God. For most of these rare instances, one might well ask whether they do not involve faulty readings of the texts or extrapolations on the part of others who repeated the words of these isolated mavericks on the basis of verbal excesses born of a moment of rage or, for some intellectuals, of a moment of conceptual inebriation. Although men of the Middle Ages often repeated the verse of the Psalms—the illiterate's primer—"The fool hath said in his heart: 'There is no God' " (Ps 13:1), the quotation should be understood as one of the many mysterious and incomprehensible expressions of a sacred text. For the clergy it was a convenient point of departure, imbued with scriptural authority, for reiterating the proofs of the existence of God. But the unbeliever (who could be found among the "others"—the Jew, the infidel, the pagan) was such an infrequent and dubious figure in the Middle Ages that he does not even appear in the gallery of marginal figures presented by Bronislaw Geremek.

What was man, then, in medieval Christian anthropology? He was God's creature. Nature, history, and man's destiny were taught from the Book of Genesis, which begins the Old Testament. On the sixth day of creation God made man and explicitly granted him dominion over nature, which meant the flora and fauna that were to nourish him. Medieval man thus had a vocation to be the master of a desacralized nature; of the earth and of the animals. But Adam committed sin at the instigation of Eve (who was in turn led astray by the serpent—that is, by evil). From that point on he was inhabited by two beings, one made "in the image of God" and the other, because he had committed the original sin, driven from the earthly paradise and condemned to suffering, in the specific forms of manual labor for the man and the pangs of childbirth for the woman, to shame, symbolized by the taboo applied to exposed sexual organs, and to death.

Medieval Christianity emphasized either the positive image of man as a divine being, created by God in his own image, associated with this creation because Adam named the animals, and called to regain the paradise that he had lost by his own fault; or else it emphasized man's negative image as sinner, ever ready to succumb to temptation, to deny God, and therefore to lose paradise forever and fall into eternal death.

This pessimistic image of man as weak, riddled with vice, and humbled before God persists throughout the Middle Ages, but it is more accentuated during the early Middle Ages in the fourth to the ninth centuries, and again in the eleventh and twelfth centuries. The optimistic image of man as a reflection of the divine image, capable of continuing creation on the earth and of saving himself, tended to predominate from the twelfth and thirteenth centuries on.

The view that Adam was condemned to toil, presented in the Book of Genesis, dominated the anthropology of the Middle Ages, but there were competing conceptions of labor and of the working man. One saw work as a curse and a penance; the other emphasized its potential as a means for an atonement that led to salvation. In her study of the sculpture of Wiligelmo on the facade of the Cathedral of Modena (c. 1100), Chiara Frugoni has pinpointed the moment when the pessimistic humanism of the early Middle Ages seemed ready to tip toward an optimistic humanism in which the image of an Adam capable of creative work was overtaking that of an Adam crushed by toil as chastisement and malediction.[2]

2. Chiara Frugoni, "Le lustre veterotestamentarie e il programma della facciata," in Marina Armandi et al., *Lafranco e Wiligelmo. Il Duomo di Modena* (Modena: Panini, 1984), pp. 422–51.

In the early Middle Ages the biblical model that perhaps best incarnated the image of man was Job. Fascination for this Old Testament figure was all the greater since a commentary on the Book of Job—the *Moralia in Job* of Pope Gregory the Great (590–604)—was one of the books most read, most utilized, and most widely popularized by the clergy. Job was the man who must accept the will of God without seeking explanations other than divine pleasure. He was in fact less sinful than other men: "That man was simple and upright, and fearing God, and avoiding evil" (Job 1:1). Overwhelmed by God's trials, Job long fails to understand, stating that his days "have passed more swiftly than the web is cut by the weaver, and are consumed without hope" and that his life "is but wind." Finally, he renounces all pride and all claims on God. As his friend says: "Can man be justified compared with God, or he that is born of a woman appear clean? Behold even the moon doth not shine, and the stars are not pure in his sight. How much less is man that is rottenness, and the son of man who is a worm!" (Job 25:4–6).

Medieval iconography, which reveals collective imagination but which also formed it, usually concentrates on the episodes of Job's story that show his humiliation before God. The most frequent image is that of Job sitting on his dunghill consumed by "a very grievous ulcer." Medieval painting portrayed Job as the wreckage of a man—as a leper.

From the late thirteenth century on, however, art portrayed man with the "realistic" traits of the mighty of this earth: pope, emperor, king, prelate, great lord, rich burgher; self-confident men proud of themselves and displaying their success; handsome when possible, but, when this was out of the question, forcing admiration for their singularity, hence even more imposing when they were ugly.

The man of suffering was no longer man, but God himself: Jesus. Latin Christianity made an important choice in the Carolingian epoch. It chose images, rejecting the nonfigurative art of the Jews and the Moslems and the iconoclasm of Greek Byzantine Christianity and firmly establishing medieval Christian anthropomorphism.[3] Relations between man and a God who appeared to him, whom he could represent in human guise, were deeply marked by this choice. A God, what is more, that, although one, was three. Although the Holy Spirit, figured through animal symbolism as a dove, escaped anthro-

3. François Boespflug and Nicolas Lossky, eds., *Nicée II, 787–1987, Douze siècles d'images religieuses* (Paris: Editions du Cerf, 1987).

pomorphism, the first two persons of the Trinity played on complementary oppositions such as old age and youth, royal power and the Passion, divinity and humanity. As Giovanni Miccoli and André Vauchez show in these pages, beginning in the twelfth and thirteenth centuries, Jesus was increasingly the Christ of the Passion, the Flagellation, the Way of the Cross, the Crucifixion, and the Pietà. In a striking reversal of images, suffering man par excellence was now the Christ, the God of the Incarnation. The image that emerges in the fifteenth century was that of Jesus draped in the purple robe and wearing the crown of thorns that symbolized derision, Jesus as Pontius Pilate displayed him to the crowd, proclaiming, according to the Gospel of John, *Ecce homo:* Behold the man. This man of an exceptional moment in human history was henceforth the symbolic figure for all men—suffering, humiliated, but divine. The great historical mystery, which theologians throughout the Middle Ages struggled to explain, was why God had accepted—even decided—to become man and to humiliate himself in Christ. *Cur Deus homo* (Why God was made man) is the title of one of the finest treatises of St. Anselm of Canterbury.

Man in medieval theology (or, in one perspective, in Christian mythology)[4] was not restricted to a face-to-face relationship with God. He was the prize in a contest that often surpassed him, the struggle of Satan, the spirit of evil, against God and against goodness. Christianity had of course rejected and condemned Manichaeism. Except in the thought of certain heretics (the Cathars, for example), there was not one God of goodness and another of evil: a God of the spirit and a God of matter. There was but one God, a God of goodness (who could, however, also be a God of wrath), who was superior to Satan, the leader of the vanquished rebel angels, but who had nevertheless left Satan extensive powers over man. It was up to man to use his own free will to accept or refuse saving grace and to resist or to cede to the sin that would lead to his damnation. Leaving aside his spiritual advocates, the Virgin and the saints (to whom I shall return), man's salvation or damnation was the stakes in a battle between supernatural armies of demons and angels standing poised to fight, ready to attack him or come to his rescue. Man's soul, their prize,

4. Jean-Claude Schmitt, "Christianisme et mythologie. Occident médiéval et 'pensée mythique'," in Yves Bonnefoy, ed., *Dictionnaire des mythologies et des religions des sociétés traditionnelles et du monde antique,* 2 vols. (Paris: Flammarion, 1981), 1:181–85 [*Mythologies,* trans. under the direction of Wendy Doniger (Chicago: University of Chicago Press, forthcoming)].

seems in some medieval authors to be the football in a hard-fought match between the diabolic team and the angelic team. Man's soul was also portrayed in the Middle Ages as a miniature person being weighed by St. Michael in the scales of judgment, under the watchful eyes of Satan, who waits for a chance to tip the beam to his side, and of St. Peter, poised to intervene on the side of good.

This Christian anthropology gave rise to two conceptions of man that tended, during the course of the Middle Ages, to become a veritable definition of man. The first of these was that of the *homo viator,* man the voyager, always traveling on this earth and through his lifespan—the ephemeral space and time of his destiny—where the choices that he made moved him toward eternal life or eternal death. Thus the monk, who was bound by vocation to the cloister, paradoxically often traveled the roads. In the thirteenth century the friars of the mendicant orders, first among them St. Francis of Assisi, were as often *in via* as they were in their friaries. Man of the Middle Ages was a pilgrim, by his nature and by vocation, and in the twelfth and thirteenth centuries he was a crusader, the highest and most perilous earthly form of pilgrim. Still, the pilgrim and the crusader have not been included among the types of medieval man presented here. We have eliminated the first because every man in the Middle Ages was a potential or symbolic pilgrim. Even if not all Christians made one of the three great medieval pilgrimages (to Jerusalem, to Rome, to Santiago de Compostela), there were innumerable other pilgrimages within a more restricted geographical range. As for the crusader, in spite of the dreams of crusades that persisted throughout the Middle Ages, crusaders were only a minority (albeit an extremely significant one) and they figured during only two of the centuries considered here.

The call of the road could also lead medieval man astray, since it could uproot him from the stability that was a condition for morality and safety. Pilgrimage could turn into errantry or vagabondage. Woe to the man *sans feu ni lieu* in the Middle Ages, particularly if he was a cleric. Wandering clerics and roving monks were among the worst incarnations of medieval man. They figure among Giovanni Miccoli's monks, and Bronislaw Geremek finds vagabond bands of clerics among his marginal figures.[5]

The second conception of man was as a penitent. Even if he was

5. Gerhart B. Ladner, "*Homo viator:* Mediaeval Ideas on Alienation and Order," *Speculum* 42 (1967): 235–59.

not a monk—the penitent par excellence—and even if he was not obsessed with the idea that work was penance, medieval man, conditioned by the notion of sin that had been inculcated in him, sought assurance of salvation in repentance. Even if he did not practice extreme forms of penance such as flagellation in private (like St. Louis, king of France) or in public (groups of flagellants were much in the news both in 1260, for example, and in 1349–50, after the first wave of the Black Death), medieval man was always prompt to respond to a calamity or a disturbing event by special penance. After the Fourth Lateran Council (1215) the obligation for all Christians to make auricular confession at least once a year and, consequently, to do the imposed penance, institutionalized the practice of penance and its performance on a regular basis.

The dogma and practice of medieval Christianity may have tended to make man a universal type recognizable in all social conditions, but he was a complex being. In the first place, he was constituted by the union of conflicting elements, the soul and the body. Much as medieval Christianity may have disdained the body, an "abominable garment for the soul" according to Gregory the Great, medieval man was forced, not only by his existential experience but also by the teaching of the church, to live with a coupled body and soul. Every part of the body, every corporeal mark, was a symbolic sign referring back to the soul. Salvation or damnation were carried out in both the body and the soul, or, more precisely, the soul fulfilled its destiny by means of the body. As Piero Camporesi has recently recalled, "the dogma of the resurrection in the body, 'the most startling sort of dogma' (Chesterton) intensified material sensations of pain and terror to an unbearable tension."[6] The bodies of saints, as André Vauchez reminds us, began the process of the resurrection of all bodies, and they gave off the famous "odor of sanctity."

The makeup of medieval man cannot be restricted to the paired body and soul—*corpus* and *anima*. There was also the spirit (*spiritus*), which introduced the breath of life and brought with it a broad range of meanings from the highest forms of classical and Christian philosophy to the almost material senses that the term assumed in the vernacular tongues, all of which, however, connected man with the third person of the Trinity.[7] There was also *cor*, the heart, lying some-

6. Piero Camporesi, *La casa dell'eternità* (Milan: Garzanti, 1987), p. 84.

7. M. Fattori and M. L. Bianchi, eds. *Spiritus, IV Colloquio internazionale del Lessico Intellettuale Europeo, Roma, 7–9 gennaio, 1983. Atti* (Rome: Edizioni dell'Ateneo, 1984).

where between the soul and the spirit, which took over inner feelings and attached itself to love and to an ever increasing range of sentiments. The heart was also opposed to the head, and it grew in prestige with the spread of the symbolism of the blood, for which it was the motor force.

Man also became a symbolic reference, both in his physical constitution and in his bodily organism. Beginning with the *Policraticus* of the Chartres humanist, John of Salisbury (1159), the human body served as a metaphorical image of society, with the king (or the pope) as its head and craftsmen and peasants as its feet. This was an affirmation of both the unity of the human organism and the solidarity of the body social. In some theological and philosophical schools man was a microcosm. In the naturalistic viewpoints that developed out of the philosophy of the Chartres school of the twelfth century, man thus acquired the new and positive image of a nature in miniature—a nature created by God, of course, and obedient to the laws God had given it, but through which man returned, on a "scientific" plane, to a central place and a plenitude from which he seemed to have fallen since the early Middle Ages.

Finally, in one way or another, medieval conceptions of man all integrated him into society. Thus they offer, *mutatis mutandis*, a point of convergence with modern historians, and in particular with the historians who have written the studies that make up the present book. Not one of these authors has conceived of or presented his profile of medieval man outside the society in which he lived. Thus Aron Gurevich, studying the conception of man in the thirteenth-century Franciscan preacher, Berthold von Regensburg, finds a conception of the person that integrates man's social nature: "the person cannot be reduced to the unity of soul and body because it includes the social function."

All the historians who have contributed to this volume have attempted—as was my intention as well—to describe and explain medieval man with the aid of realities in the economic, social, mental, and imaginal spheres whose structured union is what most historians today comprehend as history. They themselves are the heirs and the artificers of the two great sets of problems that have renewed the discipline of history in our century. The first of these is economic and social history, which is always the social base for explanation of the past; the second is the history of representations, since historians have realized that the way people represented reality has played an equally fundamental role in historical evolution. What we present here is medieval man in all his dimensions, including that of the collective imagination, which permits us at last to speak rationally (though not scientifically) about the social and mental typology of men of the past. What has made possible this documented and reasoned presentation of medieval man in ten profiles is the interchange (which has offered much to contemporary historiography) between medieval typologies and modern typologies. Only by combining the two can the historian present an image and an explanation of men of the past that avoids anachronism but that responds to both the questions posed by our own epoch and to advances in the science of history.

Human Types: From Paris to the Trifunctional Scheme The Monk, the Knight, the Peasant

When societies attempt to describe their own structures, they seek schemata that correspond to concrete social realities and that offer those who wish to conceptualize those societies or govern them adequate intellectual means for doing so.

Medieval society was, more than many others, a society of oppositions, and although it rejected doctrinal Manichaeism, it practiced a de facto Manichaeism by contrasting things as good or bad, or at least as superior or inferior.

Thus medieval Christianity often was represented in binary fashion and in antithetical pairings, the most general and the most important of which was the opposition of clerics to laymen,[8] a normal state of affairs in a society dominated by a religion with a clergy. Power was also an important dividing force, however. In the early Middle Ages power was expressed in the opposition *potens/pauper* (powerful/poor), replaced, after the thirteenth century, by the opposition rich/poor, which reflected the progress of a monetary economy and the promotion of wealth as the source or consequence of power.

Still, the realization that society was becoming more complex brought men of the Middle Ages to prefer schemes that were more fully articulated than a simple binary one. This offered an opportunity for better explanation of more complex social interplay. One of the most important of these schemes simply introduced the "middling" as an intermediate category between the great and the small: *maiores, mediocres, minores*. This scheme proved particularly pertinent in the early thirteenth century, when city burghers appeared, func-

8. Jacques Le Goff, "Chierico/laico," in *Enciclopedia Einaudi*, Ruggiero Romano, ed., 16 vols. (Turin: Einaudi, 1977), 2:1066–86.

tioning as *mediocres* between the aristocracy of the great laymen and churchmen and the mass of the peasants and city-dwellers lacking in importance.

The scheme that has met with the greatest success, both among the clerics of the age and among today's historians, is the trifunctional scheme that Georges Dumézil has seen as a fundamental structure in Indo-European culture. Dumézil recognizes a preponderant division of mental and institutional components at work in the spirit and institutions of societies that were the heirs of that culture. Three functions were necessary to the smooth operation of those societies:  magical and juridical sovereignty, physical force, and fecundity.[9] This scheme, which does not occur in the Bible, appeared in the Christian West in the ninth to tenth centuries. Introduced in a text written by Adalberon, bishop of Laon, in a poem addressed to King Robert the Pious around 1030 (*Carmen ad Rodbertum regem*), it soon became generally accepted. Adalberon distinguishes three components in Christian society: *oratores, bellatores,* and *laboratores*—those who pray, those who fight, and those who work. The scheme reflects the social situation immediately following the year 1000. First came the clergy, in particular the monks (and Bishop Adalberon recognizes their power with some bitterness). Their function was prayer, which connected them with the divine world and gave them the highest spiritual power on earth. Next come the warriors, and more particularly the new social stratum of horsemen who were to become a new nobility, the chivalric knighthood that protected the other two orders with its arms. Last came the working world, represented essentially by the peasants, whose juridico-social condition tended to become uniform and by whose labor the other two orders lived. The system provided an apparently harmonious, complementary society in which the working force enjoyed an ideological status, if not social advancement. In fact, the ideological scheme was not long in adjusting to and reinforcing social reality: by application of the biblical scheme of the three sons of Noah to the trifunctional scheme, the third order could be subordinated to the first two, just as Ham, the least respectful of Noah's sons, had become the servant of his two brothers, Shem and

9. There is an extensive bibliography in Georges Dumézil, *L'Idéologie tripartie des Indo-Européens* (Brussels: Latomus, 1958); Georges Dumézil, *Les Trois Ordres ou l'imaginaire du féudalisme* (Paris: Gallimard, 1974) [*The Three Orders: Feudal Society Imagined,* trans. Arthur Goldhammer (Chicago: University of Chicago Press, 1980)]; Georges Dumézil, "A propos des trois ordres," essays 21–25 in his *Apollon sonore et autres essais: Vingt-cinq esquisses de mythologie* (Paris: Gallimard, 1982), pp. 205–53.

Japheth. The scheme, in appearance egalitarian, reinforced social inequality among the three orders.

This fundamental scheme has provided a point of departure for the three first profiles in this book, the chapters on the monk (or on monks) by Giovanni Miccoli, on the knight, by Franco Cardini, and on the peasant and on his labor by Giovanni Cherubini.

Giovanni Miccoli presents monks' elitist mentality and their claim to social hegemony in the medieval West. Monks saw themselves as the only authentic heirs of the primitive church, and they described the conditions of human life in terms of a hierarchy of morality and merit at the summit of which they placed themselves. Rather than as an isolated and independent hermit, the monk usually lived under a rule, and he embodied the ideals of obedience and discipline. He dedicated his life to the search for God in prayer and in solitude, but he also sought peace and tranquillity; he prayed for the salvation of others, but his highest priority was his own perfection and his personal salvation. The monastery appears both as an island or an oasis and as a city—a holy city. As much as with God, the monk dealt with the Devil, whose favorite prey he was. As a specialist in satanic aggression, he protected others from the "ancient enemy." He was also a specialist in death, thanks to the death rolls, like an unending chain of prayers for the dead, kept by monasteries. He was a counselor and a mediator, primarily among the mighty. He was also a man of culture, a conserver of classical culture, and a specialist in reading and writing, thanks to the monastic scriptorium, at once library and workshop for the copying and ornamentation of manuscripts. He combined "intellectual vigor" with "emotive exuberance" and with "a skill in writing capable of expressing and noticing the niceties in sensations, disparities, or subtle and secret intentions." The monastery was the antechamber of Paradise, and the monk was the person most apt to become a saint.

The life of the knight, according to Franco Cardini, alternated between violence and peace, blood and God, pillage and the protection of the poor. In the tenth century, when the knight appeared in an individual biography (that of St. Gerald of Aurillac by Odo, abbot of Cluny), he tended to become the *miles Christi*, the knight of Christ. The reconquest of Spain and the Crusades opened vast fields for the knight's spirit of adventure, his piety, and his place in the collective imagination. He was the hero of the first great literary texts in the vernacular, of the *Chanson de Roland* and the *Cantar de mio Cid*. He forged a knightly ethic (or was it created for him?) that alternated between warlike prowess and wisdom: "Roland is fierce and Oliver is wise" (trans. Sayers). The knight played an essential part in the invention of modern love, and his sexual attitudes fluctuated between obscene violence and the refinements of the "joy" of love, particularly from a distance. He was also instrumental in furthering "youth." Inhabited by warlike fury and inspired by mystical tendencies, like Vivien, he was both "saint" and "butcher." The Christianization of the old barbaric rites for endowing the warrior with his arms created a rite of passage—investiture—essential for the young warrior. In the twelfth century, St. Bernard gave his blessing to a new chivalry in the knightly monks of the military orders. Like the monk, the knight was a hero of the *pugna spiritualis,* the fight against the Devil. With Perceval, the knight became a mystic and the knightly adventure was transformed into a religious quest for the Grail. Chivalry was to persist in the collective imagination up to Christopher Columbus, the mystical *conquistador,* and it was fed by a "mythico-folk background" and the mirage of the Orient. The chivalric imagination was invested in the hunt, in heraldry, in bestiaries, and, above all, in the tournament, which the church proved powerless to control after prohibiting it for a hundred years (1215–1316). Chivalric institutions and knightly culture were among the principal moving forces in the "process of civilization" described by Norbert Elias.[10]

Giovanni Cherubini situates the medieval peasant on the two great demographic curves of the Middle Ages, the upswing that saw the population of western Europe double from the year 1000 to the beginning of the fourteenth century and its great downward curve when it was bled by plague, famine, and war to the mid-fifteenth century. He places him in the diversity of agrarian landscapes and types of habitat—grouped or scattered—and in the struggle against nature to clear the land and reclaim polders from the sea. He shows the peasant obsessed by the task of assuring himself enough to eat and preoccupied with self-sufficiency, hence planting diversified crops but privileging the cultivation of grains. The peasant was primarily a bread producer in a society in which the first hierarchy was based on the whiteness and fineness of the bread one ate. He was a worker always threatened by poor yields and agriculture's fragility before the threats of nature. He might also specialize in one crop, a noble crop

10. Norbert Elias, *Über den Prozess der Zivilisation, soziogenetische und psychogenetische Untersuchungen,* 2 vols. (Basel: Haus zum Falken, 1939) [*The Civilizing Process: Sociogenetic and Psychogenetic Investigations,* trans. Edmund Jephcott (Oxford: Basil Blackwell, 1978; 1982)].

such as grapes or olives or a crop as humble as chestnuts. He might exploit marginal resources, like the woodsman or the shepherd who practiced transhumance. The peasant woman was primarily a textile worker, a spinner. The peasant seldom appears in texts, but he had an important place in the astonishing artistic representations of the labors of the months of the year.[11] Usually a man of the outdoors, in the winter the peasant killed his pig and ate it piece by piece by the fireside.

The peasant's social life was bounded by the lord and the rural community. He was a villager, and had been one for some time. Cherubini believes that this was the case from ancient and even prehistoric times, while other scholars date the grouping of peasants in villages as late as the eleventh century.[12] The peasant owed labor service (the *corvée*) to his lord, but he was also burdened by dues in coin and by exactions arising from seigneurial *bans* (the lord's rights over local trade), notably the lord's monopoly of milling. When oppressed, the peasant fought for social justice. He usually practiced passive resistance, but at times he broke out in violent revolt. The peasant was on the front lines in medieval man's battle against wild animals such as the wolf, the bear, and the fox. We know his mindset above all through judicial records such as those exploited by Emmanuel Le Roy Ladurie in his *Montaillou, village occitan* (1975).[13] Literary sources reveal contempt for and even hatred of the peasant, an illiterate who, they suggest, belongs somewhere between man and the beasts. The religion now dubbed "popular" but that the church qualified as "superstitions" was primarily a peasant piety. There is little doubt that the peasant followed beliefs and rites that we call "magical." This meant that the peasant, numerically in the majority in a society anchored to the land, was marginal in respect to the dominant culture and ideology, in spite of his assiduous frequentation of the village church (which inspired some clerics to trace a fantastic etymology for bells—*campanae*—from men who lived in the country: *in campo*). The peasant repaid society's contempt for him in its own

11. Chiara Frugoni, "Chiesa e lavoro agricolo nei testi e nelle immagini dall'età tardoantica all'età romanica," in Vito Fumagalli and Gabriella Rossetti, eds., *Medioevo rurale. Sulle tracce della civiltà contadina* (Bologna: Il Mulino, 1980), pp. 321–41; Perrine Mane, *Calendriers et techniques agricoles: France-Italie XIIe-XIIIe siècles*) (Paris: Sycomore, 1983).

12. Jean Chapelot and Robert Fossier, *Le Village et la maison au Moyen Age* (Paris: Hachette, 1979).

13. *Montaillou: The Promised Land of Error,* trans. Barbara Bray (New York: George Braziller, 1987).

coin, and in some documents and some of his behavior patterns we can glimpse his dislike of lords, burghers, and cityfolk. *Jacqueries* were explosions of long-standing rancor.

The Forgotten Men

In presenting here ten characteristic types of medieval man, we have been obliged to make choices and to limit ourselves to the most significant types for fear of shattering our medieval man into typological splinters.

I have already spoken of why we left out the pilgrim and the crusader. The trio of monk/knight/peasant does not exhaust the categories of the trifunctional scheme. Among the *oratores* we have not singled out the bishop (an important figure but one treated by André Vauchez in connection with sanctity), the secular priest, or, above all, the friar of the mendicant orders that arose in the thirteenth century, the Order of Friars Preachers (or Dominicans), the Order of Friars Minor (or Franciscans), the Augustinians, and the Carmelites. These were highly important figures, but only during the last three centuries of our period, when they were often found at the side of the laity. In the world of the *bellatores* we have neglected the mercenary, the paid combatant or professional soldier who appeared only late in the period (we will get a better glimpse of him when he turns into an undisciplined marauder, the member of a robber band, or an adventurer and appears among Bronislaw Geremek's marginal figures).[14] Finally, we have limited the *laboratores* to the peasants, the most important workers both qualitatively and quantitatively, who bore the brunt of the tripartite scheme of things in the eleventh and twelfth centuries. Craftsmen and wageworkers appear among the city-dwellers of Jacques Rossiaud. Perhaps the most striking object of our willful neglect is the seigneur. But how can one speak of lords without treating the immense subject of feudalism? We chose to retreat before the magnitude of the task, limiting ourselves to evoking the lord as the other side of the coin in our discussion of his relations with the peasant, or evoking him partially through his warrior function, represented by the knight. Nor did we include those specialists of the body, physicians and surgeons. We will not even offer the weak excuse that many physicians in the city environment were Jews and

14. Bronislaw Geremek, *Le Salariat dans l'artisanat parisien aux XIIIe-XIVe siècles, Etude sur le marché de la main d'oeuvre au Moyen Age,* trans. Anna Posner and Christiane Klapisch-Zuber (Paris and The Hague: Ecole Pratique des Hautes Etudes, Sorbonne, 1968); Polish edition, 1962.

that, in the rural areas, medicine was practiced primarily by amateurs to whom traditional lore and particular gifts were attributed—old women, bonesetters, healers, dealers in herbs and simples, and midwives, all of whom had learned their arts from experience. Jole Agrimi and Chiara Crisciani have written in scholarly and intelligent fashion on the place of the physician in medieval society and ideology and on how that society pictured relations between the body and the soul.[15] Marie-Christine Pouchelle has written discerningly on the surgeon of the king of France, Philip IV (Philippe le Bel), in the early fourteenth century, and on the ambiguity of the status of the physician, part man of science and part manual laborer.[16]

Among the marginal figures discussed by Bronislaw Geremek, two types, the pauper and the heretic, doubtlessly deserve to be treated at greater length than space allowed here. As for the seigneur and feudalism, the magnitude and complexity of the problems concerning poverty and heresy in the Middle Ages would have carried us too far afield. Poverty, after all, was one of the most acute social and ideological problems of the Middle Ages; there was an entire typology of the poor, and voluntary poverty was the object of bitter debate during the Middle Ages.

As for heresy, during the period that concerns us here—from the year 1000 to the end of the fifteenth century—it was endemic and took a variety of forms, peaceful or violent, widespread or geographically limited. The heretic was the man most detested by the church. He was both inside and outside the church, and he threatened the ideological, institutional, and social foundations of the dominant religion as well as the faith, the religious monopoly, and the authority of the church.

The child might also have been absent from our survey had Christiane Klapisch-Zuber not included him (or her) in her treatment of woman in her familial role, where she also considers parental attitudes toward the child. Such attitudes are perhaps still open to evaluation. I continue to think that Philippe Ariès was correct in affirming that in medieval Europe the child was not a highly valued object—which did not prevent parents from loving their children, but loving

15. Jole Agrimi and Chiara Crisciani, *Medicina del corpo et medicina dell'anima. Note sul sapere del medico fino all'inizio del secolo XIII* (Milan: Episteme, 1978); Jole Agrimi and Chiara Crisciani, *Malato, medico e medicina nel Medioevo* (Turin: Loescher, 1980).

16. Marie-Christine Pouchelle, *Corps et chirurgie à l'apogée du Moyen Age. Savoir et imaginaire du corps chez Henri de Mondeville chirurgien de Philippe le Bel* (Paris: Flammarion, 1983).

them particularly in view of the adults that they would become and that it was desirable that they become in the least possible time.[17]

Neither will the sailor be found in these pages. The sailor was long a marginal figure in a society that, except for some Celts and the Vikings, feared the sea and took its time mastering navigation, beginning with such essential inventions, in the thirteenth and fourteenth centuries, as the stern rudder, the compass, the portolan, and, much later, maps. On the ship that carried him to the crusades, St. Louis was surprised to encounter such men, who seemed to him of little courtesy or religion. Still, not many years earlier, Jacques de Vitry, in his model sermons treating the various "estates" of this world, dedicated two homilies to men of the sea.[18]

At the end of the period examined here, the development of bureaucracies and specialization in the practices of justice and finance in the states in the process of formation prompted the appearance of new types of men: judges and men of the law, and seigneurial, royal, and municipal officials. At this point, however, we approach another Middle Ages more commonly called the Renaissance or the Early Modern period.[19]

New Types of Men and the City
The City-Dweller, the Intellectual, the Merchant

One of the most important aspects of the rise of the West after the year 1000 was urban development, which reached its apogee in the thirteenth century. The city changed medieval man. It restricted his family environment, but it enlarged the network of communities in which he participated. It placed the market and money at the center of his material preoccupations, broadened his horizons, and offered him means for instruction and cultivation and a new universe of play.

Therefore, Jacques Rossiaud tells us, the city-dweller existed. He was imprisoned by space, however, in a place that could be the worst or the best of worlds, according to his occupation and his mind-set.

17. Philippe Ariès, *L'Enfant et la vie familiale sous l'Ancien Régime* (Paris: Plon, 1960; 1973) [*Centuries of Childhood: A Social History of Family Life*, trans. Robert Baldick (New York: Vintage Books, 1962)].

18. Michel Mollat, *La Vie quotidienne des gens de mer en Atlantique (IXe-XVIe siècles)* (Paris: Hachette, 1983).

19. There are two exemplary studies of France in the later Middle Ages, Bernard Guenée, *Tribunaux et gens de justice dans le bailliage de Senlis à la fin du Moyen Age (vers 1360–vers 1550)* (Paris: Les Belles Lettres, 1963); Françoise Autrand, *Naissance d'un grand corps de l'Etat, les Gens du Parlement de Paris, 1345–1454* (Paris: Publications de la Sorbonne, 1981).

For the monk who yearned for solitude the city was Babylon, the mother of all vices, and the seat of impiety. For the cleric thirsting for knowledge and eager for debate, for the Christian fond of churches and church functions, it was Jerusalem. The city-dweller was more often than not a recent immigrant, yesterday's peasant. He needed to learn to find his way around, to get acclimated. It was not often true, as the German adage claimed, that city air made men free, but the city did offer a number of freedoms. Lodging was a knotty problem and often necessitated doubling up. Beyond dwelling space lay another and clearly defined space enclosed by the city walls. The city-dweller was a man walled in. The city was teeming and it inspired some writers to numerical lyricism, like the Milanese, Bonvesin da la Riva, in the thirteenth century, who enumerated with wonder all the parts—all the marvels—of the city. The city also meant overcrowding. It was above all an economic center for the surrounding territory, and its heart was the marketplace. The city-dweller learned dependence upon the market. The urban population was a complex of small cells, of family nuclei of limited numbers. The city-dweller learned about the fragility of the family.

Above all, he learned about diversity and change. In the city there were the great, the middling, and the small, the "fat" and the "lean," the mighty and the humble. In the city money was king. The dominant mentality was the mercantile mentality, the profit mentality. If in seigneurial circles the sin par excellence was pride, *superbia*, the feudal vice, here it was avarice and cupidity, the bourgeois vices. Here one learned the value of labor and time, but above all one learned to adapt to perpetual change. Prices fluctuated incessantly and "estates" and "conditions" were continually shifting. In the city man was constantly subjected to turns of the wheel of fortune, ever present and ceaselessly revolving. Thus the city multiplied occasions for moral decision and one had to be prepared for constant violence, since "the city drove men to crime." Violence was even offered to the city-dweller as a spectacle when convicted criminals were pilloried, whipped, and executed in public.

The city-dweller lived primarily among neighbors and friends. He was immersed in the life of the neighborhood: the ward, the houses on his block, and his street. People had a number of meeting places. There were the tavern, the cemetery, the neighborhood square, and, for the women, the well, the bake oven, and the washing shed. The parish church was another pole of attraction. The city-dweller lived in an "enlarged privacy." At times the neighborhood seemed to him too small. Luckily, he could circulate throughout the city to a nearby urban "elsewhere."

The city-dweller was also a member of one or more confraternities, organizations which patched up quarrels, protected their members, and, in particular, softened and alleviated the harshness of death. He was also the target of missioners of the mendicant orders, who quite efficiently took charge of his conscience and his salvation, on occasion prying indiscreetly into his domestic life, his business affairs, and his inner conscience.

In general, however, the city-dweller benefited from a wide range of opportunities for integration offered by the city. He had full enjoyment of his status as a "ceremonial citizen." He could profit from the urban refinement that, after 1350, came to be called "urbanity" or "civility," for there existed an "art of living proper to the urban world." If he had the means, he could enjoy a variety of pleasures of the table and fully live up to the image of medieval man as a carnivore. If he was unable to resist temptations of the flesh, prostitution (increasingly tolerated) allowed him to satisfy his impulses. If he became successful in life, he had no reason for shame, for hard work was appreciated in the city, and, although usury was decried, "good" wealth was praised. The city was harsh, though, for the worker was subject to an implacable employer. The city-dweller could assure his children a good future if they attended the city schools, and for all its citizens the city was a school for behavior and *savoir vivre,* dispensing lessons in measure, order, and courtesy. Everything was better regulated in the cities and towns, beginning with time, which gradually came under the rule of the mechanical clock. The city-dweller took part, as a spectator or a participant, in civic processions and joyful festivities, in religious processions and municipal "triumphs." The ill and the poor had hospitals and hospices; the healthy had laughter and a chance to challenge reigning values in Carnival rites and charivaris. For the medieval city-dweller, the city was most often a treat. This is Jacques Rossiaud's picture of the medieval city. It may be overly optimistic, but it is true that, except in certain monastic circles, medieval ideology was "pro-urban."

Mariateresa Fumagalli Beonio Brocchieri has taken on what is perhaps the most difficult task in this gallery of otherwise comparable portraits. The intellectual, in point of fact, did not exist in the Middle Ages. There was no term for him. Nevertheless, there was undeniably a sort of person that could be defined as someone who worked "with words and with the mind," not with his hands. He might go by

various names: *magister* (master), *doctor* (doctor), *philosophus* (philosopher), *litteratus* (an educated man and, in particular, one with a knowledge of Latin).

He was a member of the clergy, and he enjoyed clerical privileges—a particular advantage, since if he went no further than minor orders, he could profit from membership in the clergy without having its responsibilities. He was a schoolman, and a man of a city school, and between the twelfth and the thirteenth centuries he moved from the cathedral school, in decline, and the city school, which lacked privileges, to the university. The university was a corporation, and the university teacher a professional man. When he broke the ideological fetters that insisted that knowledge must be imparted gratis because it was a gift of God, he was remunerated by his students, by the city, or by the church (in the form of a sinecure).

He was a bookish man not fond of lending his books and a man of words; he emphasized whatever distinguished him and set him above the manual laborer. He was already a "professor."

In the intellectual world exceptional figures were, if I may be permitted the expression, the rule. Beonio Brocchieri recalls some of the most famous of them: St. Anselm, Peter Abelard, Arnold of Brescia, and the great university teachers of the thirteenth century, Roger Bacon in particular. She treats the problems of medieval knowledge and the arrival of the "new" Aristotle.

The intellectual's life was not always an easy one. When teachers from the mendicant orders gained entry into the University of Paris, it set off a serious crisis. These men introduced intellectual novelties, which the students highly appreciated, but as members of a religious order they refused to play the corporative game, refusing to strike, for example. A grave ideological crisis followed the introduction of the ideas of the Arab philosopher Averroës. Could one admit, as Averroës would have it, the doctrine of double truth and the existence of scientific truths contrary to religious truth? In 1270 and again in 1277 the crosier of the not overly enlightened bishop of Paris, Etienne Tempier, struck Parisian intellectuals. A veritable syllabus of condemned propositions was proclaimed, circulated, and enforced. Master Siger of Brabant was imprisoned for suspicion of Averroism.

Here Beonio Brocchieri raises a question: was Dante an intellectual? She tends to say he was (as do I). In any event, he had the characteristics of one: he was "out of place"; he belonged to a corporation (the doctor's and pharmacists' guild); he was active in political life. The new task of the medieval intellectual at the turn of the fourteenth century was political, involving a choice between the pope and the emperor. As these clerics were dissatisfied with the church, they opted for the emperor and attacked the temporal power of the pope. This was true of both William of Ockham and Marsilius of Padua.

Beonio Brocchieri emphasizes three characteristics of the intellectual of the central Middle Ages. He was an international figure who often traveled from one school to another and from one university to another, thanks to his knowledge of Latin. He was unmarried, unencumbered by conjugal and familial duties, as Héloïse pointed out to Abelard. Finally, he was a man of "authorities," of obligatory texts, first among them the Bible. He was not blindly submissive to his authorities, however; he knew how to compare them, criticize them, and combine them through "rational" study, which, on occasion, had the last word.

The urban intellectual had to defend himself against the accusation of selling knowledge, "which belongs only to God." The merchant, who was even more bound to the city, had to clear himself of the accusation of selling time, which also "belongs only to God."

The situation of the merchant was more ambiguous than that of the intellectual. The old mistrust, which he had aroused as early as classical antiquity and which Christianity reinforced (Jesus had driven the merchants from the Temple), haunted the merchant, even though his status had improved economically, socially, and ideologically. From the beginning of the great surge in Western European culture, the merchant's usefulness was recognized, for example, by the Anglo-Saxon, Aelfric, in his *Colloquy* of the early eleventh century. First, his services to the community were acknowledged; then came a realization of the risks he took, as the Norwegian *Speculum regale* (The King's Mirror) emphasized in the early eleventh century. The merchant remained a pariah, however. The friars of the mendicant orders worked to justify him, calling Purgatory to his aid, but Thomas Aquinas (a Dominican) was unsure. Despite his open mind, Thomas wrote that "there is something disgraceful about trade, something sordid and shameful." The line of demarcation between the merchant and the usurer was unclear. If the merchant was king in several Italian cities ("Genoese, hence a merchant," one proverb said), outside of Italy the Italian merchant—the "Lombard"—was viewed with a jaundiced eye, and in all Christendom the image of the detested Jew exerted its influence on the image of the merchant.

An anonymous English poem of the early fourteenth century gave allegorical form to the division between the new, as yet unacceptable ethic of the "saver" and that of the "spender" praised by tradition. The merchant was part of the new ethic of work and property. He opposed talent to birth; he was a self-made man. Eventually there were merchant saints, men like St. Homobonus of Cremona in the late twelfth century. The merchant had been to school, and he encouraged the development of vernacular languages. The oldest known text in Italian is a fragment of an account book of a Sienese merchant in 1211. The merchant was a pioneer in the learning of foreign languages, in the improvement of standards of measurement, and in the manipulation of moneys. He was a writer: the archive of Francesco di Marco Datini, the merchant of Prato, contains one hundred fifty thousand business letters. He participated in the emergence of the individual and of personhood, and to the fundamental components of the person—soul and body—he added vocation and time, now bent to the individual's use.

Beyond Medieval Categories
Woman, the Artist, and Marginal Figures

Woman had no place in the trifunctional scheme. Although "woman" was certainly an operative category for men of the Middle Ages, she was long defined not by professional criteria but by her body, her gender, and her relations with certain groups. She was defined as "wife, widow, or maid." She was the victim of constraints that kinship and family had imposed upon the emergence of women as individuals gifted with a juridical, moral, and economic personality of their own. In documents of the Middle Ages, which were the product of a male-dominated society, women's voices are seldom heard, and the few that come through are usually limited to the upper reaches of the uppermost social levels. With the aid of recent contributions from social anthropology, however, Christiane Klapisch-Zuber brings back to life woman in the bosom of the family. The woman was an object of fundamental importance in marriage alliances among the feudal aristocracy. An opportunity for social advancement for the husband, she generally underwent social demotion in the marriages contracted according to this strategy. The transfer of her person and of wealth that centered on her led to her disinheritance, and an inflationary spiral of dowries led to a devaluation of the woman during the course of the Middle Ages. Still, thanks to the church, a growing obligation to assure both spouses' consent to a marriage was a revolution that raised the status of the woman, and pressure from the young gave timid assistance to the establishment of marriage based on personal inclination.

"Family order" led to a delayed marriage for men, however. Women were married very young to men who were close to thirty years of age, which meant that ten years or more separated the couples' ages. The woman was a womb; she was the victim of a high fertility rate that made her spend half her life before the age of forty pregnant. The power granted her over the household (at the heart of which was the conjugal bedchamber) was slim compensation. Mistress of the domestic space, her domain was the family's domestic economy. Submissive in her conjugal duties, obliged to be faithful to her husband and living under his authority, she found only limited compensations in love for her children, who were often sent out to wet nurses as infants and were decimated by illness in an age of a merciless child mortality rate. In the early Middle Ages, infanticide added its toll to natural death rates; later it was for the most part replaced by the abandonment of newborn infants. Foundlings were numerous in later medieval Christendom, and "women remained a mechanism subordinated to the reproduction of the family."

Enrico Castelnuovo starts from the paradox of the grandeur of medieval art and the anonymity of most of its creators. Romanticism viewed this anonymity as a disappearance of the individual in collective creation, but the Romantics' was a purely intellectual perspective. What needs to be noted is that the artist of the early Middle Ages (like his counterpart in classical antiquity, for that matter) was torn between society's disregard for a personage it grouped with manual laborers and his own need to assert his pride, establish his reputation, and encourage his celebrity, at least within the restricted circle of his clients and admirers. This was what prompted him to sign his works. Artists' names can be found in classical antiquity, but they disappeared in the early Middle Ages. In Italy they reappeared in the eighth century. The first biography of an artist—the life of St. Eloi written by his disciple, St. Ouen—dates from the seventh century. What Ouen praises in Eloi is the goldsmith, the artist par excellence, thanks to the precious material he shaped. But Ouen was also a prelate, a bishop, and a counselor to King Dagobert. Was Eloi's art inspiration enough for a biographer? Furthermore, even though the goldsmith had a certain prestige, as Marc Bloch pointed out, churches often melted down their treasures and their gold and silver pieces, counting the artist's work as irrelevant.

Before the fourteenth century, there was no term to designate the artist, just as there was none for the intellectual. The artist shared the term *artifex* with the craftsman, the Latin word *ars* referring more to technique and other tricks of the trade than to knowledge or to the as yet unspecified area that the West would later call the fine arts. There was a hierarchy among these artists before the fact. More and more, it was the architect who rivaled the goldsmith for top place on the scale, and it was in France and in the Gothic age of the thirteenth century that the architect styled himself a *maître* and even an intellectual—a *maître es-pierres*. As late as the fourteenth century, however, in the building of the cathedral of Milan the "science without art" of the French architects was contrasted to the "art without science" of the Lombard stonemasons.

Artists' signatures and mentions of artists were frequent in the twelfth century: one need only think of Lanfranc and Wiligelmo in Modena and Benedictus Antelami in Parma. Such mentions may have benefited from the promotion of the "mechanical arts" to parallel the liberal arts. Curiously, they become less frequent in the thirteenth century, when the prestige of the artist had increased, aided by a return of interest in classical antiquity, in particular in Italy, where the communal structure of cities favored the glorification of artists and cities fought over them, since monuments and works of art were thought to encourage city-dwellers' taste for beauty and their civic pride.

The only thing that delayed the emergence of the artist in medieval society was the ambiguity of his social status, perhaps aided by the slowness of the process that created the idea and the perception of beauty out of notions and impressions of grandeur, order, and richness.

Two Extremes: The Saint and the Outcast

There was no greater diversity in the Middle Ages than among those who lived on or outside the edges of society. Still, what enables us to group such persons together as a category was their common exclusion from recognized society and the process by which they were expelled to its fringes or beyond.

The first "marginal man" was the exile. Bronislaw Geremek recalls that in the early Middle Ages banishment was a sentence that substituted for the death penalty. Exile was on occasion an internal banishment; being excluded from one's usual life environment. As such it resembled interdiction or excommunication, the exclusion of a person (or a country) from the benefits of the sacraments, depriving him of the daily means to salvation and sending him off to a place where sacrality and the church were ineffective. This was an extreme case of spatial marginalization, but there were others: exile to the country or confinement to ill-famed sections of the city and, at the end of the Middle Ages, to the city ghettos. From the thirteenth century on, the "archives of repression" appeared, registering the echoes of urban violence, while in France in the fourteenth and fifteenth centuries, the pardoning of sentenced criminals that the letters of remission sought to justify brings back to life the world of outcasts who were offered a second chance to find their place in society. The borderline between the working world and the underworld was unclear, however. Becoming an outcast was often "a collateral result of pilgrimages or migratory labor." The destiny of outcasts became clear: they were "gallows birds." In the fourteenth and fifteenth centuries many outcasts joined organized bands of vagabonds, thieves, marauders, and murderers.

Short of crime, bad repute (*infamia*) generated marginality. "Infamy" was normally individual, but it could be collective, as with "impure" or "dishonest" trades, the list of which began to shrink in the thirteenth century. Opprobrium and exclusion still struck entertainers such as the jongleurs, however (in spite of St. Francis's provocative declaration that he was "God's fool"). The same was true of prostitutes (in spite of their sense of professional standards) and for usurers (in spite of Purgatory).

In a society that showed such strong ambiguity regarding the body, the ill and the infirm tended to be outcasts as well. Exclusion was clear for the most dangerous, the most scandalous, and the most wretched among them, the lepers, even if, in imitation of Jesus, St. Louis served and embraced a leper.

Geremek only touches on the most extreme cases of marginality, the heretic and the Jew, noting the signs of opprobrium that some were obliged to wear, remarking their presence in Carnival festivities, and the contrast they presented to the chief values opposed to marginality in the Middle Ages: stability, work, and recognized status.

One man—the saint—embodied the highest realization of medieval man. The saint established a contact between heaven and earth. He was, first, an exceptional corpse, a witness, according to Piero Camporesi, to "impassible flesh" whose cult developed around his body, his tomb, and his relics. He was also a man whose mediation was efficacious, a support for the church, and an example for the faithful. He was a patron for trades, for cities, and for all the communities in which medieval man was involved. When his name was given to individuals, he was also a personal patron for men and women of the Middle Ages.

The sanctity of the medieval saint was not extratemporal, however. Nor was it absorbed into continuity, as claimed by the ethnologist, Saintyves, who saw the saint merely as continuing the pagan gods of antiquity. The saint was originally a martyr. In the early Middle Ages, he bore signs of the influence of eastern asceticism; later he tended to be incarnate in the mighty as a bishop, a monk, a king, or a noble. He reflected the preponderance of the male, the adult, and the aristocrat in the Middle Ages' ideal of man. Then, after the twelfth and the thirteenth centuries, sanctity of function was replaced by sainthood through imitation of Jesus Christ. At first a "professional," the saint later settled among "common" mortals. All he needed to do was to realize, within the limits of the possible, the ideals of the apostolic life and evangelical perfection; to "follow naked the naked Christ." Sanctity became spiritualized; it was more connected to the saint's lifestyle than to his social status and more to mortality than to miracles. At the end of the Middle Ages a growing number of saints earned sainthood through the inspired word and through visions. The saints, men and women alike, were often mystics, prophets, preachers, and visionaries.

Even though the church controlled the recognition of saints from the late twelfth century on, throughout the Middle Ages the people "continued to create saints."

Chronology
The Long Time-span and Changes in Medieval Man

Thus even the saint, who seemed such a firmly established figure in Christianity, changed through time, as André Vauchez demonstrates. The periods of late antiquity and the early Middle Ages were essential for the formation of medieval man, which is why Giovanni Miccoli returns to the earliest centuries of Christianity for the first appearance of the monk. Franco Cardini sees traces of the knight in the horsemen of the Romano-barbaric world. As early as the Carolingian empire, measures were taken against vagabonds, the prototypes of later outcasts. Medieval man had an ancient heritage, transformed by Christianity. He had come a long way.

But with the year 1000 he was transformed. When functions became specialized, the laity began to play a more important role. He changed even more with the thirteenth century, when society became more complex, "estates" proliferated, human types became more differentiated, and values (within a religiousness more accepting of this world) descended from heaven to this earth. Medieval man, however, was no less profoundly religious and no less concerned about his salvation, which by that time was to be assured less by contempt of this world and more by an interest in transforming it. In the fourteenth and fifteenth centuries, finally, medieval man passed through formidable trials and was again changed by the profound crisis in the feudal system, but he was also renewed and modernized by a new world of structures and of values.

Giovanni Miccoli stops following the monk after the thirteenth century, when he ceded first place in the world of the regular clergy to the friar of the mendicant orders. Franco Cardini shows the traditional knight of the Middle Ages caught, in the fourteenth and fifteenth centuries, in the grip of exaggerations of chivalry as spectacle, of the fashion for chivalric orders, and of changes in military technology. The fourteenth century was "the age of the defeat of the knights."

For Jacques Rossiaud, the city-dweller of the fifteenth century was increasingly identified with the "ceremonial citizen" swept along in the noisy confusion of festivities, parades, and Carnival rites.

Mariateresa Fumagalli Beonio Brocchieri sees the intellectual as increasingly involved in politics (Wycliffe, Hus, Gerson), in the process of abandoning Latin, and beginning to express himself in other places than the university such as the circle, the academy, the library, or the court. Petrarch fled the city. The medieval intellectual, seized by "melancholy," gave way to the humanist intellectual and the court intellectual.

Aron Gurevich's merchant let himself be dominated by "fortune" and subscribed increasingly to the notion that time is money. He too fell pray to the "commercial pessimism" of the Renaissance, and he passed from fully developed feudalism to nascent capitalism.

Enrico Castelnuovo considers that the affirmation and the recognition of the artist begins with Dante's *Purgatorio,* when Dante finds two miniaturists, Oderisi of Gubbio and Franco of Bologna, and two painters, Cimabue and Giotto, in that place. The entire guild basked in Giotto's reflected glory.

Bronislaw Geremek sees troops of vagabonds, beggars, and felons overrunning Christianity in the Renaissance and the Early Modern period.

Some Obsessions of Medieval Man

In the last analysis, what legitimizes an evocation of medieval man is the notion that the ideological and cultural system of which he was a part and the collective imagination that inherited that system imposed upon most men (and women) of these five centuries—clergy or laity, rich or poor, mighty or humble—certain shared mental structures and similar objects of belief, of fantasy, or of obsession. Naturally, social status, level of education, cultural tradition, and historico-geographic zone all introduced differences in both the form and the content of these cultural and psychological attitudes. Still, what is striking is what those attitudes shared. Western man has still kept some of these habits of mind and patterns of behavior, weakened, to some extent, and refashioned into new syndromes. Although it is normal for us to have kept some of the traits of our ancestor, medieval man, the evocation of his obsessions is more apt to show us our differences. Medieval man is for us an exotic figure. The historian interested in restoring his image needs to call on his own sense of change and to become an ethnohistorian if he wants to evaluate his ancestor's originality.

Vices: Man of the Middle Ages was obsessed by sin. He committed sin by abandoning himself to the Devil and being defeated by sin's harbingers, the vices. He saw those vices in the form of symbolic animals or menacing allegories who embodied the capital sins (already seven in number by the twelfth century): pride, avarice, gluttony, lechery, wrath, envy, and sloth. He might also have seen the vices in the seductive and deceptive guise of the daughters of the Devil, wedded to the various "estates" of society. The Devil had nine daughters: Simony was wedded to the secular clergy; Hypocrisy to the monks; Pillage to the knights; Sacrilege to the peasantry; Deceit to the judges; Usury to the burghers; and Worldly Pomp to married women. Lechery, whom the Devil did not wish to marry off, was offered to all comers like a common whore.[20]

The Visible and the Invisible: People today, even those who consult seers and fortune-tellers, call spirits to floating tables, or participate in black masses, recognize a frontier between the visible and the invisible, the natural and the supernatural. This was not true of medieval

20. The list (which is one daughter short) is from a text noted on the flyleaf of a Florentine manuscript of the thirteenth century.

man. Not only was the visible for him merely the trace of the invisible; the supernatural overflowed into daily life at every turn. Medieval man was continually surrounded by "apparitions." There was no dividing line, let alone a barrier, between this world and the next. Apparitions proved the existence of Purgatory, and breaks in the earth's crust—the craters of Sicilian volcanos or grottos in Ireland—led to it. Even the unshriven dead, the phantoms of paganism, and the ghosts of folklore appeared, Satan at their head. Apparitions struck terror in people but they did not surprise them.

The Next World: Eternity was two steps away for man of the Middle Ages. Even if he believed less and less in the imminence of the Last Judgment, it was an eventuality he did not exclude. Hell and Heaven might be for tomorrow. The saints were already in Paradise and innumerable throngs of the eternally damned were in Hell. The spatial system of the other world became a rational system in the twelfth and thirteenth centuries. It was both a three-place and a five-place system. The three essential places were Heaven and Hell, with Purgatory, which assumed its definitive form at the end of the twelfth century, lying between them as an intermediate and temporary netherworld in which those who had died charged only with venial sins or before completing their penance passed varying amounts of time. At the final Resurrection and the Last Judgment, Purgatory would disappear, its last tenants moving on to Heaven, for which it served as the antechamber. The next world had two auxiliary places as well. The first was the limbo of the Patriarchs, the just of the Old Testament, who were unbaptized because they had lived before the Incarnation. When Jesus descended into Hell during his earthly "death," he emptied this limbo and it was closed forever, the Patriarchs passing on to Heaven. A second limbo of children who had died before they could be baptized would continue to function eternally, taking in infants who would undergo no corporeal punishment, but for all eternity would be deprived of the supreme joy of the beatific vision, the contemplation of God.

Miracle and Ordeal: God's frequent intervention—direct or indirect—in the order of nature was universally acknowledged. There was a hierarchy of intercessors, however: the Virgin Mary, the most powerful among them, could obtain any miracle from God, the principal saints also had great power before God, while certain saints, in particular local saints, had somewhat narrower specialties. Miracles were particularly numerous in areas in which medieval man was most at risk: the domain of the body, with innumerable miracles of healing; and the domain of women in childbirth and children, victims of choice, given the miserable standards of physiology and medicine in the Middle Ages. In an attempt to avoid the dubious efforts of self-styled miracle workers, the church, from the early thirteenth century on, tended to limit thaumaturgic power to saints recently dead, thus giving new impetus to the cult of relics, which could produce prodigies by their touch.

God could also allow the laws of nature to be broken under particular circumstances, should judgment be put directly into his hands: trials by water, for example, in which an accused person who did not know how to swim proved his innocence by failing to drown where "naturally" he or she should have done so, and, above all, in the trial by fire, in which innocence was recognized by having the accused hold a piece of red-hot metal in his hand or pass through flames without being burned. God's judgment could also be manifest in single combat, where one of the combatants was the accused (or his champion, substituting for him with or without payment). The church prohibited such ordeals at the Fourth Lateran Council in 1215, introducing a revolution in the administration of trials. Henceforth, oral and written testimony substituted for trial by arms or by physical ordeals, and Christianity moved medieval man one step further from magical credences and practices.

Memory: Many men of the Middle Ages were illiterate. Until the thirteenth century this was true of the overwhelming majority of the laity. In this world of illiterates, the spoken word rang out with singular force, and medieval man absorbed knowledge, anecdotes, and moral and religious instruction from sermons. The written word of course enjoyed enormous prestige, a prestige founded in Holy Writ and shared by the clergy, writing men, the monks at their head, as attested by the scriptorium, a place for writing and an essential part of every monastery. It was the spoken word, however, that was the major vehicle of communication, which presumes the existence of ways to preserve it. Medieval man was gifted with an excellent memory, which he exercised naturally or after special training. In legal cases and controversies the testimony of the aged—men of long memories in a society of short life-expectancy—was highly prized. Intellectuals, men of law, and merchants learned mnemonics, and the "art of memory" played an important role in the education of medieval man.[21] In a society in which the oath was of great importance and subject to close supervision by the church, a man who "kept his word" was well esteemed. His loyalty was attested by a long memory, and it contributed to his good repute (*bona fama*). The Christianity of medieval man was a Christianity of tradition and of memory. Did not Jesus instruct his disciples on Holy Thursday, when, at the end of the Last Supper, he established the Eucharist, "Do this in *memory* of me"?

A Symbolic Mentality: Medieval man, like Baudelaire, lived in a "forest of symbols." St. Augustine said as much: the world was composed of *signa* and of *res;* of signs, symbols, and things. The *res,* which were true reality, remained hidden; man grasped only signs. The essential book, the Bible, had a concealed symbolic structure. Every figure, every event in the Old Testament corresponded to a person or an event in the New. Medieval man was an assiduous "decipherer," which increased his dependence on the clergy, specialists in the symbolic. Symbolism ruled art, in particular architecture, for the church building was above all a symbolic structure. It was obligatory in politics, in which symbolic ceremonies such as the coronation of the king were highly important moments, and banners, arms, and emblems played a fundamental role. It reigned in literature, where it often took the form of allegory.

Numbers: Medieval man was fascinated by numbers. Until the thirteenth century it was the symbolic number that most fascinated him: three, the number of the Trinity; four, the number of the Evangelists, the rivers of Paradise, the cardinal virtues, and the cardinal points; seven, used often in religion (the seven gifts of God, seven sacraments, seven deadly sins, etc.); ten, the number of the Decalogue, the commandments of God and the commandments of the church; twelve, the number of the apostles and of the months of the year, and so forth. The Book of the Apocalypse revealed a universe of symbolic numbers containing the meaning and the hidden destiny of humanity, including the millennium, that mythical epoch of a "thousand" (that is, many) years that was both dreaded and eagerly awaited, in which ordeals suffered under the antichrist would be followed by the long reign of justice and peace on the earth.

Later, this fascination for symbolic numbers increasingly gave way, under pressure from society's new requirements (such as the merchants', the lords', and the nascent states' need for bookkeeping pro-

21. Frances Yates, *The Art of Memory* (Chicago: University of Chicago Press, 1966).

cedures), to a preference for precise numbers, numbers that could be manipulated scientifically, using algebraic or mathematical operations. This shift was aided by a growing interest in mathematics (in particular, in the Latin translation of Euclid's *Elements* and in manuals like the *Liber Abaci* of the Pisan, Leonardo Fibonacci, in 1202). Man of the later Middle Ages was possessed by a vogue, a mania, a passion for arithmetic.[22] He even introduced arithmetical madness into the religious realm when wills called for masses by the hundred, the thousand, or the tens of thousands. The arithmetic of indulgences and the maniacal calculation of years in Purgatory that raised the wrath of Martin Luther created what Jacques Chiffoleau has called an "otherworldly bookkeeping."[23]

Images and Color: The illiteracy that restricted the impact of the written word gave images all the more power over the senses and the mind of medieval man. The church consciously made use of the image to inform him and to form him, and the didactic and ideological burden of painted or sculpted images long dominated their strictly aesthetic value. In Old French the sculptor is called an *imagier.* A symbolic system that distorted forms to bring out their meaning was obligatory up to the thirteenth century, when it was replaced by a new symbolic system founded on an imitation of nature and a use of perspective that we call "realism." Medieval man transferred from Heaven to earth the sway over the universe that artistic representation gave him.

During all those centuries (toward their end, increasingly), medieval man—a visionary in both the physiological and supernatural sense of the term—was called to see and to conceptualize the universe and society in colors. Colors were symbolic, and they formed a changing value system. The primacy of red, the imperial color, declined as blue, the color of the Virgin and the kings of France, gained ground. Black and white were almost directly ideological. Medieval man was accustomed to hesitating when he saw green, an ambiguous color and the seductive but dangerous image of youth; he learned to recognize evil when he saw yellow, the color of deceit, on persons and surfaces. Striped and varicolored things indicated dan-

22. Alexander Murray, *Reason and Society in the Middle Ages* (Oxford: Clarendon Press; New York: Oxford University Press, 1978).

23. Jacques Chiffoleau, *La Comptabilité de l'au-delà: Les hommes, la mort et la religion dans la région d'Avignon à la fin du Moyen Age, vers 1320–vers 1480* (Rome: Ecole française de Rome, 1980).

ger of a moral sort. Gold, a color yet not a color, was the dominant and supreme value.[24]

Dreams: A man of vision, of symbolic thought, who lived in a universe in which the visible and the invisible, the natural and the supernatural were mixed endlessly, medieval man had a vocation as a great dreamer, but Christianity kept a tight rein on his oneiric activities. In classical antiquity, Greco-Roman man kept careful track of his dreams, interpreted them ceaselessly, and had specialists available, both learned and popular, to interpret them for him. In the fourth century the church adopted a new theory of the origin of dreams, complicating the old distinction between "true" and "false" dreams by attributing them to three sources: beneficent dreams came from God; the human body generated more suspect dreams; above all, there was the Devil, who sent temptation in pernicious dreams. Thus the church demanded that the Christian reject dreams, refuse to seek out their meaning, and close himself off from this opportunity for sin. Only privileged dreamers—kings, leaders, and, above, all, monks—could draw conclusions from dreams, either by finding messages from God in them or by triumphing over demonic trials. Dreams were thus a route barred to man of the early Middle Ages, who simply had to repress them. Monastic literature alone abounds with dreams in which the tormented soul of the monk reveals itself in strange and fantastic visions. Then, toward the eleventh and the twelfth centuries, dreams triumphed over the reservations and the fears of the church, which admitted that good or neutral dreams could overpower dreams of diabolic origin. Medieval men could then become a habitual dreamer, fascinated by his dreams and eager to interpret them or have them interpreted. Freud turned to him for answers when he wrote *Die Traumdeutung*.[25]

Social and Political Obsessions
Hierarchy, Authority, Liberty

Above and beyond the medieval schemata that have guided the original publishers and the authors of the present book in their choice of profiles, men of the Middle Ages thought, acted, and lived with sev-

24. Michel Pastoureau, *Figures et couleurs. Etudes sur la symbolique et la sensibilité médiévales* (Paris: Editions du Léopard d'or, 1986).

25. There is an abundant bibliography in the acts of the international colloquium organized by Tullio Gregory and the Lessico Internazionale Europeo on *I sogni nel medioevo* (Rome: Edizioni dell'Ateneo, 1985).

eral fundamental values that reflected the will of God as well as the aspirations of men.

Hierarchy: The duty of medieval man was to remain where God had placed him. Rising in society was a sign of pride; demotion was a shameful sin. The organization of society that God had ordained was to be respected, and it was based on the principle of hierarchy. Earthly society, modeled on celestial society, was to reproduce the hierarchy of the angels and the archangels minutely described in the sixth century by the eastern monk, Dionysius the Areopagite (for modern historians, Pseudo-Dionysius), in a work later translated into Latin. In learned or popular form according to his level of culture, man of the Middle Ages was a disciple of Dionysius caught in a hierarchical conception of the structure of the world.[26] Nonetheless, an important change is discernible in the twelfth and thirteenth centuries. A horizontal hierarchy of the "estates" of society in this world appeared to accompany the vertical hierarchy. The late Middle Ages would be invaded by the *danse macabre.*

Authority and Authorities: On the social and political levels, medieval man had to obey his superiors, who were prelates if he was a cleric, the king, the lord, the city fathers, or community leaders if he was a layman. On the intellectual and mental level he had to show loyalty to the authorities, the first of which was the Bible, followed by authorities imposed by historical Christianity: the Fathers of the church in late antiquity, the university *magistri* in the age of the universities in and after the thirteenth century. The abstract and superior value of *auctoritas,* of authority, inherited from classical antiquity, was imposed upon him, embodied in a great number of different "authorities." The greatest intellectual and social virtue required of medieval man was obedience, justified by religion.

The Rebel: Nevertheless (increasingly after the year 1000, and again after the thirteenth century), a growing number of medieval men refused to accept unchallenged the domination of hierarchical superiors and authorities. For a long time, the principal form of contestation and rebellion was religious: it was heresy. Within the framework of feudalism, it then took the form of the revolt of the vassal against the lord when the latter abused his power or neglected his duties. In

26. René Roques, *L'Univers dionysien, Structure hiérarchique du monde selon le Pseudo-Denys* (Paris: Aubier, 1954; Editions du Cerf, 1983).

the university context contestation was intellectual. Social revolt finally arrived to both city and countryside in the forms of strikes, riots, and workers' and peasants' revolts. The great century for revolt was the fourteenth, from England and Flanders to Tuscany and Rome. When necessary, medieval man had learned how to become a rebel.

Liberty and Liberties: Liberty was one of medieval man's time-honored values. It motivated his principal revolts. The church, paradoxically, gave the signal, as it was under the banner of *Libertas Ecclesiae*—the freedom of the church—that the church, the pope at its head, demanded its independence from a lay world that had subjugated it through feudalization. From the mid-eleventh century, liberty was the password of the great movement for reform begun under Gregory the Great.

Later, aware of their strength and eager to sweep away obstacles to the great surge that had begun with the year 1000, peasants and new city-dwellers demanded and obtained freedom, or, more often, freedoms. The enfranchisement of the serfs corresponded to the concession of charters or liberties to the burghers of the towns and cities. These were above all freedoms (in the plural)—liberties that were actually privileges.

Nonetheless, a new idea of liberty (in the singular), which was the modern idea of liberty, made an uncertain, timid appearance on the religious, the intellectual, the social, and the political levels. Medieval man, however, caught in a process of struggle, reform, and eternally incomplete progress, remained on the threshold of this liberty that he could only glimpse like a promised land.

ONE

Monks

Giovanni Miccoli

Monks and monasteries long ago ceased to be part of the common experience of the inhabitants of Europe. They have not ceased to exist, but they are no longer ordinarily, recurrently encountered in its historical landscape. All that remains of them are imposing vestiges here and there. In the cities monasteries are often masked; the old abbey churches have been taken over and renovated by other occupants and the immense monastery buildings have been turned to new uses after postrevolutionary suppression of the orders; in the countryside they have been abandoned and often lie in ruins in their ancient solitude, a pallid and not always decipherable witness to a presence and a grandeur the reasons for which are largely forgotten, along with their very memory.

Montalambert's indignation, more than a century ago, at seeing a monk's habit on the stage for the first time "in one of those ignoble parodies which hold, too often among modern nations, the place of the pomp and solemnities of religion" would be out of place today. Profanatory satire, however, has always been an indication of the vitality of memory and has attested to a capacity to evoke images and sentiments that today seem irremediably faded and distant. The monasteries and priories—Cluniac, Cistercian, Carthusian, Camaldolese, Vallombrosan—that populated the countryside of Europe by the thousand in the twelfth century, at the height of monastic expansion, have now been reduced to a few hundred in the entire world; the monks who people them, much diminished in number, remain as a silent presence, rarely encountered and often unnoticed, even by the Christian population. At the same time, a host of solitary monks has nearly totally disappeared: the hermits incessantly evoked in centuries of hagiographic legends and in historical chronicles, who lived outside the boundaries of institutionalized monasticism, oblivious to their common roots, burying themselves in the forests or isolating themselves on mountain heights, and who reappeared periodically among men as wild figures recalling the imminence of death and the urgency of conversion.

There was no sudden catastrophe to bring on the change, only a slow decline that began immediately after the golden centuries of monasticism. The great blows were struck from the outside—the Lutheran Reformation, which swept away monks in vast regions of central and northern Europe, and the widespread suppression of monasteries that preceded, accompanied, and followed the violent events of the "great revolution"—and accelerated a process that had begun long before, making it appear artificial. In reality, profound transformations in society had combined with radical changes in ways of living and conceiving the Christian presence in history and in the ecclesiastical policies of Rome, which was concentrating its efforts, in the new circumstances, on other and more flexible instruments for action. This complex and tortuous process did not destroy monasticism, but it drastically refashioned its role in the life of the church and signaled a different approach to society and history.

Social change and religious change had thus stood at the center of an experience that for centuries had shaped the face of Europe by the exuberant variety of its ramifications. It was a Europe that wanted to be Christian, that recognized itself as Christian, primarily because of the monastic experience and the institutions that had arisen out of that experience. A first, fundamental historical truth lies precisely in the decisive and exclusive preference shown to the cloister to guarantee the continuity of an authentic Christian presence in history. In the self-awareness that gradually emerged within monastic culture of late antiquity and the early Middle Ages, increasingly backed by a broad political and social consensus, the only true Christians were the monks. This was a slow and complex process of maturation involving experience, trial, cultural and ideological theorization, and institutional programs. This complex body of materials, variously rethought and readapted to the difficult political and social situations of post-Carolingian Europe, was the benchmark for the vigorous renewal of monasticism in the central Middle Ages in Western Europe. Between the tenth and the twelfth centuries the reduction of authentic Christianity to monastic life reached its most complete and in some ways most definitive expression. How could an operation as reductive as this take place in a society that proclaimed itself the *respublica christiana?* And who were the monks who were both the protagonists and the beneficiaries of that operation? What kind of lives did they lead? What was their Christianity—by which I mean what type of Christianized humanity did they embody and represent? Finally, what were the many complex ingredients of the singular and only partly unified mixture that was monasticism during the centuries of its greatest expansion?

These questions have no easy answers. Memory of that age passes almost exclusively through the voices of monks or of priests profoundly influenced by monks, and the actions and the works of the other protagonists in history reach us for the most part through viewpoints and criteria of judgment formed by monastic culture. This is no small distortion: monasticism had a self-awareness that offered schemata for its own representation and a touchstone for judging the world. A sort of spiritualizing yeast removed the monastery from the common measure of human works and actions. This intellectual and emotive process was not the result of a vital religious and mystical experience alone: when monasticism reduced all other reality to its own image and its own religious and cultural schemata in the aim of bending them to an explanation and exaltation of the choice and the experience of the monastic life, it discovered the subterranean ideological, political, and social roots of its own origins that provided further support to its affirmation in history.

Monasticism's mode of being has had a singular influence on modern historiography as well. The point of arrival of a spirituality, a culture, and an ideology (which must be reconstructed and understood in their roots and in their component parts) too often becomes the undisputed point of departure for historical reconstructions that are basically triumphalistic pomposity or static, contemplative reevocations of what should have been. In spite of exhaustive research on the part of historians and other scholars, only in recent decades has the long course of monastic humanity had a more adequate and accurate historical portrayal. Historicization also offers a good part of the key to understanding the reorganization of monasticism and its decline, but perhaps also the meaning of and the conditions for its continued presence (albeit marginal and highly inconspicuous) in a profoundly different religious and social context.

Documents of Monasticism in Late Antiquity and the Early Middle Ages

> And so the system of coenobites took its rise in the days of the preaching of the Apostles. For such was all that multitude of believers in Jerusalem, which is thus described in the Acts of the Apostles: "But the multitude of believers was of one heart and one soul, neither said any of them that any of the things which he possessed was his own, but they had all things common. They sold their possessions and property and divided them to all, as any man had need." And again: "For neither was there any among them that lacked; for as many as possessed fields or houses, sold them and brought the price of the things that they sold and laid them before the feet of the Apostles: and distribution was made to every man as he had need." The whole Church, I say, was then such as now are those few who can be found with difficulty in coenobia. But when at the death of the Apostles the multitude of believers began to wax cold, and especially that multitude which had

> come to the faith of Christ from diverse foreign nations, from whom the Apostles out of consideration for the infancy of their faith and their ingrained heathen habits, required nothing more than that they should "abstain from things sacrificed to idols and from fornication, and from things strangled, and from blood," and so that liberty which was conceded to the Gentiles because of the weakness of their newly-born faith, had by degrees begun to mar the perfection of that Church which existed at Jerusalem, and the fervour of that early faith cooled down owing to the daily increasing number both of natives and foreigners, and not only those who had accepted the faith of Christ, but even those who were the leaders of the Church relaxed somewhat of that strictness. For some fancying that what they saw permitted to the Gentiles because of their weakness, was also allowable for themselves, thought that they would suffer no loss if they followed the faith and confession of Christ keeping their property and possessions. But those who still maintained the fervour of the apostles, mindful of that former perfection left their cities and intercourse with those who thought that carelessness and a laxer life was permissible to themselves and the Church of God, and began to live in rural and more sequestered spots, and there, in private and on their own account, to practise those things which they had learnt to have been ordered by the apostles throughout the whole body of the Church in general: and so that whole system of which we have spoken grew up from those disciples who had separated themselves from the evil that was spreading. And these, as by degrees time went on, were separated from the great mass of believers and because they abstained from marriage and cut themselves off from intercourse with their kinsmen and the life of this world, were termed monks or solitaries [μονάζοντες] from the strictness of their lonely and solitary life. Whence it followed that from their common life they were called coenobites and their cells and lodgings coenobia. That then alone was the earliest kind of monks, which is first not only in time but also in grace. (trans. Gibson)

These were the terms in which John Cassian, early in the fifth century, summarized, for the use of the monks whom he intended to organize and teach in southern Gaul, memories of the origins of the monastic communities as he had garnered them, in the course of his long experience in the East, from the tradition of the ancient Fathers. Cassian brought system and a coherent historiographical schema (which was also an efficacious didactic myth) to widely held ideas and credences. He pictured the monastic experience as an attempt and a desire to perpetuate the modes of being and the fervent renunciation of the first Christians and as the only form of life that would guarantee, by its very organizational structure and its separation from the rest of society, a continuity with a model of perfection otherwise irremediably contaminated and dispersed in the historical success of Christianity.

For Cassian, the choice of celibacy and asceticism and the renunciation of all forms of private property, with the consequent commonality of property, were the reasons for that continuity and assured its future. It should be superfluous to note that this summary is a great simplification of the actual process. Both eastern monasticism of the fourth century and the irrepressible and chaotic expansion of monasticism in the West between the fourth and the fifth centuries had roots, developments, and characteristics that were a good deal more complex and more fully articulated. Cassian's argument is a reflection of the task—at the time well begun and headed for success—of capturing and absorbing into ecclesiastically disciplined frameworks the unsystematic and convulsive forms of individualistic asceticism typical of the first anchorites in Egypt, Syria, and Mesopotamia. It also registers a stage in the elaboration of theology and ethics in which themes and commonplaces of Stoic and Neoplatonic thought had been combined skillfully with mystical and ascetic elements from Christian tradition to produce an intellectually and socially aristocratic synthesis that founded a form of life apart from both the cares and the worries of the world and the "weaknesses" and the "woes" of common mortals, in the interest of total dedication to the search for God through contemplation in tranquillity.

The themes and experiences that Cassian introduced into the West are not immediately perceptible as particular or specific in comparison to the Greek Fathers of the fourth century, who continued, through the many Latin translations of their works, to offer conceptual instruments and means of expression to monastic culture in the Western Middle Ages. What was decisive for monastic culture, however, was the self-awareness in the historiographical scheme Cassian had constructed. The idea of monasticism's exclusive possession of authentic Christianity and its consequent potential for contesting the state of the church outside the monastery were fundamental components (which cropped up in various ways and in combination with other elements) of the extraordinary flowering of monasticism in the eleventh and twelfth centuries.

Two other aspects of Cassian's account deserve comment, however, because they are indicative of choices and attitudes that would contribute much to the development of monasticism and to the way monks related to their times. On the one hand, the clear designation of community life—the cenoby—as the original and the preferred form of monasticism implied the creation of organized structures that tended to be arranged according to a *regula* (Gregory of Tours tells of *regulae* that he wrote for the communities he founded in Marseilles), as was already occurring in the East, and as Augustine was doing for his church in Hippo. These rules thus went beyond the spontaneous forms of free ascetic initiative that had inspired (and in part continued to inspire) a flight to the "desert." Rules and organization, however, involved a radical change in basic mental orientations and in the very constitution and experience of monastic life, since one of their essential elements was the criterion of obedience and discipline.

The free experience of God that had been the aspiration and the crowning reward of the solitary life was thus consciously organized as a method and placed under the direction and supervision of a hierarchic superior, while renunciation of the world and the struggle against its enticements and one's own inclinations necessarily led to renunciation of one's own will and its abandonment into the superior's hands. Although Gregory the Great noted, nearly two centuries later, toward the beginning of the *Dialogues*, that isolated exceptions to the fundamental norm of ascetic education existed, he prudently observes, "According to sound monastic practice, a person should not presume to become a superior until he has learned submission; if he does not know how to obey, he should not be requiring obedience of others" (trans. Zimmerman). "Ascetic imitation replaced ascetic initiative" (Courtois), and the choice of the monastic life as a personal realization of the Christian life, thus as confirmation and embodiment of the promises of baptism (it was in fact referred to as a "second baptism"), became in some fashion a point of arrival, the stage at which most monks could stop and indeed had to stop on the uninterrupted scale of an arduous and solitary ascension toward the divine, an experience that remained the privilege of an exceptional few.

This opened monasticism to broader possibilities for expansion and recruitment, promptly fulfilled by a flurry of new monastic orders founded between the fifth and the sixth centuries, aided as well by increasingly precarious conditions in civil life. In my opinion, it is difficult to deny that the monk of that period was not simply a soul seeking God in prayer and in solitude, but very often also a man in need of peace and tranquillity in an increasingly difficult and hostile world. The first female communities were founded for reasons that were in great part analogous, but with the addition of a strong, persistent, and long-lasting subordination to the male model. Harsh social conditions also contributed to the proposal and elaboration of precise codes of behavior—the rules—as did the proliferation of new centers that attracted an increasing population in hard times. Between the fifth and the seventh centuries at least thirty extant texts for rules offer a mix of borrowing, adaptation, rewriting, and reelaboration that is difficult to untangle. The enormous variety in ascetic orientations and in the traditions of spirituality on which these rules were based and the very different conditions under which the various monasteries were founded must not prevent us from seeing what they had in common. The monastery tended to become a world apart, self-sufficient and perfectly regulated in all its parts; a center for prayer, for labor, and, one must add, for culture.

We need to resist both mythologizing and generalization, however. The ambitious program of Cassiodorus, the classically-minded and authoritative minister for the Gothic kings in Italy, to make the monastic community of Vivarium a center for the conservation and transmission of classical culture (albeit for its recuperation and integration into Christian tradition) failed to hold firm against the disintegration and collapse of civil structures that followed the Lombardic invasion. The Benedictines, at least originally, contemplated nothing of the sort, and only partially can such aims be considered to have been realized by subsequent monastic culture. Still, the fact that the rules generally provided that all monks had to learn to read—at least all those under the age of fifty, as the *Regula magistri* specifies, thus attesting that a number of adult illiterates also chose the monastic life—placed monks on a level of instruction above that of the common herd. There was, in fact, a strict connection between the ability to read and the religious life of the monk, as rules in the Western tradition generally set aside from two to three hours daily for spiritual reading, and reading was the necessary preliminary to *meditatio,* the oral repetition of biblical texts committed to memory. This meant that the monastery needed to have the means—a library, a school, a scriptorium—that quite naturally made it an exclusive and culturally privileged place.

The monastery thus appeared more and more as an island within a society that it preferred to ignore, except for material necessities and what was needed for the spiritual well-being of the monks. Hence the customary obligation of hospitality and the rules for assisting the poor; hence, above all, the holdings (great and small) that guaranteed daily subsistence and provided for the practical needs of the monks. According to Gregory of Tours, St. Lupicinus would accept from Chilperic, king of the Burgundians, only what the land produced, so persuaded was he that monks should not own fields or vineyards. Monastic rules of roughly the same period, however, are usually limited to prescribing renunciation of all forms of individual property for the monks without excluding collective ownership.

Monastic centers and rules sprang up everywhere, at times placed under the nominal authority of some prestigious ancient Father, as with the Rule of Macarius (in reality the work of Porcarius, abbot of Lérins, who lived at the turn of the fifth century); at other times referring to more mysterious but no less authoritative sources, as for the *Regula quatuor Patrum* or the *Regula magistri*. Thanks to the systematic backing of Rome and to the efforts of the Carolingians, the *Regula S. Benedicti* of the mid-sixth century, was to be, for several centuries to come, the normative text for the great majority of the monastic "families" in the West. The reasons for its success, however, also lay in its precise dispositions and its efficient organization of the whole of cenobitic life, in the balanced code of conduct that it proposed, and in the ample discretion conceded to the abbot to adapt it to differences of person and of place. The *Vita S. Benedicti* inserted into Book II of the *Dialogues* of Gregory the Great further reinforced the spread of the Benedictine Rule by connecting it to the concrete experience of one man and one environment.

The last aspect of Cassian's discourse that, in my opinion, should be noted (because it points to an attitude that became central in the monastic experience as it was later defined and was periodically reasserted and reproposed and periodically questioned) is the exclusive concentration of those first "monks" on their own perfection and salvation. Cassian is clear on the question. The only proper reaction to the decadence and corruption of the Church of Jerusalem was flight, and the one problem that obsessed those first "monks" was to keep the ancient rigor uncontaminated and preserve themselves from such "contagion." Elsewhere Cassian defines as a "diabolical illusion" the call to convert others that persuaded monks to leave the community: what mattered was one's own "correction," which could not be realized among the daily activities and tribulations of worldly life that would confront one in the task of converting and guiding others.

Cassian's position is rigorously consistent within his logical system, which is impregnated with Neoplatonic elements picked up from Origen and Evagrius: one cannot jeopardize the conquest of God, which the cenoby made possible, to pursue advantages and gains that are less important because they concern mere creatures. This was not only an ecclesiological doctrine restricting opportunity for Christian perfection to the choice of the monastic life; it was also an ethic and an anthropology. In this viewpoint, humanity was irremediably distributed into "conditions" of life in a hierarchy of morality and merits not susceptible to modification or change of place. In the final analysis, those living at the lowest levels of the "common condition" did not merit the attention or the interest of those who had attained the highest level. Did this aristocratically elitist argument contain an acknowledgment of the real situation; of the difficulties involved in Christianization and of the growing crisis that had struck ecclesiastical and civil structures? It is possible and perhaps probable. The price that monks paid was that they were shut off—not merely separated—from other men and from their own times. The superior grace that they proclaimed for themselves led to a more rigid superiority in social status.

Cassian's positions refer to a reality still in a phase of slow and uncertain construction, and they aim at supporting and corroborating awareness of a way of life based on a variety of motivations and as yet divided among different trends. In the central Middle Ages, when his arguments became an integral part of the ideology of monasticism, they brought a proud claim to social hegemony to a quite different monasticism, much more solidly built and more socially recognized than at its unsure beginnings, but they also brought a contradictory and agonizingly difficult relationship with society and with history.

These were, of course, not the only notions that Western monasticism inherited from the religious experience of the society of late antiquity. It was also between the fourth and the fifth centuries, with the advent of the tumultuous experiences of the first anchorites and with the writing and distribution of the earliest "models" of monastic biography (the *Vita S. Antonii* of Athanasius first among them) that a connection began to be drawn between the figure of the monk, personal "sanctity," and the exploitation of charismatic and supernatural powers, a connection that later would be fundamental to medieval religion and to the relationship between the monastery and society. Veneration, cultic forms, and expectations and hopes that focused on the tombs and the sanctuaries of the martyrs and confessors of the faith were enlarged to include new and more recent witnesses to God and "friends of God"; new and different "athletes of the faith."

The growth and spread of the cult of the saints was not directed at monks and anchorites alone; it also included churchmen, in particular bishops who were considered charismatic and beneficent people during their lifetimes and, through their acknowledged sanctity, were thought to prolong and increase their powers after death. With the specific involvement of monasticism, however, and thanks to a combination of motivations and forces that underlay the emergence of the monastic movement, the cult of saints underwent a radical change. This cult, which had been a religious and social phenomenon centering on actual persons and real-life experiences from the recent or remote past—persons who offered a special relationship and promised aid exclusively through the mediation of "relics," holy sites, and cultic memory—became extended to people and situations whose physical reality, so to speak, reached into the present time, no longer fostered exclusively by groups of disciples and by communities that kept the memory of the holy teachers alive. Henceforth, not only did groups of disciples and communities act as custodians for the memory of their saintly leaders; those holy men could be identified while living by their choice of a life foreign to the standards of common men and could manifest their full powers for regeneration and salvation during their lifetimes.

The cult of saints was formed out of a particularly complex set of themes, impulses, and suggestions taken from a variety of places and sources. The history of sanctity and of the cult of sanctity unfolds on many levels, even if sanctity expressed profoundly unified and widely shared needs and expectations. To understand the structure of the medieval monastic ideology, however, we need to grasp the privileged (if not exclusive) relationship that was gradually established between the monastic life and sanctity. Although the saint was a man who had distinguished himself for the fullness of his faith, the excellence of his Christian life, or the wealth of grace and the breadth of the powers with which God had rewarded him, the interpretation of the monastic life—the only full and authentic form of Christian life—suggested that only through that life could manifestations of sanctity remain present and active in the life of men.

The perpetuation of the ancient cults in places sanctified by tombs or by charismatic signs, symbols, and objects thus intersected with new cults and new sites, was enriched by them, and was continued in the living reality of the religious communities, which not only preserved the tombs, the "relics," and the memories of their saintly founders, but were themselves centers of the holy life and, by that token, provided boons, graces, and hope for comfort and salvation to whoever entered into contact with them. The *Dialogues* of Gregory the Great are largely an exposition of the *signa* and *virtutes* of ascetics, founders of monastic communities, and monks. Such men showed the living power of God in history, and signs of that sort in turn attested, for the instruction of all, to the goodness and excellence of their lives. The monasteries became places of veneration that could be terrible for their desecraters but that guaranteed their benefactors prayers and spiritual favors. The ancient entreaty of St. Paul to come to the aid of the "saints" of Jerusalem with "material things" (Rom. 15:25–27) translated in current terms as a duty to support monastic communities with offerings and donations, thus somehow enabling the donor to share in their merits and to profit from the grace granted them. This gave the monastery, as a center for prayer and asceticism, the task of compensating for the prayers and the penance that common mortals were incapable of performing, and it established a privileged relationship between sovereigns, nobles, and monastic foundations that was to be a decisive factor in the expansion of Western monasticism.

Religious implications and hopes for salvation lay behind the exceptional drive to found monasteries that possessed kings and *potentes* of barbarian Europe in the sixth and seventh centuries. The purposes and interests underlying such initiatives were a good deal more complex, however, not only according to the observations of some perspicacious contemporary witnesses but probably in the calculations of the founders themselves. In his *Historia ecclesiastica gentis Anglorum* Bede states that the advent of an age of peace and serenity would both be signaled by and result in many of the great (along with people of all social strata) laying down their arms and submitting, they and their children, to monastic discipline. Bede closes his long account with the somewhat mysterious words, "The future age will see what will be the outcome of all this." He remained clearly optimistic, however: the outcome would be affirmation of the Christian faith and involvement of the entire earth in the exultation at the reign of Christ. During those same years, however, in a long letter to Egbert, archbishop of York, Bede expressed an opinion on the causes and consequences of monastic expansion that seems radically different. It was a gigantic speculation favored by previous kings and bishops: with the pretext of founding monasteries great lords had obtained enormous landholdings from the crown and had administered them, along with the monasteries on them, for their own benefit, rendering them hereditary and filling them with monks of the commonest stuff, recruited without discrimination. Bede proposes remedies, insisting, among other things, on the duty of the bishops to supervise the monasteries. At the time this seemed the bishops' evident and unquestioned right (interfering great lords aside); it was only much later that it became an extremely delicate problem of internal equilibrium for the church as an institution.

Bede is particularly lucid when he analyzes the spread of monasticism in England, where specific and clearly defined political and social interests were involved. His only criticisms of the process bear upon certain distortions that he thought needed correction. The apparent contradiction with the *Historia* dissolves, however, with consideration of the different perspectives of the two texts: the letter speaks about what is to be done immediately but is being blocked; the history looks at the long time-span, evaluated optimistically in an all-embracing vision (Gustavo Vinaj). The difference in Bede's judgments is a clue—as are their limitations—to an attitude that was to be long-lived in monastic culture. A monk himself from the age of seven and profoundly sympathetic with and deeply satisfied by the religious, cultural, and social benefits that the monastery offered him (benefits which most men lacked), Bede was incapable of seeing that those very characteristics of monastic institutions were the incentive for the corrupting mechanisms whose outcome he criticized. He insists on the monks' choice of poverty, but he seems unaware that the monastery was by its nature a privileged center of wealth and power.

To speak of a culture of intention would perhaps be going too far. The fact remains that evaluation of the same acts shifted according to the end that inspired them, and that from the monastic point of view the purity of an opinion could be measured by the respect it showed to "men of God." I have no intention of indulging in facile historiographical moralism: what is important is to become aware of the logical and structural processes that produced and justified the paradoxical situation in which the monastery was the private property of lay potentates. Wilhelm Kurze, to explain the growing support that the Lombard kings and dukes offered monastic expansion after their conversion to Catholicism during the course of the seventh century, has rightly insisted on the complex interplay of political and economic considerations, even though he finds a unifying element in the "elementary nature" of the religion of the time. For great lords and kings, the opportunity to give their lands a less precarious economic and administrative organization through the founding of monasteries combined with the spiritual advantages that they expected to gain.

The same mechanism operated throughout barbarian Europe, in differing degrees and at different times. The "missions" of the Irish and Anglo Saxon monks who invaded the Continent between the late sixth century and the eighth century found strong local support in the rulers of the land, the Franks in particular, as well as from Rome. From Columban to Boniface, in little more than a century and a half monastic foundations increased remarkably. Luxeuil (590), Bobbio (613), Saint-Denis (650), Jumièges (654), San Vincenzo al Volturno (703–8), Reichenau (724), Fulda (741), Saint Gall (750) are famous names, but there were by that time hundreds of monasteries.

The first great wave of monasticism reached its height during the decades of Carolingian hegemony. With Charlemagne and his immediate successors the foundation and the possession of a monastery became a specifically royal prerogative, and in the great royal or imperial abbeys hosts of monks prayed to God for the sovereigns and assured their works celestial protection. The effort to provide a cultural base for their rule further encouraged monastic foundations, and the commitment to give them more solid and uniform discipline encouraged adoption of the Rule of St. Benedict. This was the last great legacy that the early Middle Ages left to the later, full development of monasticism. In the Carolingian age, Western monasticism was nearly exclusively Benedictine monasticism, which obeyed a precise logic of its own in both organization and establishments, in spite of the persisting variety of applications and interpretations of its rule.

The chief architect of this institutional organization and imposition of discipline was Benedictus of Aniane, who entered the monastery of Saint-Seine, near Dijon, as an adult after serving at the court and in the army of Charlemagne. For his work he has been called, with some exaggeration, the second founder of Western monasticism. In a fluid, multiform situation, he imposed a degree of uniformity on practice by drawing up precise but amplified rules specifying and organizing the daily ritual of the monks and noting times appropriate for each act (Jean Leclercq). Benedictus's consistent aim, according to his disciple and biographer, Smaragdus, was to create a set of daily practices (*consuetudo*) within a monastic community through observance of a unique and common rule. His success would have been unthinkable, however, without the political backing and the generous financial support that Charlemagne and Louis the Pius offered the monasteries, or without the *iussio imperialis* that obliged the monasteries of France and Germany to adopt the norms that Benedictus proposed at the synod of Aix-la-Chapelle in 817 (Schmitz).

Veritable "holy cities" arose, and near the monasteries sizable agglomerations that could almost be called urban sprang up, organized into wards and defended by their own small army of *milites*. Saint-Riquier in the Ponthieu region was completed in 788, and its triangular *claustrum*, the angles of which were marked by three vast churches, lodged at least three hundred monks. Surrounding it, there grew up a town of some seven thousand inhabitants, distributed into various *vici* (neighborhoods; quarters) according to their trades and to the services they owed the monastery. There was a *vicus militum*, which lodged a hundred soldiers, and there were sections for blacksmiths, weavers, leatherworkers, shoemakers, saddlers, bakers, taverners, vintners, and merchants. There were even *servientes per omnia* to do the humblest tasks (Hubert).

Saint-Riquier was certainly not an isolated case. The figures proclaim the extraordinary expansion of monasteries: Lorsch could call 1,200 *milites* to its defense; Anselm, in the long decades that he spent at Nonantola, had more than a thousand monks grouped around him; Lobbes had jurisdiction over seventy-two parishes. Even the pompous formulas applied to some monasteries of the time, harking back to prestigious models—*altera Roma, Altera Aegyptus*—attest to their remarkable size.

This growth was impressive, and it continued almost uninterruptedly. If we look at the underlying causes of monastic expansion at its height, however, a change is clearly discernible in the accentuated ritualism that Benedictus of Aniane introduced—a change that would influence the very nature of the monastic vocation. The monastery did not cease to be a place for asceticism and individual penitence, for refuge and for protection against the ferocious mores of a military society, but it became primarily a place for the collective and public prayer that both men and society needed for their very survival. A veritable citadel of prayer, it fulfilled a function held basic to the interest of all: adoring God, obtaining his favors and his graces, and combating the inexhaustible presence among men of the "ancient enemy."

The crisis that struck and overwhelmed the political structure set up by the Carolingians and the destruction wreaked on both civil society and monasteries by the Saracens, the Hungarians, and the Normans broke the continuity of many monastic foundations and obliged the next generation of monks to start over in scenes of desolation and ruin. These tribulations failed to interrupt the continuity of memory of the logic that encouraged, supported, and lent direction to monastic institutions. In the slow work of the reconstruction of authority between the tenth and the eleventh centuries that put a new face on Europe, the monastery, whether it was promoted by a bishop, a lord, or a king, occupied a decisive position further strengthened by the extreme weakness of civic structures. Central authority was nonexistent, the bishops, embroiled in struggles between local potentates (from whose numbers they themselves sprang), played an insignificant role, and the cathedral schools, which had been one of the finest fruits of Carolingian reform, were in decline or in ruins. The monastery offered a model that was a fascinating alternative to the prevailing disorder. In spite of everything, it had retained a capacity for cultural formation and economic and civil organization of the territory that made it a privileged point of departure for a slow recovery. The monasticism that was to emerge from this revival was in many ways a monasticism of different men, however. Not only was it better organized and more compact; it had an existential attitude of its own, a self-awareness, and a capacity for hegemony and action that profoundly differentiated it from the monasticism from which it had nonetheless inherited much.

The Aurea Saecula

Beginning with the tenth century the main outlines of monastic recovery grew clearer as monasteries were founded or refounded. The process was slow at first, then increasingly rapid, and it followed the time-tested scheme. Kings and great lords (bishops and popes also took the initiative or lent support) counted on the monastery to be a religious center of prayer, an agricultural enterprise, and a site from which to expand and reinforce political control of the surrounding territory. In taking over the founding of monasteries (a royal prerogative in the Carolingian period) and pursuing it for their own benefit, the lords who held title to the great territorial principalities built on the ruins of the former empire attested to their high rank, their power, and their autonomy. In a context of contradictory, intersecting, or juxtaposed authorities and relations searching for new spaces and new instruments for affirming their power, the very complexity of the function of monastic institutions prompted totally opposite attitudes, and there were also lords, bishops, or *milites* who attacked, pillaged, and ravaged the monasteries and squandered their wealth.

Recovery alternated with destruction, and both were linked to the many interests concentrated around the monasteries and to the lack of solid central powers. For at least two centuries, tensions and conflicts ebbed and flowed and were noted in abundant detail in monastic chronicles and biographies. The road nevertheless led irresistibly forward; there were occasional setbacks, but also new trails were blazed. Awareness grew of a gradual decline in monastic discipline brought on by the subordination of the monastery to the powers and the interests that surrounded it. Those same powers and interests were often responsible for its existence, but that did not make them any less of a threat to the monastery's autonomy and the regularity of its discipline. As pressure for reform matured, there were increasing demands to assert the primordial and constitutional superiority of monasticism and, as a corollary, to achieve the monastery's autonomy from the political and institutional context in which it was set. The two great courts of appeal for "monastic liberty" were thus the royal or imperial power (following the Carolingian tradition) or papal power.

During the tenth century those powers were in a phase of eclipse and intrinsic weakness, and when the first centers of reformed monasticism turned to them for support, the consequences were important for their gradual recovery. The first explicit theories viewing the church as one great diocese of Rome came from Cluniac monks.

Monasticism had other concerns, however. The need for defense against the interference and the ambitions of local powers prompted the monasteries to move toward concentration and interconnection. They gradually ceased to be self-contained centers under the jurisdiction of the diocesan bishop and subject to intimidation in a variety of ways by the local lord, clerical or lay. They tended to coalesce around one main monastery, organizing into great congregations that hoped to persuade Rome to grant them exemption from the jurisdiction of the local Ordinary. This acted like a centripetal force: the congregation attracted new monasteries; its increased strength brought it increased attention and interest and lent it greater weight in religious and political matters.

The case of Cluny, founded in 910 by the abbot Berno of Gigny with the support of William of Aquitaine, is both striking and exemplary. In little more than a century it became the *ordo*, the *ecclesia cluniacen-*

sis, gathering together hundreds of monasteries throughout the West from England to Italy; between the eleventh and the twelfth centuries it became the most important and authoritative religious congregation in all Christendom. It was not unique, however: from Saint-Victor of Marseilles to Vallombrosa, from Saint Benignus of Dijon to Hirsau and Gorze, from Camaldoli to Cîteaux, the great centuries of monastic expansion saw a proliferation of solid congregations grouped around one major center radiating its influence and imposing its customs far and wide.

The massive presence of these orders had a profound influence on both ecclesiastical and civil society, not only through the model that their way of life provided but also by the growing number of monastic personnel that entered the ranks of the church's hierarchy. Of the six successive popes in the decisive half century of the struggle for reform from Gregory VII to Calixtus II, only the last could not boast of a monastic background. "Episcopari monachos nostros nec novum nec admirabile nobis est," Peter the Venerable remarked in 1138, not without pride, defending the election of a Cluniac monk as bishop of Langres against the criticism of Bernard of Clairvaux.

Monastic presence reflected a powerful cultural movement to gain command of all life in society and organize it according to monastic views. The legacy of the church Fathers and the early Middle Ages was reinterpreted and reformulated in terms of monastic hegemony: theology, cosmology, anthropology, morality, and the law were recast to provide a foundation and a justification for the preeminence of monks within the rigid social categories that subdivided and disciplined society. The monastic citadel stood in contrast to an inimical "world" deserving only of contempt and to a history irrationally disposed as a series of violent acts, woes, and catastrophes. Only the monastery was capable of giving meaning and perspective to that world and to that history because it was the only full response to Christ's call and was directed toward the eschatological fulfillment of an otherworldly goal.

The hierarchical scheme of the three *ordines* proposed by ecclesiastical culture of the Carolingian tradition that divided society into men of prayer (*oratores*), men of war (*bellatores*), and men who worked the land (*laboratores*) was revised in monastic circles to put monks at the top: "Among Christians of the two sexes we know well that there exist three orders and, so to speak, three levels. The first is that of the laity, the second that of the clergy, the third that of the monks. Although none of the three is exempt from sin, the first is good, the second is better, and the third is excellent" (*PL*, 139, col. 463). Abbon of Fleury, the abbot of Saint-Benoît-sur-Loire at the end of the tenth century, went on to refer to Jesus' parable of the sower and the different yields from seed to express the idea of different and precisely defined rewards awaiting Christians in the other world according to their status in this life—in the ratio of 100 for monks, 60 for the clergy, and 30 for the laity.

Reflections on the theoretical divisions of humanity have a long history and have been applied in many ways, but in this period they found monastic culture marshaled in defense of its own scale of values. That culture did more than profoundly undervalue secular society and depreciate all efforts that did not originate in the cloister and continue to radiate from there; it also overwhelmingly favored the spirit over matter and the soul over the body, implying a tendentiously negative judgment of any human category that did not have chastity—or at least the unmarried state—as its first requirement. It is not by chance, incidentally (in fact, it reflects attitudes and options with deep psychological roots) that woman in monastic biographies and chronicles, when she was not the loving and prescient mother of a saint or a nun, was for the most part a deceitful and savage creature, constantly prey to the senses and to an uncontrollable emotivity, and fated to corrupt men by luring them with pleasures of the flesh. Men, society, and history were analyzed and conceived of exclusively in reference to man's celestial destiny; life on earth was viewed in new terms and portrayed according to the rigid hierarchical divisions that were imagined to be true of Heaven. The abyss between Heaven and the earth would remain unbridgeable, however, were it not for the foretaste of Paradise that the cenoby offered men within their historical experience. To those who entered the cloister, it offered an initiation, even in this life, to the delights of the future life; to those who remained on the outside, it gave hope for future salvation in spite of all, thanks to their relations with those who had had the grace and the merit to have elected the monastic life. The monastery was a privileged place in which earthly life and the beatific life were joined almost indissolubly, assuring its inhabitants a passage to the better life; a passage that was otherwise perilous and uncertain. But it also was a place in which the prayers of those within the monastery could guarantee aid and comfort to those who, even though they lived in the world, had done something to merit help.

In reality, the confines were not that clearly drawn. People from all walks of life and with a variety of connections to the monastery grouped around it, forming something like concentric circles of interest. Some people's needs could be satisfied by temporary aid or asylum; other humble folk whose autonomy or subsistence were threatened could "give themselves" to the monastery, offering themselves, their meager possessions, or their small landholdings in exchange for protection, aid, and prayers. Material concerns were obviously of prime importance among these newcomers, though not to the point of obliterating the complex of expectations and images that linked vast strata of society to the cloister. Still, this influx affected the composition of the monastic family itself when some congregations—Vallombrosans, Cistercians—introduced the *conversus*. The term was usually used as a qualifier and originally indicated a monk who had joined the order as an adult. The *conversus* was contrasted to the *nutritus*, the monk educated in the monastery from childhood, and the number of *conversi* seems to have declined during the tenth and the eleventh centuries, as noble recruitment to the monastery increased. In the new use of the term, to the contrary, the *conversi* were illiterate laymen accepted as monks but not admitted into the chancel who were asked to provide humbler services and were allowed only limited participation in the cult. To some extent they substituted for the *servi* of Cluniac monasteries, but they also were a result of recruitment from a broader social range. An ongoing quest for protection and security within the monastic environment combined with new demands for the religious life that permeated much of society. It is difficult to determine the extent of phenomena like those attested by Bernold von Constanz at the end of the eleventh century, where families and entire villages seeking a more rigorous religious life organized into *fraternitates* linked to the monastic world. The novelty of certain forms of organization and living in common reflects long-lasting and widespread basic tendencies. There was a broad, ambiguously defined area within the compass of the monasteries the nature of which becomes clearer only when we look higher on the social scale. Kings and great lords established close connections with the cloister in quite specific ways. Their custom of taking on the monastic habit at death's door is a clear indication of a search for guarantees for their destiny in the next world, guarantees offered not only by the habit but also by monastic burial and the prayers of the monks. Similarly, donations of revenues or property recommended the donors to the prayers of the monks.

> Honour the servants of God in word and deed. Especially, revere and help in every way you can our lords and brethren, the monks who minister in this church, supporting them with your counsel and help if they have need of it. Grant freely that they may enjoy in peace and quiet the goods that my father and I have given them for our salvation. Never try to deprive them of any possessions or revenues, nor allow any of your men to do them any wrong. For if you take care to be a true patron to them, they will never cease to pray God for you. (Ordericus Vitalis, *The Ecclesiastical History,* trans. Chibnall [Oxford: Clarendon Press, 1972, 1978], 3:195 [*PL,* 188, cols. 442f.])

It was in these terms that the noble Ansold, lord of Maule, reaching the threshold of death after an adventurous life of voyages and battles, recommended the monks of Saint-Evroult to his son as he donned their habit "to finish his life with them, so that he could receive the reward that God promises to his own" (ibid.). This is only one among many analogous episodes recounted in detail by the Cluniac chronicler Ordericus Vitalis; innumerable diplomatic sources and chronicles also attest that this was an established and widespread custom in the better society of the time. In this way a privileged and lasting fraternal bond stretched uninterrupted from life to death. Alfonso, king of Castile, made abundant gifts to the Cluniac congregation "ut neminem regum vel principum sive priscis seu modernis temporibus ei comparare possimus." He managed to assure himself an imposing list of monastic services on his behalf: the recitation of an entire psalm at terce ("Exaudiat te Dominus") and of the collect "Quaesumus, omnipotens Deus" at high mass; the washing of the feet of thirty paupers on Holy Thursday *pro eo;* the feeding of one hundred poor people—again, *pro eo*—by the *camerarius* on Easter Sunday. Furthermore, a meal for the king was to be served daily in the refectory "quasi si nobiscum epulaturus sederet" to maintain a monk for the salvation of the king's soul "tam in vita quam in morte." In the church of Saints Peter and Paul, built with his contributions, one of the most important altars bore his name, and on it a daily mass was to implore God for his eternal salvation. These benefits, in which the queen also shared, were to be broadened after his death by masses offered for his soul, choral prayers, multiple distributions of food to the poor, and the concession of a more abundant dinner for the monks on the anniversary of his death (*PL,* 159, cols. 945f.).

Alfonso offers an exceptional picture, comparable to few others in its prodigality. Still, the connection and relationship between monks and their benefactors that we see in him was by no means exceptional. Taken singly, the works carried out for the benefit of Alfonso or on his behalf were repeated for many of the greater (and lesser) lay lords who offered donations, favor, or protection to that particular monastery. *Libri vitae, libri memoriales,* necrologies, obituaries, *libri confraternitatum,* and *libri sepulcrorum* all attest fully that monastic communities and their benefactors were bound to one another by the connection between the benefits of monastic prayer and charity.

Both life inside the monastery and its role in society thus took on an eminently cultic and assistive dimension, and the portion of the monastic day dedicated to liturgy expanded noticeably, in the Cluniac congregation in particular. Even monastic recruitment (which by that time, following a custom that had begun in the early Middle Ages, focused particularly on the very young) found a specifically religious motivation in such social functions. When parents offered one of their sons to God (often with a substantial donation to assure his education and maintenance), it was a quite special way of assuring both a friendly presence in the "holy college" of the monks and a privileged vehicle for prayers and intercession.

Guarantees for the otherworld were solidly connected with concrete advantages realizable in the present one. Prayers were accompanied by the special talents, the backing, and the concrete forms of aid that the monks could offer their benefactors, thanks to the monks' power, their culture, their prestige, and their authority. William of Normandy, after his conquest of England, turned to the monastic communities he had founded for assistance in renewing the episcopate of the realm, but he also called on monastic personnel to organize a wiser and more prudent administration of the crown's holdings (*PL,* 159, cols. 817D–818A). Count Theobald, one of the most powerful lords of France, was renowned for his generous support to the newly founded Cistercian congregation and for the friendship that bound him to St. Bernard. When the king turned his forces against him and Theobald found himself in grave difficulty, some commented ironically on his past generosities: he had no need to arm troops—instead of knights on horseback and crossbowmen he had monks and *conversi!* The monks' prayers did not seem to do him much good, and in order to save himself, as one bishop sneered (his realism concerning the art of government obviously suggesting a skeptical vein), God would have to appear in person, take up a mace, and not spare his blows, "but up to now He has done nothing of the kind." In the hagiographer's apologetic and edifying account, St. Bernard saved the situation, not only with his prayers but also with his active intervention, pacifying the contenders and freeing Theobald from his difficulty (*PL*, 185, col. 328f.). Pious bombast aside, traces of the saint's decisive interventions in political clashes are too frequent and attestations to them too consistent to be written off.

St. Bernard was without any doubt an exceptional figure, but similar roles for abbots and monasteries crop up again and again during at least two centuries. It was certainly not by chance that Hugh, the great abbot of Cluny, sat at Canossa at the side of Gregory VII and was an active protagonist in the absolution and reconciliation of Henry IV, nor that the old emperor, in flight and pursued by his son, turned to Hugh for comfort and support. These are well-known facts. Similarly, it is well known that such men as Romuald, William of Volpiano or Desiderius of Monte Cassino, Wilhelm von Hirsau or Suger of Saint-Denis, or Peter the Venerable acted as counselors, mediators, peacemakers, and active protagonists (at times behind the scenes) in the great questions of their times. These were great men and outstanding figures in a monasticism that in reality counted innumerable actors, some of them minor in appearance only, who moved in the same directions and with the same intentions as the major figures.

The prestige, authority, and force of decision of such men would be incomprehensible without the fascination that they were able to inspire, which, in my opinion, had a deeper source than simply their aura of sanctity or the reputation of disinterested rigor that surrounded them. These monks give an impression of a density of personality, an introspective wisdom and a power of analysis, a capacity for detached realism in reading the soul's impulses that make them somehow superior to the others and that one might even say attest to the presence of a human stuff, a level of maturation absent elsewhere. This is not terrain that is easy to tread or to investigate. Nor is it enough, obviously, to speak of the strong sense of self-awareness that animated monastic culture. The lack of any documentation that does not spring from that same culture undeniably complicates research. Nevertheless, many marginal indications support this impression if one follows the trail of the uncontested dominion over the written word that was the exclusive prerogative of such men. Many small bits of information, in themselves irrelevant, combine to offer an eloquent picture of mental agility, subtlety of interpretation, and acute insight to portray the real stature of their mode of being and their operating style. One example is the vivid picture that Hugh of Cluny paints, defending himself before the Council of Reims in 1049 from the charge of having maneuvered basely to promote the abbey: "The flesh wanted it, certainly; the mind and the reason rejected it" *PL*, 159, col. 865D). There is the biting irony with which Suger, in a few realistic strokes, sketches the members of the haughty imperial embassy that had come to France to negotiate with Paschal II: the noisy corpulence of Duke Welf, an incredibly tall, broad-shouldered man, the ingratiating eagerness to please of the bishop of Trier, an expert in solemn speech, the entire group "so tumultuous that they seemed sent more to inspire fear than to reason peacefully" (*Vita Ludovici Grossi regis,* 9). There is also the pained and disenchanted awareness with which Suger (again) comments on the atrocious betrayals that peppered familiar relations within the feudalism of his age: "The scarcity of faith makes it so that more often evil is rendered for good than good for evil: the one is divine, the other is neither divine nor human, nevertheless it is done" (ibid., 17). Finally, there is the subtle delineation, in a letter of Peter the Venerable, of the obscure zones of the soul incommunicable even to one's dearest friends (Ep. 54), or the balanced wisdom of Bruno, the founder of the Carthusian Order, who understood the importance of the delights of nature for the repose of a spirit wearied by meditations and vigils. Intellectual vigor and emotive exuberance joined in these men with a skill in writing that discerns and expresses the niceties of sensations, disparities, or subtle and secret intentions. This aspect of the monastic universe deserves systematic investigation. All evidence points to it as having been an essential component of monasticism's hegemony over contemporary society.

The tasks of mediation, pacification, and orientation were thus fundamental to the relation between monasticism and the secular powers, almost as if monasticism sought to transfer out of the cloister the peace and the fraternal and ordered community that remained among its most tenaciously pursued goals. This does not mean that those monks and those monasteries had not chosen sides, nor that their involvement in historical events remained limited to the role of arbiters above all factions. Monasticism constituted too full a reality and too complex a presence not to become an important pawn (often a decisive one) in struggles for the redistribution of power, just as self-awareness and an awareness of the existential and symbolic significance of their own state was so high among monks that they quite naturally demanded the right of prophecy and binding judgment over the actions of men. When monks' lives were jeopardized by undisciplined *milites* in search of fortune and the monasteries' property rights were infringed by unscrupulous and ambitious lords, monastic culture invariably attributed such acts to blind violence or diabolical malevolence. Monastic chronicles usually note that the guilty parties brought disgrace upon themselves and were punished by the work of God or man operating as the right hand of divine justice. A touchstone for the religion, the righteousness, and the justice of other men, the monastery claimed to remain apart, above the complex, conflicting interests and ambitions that rent a chaotic feudal society, in ferment during those centuries. In reality, however, it remained a pawn and an important element in strategies well known to the historian: the organization of factions and the establishment of potentates, for example, or the formation and alignment of the various groups and alliances that confronted one another in the great political and religious struggles of the period. In these struggles, monasticism showed the force and the prestige that it had achieved, but it also displayed all the qualities that had permitted its expansion and its development and that continued to burden its future.

We need to press further if we want to understand the position of the monastery in the political and religious context of its age or to penetrate the complex human reality that found expression and a habitat in the cloister. There is no greater distortion than a univocal, single explanation for great social phenomena—which is precisely what the monastic universe was, particularly between the tenth and the twelfth centuries. It was presented as a life and a career apart, beginning with its recruitment, entirely or in great part from the very young, since adult vocations, as we have seen, seem to have been the exception for the greater part of this period, at least in monasteries that drew from the nobility. It was almost as if monasticism were a reality that in some way claimed to remain closed, impermeable to the memory and the ordinary experience of common mortals. The monastic vocation was justified as the choice of a perfection that understood and was fully prepared to measure the abyss that separated the monastic world from the rest of human experience. Monasticism founded a self-conscious elite who believed they were carrying out an indispensable task decisive for the destiny of all men in the next world. This was why they felt impelled to demand—in constant tension with monasticism's original goals of abandoning the world—a position of preeminence, of judgment, of orientation if not command of the historical present.

Nonetheless, the monastic universe was not formed uniquely of men who had made a personal choice, for their own reasons and with their own individual memories, nor could it be defined by their difference or their opposition to the world around them. Because that difference was expressed in a daily round of acts and rhythms that were removed from time and from common measures, it gave rise to a style—to gestures, attitudes, tastes, and sensations—that was regarded as a compact and coherent whole offered to the veneration and the admiring contemplation of others, but that was not susceptible—at least as things ought to be—to real communication or interchange with society at large. Analysis of those elements and identification of the often unstable and difficult balance that gave them cohesion allow us to penetrate the reality of monasticism more deeply; to grasp the processes by which it grew and evolved, the roots of its crises, and the reasons for its slow but irresistible reorganization—in other words, to come closer to what has been defined (not completely felicitously) as the "monastic mystery" (unless "mystery" simply indicates the limits of knowledge and judgement that inevitably bar the historian's path).

The Crisis of the Monastic System

The monastic life—a desire for God and a foretaste of eternal things—claimed a privileged relationship with the absolute, signaled by renunciation of the world and all transitory things and the election of "voluntary poverty" as an expression of the *sequela Christi.* The theme of the total gift of oneself, the only gift to be made to Christ, yet one that would always remain totally inadequate to the immeasurable greatness of Christ's sacrifice, was a constant in ascetic reflection, and it underlay the highest expressions of Christian life. On occasion, however, culture and history offered their criteria and their experience to the realization of that gift. "'Here, we have abandoned all things and have followed thee': These are the persuasive words of voluntary poverty, which have begotten the monasteries, which have filled their cloisters with monks, which have peopled the forests with anchorites" (*PL,* 144, col. 549). Nicolas de Clairvaux, St. Bernard's secretary, summarizes monasticism's explanation of its own existence and vocation in these totally traditional terms. His explanation is inadequate to explain how this occurred, however. It ignores the sociological and cultural conditioning that allowed monasticism to persist in a certain fashion and not in another. It fails to clarify the processes of acculturation that determined why the *sequela* was realized in that particular way and following those specific criteria. It does not state why the *sequela* existed in a context and according to an interpretation that drew ironclad rules for its application from the framework of the religious orders and from within the rigid structure of social hierarchies. Hence the "poverty" in question had nothing in common with the total absence of means and possessions, with no guarantees or any form of power, of the secular poor. Monastic poverty was rather an abandonment of lay society and its customary sites; a rejection of its daily life and its goals; a choice of an individual discipline of asceticism and obedience; a high priority given to the search for God in prayer and contemplation; the reestablishment of an order and a scale of values that sin and the constant enticements of Satan had upset and tampered with: "Far from the tumults of the fray, they elude, with patience, the deceitful enchantments of the demons. Assiduous in Scripture, first in obedience, fervid in charity, they contemplate from the entry gate the delights of the blessed city" (*PL*, 144, col. 901). Thus for the monks it was less a question of renouncing the instruments and the means offered by history and by men's labor than it was of knowing how to use those means for the exclusive purpose of affirming and accomplishing their own ultimate goal. That logic lay behind the power and wealth of the monasteries; the opulent grandeur of their churches and the splendor of their cult; the size of their great guesthouses that stood ready to welcome poor pilgrims but also contained separate quarters that offered a worthy welcome to the great of the world; the hundreds of men who tilled their fields when Benedict's invitation to manual labor had shifted into other, more noble tasks; even the monks' involvement in political events and the struggles of both lay and ecclesiastical society. At the same time the monks claimed that monasticism's underlying rejection and renunciation of the world remained intact. From their point of view the monastery, with the solid, massively physical presence of its churches and its cloisters, with its throngs of monks absorbed in prayer or bent over their texts, ceaselessly contemplating the mysteries of the word of God, rendered visible within history the concrete reality of a human nature removed from the disorders and the violence of sin. It created islands of "rationality" in a society otherwise prey to the constant incursions of the Evil One.

Among the "similes" of Anselm of Bec lovingly gathered together by his disciple Eadmer there is one that expresses extraordinarily well the search for security and protection that was concentrated within the monastic walls. It is the story of a king who owned a town in which there was a castle with a massive keep capable of resisting any assault. Outside the town were houses, some solidly build, some less so. This king had a powerful enemy whose frequent forays found easy prey in everything that lay outside the town. Often, however, he managed to penetrate inside the walls, occupying the more poorly defended houses and capturing their inhabitants. Only the castle, closed to all relations with the outside, deaf to cries for help, remained out of his reach and offered full and absolute safety to those who had taken refuge inside. The moral of the tale is easy to divine:

> That king is God, who is constantly at war with the demon. In his kingdom he has Christianity and in Christianity, the monastic life. Above the monk's state there is only the life of the angels. In Christianity some are strong in virtue [but] the weak are many. In the monastic life, however, strength and security are so great that if someone, taking refuge in it, becomes a monk and persists in his choice without turning back, he can never be harmed by the demon. . . . All these things God has under his power. But his enemy, the devil, has so much power that he can carry away, without encountering any resistance, all the Hebrews and the Pagans, whom he finds outside Christianity, casting them down into the inferno. Often he even penetrates inside Christianity [and] with his temptations he seduces those whom he finds to be weak and he takes prisoner the souls that inhabit their bodies. Though reluctantly, he abandons those who are strong and well defended when he cannot win them over. Against the monastic state he is not able to mount the slightest attack, nor can he harm those who have become monks, unless they return to the secular with their bodies or their minds or through some emotional attachment to their own kin. (*PL*, 159, cols. 647f.)

One could easily find in hagiographic and monastic literature a vast number of examples that appear to contradict this picture—of monks, that is, constantly attacked and besieged by the temptations of the Evil One. Obviously, that is not the point. Anselm—like the authors of that literature, for that matter—was interested in portraying the invincibility inherent in the monastic state. He also insinuates, by his use of contemporary figures and familiar situations, that monks were aware of their strength and their privileged status as compared to other mortals. The monastic vocation realized individually and most completely the call and the promise offered to all men; it also claimed to embody, by safeguarding the celestial destiny of those who answered its call, what was most deeply ingrained—even if too often obliterated or forgotten—in men's secret aspirations.

Monastic preaching insisted forcefully on the point that the monastic vocation was a matter of election and grace that depended on the mysterious will of God. It was also an occasion for special election, however, and the monastery was the only site for the formation of superior men gifted with an intellectual preparation, intellectual capacities, and possibilities for human expansion that eluded other men. It was not by accident that of the seven gifts of the Holy Spirit, understanding and wisdom, which were the highest among them, were held to be the exclusive privilege of the contemplative life, thus of the monastic state. Understanding permitted the grasp of the reasons behind divine precepts and the lack of reward for good works; wisdom made reason's understanding sweet and pleasurable, and it assured that what the intellect had understood would be followed purely out of love of rectitude (*PL,* 159, col. 681). The superiority of the monk lay in his intellectual and moral stature. It was honored and recognized, and only in the monastery did it find scope for full realization. Gerbert, at the turn of the tenth century, had kings, emperors, and popes competing for his friendship, but his culture was the result of a painstaking preparation that took him to the great, declining monasteries of the West in search of new books and new masters. When Lanfranc became archbishop of Canterbury after having been abbot of Bec and of Saint-Etienne in Caen, he went to Rome. Pope Alexander II stood up to receive him, to the astonishment of the papal court, who were well versed in the Roman curia's rules of etiquette. "It is an honor that we render not to the archbishop," Alexander said, "but that we owe to the master of our studies" (*PL,* 159, cols. 352f.).

The choice of the monastic life was also the choice of culture and knowledge. For the sons of the nobility it represented the only real alternative to the warrior's profession. Little wonder that nearly all the monastic biographies of these centuries emphasize their hero's repugnance toward chivalric exercises and knightly violence and his irresistible natural vocation for reading, meditation, and prayer. A vocation for sanctity went along with a vocation for culture. Columban could still retire from the world to defend a culture he had already acquired (Gustavo Vinaj), but four or five centuries later it was only by retiring from the world that one could hope or think to acquire a culture.

One should not misinterpret the concept of "vocation," however.

What for a few was a choice made consciously and personally as an adult meant for most monks setting out on a road chosen by and directed by others. It was the outcome of a vocation that might be called objective, which the ruling groups imposed upon a certain number of their own in order to respond to religious and social needs that were collective but out of the reach of most men. The custom, widespread among nobles and knights, of entrusting their sons to the monastery at a tender age to have them initiated into monastic life corresponded to the need for a long intellectual apprenticeship that found only within monastic walls the necessary traditions and instruments which that preparation required. Precocious vocations were also the result, as we have already seen, of a notion of a profound solidarity binding and uniting all humanity in an order that pertained both to man's earthly life and his destiny in the life beyond, which required a variety of functions and tasks, all of them indispensable. The monk who lived within the religious community was well aware that he needed seculars to provide him with food, clothing, buildings, and defense. By the same token, he was aware that his spiritual life (*spiritualis conversatio*) was not an aim in itself but also affected those who assured him such *supplementa*. Similarly, "those who are placed in worldly affairs" should be conscious of their dire need for the prayers of the "spiritual men" "in order not to risk, hard-pressed as they are among the delights, the cares, the innumerable perils of the present life, remaining deprived of the glory of eternal salvation" (*PL*, 146, col. 121B–C).

This religious and social equilibrium was only apparently peaceful or stable. Tensions and contradictions inherent in the very system that created that equilibrium arose within the monastery and between the monastery and the society around it. They were rooted in the monastery's recruitment system, in its methods for the formation of monks, even in its consciousness of offering the best road to salvation through isolation from the world. Tension also originated, however, in the monastery's claim to embody the perfect Christian life, setting the pace for others according to models of comportment and relations (destined for a long and complex evolution) that had gradually concentrated within the monastery expectations and demands that had arisen elsewhere.

For many, as we have seen, the monastery was not a final haven resulting from an initial personal choice. When they were placed in the cloister by their families at an early age, they had to become monks gradually; they had to accept the idea of fashioning themselves into monks, of fitting themselves for a model of life that had the conquest of the absolute as its unique reason for being; they had to put themselves to the test, rising above the lacerating and painful condition that Columban described in its full paradoxicality as proper to man preoccupied with his eternal destiny—being duty-bound to detest what he sees and not being able to have concrete experience of what he must necessarily love (*Instructio* III, 3). This was one reason why monastic pedagogy was so largely constructed on the themes of loyalty and irreversibility—loyalty to the monastic state and the irreversibility of the way of perfection once one had set out on it. Even though loyalty and irreversibility obviously demanded the individual's assent and the participation of his will, nevertheless, in a certain sense they existed outside his will, operating, so to speak, by the objective fact of his presence within the monastery, which in this perspective was even more clearly a place and an opportunity for salvation.

Peter the Venerable, the last great abbot of Cluny, had something to say on this point as he parried the Cistercians' reprimand for having accepted novices without waiting until the end of the trial period stipulated by the Rule. No one, he states, who asks for the way to salvation should be denied or delayed; assuming a harsh and severe attitude might induce him to remain in the world and follow Satan. Not deferring the acceptance of novices came of the belief that good must be given even to those who do not really want it. It often happens, Peter continues, that after a certain time some who have submitted to the monastic yoke, oppressed by temptations or by sorrows, might return to the loathsome world they had left if they did not know that they could not reverse the step they had taken without committing themselves to eternal damnation, "and if on occasion they presume to do so, later, however, driven by great fear, they will return to their own sheepcote, and because they do not know how to save themselves otherwise, willing or unwilling, they will keep the promise they have made" (*Ep.* 28).

The Cistercians criticized this stand and many other aspects of Cluniac life: promoting adult vocations aimed also at a return to an emphasis on penance and labor in monastic life. Since the monastery was held to represent the high road to salvation, even the Cistercians tended to attract and accept as many recruits as possible, not stinting in their solicitations and pressures. Anxiety over the salvation of others was translated into a strong upswing for monasticism.

Bernard of Clairvaux was in many ways an extraordinary personage, extreme in his outbursts and his harsh statements, cutting, and rigid in his deductions, thanks to his exclusive dedication to monasticism and his program for the angelic life. Only long experience of government managed in part to mitigate these qualities as the years went by. The story of his "conversion" and that of his followers is nonetheless significant, and it remains emblematic of attitudes widespread in monastic culture, even if in him those attitudes were in some ways carried to extremes. The personal choice that led Bernard to Cîteaux at the age of about twenty was not enough to satisfy him, and he worked, insisted, and thundered until his entire family followed him—father, uncles, brothers, and cousins. He even showed his sisters the way to the cloister. One sister, who was already married, resisted him; he treated her as a diabolical seductress and finally bent her to his will, persuading her to wrest consent from her husband to her becoming a nun (*PL*, 185, col. 244f.). There was no pressure, no prayer, no threat that he did not use, no occasion that he did not exploit to reach his ends. His worthy biographer doubtless exaggerates, but he gives an excellent idea of an overwhelming zeal: "Mothers hid their sons, wives shut up their husbands, friends sent away friends because the Holy Spirit gave his voice such a ring of virtue that only with great difficulty could any affective tie resist him" (*PL*, 185, col. 235C–D). Similarly, Romuald, more than a century earlier, stricken with anxiety for the salvation of others, aspired, according to Peter Damian, to "convert the entire world into a hermitage."

The extraordinary growth of monasticism in those centuries doubtless also had—as we have seen several times—other motivations and reasons for being. A few shrewd contemporary observers in the eleventh and twelfth centuries even connected it with a need to shore up defenses against a demographic growth too rapid for the available resources. Nonetheless, I do not believe we can undervalue the constant pressure and the psychological coercion in the presentation of the cloister as the only authentically Christian life of penance and atonement for weaknesses and sins; as the only real alternative to the irrationality of a violent, cruel society; as a life that made any monk who abandoned it a desperate being doomed to eternal damnation.

The existential and psychological outcomes of those qualities and criteria are not easy to measure. Othlo of Sankt Emmeram came to doubt the existence of God because he felt his life—from childhood—within the walls of the cloister to be so empty of meaning. We can never know to how great an extent his long crisis resulted from his own particular life-story, or whether his was one of the rare cases in which widespread situations and common problems found expression in a dramatic and exemplary account. His decision to write his story for the instruction of his fellow monks would seem to indicate the latter.

There were other indications of restlessness and malaise in the complex reality of monasticism. Its educative system claimed to focus exclusively on the contemplation of God and on a deep assimilation of God's word through a constant and repeated rereading of Scripture (*meditatio* and *ruminatio*). The presence of ancient pagan authors was justified in this context only as they contributed to the linguistic and literary formation of the monks; they had no autonomy in the monastic scheme of things. What was true in principle was not always true in fact, however. The concentration of every possibility for cultural life in the monastery and its claim that all human values and experiences were subordinate to its theological and spiritual system gave rise to discrepancies and hidden contradictions, traces of which emerged sporadically. Clues, some masked, some explicit, attest to an emotive gap; to a search for a more fantastic, more human alternative. Even pedagogical texts might offer an opportunity—even if only on the individual level—to break with the compact system on which the monastic world was based.

Monastic reformers were fully aware of the problem. In 1199, for example, the Cistercian chapter felt it necessary to stipulate that monks who wrote verse had to be transferred to another house, and that they could be readmitted into their monastery of origin only by decision of a general chapter. More than a century earlier, in the biography of Hugh of Cluny, a codex of Virgil is held responsible for the decline of monastic discipline at the monastery of Saint-Marcel in Chalon-sur-Saône (*PL*, 159, cols. 871f.). Othlo, who appears to be a dependable observer, noted as he entered a monastery that some of the monks were assigned to reading pagan authors exclusively (*PL*, 146, col. 29A). Although Othlo states his own intention to read nothing but the Bible, he confesses that his chief preoccupation in choosing the monastery in which his made his profession had been to make sure that it was furnished with a sufficient supply of good books (*PL*, 146, col. 35A). At the end of the eleventh century, the catalogue of the library at Pomposa (the compiler, in a fit of enthusiasm, claims it was richer than the library in Rome) lists with scornful care the brothers' objections when the abbot, Gerolamo, used the monastery's resources to acquire the works of pagan authors. Gerolamo's defense is predictable, though neither very persuasive nor exhaustive: the house of the mighty, he argues, should have clay vessels as well as gold and silver ones. Gerolamo acted as he did so that his monks could find pleasure and exercise their minds according to their inclinations and deserts. What was more, when they were read with pure intentions, the books of the gentiles were edifying: did they not demonstrate that secular pomp was naught? (Mercati). In spite of emphasis on the allegorical reading of pagan authors and in spite of monasticism's optimism about its powers of assimilation, it is still difficult to believe that Ovid was read and enjoyed in strict obedience to the limits set by an anonymous *accessus ad auctores* of the twelfth century: "bonorum morum est instructor, malorum vero extirpator." Nor is it easy to believe that such criteria were the only ones that governed the reading of a work.

Even if we find it impossible to measure the influence of such perplexities and aporias in monastic life, that does not prevent us from noting that such problems were primarily connected with the monastery's cultural monopoly. From this point of view, when the concrete needs of both religious and civil life were worked out, ideologically and institutionally, to include more varied and complex views on piety, culture, instruction, and taste, monastic expansion was curbed, recruitment declined, and one of the elements that had assured the success of monasticism was taken away. The most visible cracks in the monastic system, which had opened up as early as its "golden age," came from its claim that its criteria and its mode of being embodied Christian perfection; that it alone realized the *sequela Christi* within history. The opulence of certain monasteries prompted a movement for monastic reform, an accentuation of the ascetic and penitential aspects of monasticism, and a return to the letter and the spirit of the Rule. The opposite tendency to exclusivity, which had accompanied the expansion and the success of monasticism, also remained strong, however; nor was the monastery's claim to social and cultural hegemony—one of the most obvious side effects of its success—impaired. The idea and the practices of "voluntary poverty," as they had been worked out in Benedictine monastic experience, deeply permeated the objectives of the socially dominant hierarchies, where the respect for the *pauperes Christi,* their prestige, and the recognition they received operated as a touchstone by which the piety of others could be measured. The institution of monasticism had an internal logic that, so to speak, imposed a particular line of development: the Cistercian congregation, fifty years after its constitution, already showed signs of taking on a mode of life and a wealth for which, at its rise, it had bitterly reproached Cluny.

It was precisely these aspects of monasticism that were no longer acceptable in a changed situation and that no longer satisfied the new religious and social demands that slowly emerged during those centuries. The monastic system both exploded and disintegrated—if this can be said of a process that was slow and gradual. One force for change came from within the monastery, when monastic life was questioned on the basis of its own intellectual tradition, using the very texts that had nourished monastic spirituality. With renewed demand for the Christianization of society, the aristocratic bent and the elitist exclusiveness of the monastery came to be contested, and people became aware that to equate the apostolic life and monastic life—one of the main features of the monastic ideology—was both ambiguous and inadequate. Peter the Venerable, writing to Bernard of Clairvaux (in full knowledge that Bernard would fully agree with him), asks rhetorically, "Quid est aliud dicere, 'omnia quae habes da pauperibus et veni sequere me,' nisi esto monachus?" (*Ep.* 28). But what was still an undisputed axiom for those two men was no longer axiomatic for many others. In many areas, the decades of the struggle for reform around the turn of the twelfth century had already invited or obliged monks to leave the cloister, either for the active exercise of preaching or in a direct commitment to the *cura animarum,* both of which proved contradictory to and incompatible with monastic tradition.

The movement out of the cloister, which arose in the monasteries themselves, encountered needs and motivations emerging out of a society growing in both size and complexity. The secular clergy tended to be organized and disciplined along broader lines than the monastic scheme of perfection: a new desire for evangelical authenticity led to the discovery of the preaching mission and prophecy as fundamental components of the *vita apostolica.* Lay groups demanding more active participation in religious affairs found the monastic model constraining. Pauperism became a pressing reality that economic conditions made more acute and that affected a more diversified population. It posed a problem not only in the old terms of assistance and good works but also as a human question and a problem of religious redemption and salvation. The *conversatio inter pauperes*—life as a pauper amid the poor—was depicted as a more authentic, more faithful path for evangelical witness. The point of arrival of this process lay in the extraordinary experience of Francis and his first companions, an experience of an enormous impact and importance, even in its later developments and even when it had been subjected to discipline and reshaped to fit norms that more nearly corresponded to firmly established ecclesiastical tradition.

Precisely because the various forms of religious life still needed to be organized according to a "rule" constructed on a model of obedience, angelism, conventual stability, clear separation from the rest of humanity, community property, and disciplined asceticism, the monastic tradition continued to exert a profound influence on the modes and terms of the Christian presence in societies of Western culture. Although monks and monasteries were gradually reorganized to play a less central, less dominant role in both the church and society, the spirituality that they elaborated and proclaimed during the centuries of their hegemony left a decisive legacy that defined the Christian life, as distinguished from the secular life. It was a far-reaching wave that does not seem to have exhausted its force even now. It would be hazardous and presumptuous to claim to judge in a few words the importance of that spirituality or its significance for the multifaceted story of the Christian experience in history. It is a fact that in recent decades the demand to move beyond this tenacious and subtle conditioning seems more accentuated. Nor is it perhaps a coincidence that attempts to do so have been met, on the other side, by initiatives for monastic renewal aimed at aiding the monastery—stripped, of course, of any pretense of totality or exemplarity—to regain its function as a clear prophetic and eschatological sign of an inspiration that springs from a deep vein of ancient tradition.

BIBLIOGRAPHY

Il monachesimo e la riforma ecclesiastica (1049–1122), Atti della IV Settimana internazionale di studio—Mendola 23–29 agosto 1968. Milan: Vita e pensiero, 1971.

Il monachesimo nell'alto Medieovo e la formazione della civiltà occidentale. Atti. Settimane di studio del Centro italiano di studi sull'alto Medioevo, IV. Spoleto: Centro Studi Alto Medioevo, 1957.

Crouzel, Henri, et al. *Théologie de la vie monastique. Etudes sur la tradition patristique.* Théologie 49. Paris: Aubier, 1961.

De Vogüé, Adalbert. *Les Règles monastiques anciennes (400–700).* Typologie des sources du Moyen Age occidental, facs. 46. Turnhout: Brepols, 1985.

Duby, Georges. *Les Trois Ordres ou l'imaginaire du féodalisme.* Paris: Gallimard, 1978 [*The Three Orders: Feudal Society Imagined.* Trans. Arthur Goldhammer. Chicago: University of Chicago Press, 1980].

Leclercq, Jean. *L'Amour des lettres et le désir de Dieu. Initiation aux auteurs monastiques du Moyen âge.* Paris: Editions du Cerf, 1957 [*The Love of Learning and the Desire for God: A Study of Monastic Culture.* Trans. Catharine Misrahi. 3d ed. New York: Fordham University Press, 1982].

Vauchez, André. *La Spiritualité du Moyen Age occidental. VIIIe–XIIe siècles.* Vendôme: Presses Universitaires de France, 1975.

Vinaj, Gustavo. *Alto Medioevo latino.* Naples: Guida, 1978.

SUGGESTED READINGS

Constance Brittain Bouchard, *Sword, Miter, and Cloister: Nobility and the Church in Burgundy, 980–1198* (Ithaca: Cornell University Press, 1987).

Christopher N. L. Brooke, *The Monastic World, 1000–1300* (London: Elek, 1974).

Marjorie Chibnall, *The World of Orderic Vitalis* (Oxford: Clarendon Press, 1984).

G. R. Evans, *The Mind of St. Bernard of Clairvaux* (Oxford: Clarendon Press, 1983).

Noreen Hunt, *Cluny Under Saint Hugh, 1049–1109* (London: Edward Arnold, 1967).

Noreen Hunt, ed., *Cluniac Monasticism in the Central Middle Ages* (London: Macmillan, 1971).

David Knowles, *Cistercians and Cluniacs: The Controversy between St. Bernard and Peter the Venerable* (London: Oxford University Press, 1955).

———, *The Monastic Order in England, 940–1216*, 2d ed. (Cambridge: Cambridge University Press, 1963).

Clifford H. Lawrence, *Medieval Monasticism: Forms of Religious Life in Western Europe in the Middle Ages* (London: Longman, 1984).

Barbara Rosenwein, *Rhinoceros Bound: Cluny in the Tenth Century* (Philadelphia: University of Pennsylvania Press, 1982).

Richard William Southern, *Western Society and the Church in the Middle Ages* (Harmondsworth: Penguin, 1970).

TWO

The Warrior and the Knight

Franco Cardini

It was doubtless a great and revolutionary change when, during the tenth century, the old division of Christian society into *liberi* and *servi*—a dichotomy that predated the Hebraic, Roman, and Germanic civilizations from which the West drew its cultural origins—was almost totally replaced by a more practical and meaningful division into *milites* and *rustici*. The dividing line was no longer normative and institutional, but now separated social functions and ways of life: on the one side were (the few, basically) who possessed the privilege of bearing arms and of fighting and for that reason were normally exempt from feudal *bans;* on the other, those (an overwhelming majority of the laity) who were expected to produce enough to satisfy both their own limited needs and the more demanding and sophisticated requirements of the few, who were privileged to live on the fruits of the labors of the many.

The world of the tenth century (and even of the latter half of the ninth century) was harsh and dangerous; mere survival was a constant preoccupation and a vexing task. Vikings, Magyars, and Saracens plundered the coasts and tormented the hinterlands of eastern Mediterranean European societies. Their raids were accompanied by (and, when they had passed on, replaced by) continual struggles within rapacious and violent aristocracies who were only superficially Christianized, even though they were proud of the monastic institutions they had promoted and prouder still of the rich booty of relics gathered from far and wide and displayed, venerated, and honored like objects charged with magical powers. Europe at the time was dotted with castles, to the point that some regions, such as Castile, even took their names from them. These were fortified sites in which people could take refuge, tightly packed together, while barbarians and "tyrants" loosed their fury on the countryside. Nonetheless, it was to a great extent precisely the uncomfortable and precarious conditions of castle life that taught the people of Europe the practices of self-defense and self-government.

Harsh times also lay behind the emergence of long-lasting and deep-seated traits such as the division of society by men's functions into the three "orders" of the *oratores*, the *bellatores*, and the *laboratores*. By this period praying, fighting, and laboring in the fields were considered—though on different levels of dignity—the three fundamental aspects of civil life and the three pillars of the Christian world. The studies of Georges Dumézil have splendidly and definitively confirmed that this tripartite and functional division had its remote source in Indo-European culture. My purpose here is not to trace such constants, but rather to note what was specifically medieval in a process that took not centuries but a millennium; a process that lent positive value to war and the warrior and that, between the tenth and the twelfth centuries, permitted Christian society, despite its higher ideals of peace, to elaborate a set of ethical and theological values aimed at the sacralization of the military.

We can begin, then, with the tenebrous period of the barbarian incursions and the so-called "feudal anarchy" that extended from the late ninth century to the eleventh century; with the world *miles*, which gradually replaced all the other terms for the warrior (*sicarius, buccellarius, gladiator*) that had been used up to then to qualify the armed men gathered in close companies around a *dominus*, a sire. Tacitus had already described the Germanic *comitatus*, which in the early Middle Ages had a number of variants from the Frankish *trustis* to the Russian *družina*. In time an ethic developed within this concept that included courage, faithful friendship, and affection toward the sire, considered less a *dominus* than a *senior*, the leader of the band, the "elder" from whom gifts and protection could be expected. These *Männerdünde*—"societies of men"—preserved earlier initiatory rites for admission to the circle of those held worthy of bearing arms: rugged trials of strength and of the ability to withstand pain, ritual wounding, and tests of skill at the limits of what the Christian church could consider legitimate. At one time (again, Tacitus is our informant) all young warriors of the forest and the steppes had had to affront trials of the sort. Beginning with the eighth century, however, the increasing use of the horse in warfare and the consequent increase (rather than a decrease) in the warrior's costs for offensive and defensive equipment (demonstrated by the Carolingian *Capitularia*) set off a trend toward specialization in the profession of arms, consequently toward overall demilitarization in Romano-barbarian society. This meant that only among the new elite groups of warrior companies gathered around powerful nobles were the old traditions maintained. The solemn consignment of arms had even become the exclusive province of rituals to signal the young lord's entry into the world of power. This was the basis of the ceremony usually known as "dubbing" and that, together with horseback combat and certain external signs of status and a particular way of life, defined the knight.

The professional warrior between the tenth and the eleventh century was thus ordinarily a member of a company guided by a great lord or garrisoned in his dwelling, hence he might or might not hold lands in vassalage from his *senior* or receive arms, horses, and equipment as a sort of stipend. He might live close to his *senior* a great part of the time, or he could lead his own life on his own lands or lands conceded to him. He might be a free man or a serf (as with the so-called *ministeriales*).

As far as the strictly martial aspects of the knighthood are concerned, scholars have now abandoned both extremes of evolutionism and determinism. No one now believes in the thesis of a chivalry born "naturally" during the eighth century out of the need to combat the swift incursions of the Arabs in Spain, and almost no one still maintains that it was the inevitable result of the invention of one object—the stirrup—which permitted greater stability in the saddle and hence led to the development of the headlong attack in which a knight coming at a gallop could overwhelm any obstacle in his path with the powerful thrust of a lance couched against his chest. Today we are more interested in attempting to understand the prestige of the combatant on horseback by investigating the persistence of a sacrality that had been connected with the horse in the culture of the steppes. We are also interested in investigating the connection between the ever-rising costs of war and of military equipment on the one hand (the horse itself, iron weapons and armor, the padded and reinforced jacket called the *bruina*) and, on the other, the definition of the hierarchy of vassalage dependency, in conjunction with an increasing socioeconomic and sociojuridical distance between those who could bear arms and those who could not.

Clashes between great lords who held a *ban* granting them territorial jurisdiction, each with his armed followers, became characteristic of life in the tenth to the eleventh centuries—that is, in the long period corresponding to the fragmentation of public powers and so-called "feudal anarchy." This was the time in which men-at-arms were above all *tyranni* or *praedones.* The bishops in particular increasingly denounced their violent attacks on the defenseless and, more generally, on all whom the church defined as *pauperes,* such as the clergy itself, widows, orphans, and all who were unable to defend themselves or lacked protection.

It was, in fact, the bishops of certain dioceses who initiated the movement for the *pax* and the *tregua Dei* between the late tenth and the early eleventh centuries, and they were soon seconded by aristocrats and *milites* who rallied to their program and by laity of even modest social status, who were preoccupied by the endemic violence that prevented the relaunching of trade and economic life. Sanctuaries, hospices, markets, fords, and roads were placed under the special protection of the *pax Dei*, which meant that anyone who committed acts of violence in those places risked excommunication. The provisions covered all categories of *pauperes* (a world connoting weakness more than impoverishment, as we have seen); and it eventually came to be established that warlike acts, already prohibited by the *pax* in certain places and toward certain persons, were forbidden on specified days of the week as well. Killing was a mortal sin at all times and in all circumstances, but the *tregua Dei* meant that assassination between Thursday afternoon and Sunday afternoon also entailed excommunication. In this way, even without flatly prohibiting war (which would have been unthinkable in a society dominated by warriors), fighting was restricted as much as possible and was forced to give way to the needs of social and economic recovery and church reform. (These were, in fact, the years of the vast movement for reform launched by the monastic congregation headed by the abbey of Cluny in Burgundy that was aimed at *libertas Ecclesiae*—freeing ecclesiastical institutions from subjugation to lay powers.)

The provisions of the *pax* and the *tregua Dei*, developed in a series of local councils attended by both clergy and laity in each region, could never have been promulgated or accepted if warriors had not been won over to the cause and if they had not been willing to use force to impose the pacification program on *tyranni* who continued to shed Christian blood in their private quarrels and on aristocrats who persisted in their violent ways even after swearing pacts of peace and truce (in which case they were then called *infractores pacis*). The same sort of thing occurred in Italy, where there was armed support for the program of the reformist clergy in the so-called "investiture controversy." Although the bands of *milites* already had an ethic based on courage, fealty to the chief, and affection for companions in arms, the ecclesiastical canons of the councils for peace provided a more strictly "chivalric" ethic based on service owed to the church and defense of the weak—the *pauperes*—to the point of self-sacrifice. Roughly between 1070 and 1090 Pope Gregory VII, taking as a model such figures as the *miles* Erlembaldo Cotta, the military head of the Milanese Patarenes, elaborated the new concept of the *miles sancti Petri*, a development of the concept of the *miles Christi* but also a substantial modification of it. *Miles Christi* long referred to the martyr; later the term was applied to the monk or the ascetic—in short, to anyone who devoted himself to prayer and things of the spirit, combating sin by confronting the *pugna spiritualis* in the silence of his heart. In this sense *militia Dei* and *militia huius saeculi*—dedication to the religious cause or to this world's causes—had long been understood as antithetical. The church, deeply involved in a struggle for reform and for liberation from the control of secular rulers, now felt that it needed all forces capable of lending support to its new program, warriors included. This was why Pope Gregory severely reproached one noble who had decided to abandon the world and close himself up in an abbey. What until then would have seemed a holy and heroic decision now appeared as desertion of the frontlines. A new type of *miles Christi*—or rather, *miles sancti Petri*—arose, willing to use his sword in the service of the priesthood. This may have been when the dubbing of knights, which until then had been a secular ceremony carried out within groups of professional fighters freely deciding to co-opt a new companion in arms, began to involve religious recognition by the Church. According to such sources as the Romano-Germanic pontifical of Mainz of the tenth century, the church had for some time blessed arms, just as it did work tools and household implements.

The new church that emerged from the reform was harsh with *tyranni* and *praedones*, but it proved notably more benevolent toward laymen who put their military skills and their courage at its service. One hagiographic text, a life of St. Gerald of Aurillac written by Odo, abbot of Cluny, could serve as a model for this new attitude. Before he came to the monastery, Gerald had led the life of a warrior, and even in that life, according to his biographer, he had served God satisfactorily. The farewell to arms as a sign of *conversio*, following the edifying pattern formulated in the *Vita Martini* of Sulpicius Severus, thus seemed a thing of the past. Now sanctification was possible even while one served the church, weapons in hand.

This changed attitude was not the simple result of new demands that surfaced through the *pax Dei* movement or during the investiture controversy. Western Christendom was undergoing a phase of vigorous expansion in the eleventh century, one expression of which lay in military operations led by groups of knights or by the sailors of the maritime cities (of the Tyrrhenian Sea in particular) against an Islam that, after its extraordinary expansion in the seventh through the tenth centuries, was in a phase of stagnation in its conquests and crisis in its internal structure. The moment for a Christian counteroffensive seemed to have come. It came in Islamic Spain in the eighth century with the *Reconquista*, with the aid of propaganda (to some extent favored by Cluny) for the pilgrimage to the sanctuary of Santiago de Compostela in Galicia. It found further support in the thirst for adventure and hope for booty of groups of knights—French, for the most part—who offered their services as mercenaries to the Christian nobles of León, Castile, and Aragon. Not only did the tensions and battles of that period produce the Christian and national epic of the *Cantar de mio Cid,* there was a vast harvest of epic poems and legends in which the Christian faith and a sense of miracle, reinforced by a good many accounts of apparitions and by the cult of relics and sanctuaries, were translated into a new "warlike Christianity." The exaltation of Christian spirituality coincided with military glory in this new image, and the Virgin and St. James often appeared on the field of battle, surrounded by fluttering white banners and accompanied by the "military saints"—George, Theodore, Mercurius, Demetrius, Martin, and others—to incite the Christians to greater efforts as they struck down or routed the infidels. A similar climate reigns in some of the narratives of the Norman conquest of Sicily, in sources recounting the deeds of Pisan sailors attacking al-Mahdiah in 1087 or, twenty-five years later, the Balearic Islands, and even in the most famous epic poem of the period, the *Chanson de Roland.*

The Christian hero, Roland, Charlemagne's nephew, has some tenuous connection with historical fact, though documentation is scant. It is not important for our purposes to know whether a person of that name really existed in the entourage of Charlemagne, or whether his fame is to any extent justified by his deeds. What matters is that his death, which took place in the eighth century during an ambush at the Pass of Roncesvalles in the Pyrenees, almost immediately gave rise to an epic tradition that was taken over in the eleventh century as a paradigm of martyrdom for the faith. Roland's death, narrated in moving verse in the *Chanson,* was that of a saintly vassal of a warrior God. Before his eyes close, the paladin sings a veritable love song to his shining sword, Durendaal, whose hilt contains precious relics, after which he offers his gauntlet to God in an ultimate act of *fidelitas,* raising it toward the heavens, which then open and a host of angels descends to welcome the hero and carry him off to the gates of Paradise.

For decades scholars have debated the role of epic poetry, the originality of the *Song of Roland,* and the relation of the work to a preceding warrior tradition perhaps going back to ancient Germanic paganism. One thing is certain, however: the angels who descend to Count Roland and escort him to heaven are not the Valkyries in disguise. They are Christian angels, refashioned, reinterpreted within a set of conceptual values and sensitivities that owed much to the ancestral warlike tradition but even more to an ecclesiology in which the Old Testament was a greater inspiration than the New. The warrior St. Michael in the epic is the biblical "Prince of the armies of the Lord," and the Christian God of Roland, even if he is often lovingly referred to as the "Son of Mary," is in reality the terrible God of Israel, the *Dominus Deus Sabaoth*, Lord of battle and of vengeance.

At this point, however, a problem arises: was it truly the hierarchical and hierocratic Gregorian church, as it emerged from the reforms of the eleventh century, that "invented" the ideals of chivalry, greatly modifying the older feudal-military ethic (indeed, at first opposing that ethic) and elaborating a system of warlike virtues based on the ideals of defense of the weak and martyrdom for the faith to oppose the old value system based on courage and on professional cohesion and initiation? Theses of the sort have in the past drawn support from the realization that the *chansons de geste* owe much, conceptually and stylistically, to liturgical formulas and hagiographic texts, and that consequently they could serve the purposes of a propaganda administered from ecclesiastical circles. Many scholars today hold the opposite view; that is, the *chansons* are the ancient voice (reinterpreted and refined between the eleventh and twelfth centuries and perhaps even brought up to date by new ways of feeling powerfully expressed in the leitmotiv of religious heroism) of a largely autonomous secular culture. Thus it may have been the liturgical formulas and the hagiographic literature that adapted to the *chansons*, making use of the popularity of epic poetry to become more solidly implanted in collective consciousness and the collective imagination. In this view it is not so much a question of the Christianization of chivalric culture as the militarization and heroicization, so to speak, of some models of Christian witness judged to be particularly capable of impressing and moving people—in short, of serving as instruments of propaganda.

The *Song of Roland* offers a first important model of the codification of the *ritterliches Tugendsystem*—the chivalric system of ethics. It turns around the two poles of *prouesse* (valor) and *sagesse* (wisdom), or the particular variety of wisdom sharpened by experience usually expressed in terms of prudence. The terms are complementary; when they are both present and in harmony, the result is *mesure*, controlled equilibrium. The valiant knight who is not wise is a madman; the wise man who cannot show proof of valor is vile. In practice, however, few knights possessed both of the basic virtues in perfect harmony: harmony arose instead out of the fellowship of arms among knights of complementary characteristics and out of companionship between a predominantly strong knight and a predominantly wise one. As treatises on the question from the Gregorian reformer Bonizo of Sutri to Ramon Llull (who proposed a mystical interpretation of the knighthood) insisted, the perfect knight was less an individual than he was the result of what Cicero, St. Bernard, and Ailred of Rievaulx all defined as *amor socialis,* which coincided with the *notitia contubernii,* group spirit or *esprit de corps.* This is perhaps both the innermost and the most obvious meaning of the image of two knights on one horse on the seal of the Order of Templars. It was in the name of fraternal friendship and warm solidarity that one author of the fourteenth century exclaimed, in praise of chivalric values and with no hint of the aestheticism that led to similar declarations in the nineteenth and twentieth centuries, "What a sweet thing war is!"

I might add, to confirm how profoundly "secular" and how superficially Christian the world of Roland was, that the "young, fresh war," the "beautiful war" that Marc Bloch found so little to his liking was not an invention of the decadent hysteria in vogue several decades ago. The same attitude can clearly be found in ancient epic tradition; it is present, in one particular form, in the medieval chivalric world, a form for which Erasmus' wise adage, *bellum dulce inexpertis,* does not seem to apply.

One of the most characteristic elements of chivalric poetry (which was to return in the troubadors' *fin'amor*) was *joie,* usually associated with youth. To see these values as uniquely sexual, or even erotic, emphasizing the connections between youth and enjoyment of life, would be a misunderstanding, however. In reality, "youth" was closely related to the *iuvenes,* the newly dubbed knights who wandered in turbulent groups in search of an adventure that was often tantamount to violence and tyrannizing. "Joy," as we find it in some *chansons de geste,* referred less to a pleasant and optimistic state of euphoria than to a ferocious excitement, a wild exaltation not far from the *wut* of German pagan tradition, the warlike furor or trance, the shamanic valence of which some scholars have noted. It is hardly surprising to encounter elements of the sort in a text like *Raoul de Cambrai,* a somber story of atrocious revenge. A like climate, however, pervades the *chansons* (in many aspects edifying) of the cycle of William of Orange, a warrior converted to the cloister. Even a poem like the *Aliscans,* which recounts the martyrdom of its pure young hero, Vivien, shows him as nearly a saint in the logic of the narration, but still a terrible butcher in certain episodes.

In short, although the *chansons* open an extraordinary window onto the mentality of courts and markets, of knights, and of laymen of lower status who took pleasure in hearing the narration of chivalric deeds, we need to be careful not to take their sincere and even ardent Christian inspiration as the result of a theologization of the martial spirit on the part of the church. Not only in a great many episodes such as the scenes of forced baptism of the Saracens, but more generally, in the underlying spirit that animates this literature, the type of Christianity it proposes is explicitly secular and often based in folk culture. Doctrinal preoccupations are absent, however, and it frequently has anticlerical currents, at times irreverent, at other times calling for a sacrality specific to the knightly profession, different from and perhaps even better and more pleasing to the Lord than the ministrations of the priests. This can be seen, for example, in the mood of the fairly frequent scenes in which wounded knights on the point of death confess and absolve one another, even giving one another communion, using a blade of grass from the battlefield as Host.

A similar logic imbues the *chansons* of the cycle dedicated to the First Crusade, which pulse with the epic intensity of the vast undertaking between 1096 and 1099 that some have seen—quite rightly and legitimately—as the direct and immediate result of the Christianization of the knighthood. Today we know that in the First Crusade (as in France during the disputes concerning the *pax Dei,* in Italy with the investiture controversy, and in the Spain of the *Reconquista*) groups of "poor knights" (mentioned in the *chansons* as well), took an active role. The adjective "poor" is not to be interpreted literally. Such knights were not necessarily indigent, nor members of the lesser aristocracy, although contemporary documents do attest to the existence of warriors of low socioeconomic status, who perhaps lacked even a modest number of followers, or who even owned nothing but a horse and the armor they wore. The "poor knights" were so called because they had accepted the austerity program of the reformed church and had put aside their thirst for glory, wealth, and adventure to devote themselves to the church's aims even while they remained laymen and warriors. Their vocation, in other words, had much in common with many lay devotional confraternities of the time. We have good reason to believe that many members of the knighthood were involved in the new climate in Christendom on the morrow of the reformers' triumph—and it should be noted that the reformers were a composite group, hence to call all eleventh-century reforms "Gregorian" is unacceptably reductive. Nonetheless, the most interesting epic poem to come out of the crusade, the *Conquête de Jérusalem,* shows no sign of being affected by the deeper implications of the reform. It offers the usual prodigies (angels and saints descending to the battlefield to fight at the side of the Christians) and the stylized, formal, but also violent emotionality typical of epic heroes (who are moved, swoon from emotion, sob), but it also offers scenes of ferocious cruelty. To do it justice, however, we know that the conquest of the Holy City was in fact accompanied by terrible massacres in which the crusaders slaughtered Muslims, Jews, and Eastern Christians indiscriminately. Aside from Godfrey of Bouillon, the principal hero of the *Conquête* was Thomas of Marle, who was first to mount the walls of the city, carried almost as if he were flying on the blades of his men's lances, but who had no compunction about massacring women. We see him imbued with pious fervor and moved to tears before the Holy Sepulcher, but he also wore a magic talisman that promised him invulnerability in battle. In historical reality, we do not know whether Thomas of Marle was first to scale the walls of Jerusalem, a merit later contested by legions of heroes actual or fictional. What we do know about him or of his historical personage (Guibert, abbot of Nogent, chronicler of the crusade and autobiographer, speaks of him at length) makes one shudder. He was a feudal lord whose barbarous and savage deeds make those of the epic hero Raoul de Cambrai pale in comparison. Obviously, there is nothing intrinsically contradictory in Thomas's tears before the Holy Sepulcher (this may well be an authentic historical episode, and we have no reason to doubt his sincerity). We do need, however, to guard against anachronism in the reconstruction of mental, affective, and emotional life in the eleventh and twelfth centuries, and to remember that people of that age thought in quite different fashions from our own and did not share our concept of coherence.

Thomas of Marle may have been a valiant crusader, but he was certainly not a "poor knight" of the type of Gautier Sans Avoir (Walter the Penniless), who led troops of *populares,* perhaps even of ruffians, to the First Crusade and who, far from being a penniless adventurer, seems to exemplify members of the military aristocracy who were truly and sincerely won over to the cause of ecclesiastical reform and intended to devote the rest of their lives to the service of the new ideal. Of the same stripe must have been the handful of warriors and lesser aristocrats in the second decade of the twelfth century (in great part from Burgundy and Champagne) who gathered around one of their peers, Hugues de Payens. These men were either former crusaders or new arrivals in the Holy Land on one of the many pilgrimages organized after news of the First Crusade's successful conquest of Jerusalem in 1099 had spread through the continent of Europe. Instead of finding enthusiasm in Palestine, they found widespread disorder, desolation, and abandonment. Indiscriminate massacre of the native population, together with the exodus of terrorized survivors, had reduced those once flourishing lands to miserable poverty. Furthermore, when Islam had recovered from the surprise that was in great part responsible for the success of the crusade, it began to reorganize and plan for reconquest. Once the pilgrims had fulfilled their vow to visit the Holy Sepulcher they returned home: who, then, was to defend the conquests of 1099?

The monastic-military (or religio-military, religio-chivalric) orders were born of the need to garrison troops in the territories that had been won in order to defend pilgrims, to assist the weak and the sick, and to extend "permanently," so to speak, the mobilization that had made the crusade possible. In many ways these orders can be considered the most characteristic product of the ethic elaborated in the "leagues of peace" that sprang from the ecclesiastical reformers' efforts to subordinate the knighthood to their programs. From another point of view, however, they went far beyond those limits, even in their immediate results, inasmuch as they reflected a total and integral *conversio* of at least some religiously inclined European knights. It was no longer a matter of subordinating and making use of the knights, then, but rather of bringing them into the church. The difference is great: even though Gregory VII had spoken of a *militia sancti Petri,* he would perhaps not have welcomed a solution so extreme and, in its way, extremist.

The connection between the free and perhaps spontaneous confraternities of "poor knights" of the time of the "leagues of peace" and of the investiture controversy, on the one hand, and, on the other, the religious orders of knighthood is evident as early as the fellowship organized around Hugues de Payens. It appears that he and his followers at first assumed the name of *pauperes milites Christi,* vowing defense of the Holy Sepulcher and of pilgrims, but when the rule of the association was formally accepted at the Council of Troyes in 1128 it was transformed from a *fraternitas* into an authentic *religio,* an order. Since in the meantime Baldwin II, king of Jerusalem, had granted the knights lodgings in adjacent sites within the walls of the *Haram esh-Sharif*, near the two mosques of the Dome of the Rock and al-Aqsa (for the crusaders, the *Templum Domini* and the Temple of Solomon), the order assumed the name of "Templars." The Order of Knights Templar was dissolved in 1312 by order of Pope Clement V, following a series of scandals in which it had been involved, above all, it seems, because Philip IV of France coveted the extraordinary wealth it had accumulated.

The Order of Knights Templar was only one of the many religious orders of knighthood founded during the twelfth century in the Holy Land and in the Iberian peninsula and later in northeast Europe as well, where their role was to carry conquest and colonization into the Slavic and Baltic world. They were established throughout Europe, however, thanks to their initial success and to their many endowments in money and in lands, but also because of the conversion of members of the military aristocracy, attracted by their reputation for austerity and ascetic courage, who flocked to swell their ranks. The reputation for greed, violence, and corruption that some orders later earned,when times had changed (in which it is not always easy to distinguish historical reality from the biased propaganda of rival political forces), does not diminish their original significance.

Several of these orders deserve mention: the Hospitallers (dedicated to lodging and assisting pilgrims) of St. John of Jerusalem, called "of Rhodes" from the fourteenth century and "of Malta" in the sixteenth, as their headquarters shifted, became famous for their fleet. The Order of the Hospital of Saint Mary, known as "the Teutonic Knights" because its membership was made up exclusively of knights of Germanic origin, was also founded in the Holy Land. In Spain the orders of Santiago, of Calatrava, and of Alcántara were formed with the primary aims of lodging and defending pilgrims on their way to Santiago and of combating the Moors; Portugal had the orders of Montesa and Aviz; in northeast Europe, where the Teutonic Knights soon became established, there was the *militia Christi* of Livonia, called the Order of the Brethren of the Sword or the "Swordbearers" from the emblem they adopted, a vermilion cruciform sword on a silver field.

There are entire libraries of works on the experience of the religious orders of knighthood, though not all are equally trustworthy. Some scholars have traced their origin to the Muslim *Ribat*, fortresses of warrior mystics found in particular at the frontiers between areas of Christian and Muslim domination in the Iberian peninsula. That there were contacts and reciprocal influences between Christians and Muslims at the time of the crusades and the *Reconquista* is beyond doubt, even if their nature and their intensity are still hotly debated. Still, apart from a certain typological similarity, which can be explained without appealing to reciprocal influence (also because Christianity had no concept of the *jihad* or "holy war"), the fact remains that lay religious associations had existed since the eleventh century. That experience and the practical demands of defense—both in the Holy Land and in Spain—are enough to account for the emergence of those new fellowships, solidly grafted into the trunk of monastic tradition but at the same time endowed with their own revolutionary energy. One constant in Christian religious orders has always been a refusal of all compromise with war; the religious orders of knighthood, to the contrary (in which both clergy and laymen were admitted as knights and *servientes*) claimed contingent necessity to prescribe for their lay members a vow of combat as well as the vows of chastity, obedience, and personal poverty customary in the monastic tradition. The Templars even had special provisions for admitting married knights. Furthermore, orders such as the Templars and the Hospitallers of Saint John had a unique supranational structure: they came under the direct jurisdiction of the Holy See, which made them "states within the state" and in the long run created enormous problems for them.

At least at first, the military orders seemed to embody the ideal of the "divine knighthood," the *militia Christi,* as opposed to the *militia saeculi,* whom ascetics and rigorists in the Church never missed an occasion to reproach for their aimless violence, their fatuity, their cult of worldly glory, and their pursuit of pleasure. The rigorists even picked a quarrel with some of Gregory VII's most faithful followers and accused the pope (with some reason) of being ultimately more preoccupied with utilizing the knighthood for his own political ends and of not promoting the true Christianization of knights.

Non militia, sed malitia. That cruel play on words reflecting the implacable stylistic virtuosity of the ascetics dates from a few years after the Council of Troyes that gave legal status to the Order of Templars. It comes from the pen of a man who had offered protection and inspiration to the Templars, Bernard of Clairvaux, whose maternal uncle had been among the original collaborators of Hugues de Payens. In a treatise entitled *Liber ad milites Templi de laude novae militiae* Bernard displays a certain poetic force, particularly when he evokes the holy sites that he had never seen but that he loved and knew through Scripture. He also outlines a new and ideal knighthood composed of warrior-monks totally unmindful of the world and wholly dedicated to the cause of the war against the infidels and the loving defense of Christians. The *militia saeculi,* Bernard says, was not only impious in its worldliness and its insane dedication to fratricidal wars between Christians; it also lacked the virility demanded of the warrior and was in fact conspicuous for the attention knights paid to their hairdress and clothing. His satirical description of the handsome lay knight (a biting condemnation of the very culture that was gaining ground in contemporary courts) is harsh indeed: his soft hands enclosed in iron gloves, his beautiful, perfumed hair covered by his finely-worked helmet, his ankle-length coat of mail, covered, in the latest fashion (perhaps following an Oriental style) with a surcoat of sumptuous colored or quilted silk, his great blazoned, almond-shaped shield ready, the lay knight galloped through fields of flowers toward eternal damnation.

Bernard compares this knight to the Templar, who paid little attention to his hair and in fact wore it cut short both as a sign of penitence and so that his helmet would fit more closely; who gave no thought to having a freshly shaved, smooth face, but let his beard grow full (the custom in the East, but not in the West); who wore no colored garments nor damascened armor since the rule explicitly prohibited gilt and ornament; who hunted only ferocious animals, since big-game hunting was considered useful training for war (wild animals, aside from symbolizing the *pugna spiritualis,* were often seen in contemporary allegorical tradition as symbols and figures for the Devil); who was terrible as a lion for his enemies, the infidels, but mild as a lamb for Christians. The Templar was a monk, yet he killed. This was somewhat sad, the abbot of Clairvaux admits (with some embarrassment?), but Bernard was of course not about to allow the infidel a right to live. Moreover, he continues, the elimination of the pagan in arms was necessary in order to defend Christians and prevent injustice. Rather than thinking of killing a human being when he "suppressed" the enemy, the Templar should keep his mind on suppressing evil in all its forms, and clearly the pagan was in some measure a carrier of evil. His death was thus more a "malicide" than a "homicide."

Although Bernard justified and even praised the institution of the knight-monks, he by no means defended the knighthood itself, nor did he draw up any proposal for the thoroughgoing Christianization that he advocated. To the contrary, when he proposed to move the *bellatores* into the order of the *oratores* and when he suggested an arduous and somewhat paradoxical solution for war in terms of prayer and ascetic experience, he expressed a total condemnation of the knightly profession as an existential reality and a mode of life.

This does not mean that his testimony was received in this sense, nor that this is the objective historical meaning to be attributed to it. What is true is that the model proposed in the writings of Bernard of Clairvaux (also in terms of style) and his mystico-ascetic teachings contributed greatly to the establishment of "courtly" culture and poetry, and that his veneration of the Virgin set the example for the chivalric concept of disinterested service to the lady, seen as superior and unattainable. It is true that Erich Köhler and Georges Duby have taught us to look behind the screen of literary forms to seize the social realities that underlie them and for which they are the metaphor. It is no less true that in the logic not only of court life but also of courtly poetry itself, service to the lady turned out in practice to be less spiritual and disinterested than it might seem if the poetry is taken literally. In fact, analysis of the poetic works produced in such circles and of their underlying ideological system has demonstrated that courtly verse is permeated with an intense and even heavy eroticism. In spite of this, the teachings of the great Cistercian mystic and the fascination of his images outlasted the twelfth century and, together with other elements (for example, the paradigm that Ovid's verse offered), they gave the courtly world its intellectual unity.

This explains the apparent paradox in the fact that even though St. Bernard totally rejected the experience of worldly knighthood, directly or indirectly the writers of treatises on chivalry and chivalric romances relied on certain elements in his personality and his writings to lend legitimacy to the system of images they elaborated.

There was a clear revival of mystical and sacred themes among secular authors (or, in any event, in writings destined for secular readers) during the twelfth century and part of the thirteenth. At the same time, the ceremony of the dubbing of knights acquired forms increasingly similar to those of the sacraments, baptism in particular. Despite efforts in that direction, however, dubbing never became truly sacramental, nor was it ever celebrated obligatorily in church or in the presence of clergy, even though the pontifical of Guillaume Durand provided a liturgical organization of the rite. An anonymous text of the early thirteenth century that may originally have been produced in the Holy Land of the crusaders, the *Ordène de chevalerie* whose protagonist was the crusader Hugh of Tiberias, presents Saladin himself as eager to receive "the order of chivalry." Hugh dresses him in a white tunic and a vermilion cloak, fits him with brown hose, girds him with the ritual belt, and places gilded spurs at his heels. He then introduces him to the mysteries of the purifying bath and the restorative bed (symbolizing the Paradise that awaits the purified). He refuses to administer the *collée,* however—the *alapa militaris,* a blow given with the right hand to the back of the neck of the initiate, which was obviously considered the fundamental act in conferring the knightly *caracter.* Why this omission? Hugh of Tiberias was Saladin's prisoner, the author explains, and he had no right to strike a man who was for the moment his liege lord. The truth of the matter may be different: Saladin, for all that he was the most generous, noble, and valiant of men (thus in possession of all requisites to become a knight), was nonetheless not a Christian. The definitive and fundamental rite of the new baptism that was knightly ordination was thus withheld from him. This was not the first time that Christian chivalry wept for the religious abyss that separated it from the Muslim heroes: the *Conquête de Jérusalem* had already said of the valiant pagan warrior Cornumarant, "If he had believed in God, no one would have been as valiant as he." In the allegorical literary genre that immediately took over chivalric theoretical treatises, every piece of clothing, every weapon and piece of armor, every gesture became a symbol of Christian virtues and requirements. The sword became the glaive of the spirit, the helmet faith, and so on. The model for all this symbolism was the celebrated letter of St. Paul on the *arma lucis.*

The ethico-allegorical interpretation of the knighthood and of the knight's arms and armor was to have a long life. We can find it again in a treatise of Ramon Llull, the *Libre de l'orde de cavayleria,* which was to become bedside reading for the entire European noble class in the fifteenth century and, after William Caxton had printed his edition, into the early modern period. We meet it once more in Bernardino of Siena, in Catherine of Genoa, in Ignatius of Loyola, in Teresa of Avila, in Benoît de Canfield, and in Lorenzo Scupoli. It was an ambiguous tradition: it invited an objective depreciation of the experience of war, considered as pure allegory for the *pugna spiritualis,* yet it invested arms and combat with a profound spiritual dignity.

Another invitation to a mystical interpretation of worldly chivalry came—still in the early thirteenth century—in another text of probable Cistercian authorship (or at least inspiration), *La Queste del Graal.* This work takes up themes that Chrétien de Troyes had launched in the last quarter of the preceding century in his romance *Perceval,* which was in turn based on the Arthurian legends and on a mythic and folk tradition of Celtic origin, resolving them in ascetic terms. As Pierre Gallais has noted, it also contains notable elements that call to mind Arabo-Persian antecedents that can be inferred to have filtered into the West through contacts in Spain or in the Holy Land of the crusades. The mysterious presence of the Grail—at times a goblet or a bowl endowed with magic qualities, at other times a stone with arcane powers—was unfailingly interpreted symbolically as the Eucharist.

If the knight of the epic *chansons* was all warlike ardor and Christian faith, reflecting the Christianity of the *Reconquista* and the crusades, the knight of the Arthurian romances (like the knight of Provençal courtly poetry) was of a much more complex nature. It is not surprising that he has interested anthropologists and psychoanalysts as well as historians and philologists. Along with hunting scenes and encounters that resemble duels more than battles, these narratives quiver with erotic and spiritual tension directed at conquest of the lady, and through her, at self-affirmation. The knight remains a warrior hero, but above all he becomes a human type in search of an identity and a self-awareness that elude him. His experience thus unfolds as adventure and quest. Restless, solitary, constrained to journey from one initiatory trial to another through a dreamlike landscape of forest and heath, the "knight errant" has too long been considered a wholly literary figure, atemporal, improbable even as a model, and absolutely impossible to propose as the reflection of any sort of genuine reality.

This is far from the truth. New techniques for interpreting literary texts and interrogating the past show us a different reality, in these problems as in others. Psychoanalysis, semiology, and cultural anthropology combine forces to invite us to read those "improbable" Arthurian texts with the new eyes. Erich Köhler in the sociology of literature and Georges Duby in history have taught us to grasp what might be defined as the concrete forms of the adventure lying beyond the dreams and the fictions of literature—dreams and fictions, however, that were in constant touch with reality.

Admittedly, chivalric adventure is strewn with fairies, dragons, monsters, enchanted castles or gardens, dwarfs, and giants. They are more metaphorical than fantastic, however.

Adventure was a historical fact. Georges Duby has demonstrated that between the eleventh and the thirteenth centuries the most active sector of the lesser aristocracy in Europe—French, in particular, but following the French model, Anglo-Norman, German, Spanish, and Italian as well—was made up of *iuvenes*, freshly dubbed knights. When these knights received their arms during the ceremony of investiture, they left their familiar environment to band together, in groups of varying size, to follow dreams, perhaps, but also attempting to realize concrete ideals (not always achieved) of security and social prestige. Their optimal point of arrival was a good marriage, if possible with a lady of a higher condition than theirs and with more ample economic resources: behind the refined screen of *fin'amor*, discussed with great display of learning in texts of the later twelfth and the early thirteenth centuries such as the famous *De Amore* of André le Chapelain, lay an urgent will to found a household and establish a social position. In other words, the point is not to discuss whether courtly love was in fact a mystical sublimation of eros or a mask for sensual and sexual tension intensified to the limits of licentiousness; it is, rather, that the culture of courtly love had a clear function in a world that thought in exogamous terms and had need for sociocultural affirmation. The feudal lady, beautiful but cold and inaccessible, was a metaphor for a much less inaccessible heiress whose hand could be won by demonstrating one's audacity and valor.

This led, paradoxically, to a strange contrast between the professional, almost vocational dimension of being a knight and the existential impermanence of the knightly condition that ended with marriage and settling down. The twelfth and thirteenth centuries, traditionally regarded as the height of the knightly age of the European Middle Ages, doubtless signaled the triumph of the knighthood. Poets, the authors of treatises, even theologians and hagiographers seem to speak of nothing else; chroniclers and painters reflect the shining splendor of the ceremony of dubbing; high nobles and even great monarchs from Richard the Lion-Hearted to St. Louis neglected their glorious titles to bear the simple title of knight. It was a title coveted by social strata on the rise, by the newly rich of urban societies—the *gente nova*—in particular. We shall soon see that the broader distribution of the outward signs and the practices of chivalry (predictably, accompanied eventually by their devaluation and vulgarization) was discouraged by the nascent feudal monarchies. We shall also see that such obstacles were gotten around in one way or another by social groups in search of distinction and quite capable of creating their own political institutions and finding revolutionary ways to confront socioeconomic situations, but who were nonetheless tenaciously attached to tradition and dependent upon others when it came to elaborating their own culture.

Matrimonial prospects aside, the chivalric adventure was essentially a search for new sources of wealth and new opportunities for employment. Mercenary military service was already widespread in the twelfth century, but it existed even earlier. The Norman knights who swarmed toward Puglia and Byzantium in the eleventh century offered their services to whoever paid them best, beginning with the *basileus* of Constantinople. There were also opportunities in the various military campaigns in Spain or, particularly between the thirteenth and fifteenth centuries, in northeast Europe in campaigns against the pagan Slavs and Balts. Naturally, there was the crusade itself, which, according to Adolf Waas, permitted the development of a veritable *Ritterfrömmigkeit*, a characteristically chivalric religious *pietas* expressed in many songs about departure for the crusade written by poets who were also feudal nobles and knights: Hartmann von Aue, Friedrich von Hausen, Walther von der Vogelweide, Thibaut de Champagne, Conon de Béthune, and so forth. Service to the Most High was identified with service to a strong, generous, and splendid feudal lord; service to the Virgin Mary was service to the lady in celestial form. These and the search for a divine homeland by a pilgrimage to Jerusalem, willingness to face martyrdom, but also loyalty to companions in arms and noble admiration even for enemy warriors worthy of praise and honor (Saladin's high reputation in the West, later consecrated by Lessing, begins here) were the basic ingredients of crusade-oriented chivalry as the "worldly" knighthood typically perceived them. Even though the religious orders of knighthood also sprang from the experience of the crusades, their particular brand of spirituality was powerless to influence this way of thinking.

The chivalric aspiration for adventures in distant lands—and for *amors de terra lonhdana*, as the troubador, Jaufré Rudel, put it (he was in love, tradition tells us, with a Franco-Lebanese feudal lady he had never seen)—was translated into an invincible attraction for the mysteries and the marvels of an Orient that by then extended well beyond Jerusalem and the Holy Land. The cultural revival of the twelfth century, together with the many Greek, Arabic, and Hebrew texts that began to circulate through Europe at the time, albeit in bad or unfaithful translations (in Spain there were even first attempts to translate the *Koran*), kindled interest and fueled fantasies about an Orient that was indeed an "oneiric horizon," but that was beginning to be discerned more clearly in versions that were indeed fabulous but that in some points coincided with reality. The Far East, the deeper Asia with which contact was established after the crusades, was a land of spices that reached Europe from India by caravan over the "Silk Road" and by water over the routes of the Indian Ocean, already closed to Westerners. It was also the Asia of the cycles of legends, which also had a connection with spices. Spices were believed to come from the Earthly Paradise, thought by contemporary geographers to be the source of the great rivers of the *partes infidelium*, the Ganges, the Tigris, the Euphrates, and the Nile. Unending territories inhabited by monsters but overflowing with treasures and, isolated in the farthest reaches of the Orient, the Earthly Paradise—this was the imaginary geography of Asia that returns in many versions of the "romance of Alexander" or in curious works like the "letter of Prester John." This letter, supposedly sent to the pope and then to one emperor or another, described the immense wealth and the mysteries of a reign that voyagers of the thirteenth and fourteenth centuries—Marco Polo first among them—were long to sigh over. Behind the putative author of the letter, a fabled sovereign of a countless people of Christian faith, lay the historical existence of a Nestorian Christian community that extended from Persia all the way to China.

Epic poems and romances were profoundly marked by this fascination with Asia, and they popularized the legends of the Earthly Paradise, the kingdom of Prester John, the land of the Amazons, and the secret and terrible empire of the Old Man of the Mountain, leader of the sect of the Assassins. The attraction for distant lands and their customs was to have a decisive influence on European culture between the eighteenth and the twentieth centuries and to give rise to an exoticism that contributed to colonial conquests. That attraction was rooted, however, in medieval chivalric literature, which in turn borrowed from ancient geographical literature and from the spirituality of the crusades, but which in some ways closely resembled a proselytizing spirit that, in other ways, seemed totally unrelated to it but that was at the same time sensitive to the copious testimony of voyagers and, indeed, of missionaries. The spirit of adventure of the crusaders and of chivalry was passed on, in the era of the great geographical discoveries and transoceanic voyages, to Henry the Navigator, Christopher Columbus, and the *conquistadores* (who used it as an alibi for violence and despoliation but nonetheless remained faithful to it in their fashion).

Adventure was also a part of daily life and had no need of wars or crusades. It existed in the hunt, especially in hunting the great and noble beasts of the forests of Europe—the stag, the boar, the bear—whose symbolic connotations, borrowed from heraldry, and mythico-folk background were adopted by allegorical bestiaries and by hagiography. Thus there are often echoes of the hunt in romance, where it takes on the character of an initiatory experience. Adventure lay above all in a characteristic activity that was in some ways a sporting event, in others useful training in martial arts, but was most significant on the level of its dramatization of social functions and of the aristocracy's self-image: the tournament.

It is difficult to say when the practice began of holding encounters between opposing groups in an enclosed field. Such encounters were called *hastiludium* from the characteristic contest between knights armed with a heavy wooden staff (*hasta*) who tried to unhorse their adversaries; in Anglo-Norman sources they were called *conflictus gallicus,* indicating that the practice was imported into England from France. Nor is it known when the joust arose to accompany the tournament proper—that is, the series of encounters in single combat between pairs of knights that proved both more orderly and less cruel than the *mêlée,* the mass combat typical of the tournament. From a purely typological point of view it is fairly simple to hypothesize that the tournament arose early as a form of training for war. The fact that it was contested in an enclosed area (and that jousting narrowed combat to single "champions") has led to comparison with the juridical duel of the "judgment of God." We do know that the vogue for tournaments—unknown until the late eleventh and early twelfth centuries—seems to have suddenly burst forth at that time. Absent in the older *chansons,* the tournament fills later chivalric literature with clouds of dust raised by the horses' hooves, the shouts of the participants, the encouraging cries of the public, the herald's strident announcements, the thundering clash of arms, and the crack of splintered lances flying skyward. From that moment on, heraldic symbology spread rapidly, doubtless also in response to the need to distinguish the various champions in the melee. Entire generations of knights were mowed down in tournaments—perhaps more than in battle—helping to prevent the scattering of inheritance, thus maintaining strong lineages and consolidating family wealth. In battle, the knights' aim was not to kill one another but to take enemies prisoner in order to collect their ransom. In jousts and tournaments lethal incidents, to the contrary, must have been extraordinarily frequent, as were serious consequences when a knight fell from his horse at full gallop and collapsed under the weight of his iron armor.

Historians have long hotly debated these martial games: did they have real value as training? If so, to what extent? The problem is not negligible, since it involves another and broader question: did armies of the tenth to the thirteenth centuries, in which knights were the crack troops, even the true combatant nucleus (given that all other fighters—infantrymen, sappers, artillerymen who handled the siege engines and the catapults—were really there to back up the knights), know the value of tactics and strategy? Or did strategy come back into fashion only from contact with the Byzantine and Muslim East, where the Greco-Roman military arts had been kept up and brought up to date? This happened above all in the thirteenth and fourteenth centuries, when, for example, translations of Vegetius' *De re militari* were available in versions that even had a certain literary value, as in Jean de Meun's and Christine de Pisan's French translation under the title *L'Art de chevalerie*). Certainly, the great era of tactical and strategic treatises was the fourteenth and the fifteenth centuries, when the prospect of a new crusade often prompted works like the manuals of Benedetto Zaccaria, Pierre Dubois, and Marino Sanudo the Elder. This does not mean, however, that the knights of earlier times were ignorant of tactical questions and strategic problems, or that they limited themselves to frontal attacks in the elementary formations of the "wall" or the "wedge," thus reducing military encounters to pure contests of physical strength and skill on horseback.

It is true that if we looked for theoretical statements in the *chansons* and the romances, we could easily compile a florilegium of heroic maxims in which all artifice or stratagem is equated with treachery and betrayal. Even the later chroniclers (in fact, later chroniclers in particular if we think of the great Froissart, the bard of the "autumn of chivalry" in the age of the Hundred Years War) took pleasure in compiling instances of valor uniquely involving a provocation to combat. It has been said that this was why the flower of European chivalry let itself be wiped out or taken prisoner by the Turks at Nicopolis in 1396. The Turks fought in their own style, using archers on horseback to make rapid strikes and thin-spread formations that opened up before the heavy charges of the Christians, weighed down head to foot in heavy armor, only to close behind them and squeeze them in a vise. In the fourteenth century, however (and we shall return to that period soon), the knighthood was being redefined as a social distinction and in crisis as a military force. If we look closely at the knighthood in the centuries of its greatest vogue, we can see that horseback warriors were far from ignorant of *ruses de guerre*. In this sense the tournament could indeed constitute a good opportunity for training, since it often took the form of a veritable battle (I was about to say, "a simulated battle," but when we read certain descriptions, we wonder how accurate the term would be). Indeed, contrary to a persistent romantic image, participation was not always limited to knights alone; they often had helpers on foot, even in good number. As for the "enclosed field," at times the term could indicate a vast terrain with meadows, woods, and clearings, on occasion even encroaching on inhabited areas. In short, it was not a modest, well-defined arena or "list" but a true battleground.

The knights and troubadors, heralds and minstrels who flocked to the tournament never ceased singing its praises as a school of courage and loyalty. They even proposed it as a mirror of Christian values, since it provided training for the crusade and an occasion for making plans for an overseas expedition. It did on occasion happen that during or at the conclusion of a tournament a group of knights would vow to depart for the war against the infidel, and the chivalric tradition showed fondness for vows of this and other sorts (vows based on piety, promising erotic rewards, or involving a display of courage for its own sake).

For a long time the church took a much less kindly view of tournaments. Innocent II condemned in no uncertain terms the "detestable fairs and markets commonly called tournaments, in which knights customarily gather together to exhibit their strength and their impetuous recklessness." The date was 1130, when the fashion for tournaments reigned throughout the West, in the Holy Land under the crusaders, and even in the part of the Byzantine and Islamic world that had had contacts with the crusaders. The condemnation was repeated in the Second Lateran Council of 1139. Anyone killed in a tournament was denied the right to burial in consecrated ground, but the religious orders of knighthood, appealing to their ample autonomy as orders directly responsible to the Holy See, agreed to depart from this norm, and they welcomed knights killed in tournaments in the cemeteries that surrounded their headquarters. Preachers and authors of theological and moral treatises and saints' lives competed to exhort men to forgo martial sports. They also spread fearful rumors: in one place where a particularly cruel contest had been held demons had been seen flying through the air, holding a tournament of their own to spine-chilling cries of joy; other demons (in the shape of crows or vultures this time) had been seen circling around the tournament lists obviously in search of souls to snatch, tearing pieces of flesh from the corpses of the fallen like birds of prey. There were even reported to be nobles who had briefly come back to life, rising from their catafalques to tell in a few shattering words the fate in the afterworld of those who reveled in such atrocious contests. In the thirteenth century, Jacques de Vitry detailed at length how all the seven deadly sins were committed in a tournament: pride, because this type of competition sprang from an exaggerated desire for glory and honors; anger, because combat, even when governed by rules, fatally generated hatred and a desire for revenge; acedia, because defeats easily led to prostration and despair; envy and greed, since the combatants competed for a rich booty of the arms, armor, and horses of defeated competitors and rich prizes were offered for the winners; gluttony, because these festivities were usually accompanied by great banquets; finally, lust, since the competitors usually fought to please their ladies, whose "colors" or other tokens—veils, sleeves—they bore in combat on their helmets or their lances.

The gage of love ostentatiously worn in a tournament, together with the heraldic blazon on his shield, his surcoat, and his horse's caparison, identified the knight when he took part in such martial sports. Erotic tension stretched to the breaking point was a fundamental characteristic of this type of knightly activity, and when the church opposed tourneys, it was proposing an ethical and social discourse much more profound and complex than we might think if we judge the church's prohibitions merely as religious policies aimed at reducing violence and bloodshed among brothers in Christ. Chronicles often speak of inextinguishable hatreds originating in a tournament and of tournaments used as an excuse for taking revenge on an enemy. Rivalry in love must have been one of the commonest motives in such instances, and students of animal behavior have shown that males' desire to display their strength before females, which reiterates the right of the adult male to enjoy females, underlies what they call, not by chance, "animal tourneys." One anecdote should suffice to show the levels of erotic tension that could be reached. In the mechanism of the "obliging gift" dear to both chivalric literature and folklore, the lady asks a boon of her champion but does not specify what it is. When he assents, she reveals the nature of the promise he has made, usually a particularly difficult test or some special behavior during the tourney, as in the *Lancelot, ou le chevalier à la charette* of Chrétien de Troyes, in which Guinevere obliges Lancelot to feign cowardice in combat. In our anecdote, the lady commands the knight to leave off his heavy armor in the lists and wear only her shift to protect him. Her wish granted, she exchanges the courtesy by arriving at the feast that follows the contest dressed only in the same shift, now stained with the lifeblood of her champion. We have no need of Freud to pierce the transparent, heavily erotico-sexual significance of the entire episode.

The tournament had penetrated aristocratic culture deeply, but it also permeated the culture of the burghers and the common people, where imitations and parodies of chivalric contests were common events. It also entered into the life-style of members of the governing groups. One thirteenth-century poem narrates the deeds of a knight who, thanks to Georges Duby, is now the most famous "tournament contestant" of the Middle Ages—William Marshal, who rose to be mentor to the young king, Henry III of England, and who died in 1219 at over seventy years of age (over eighty, according to him). Marshal's case is certainly exceptional; still, it shows well how, from one tourney to another, one court to another, one victory to another, one prize to another, and one kinship group to another the *iuvenis* could become wealthy and settle down. The knight's condition was a paradoxical one: once dubbed, he remained a knight forever, somewhat like a priest, despite the fact that the dubbing ceremony was not sacramental in nature. At its most solemn, dubbing did its best to follow the patterns of a sacramental rite, and there was no lack of theorists ready to argue that knighthood was a sort of lay "priesthood" dedicated to God, to the liege lord (later, with the establishment of absolute states, to the king), and to high-born ladies. We have already seen that kings condescended to being known by their knightly title alone. It was also true that the knight's career was soon ended. In fact, it was decidedly brief, coinciding with the period of the band of *iuvenes* and of the search for adventure of which the tournament is perhaps the most common and also the most concrete representation. If fortune led him to contract a good marriage, the handsome warrior was happy to hang up his heavy girdle, his sword, and his gilded spurs, saving them for a solemn occasion now and then, and to devote himself to the administration of his own inheritance and the wealth he had acquired through his wife.

Not only did the Church condemn tournaments in no uncertain terms, rulers also put out decrees. They failed to empty the lists, and they did not even manage to lessen the danger and aggressiveness of the tourneys. The heavy tournament armor that knights began to wear in the thirteenth century (for reasons we shall go into) may have played a role in these high tolls. A knight entirely covered with steel plates (that is, who wore the plate armor perfected during the fifteenth century) did not necessarily risk less harm if he fell from his horse than his counterpart of the eleventh and thirteenth centuries who wore the relatively lighter mail hauberk. The various ordinances did their best to prevent flareups of personal enmity or vendettas during contests of knightly skill, aided by the progressive replacement of arms *à outrance*—battle weapons—with tournament arms—the "courtly arms" or arms *à plaisance*, such as the blunted sword or the lance capped in a variety of ways or else wrapped so that it could strike the adversary's shield and even unhorse him, but not pierce him. Above all, the number of serious accidents was lowered by the gradual (but never total) replacement of the *mêlée* with jousting in single combat: jousting made everything more orderly, better regulated, and less dangerous than mass combat.

Given that tourneys had come to be such an integral part of social relations among the aristocracy, the church found it difficult to maintain its prohibition after tourneys had lost some of their danger and the simulated battles had tended to become more like sporting matches and spectacles. Knights, for their part, emphasized what to them was a total harmony between religious faith and the practice of tourneys: matches served to propagandize crusades, and they usually began with religious functions (which meant, among other things, that for one reason or another not even the clergy scrupulously respected the ecclesiastical prohibitions). There soon arose a counterpropaganda to the legends of demons flocking to tournaments. One well-known and moving episode in the *Dialogus miraculorum* of Caesarius of Heisterbach, perhaps the finest text among religious legends of the thirteenth century, is a case in point. A knight on his way to a tourney with some friends passes before a chapel dedicated to the Virgin and cannot resist the impulse to render homage to her. Absorbed in prayer, he is unaware of the passing time. He arrives, sorrowfully, too late for the contest, only to find everyone celebrating his deeds. While he was praying to the Virgin, she had jousted for him, in his armor and wearing his insignia, and had won the tourney.

When Pope John XXII abrogated the ecclesiastical prohibition of tournaments in 1316, the struggle against religious rigor had long been won and tourneys had become something quite different from what they had been in the past. Nor was fourteenth-century knighthood what it had been two centuries before, either in its social structures or its influence on European life. We shall return to the question.

The tournament had given rise to its own literature, which can be divided into several genres. First of all, there were veritable blow-by-blow accounts in verse, the speciality of the "heralds"—poets and contest judges expert in the rules of combat and in identifying the insignia of the various participants. The most famous of these is *Le Tournoi de Chauvency,* written by Jacques Bretel to celebrate a tourney held at that place in 1285 that included two full days of jousting, followed by a day for the great mass combat. Texts of the sort are an interminable series of descriptions of encounters and detailed enumerations of heraldic colors and figures. To our tastes they are a soporific bore, but the thirteenth century found them intensely interesting.

Another notable literary genre "moralized" the tourney by giving it allegorical meaning. As we have already seen, the *pugna spiritualis* lay at the base of the Christian legitimization of knighthood, and Bernard of Clairvaux had few qualms about defining the massacre of infidels in battle as "malicide," not "homicide." In like fashion, Romanesque portals and capitals abound in allegorical figurations of the combat between the virtues and the vices, represented as opposing warriors or as knights and monsters. This was an inviting interpretation of the tourney, as it opened the way to infinite possibilities for allegorization: the combatants could be allegorized, as could their clothing, their colors, their insignia, and the blows given and received. Huon de Méry's poem, *Le Tournoiement d'Antéchrist,* offers one example of this: Christ's shield bears a vermilion cross twisted around with a token from the Virgin; he jousts against Satan, whose insignia is a strip of Persephone's tunic (in another version the Devil is "the knight of the dragon" and has a dragon as his blazon). The archangels and the cardinal and the theological virtues fight at Christ's side, along with the specifically knightly virtues of *Prouesse, Largesse, Courtoisie,* and *Débonnaireté.* The knights of the Round Table descend into the lists to fight by their side.

Allegorical representations of this sort, which we are used to reading about or seeing depicted, must on occasion have been dramatized. The tourney lent itself marvelously to spectacle; it was already in part spectacle by its very nature, perhaps even more than it was simulated battle. Philip of Novara describes a tournament organized in 1223 in Cyprus to celebrate the dubbing of a young man of the house of Ibelin, crusader barons of Beirut, in which knights impersonated the characters of the Arthurian cycle. The knight Ulrich von Lichtenstein became famous for two voyages throughout Europe in 1227 and in 1240, known respectively as his *Venusfahrt* and his *Arturfahrt,* during which he dressed first as Venus and then as King Arthur and went from castle to castle and city to city challenging all comers. Later there were veritable theatrical representations. On one occasion, in 1490, two teams of Bolognese knights, one side dressed in blue in honor of Wisdom, the other in green in honor of Fortune, faced off in what might be called a humanistic version of the *pugna spiritualis.* More important, there were true blends of theatrical spectacle and the tournament, called in Italy *tornei a soggetto,* in France, *pas d'armes,* and in Spain *pasos honrosos,* famous examples of which occurred in France at the time of the Hundred Years War or in the so-called *cavallerie* of Ferrara in the early sixteenth century. A plot was invented—often a very slim plot indeed—such as a castle to attack or defend, a tower, a bridge, or a fountain to safeguard, a maiden to save. The various encounters between knights, dressed according to the scenic demands of the plot, fitted in with the flimsy story line. In time these spectacles became the special province of the courts, but between the thirteenth and the fifteenth centuries they were played out also in the city, before a populace who seemed to enjoy them just as much as they did the many burlesque and parodic tourneys organized by burghers and even by ruffians and marginal sorts. Other poetic works speak of tournaments of birds, of clergy and knights, friars and nuns, and so forth. On the folklore level, the tourney to end the winter, one that took place between Carnival and Lent (an amusing version of which is narrated by the *novelliere,* Sabadino degli Arienti), soon became famous. There were even "tournaments of ladies" in which poetic and musical compositions served as an excuse to organize dances.

The connection between allegory, theater, and martial games in the fifteenth century can be grasped by looking at two complementary works by René d'Anjou, duke of Lorraine and titular king of Naples. The first, the *Livres des Tournois,* is perhaps the fullest and most complete theoretical, descriptive, and normative treatise on the science of tourneys ever written. (It contains important sections on dress, insignia, and "courtly" arms, which were often not made of metal but used boiled leather for defensive armor and wood for offensive weapons.) The second, the *Livre de Coeur d'Amour épris,* uses the form of the chivalric romance to narrate the complexities of falling in love and describes the phases of courtship and progress in the erotic relationship in terms of voyages, duels, and initiatory trials.

When we describe an event that begins with battlefields barely disguised as tournament lists and arrives at the spectacle-games of the court, we are also drawing the parabolic curve of chivalric culture between the twelfth century and the sixteenth century and, at the same time, the loss of concrete military and social values to which those dignified with knighthood were subjected.

It was Marc Bloch's famous thesis that late medieval nobility originated in the knighthood—a thesis later denied or modified by an entire sector of medieval studies, German in particular, and recently reexamined and to some extent rehabilitated, as shown in a masterly study by Giovanni Tabacco. It is certain that once the dignity of knighthood (entry into which was signaled by the ceremony of dubbing) began to take on social and cultural importance and knighthood itself seemed to be changing from a free confraternity of armed men banded together around a chief to become an institution, the rulers of feudal Europe took over the selection of new knights (still a composite group) to be awarded the *cingulum militare,* thus depriving the knights themselves of their right to co-opt recruits. The first well-documented restrictive provisions (usually referred to by the German term, *Abschliessungen,* or "closings") came from England, Norman Sicily, and Swabian Germany of the mid-twelfth century, but there are clear indications that they existed earlier in some areas of Europe. In practice, the right to the knight's girdle and spurs began to be denied to anyone who did not already have a knight among his direct ancestors. Although knightly dignity itself was never declared hereditary, the requisites to accede to the knightly condition were declared so, along with the privileges and the duties connected with knighthood. In the long run, the duties proved to be more onerous than the privileges were rewarding. The ceremony of dubbing, which included the bath, the vigil of arms, the gifts (clothing, for the most part), and the banquet that the new knight was obliged to offer his guests, required a notable expenditure, unless an occasion for more summary dubbing could be seized—on the eve or the morrow of a battle, for example, or at the ruler's passage through the territory. This explains why many thirteenth-century men, particularly in England, who had a right to the dignity of knighthood—"esquires," *damoiseaux, scudieri,* and so forth, men who ranked immediately below the knights and could aspire to wearing the gilded spurs one day—

preferred to continue to aspire to knighthood for the rest of their days. As everyone knows, the British "squire" became a characteristic figure of the lesser aristocracy.

Above and beyond the common term *miles,* which was applied to all members of what ideally was supposed to have been a supranational brotherhood in arms linked by the insignia and the tradition of knightly investiture, knighthood began to show regional and national traits. Since knighthood tended to be transmitted hereditarily, it found in heraldry its most characteristic ideological and cultural expression. The need to foster new blood in society, particularly in the period of intense social and economic mobility during the thirteenth and the fourteenth centuries, was satisfied in France by special *lettres d'anoblissement* that granted exceptions to the restrictive norms and gave people of humbler origin an opportunity to accede to the dignity of knighthood and choose a crest, the basic requirements for what was to become the nobility. In the cities of northern and central Italy as well, where toward the end of the Duecento the dignity of knighthood was considered by the various "people"'s governments (which spoke for the entrepreneurial and merchant class) as one of the distinctive signs of the "magnates" whom they were determined to exclude from the exercise of power, the burghers—the *gente nova*—soon began to covet the title as they invested capital in lands and castles and imitated the life-style of the aristocracy in France or Germany or the analogous feudal and seigneurial aristocracy of the Italian peninsula. Soon armed knights "of the people" appeared, and in 1378 in Florence the *ciompi*—unskilled wool workers—claimed a right to the sovereign act of creating knights of their own. Knighthood, what is more, was a requirement for certain posts such as *podestà* or *capitano del popolo,* positions that involved service in another city than one's own.

In time the term "knight" (*cavaliere, chevalier,* etc.) no longer seemed sufficient to indicate the holder of the dignity of knighthood. Fighting on horseback was practiced by others than knights, and the need arose for distinguishing, for example, between simple *milites* and "outfitted" *milites* who had been dubbed or, later, *equites aurati,* which vernacular Italian sources translated as *cavalieri a spron d'oro* (golden-spurred knights). These were social distinctions, however, and those who had the right to them were not necessarily to be found on a horse. In the practical operations of municipal, seigneurial, or mercenary military formations, legitimate title to knighthood commanded a higher rate of pay, but little or nothing more. Abuses must of course have been many.

In the late Middle Ages horsemen were still considered the backbone of armies. According to their rank, knights in Italy were considered *banderesi* (who had the right to a banner, symbol of their jurisdiction over their lands, hence of their command over a certain number of followers) or *baccellieri*, a term usually explained as a synonym and homophone of the French *bas chevalier.* In reality, the gap between "high" and "low" nobility had by that time increased. Aside from the many men of humble or at least non-noble extraction promoted to knighthood by the royal will, it was already clear that knighthood, with all its many variants, was becoming the sign of a lower stratum (at times very low indeed) of an aristocracy in crisis. Land and arms, the base of the aristocracy's power and prestige, were no longer adequate in times dominated by intensifying programs for centralization as monarchies shifted from feudal to absolute (in Italy, regional states dominated). They were no longer adequate in a monetary economy managed by bankers, merchants, and entrepreneurs who may indeed have loved chivalric pomp, heraldic insignia, and the civic prerogatives of knighthood, but who would not have dreamed of making it the basis of their existence and even less of giving battle.

In France, however, the *bas chevaliers* who held fiefs often barely large enough to arm one warrior (a "shield" fief) long found employment, remunerative in its way, in the Hundred Years War. In Germany, knights both free and nonfree (the *ministeriales*), who had always been strictly segregated from the high nobility and locked into their role as a subordinate nobility by the system of *Heershild,* drew a living from land that at times was truly poverty-stricken, consoling themselves with participation in tourneys, which had become an authentic institution. All too often indigent and hounded by debts, they turned to robbery and plunder as *Raubritter,* particularly at the expense of rich city merchants, whom they scornfully called "sacks of pepper." The merchants reacted by organizing punitive expeditions against the castles, by engaging knights from among other marauder groups who were needy enough to betray their rank (the other knights called them "blood merchants"), or by bringing outlaws to justice, including those with knightly girdles and gilded spurs. This explains the high number of haughty but desperate nobles, skilled only in fighting, who signed up as soldiers of fortune in mercenary companies—societies of mercantile structure, as Mario Del Treppo has demonstrated, but in which there nevertheless survived, in vulgarized form, some glimmer of the ancient knightly virtues.

In Spain knights were undergoing an analogous dramatic decline. The proud *hildagos,* unlike many of their peers in other areas of Europe, never could have become prosperous gentlemen farmers (or even less prosperous ones), and they continued to believe that living by the sword was the only life worthy of them. When the marriage of the "Catholic monarchs" Ferdinand of Aragon and Isabella of Castile put an end to the long period of unrest and civil war that followed the *Reconquista,* many of the *hildagos* took refuge in companies of select foot soldiers—the *tercios* of whom Emperor Charles V was so rightly proud. Others ended up pursuing chivalric adventure overseas, adventures that combined echoes of the medieval cosmographical legends of Asia (long confused with the New World) involving the Earthly Paradise, the Fountain of Youth, and Amazons, with a reality made up of the massacres and the pillage that characterized the deeds of the *conquistadores.* Even that—like the wars of the Indian subcontinent for romantic young officers of Her Britannic Majesty, who lived in a nineteenth-century climate of revival of knighthood—was a concrete form of the adventure.

In the constant misunderstandings and contradictions that make up the history of knighthood, it should be noted that medieval aristocratic culture was permeated with chivalric values and ferments. It is significant, however, that Thomas Malory could write, in England, the most important work of late chivalric literature before the masterpieces of Ariosto and Cervantes in the fifteenth century and that he dedicated it to the death of Arthur and to the end of the glorious customs of knights on horseback. In the real world knighthood had become a sorry thing indeed—a series of exterior trappings that could be bought and sold; an instrument for social promotion; an incoherent congeries of warriors overweeningly proud of their rank but lacking means and in continual search of systems to scratch out a living. One exception between the sixteenth and the seventeenth centuries was the lesser nobility in Poland, the *szlachta,* whose social persona was saved by their country's continual instability (which kept up the demand for warriors) and by the "price revolution" in the West, which notably raised the value of both the land to which they had remained faithful and its products.

The rulers of the nascent centralized nation-states of Europe reacted to the crisis in knightly society on two different levels. First, they worked to empty the power and prerogatives, both juridical and sociopolitcal, of the lesser nobility of all meaning (and of the higher nobility as well, when possible). This was a long and fairly continual process that nevertheless contained moments of stagnation and occasional reversals, as in the well-known "refeudalization" of the proto-modern epoch. Second, in an attempt to bind the nobility more closely to the monarchy, the rulers created a quantity of "court orders" on the model of the religious orders of knighthood or on the models proposed by chivalric literature (the most typical of which was of course the Round Table). These had splendid ceremonies rich in images, sumptuous insignia, and resplendent clothing, but their entire meaning was connected with the mechanisms of the court. These orders—of St.George or of the Bath in England, of the Star in France, of the Ship in Angevin Naples, of the Crescent in Lorraine, of the Golden Fleece in Burgundy and later in Hapsburg Austria and Spain, and so forth—were the direct ancestors of modern honorific orders of knighthood and their systems of decorations. The code that governed these orders combined the Christian faith and service to women (the constants of secular chivalric mythology) with loyalty to the king, and in this sense they played an important role in converting to the monarchy in *ancien régime* countries a nobility that until the late fifteenth century had less than unanimously rallied to the throne and the reigning dynasties.

A substantial transformation in military technology underlay the "decadence" of the knighthood and its partial demilitarization between the thirteenth and the sixteenth centuries, however. Some hint of this had come as early as the twelfth century, when the crossbow, which, in its portable form, had come from the steppes of Asia, was introduced at sieges and on battlegrounds. The church long considered the weapon illicit, given the lethal force of its blows, but in spite of the church's prohibition of its use in conflicts between Christian forces, the crossbow took hold, along with the English longbow with the great range and high speed of its arrows (two qualities not shared by the quarrels the crossbow shot). Projectile weapons obliged knights to wear heavier armor. In addition to the chain-mail hauberk (which was transformed from the mail shirt of the eleventh and twelfth centuries to something like a tight-fitting metallic jumpsuit), knights wore a coat of iron plates molded to the body at the critical points of the neck, the chest, the back, the elbows, the wrists, and the knees. Reinforced defensive armor made the shield less necessary. It was already awkward in frontal combat when the knight, his heavy lance couched against his chest with his right hand, needed his left hand free to control his horse. The shield thus tended to disappear from combat, although it remained important in heraldry, shifting from a large, almond-shaped form in the eleventh and twelfth centuries to a small triangular shape in the thirteenth century, and later it took on fantastic and aesthetically pleasing shapes with no function in the open field or the tournament, where it was no longer used. This slow process led, in the fifteenth century, to the use of full plate-armor. The knight, covered from head to foot in steel, was an unstoppable projectile when he galloped full tilt into battle; when unhorsed or surrounded, however, he became a poor crustacean and an easy prey for common foot soldiers. This often happened, up to the famous "battle of the Golden Spurs" in Courtrai (Kortrijk) in 1302, in which burgher infantry gave the noble horsemen a hard lesson and a sound thrashing. The fourteenth century was the age of the defeat of the knights, who often were obliged—as at Crécy—to get down from the saddle, break off the lower part of their attack lances, and defend themselves against the enemy as best they could, something like a heavy infantry. Not only did the cost of defensive armor rise rapidly and suddenly, its increasing weight made it impossible for knights to remain long in the saddle, and it obliged them select varieties of horses that were ever stronger and more resistant to fatigue, but slower, which exposed the horseman to enemy arrows for a longer time than before. The remedy was to shorten the charges so as to come into contact with the enemy sooner, but when the knights were confronted by enemy archers and crossbowmen in tight ranks, shielded by great rectangular shields called pavises, the attack could turn out to be useless or downright disastrous. The same was true when a knight launched at a gallop was stopped short by a wall of long pikes of the municipal (later, a mercenary) infantry. Both the Swiss and the "lances" of southern Germany were famous for fighting in compact battalions of mercenary pikemen. Knighthood still had its trappings, its tournaments, and its challenges to single combat, but real war between the end of the Middle Ages and the beginning of the modern era was quite another thing. With the fourteenth century, firearms gave the deathblow to the military usefulness and the moral prestige of horse combatants: Ariosto gave voice to the swan song of medieval chivalry when he called the arquebus a "cursed, abominable contraption," but the gentle and valiant Bayard, protagonist of knighthood's last season in the sun, was fated to fall, struck by a falconet, a light artillery piece. His death was emblematic.

Did the beautiful knightly adventure die, then, among bristling pikes and smoking bombards, among fortified bastions and the tyranny of the absolute sovereigns of the sixteenth century? Yes and no. The combatant on horseback went into a long eclipse after the early sixteenth century, but to some extent he rose again in the following century as a pistoleer, a lancer, or a dragoon (or as a hussar or a uhlan imported from the steppes). Horses that were more maneuverable, cuirasses, and pistols later brought the horseman back to European battlegrounds. As for the distinctions and decorations of knighthood, their fascination and their prestige have lasted almost to our own times, fed by a rich and often beautiful mythology and literature that had an important voice in the cultural panorama of Europe. The death of chivalry was lamented in the age of Marie Antoinette and in that of Marshal Radetzki, and both Eugène of Savoy and Ludwig of Bavaria were heralded as the "last" chivalric knights. As legends, honorific decorations, and revivals come and go, the fascination of chivalric civilization lives on in the contemporary world, even adapting to the myth of the cowboy or to the world of the comic strips or science fiction.

Chivalry was stillborn: immediately after its birth it wept for the inanimate corpse of Roland, fallen at Roncesvalles. It even wept over a hero who had fallen some time before, since the historical Roland lived in the eighth century and the *chansons* date from the eleventh century. "Great goodness" was always in "the knights of yore." That was one of the rules of the game, since chivalric mythology was part of a way of understanding history by continual reference to the theme of the *mundus senescens* and the corruption of the present, invoking the arrival of a hero *sans peur et sans reproche.* Awaiting the knight was part of a profound need for hope of salvation, and it is no accident that psychoanalysts are among the most recent exegetes of the myth of St. George. At the same time, however (and in terms of concrete historical development, not of psychoanalysis), chivalric institutions and the culture that lent them prestige between the eleventh and the eighteenth centuries and perhaps beyond have proved to be one of the most vigorous motive forces in Western man's search for individuality and his conquest of self-awareness—what Norbert Elias has called the process of civilization. It is an important contribution, which we cannot ignore and which even we of the contemporary world cannot renounce.

BIBLIOGRAPHY

General histories of chivalry are nonexistent, and may be an impossible task. Useful for an overall view, however, is Maurice Keen, *Chivalry* (New Haven: Yale University Press, 1984). Dubbing ceremonies are treated in two works by Jean Flori, *L'Idéologie du glaive: Préhistoire de la chevalerie* (Geneva: Droz, 1983), and *L'Essor de la chevalerie: XIe-XIIe siècles* (Geneva: Droz, 1986). For the tournaments, the reader is referred to Josef Fleckstein, ed., *Das ritterliche Turnier im Mittelalter: Beitrage zu einer vergleichended Formen– und Verhaltensgeschichte des Rittertums* (Göttingen: Vandenhoeck and Ruprecht, 1985). The chivalric sense of adventure is treated in Mario Del Treppo, *I mercanti catalani e l'espansione della Corona d'Aragona nel secolo XV* (Naples: L'Arte Tipografica, 1972); Georges Duby, *Guillaume le Maréschal, ou, le meilleur chevalier du monde* (Paris: Fayard, 1984) [*William Marshal: The Flower of Chivalry*, trans. Richard Howard (New York: Pantheon, 1986]; Erich Köhler, *Ideal und Wirklichkeit in der höfischen Epik: Studien zur Form der frühen Artus- und Graldichtung* (Tübingen: Max Niemeyer, 1970); Giovanni Tabacco, "Su nobiltà e cavalleria nel Medioevo. Un ritorno a Marc Bloch?" *Studi di storia medievale e moderna per Ernesto Sestan*, 2 vols. (Florence: Olschki, 1980), 1:31–55. On medieval war an excellent starting point is Philippe Contamine, *La Guerre au Moyen Age* (Paris: Presses Universitaires de France, 1980) [*War in the Middle Ages*, trans. Michael Jones (New York: Basil Blackwell, 1984].

SUGGESTED READINGS

Richard W. Barber, *The Knight and Chivalry* (London: Longman, 1970).

John Beeler, *Warfare in England, 1066–1189* (Ithaca: Cornell University Press, 1966).

Marc Bloch, *Feudal Society* (Chicago: University of Chicago Press, 1964).

Georges Duby, *The Chivalrous Society* (Berkeley: University of California Press, 1977).

———, *The Three Orders: Feudal Society Imagined* (Chicago: University of Chicago Press, 1980).

C. Stephen Jaeger, *The Origins of Courtliness: Civilizing Trends and the Formation of Courtly Ideals, 939–1210* (Philadelphia: University of Pennsylvania Press, 1985).

Sidney Painter, *French Chivalry: Chivalric Ideals and Practice in Medieval France* (Baltimore: Johns Hopkins University Press, 1940).

Timothy Reuter, ed., *The Medieval Nobility: Studies in the Ruling Classes of France and Germany from the Sixth to the Twelfth Century* (Amsterdam: North Holland, 1978).

Jonathan Riley-Smith, *The First Crusade and the Idea of Crusading* (Philadelphia: University of Pennsylvania Press, 1986).

Malcolm Vale, *War and Chivalry: Warfare and Aristocratic Culture in England, France, and Burgundy at the End of the Middle Ages* (Athens: University of Georgia Press, 1981).

THREE

The Peasant and Agriculture

Giovanni Cherubini

To speak of the peasant and of agriculture for the whole of Europe during the last two or three centuries of the Middle Ages is a nearly impossible task, particularly in the space available. Agrarian life and environmental conditions varied greatly from one end of the continent to the other, so that even if the vast majority of peasants could be said to have been small-scale farmers—"primary" producers, as distinguished from both tribal hunters and gatherers and nomadic shepherds, on the one hand, and, on the other, from paid laborers and capitalistic or collectivistic farmers—some of the specific traits in the portrait of a man of the fields varied from one region to another. Through time there were even changes in the geographical boundaries of Latin Europe (to which these remarks will be limited). When Islam was forced to withdraw in the thirteenth century, Europe again included nearly all the Iberian peninsula, and Latin Christianity had already reconquered Sicily. In central Europe and by the Baltic Sea, Latin culture abutted Greek Orthodox Christianity (along boundaries not yet precisely defined) and pagan populations that were forcibly Christianized by the Teutonic Knights during the centuries that concern us here. All of Russia and the territories of the Byzantine Empire remained outside the boundaries of Europe as we now understand it, although these lands were linked to Latin culture by the ephemeral empire set up by westerners after the Fourth Crusade, between 1204 and 1261. (Some reference will be made to these non-European lands.)

Marked differences in geographical settings, soils, climates, population density, and agrarian technological development in the various zones of the continent add to the difficulty of identifying common traits among the European peasantry. The low technical level of medieval agriculture in general gave these factors a greater influence on agricultural activities and on people's lives than they have now.

From the viewpoint of agricultural exploitation, Europe can be divided roughly in two by the criterion of altitude (if regions of prohibitively harsh climatic conditions such as most of Norway, Sweden, Finland, and northern European Russia are excluded). Arable lands in the first of these areas—in most of Spain, southeast France, most of Italy, Greece, the Balkan peninsula south of the Carpathian mountains—lay at least 500 meters (1,640 feet) above sea level, and these regions included vast mountainous areas, the only exceptions being the plains of the Po valley and the Danube basin. The second part lay to the north of the first, beginning in southern England and at the western coast of France and stretching to the Urals and the Caucasus, and including vast lowlands rarely over 200 meters (650 feet) above sea level. Yearly precipitation was very unevenly distributed: more regular in the great plains of western and central Europe, it was extremely irregular closer to the Mediterranean, where rainfall was concentrated in autumn and spring, with occasional violent, damaging storms in late summer. Mountainous areas of the first zone could not be cultivated above a certain altitude, and the soils of the central and western high plains and the "black lands" of Russia were much richer naturally than the lighter soils of the Mediterranean. Furthermore, some plains lands of potentially high productivity were uncultivated at the time because they were marshy, as for example in Italy in the lower Po Valley, the Valdichiana, and the Tuscan Maremma.

Our task is also made difficult by the uneven store (or the uneven paucity) of documentary sources on demographic density, population distribution, and population trends during the course of these centuries.

Furthermore, agricultural land, forests or untilled lands, and pasturage for sheepherding (stationary, seminomadic, or practicing transhumance) combined in varying proportions in different regions. In some areas agrarian colonization was predominantly or exclusively internal; in others, for example in the German advance into Slavic lands or the Christian reconquest of the southern Iberian peninsula, colonization accompanied and reinforced political penetration; in still others it moved from regions of older settlement such as the shores of certain Norwegian fjords or the plains of southern Sweden to penetrate into higher or more northern zones that were unpopulated and still covered with forests. Not everywhere did agricultural production and peasant labor have the task of maintaining a large urban population. In some regions, finally, peasants of different races lived in contact with one another, as in Sicily, Spain, and the Germanized Slavic lands, with results that are not always clear for our portrait of men of the fields.

*

A series of often ingenious hypotheses and deductions from the few data available has led scholars to hold that by and large, after several centuries of slow but continual population growth, Europe reached a demographic high around the first decades of the fourteenth century. Although it had forerunners, the great wave of plague in 1347–50, followed by other widespread epidemics, is held to have reduced the population of Europe at the mid-fifteenth century to one-half or two-thirds of what it had been at the beginning of the fourteenth century. Population subsequently made gains. At its demographic height, Europe had no more than 73 million inhabitants—a figure that many have judged to have exceeded, at least for many areas, the productive potential of its agriculture—and, at its low point in the mid-fifteenth century, no more than 50 million. Indirect proof of an increase in European population beginning at the tenth or eleventh centuries can be seen in an increase in the urban population and in the number of cities and towns, the shrinking of forests, marshes, and untilled lands and the extension of cultivated fields, the transfer of individual peasants, groups of families, or entire communities to new soils (with the consequent founding of churches and villages), and an increasing subdivision of households and families. In one area directly connected with the history of country areas—land clearing—scholars have now amassed an abundant documentation, making use of sources that pertain clearly to this topic. Village names throughout the continent bear witness to the peasants' heroic battle against an omnipotent nature, waged on their own or coordinated by lords, abbeys, or cities (as in the Po Valley in Italy). There were "new towns" everywhere—the *bourgs* in the French provinces of the west, the *abergements* in eastern France (Burgundy, above all), the *bastides* of southwest France. In lands where German was spoken there were new nuclei bearing the name of a man coupled with the suffixes *-berg, -feld, -dorf, -rode,* or *-reuth.* The most important event in the even more arduous struggle against sea water and the marshes was the construction of the polders of Flanders and Zeeland; but in England's fens and in Brittany and Poitou as well, peasants successfully drained the salt marches, and Italian peasants of the entire Po Valley and elsewhere drained bogs, built dikes, and channeled rivers.

When population decreased dramatically, however, herding increased in proportion to agriculture, marginal or less productive arable lands were abandoned, and entire villages disappeared, although such phenomena did not occur with the same intensity everywhere or with identical consequences for agrarian economy and the shape of villages. These major population swings aside, and despite the emergence of heavily urbanized areas such as Flanders, Tuscany, and the Paris basin, late medieval Europe continued to be profoundly rural, since perhaps nine-tenths of the population lived on what it produced by laboring in the fields. This agricultural population was very diversely distributed from one place to another. Not only did population density vary notably from one entire zone to another—for example, from the thickly populated lands of the Île de France to the more sparsely settled areas of eastern Europe, Norway, or Iceland—it also varied within a region or between contiguous regions where changed environmental conditions connected with agricultural exploitation came into play.

The overall population figures for the larger geographical sectors of the continent proposed by one of the greatest experts in historical demography (J. C. Russell) confirm this profound diversity. According to these estimates (which are, of course, approximate), the population of southern Europe (Greece, the Balkans, Italy, the Iberian peninsula) approached 25 million in 1340 and shrank to 19 million in 1450; western and central Europe (France, the Low Countries, the British Isles, Germany, Scandinavia) had a population of 35.5 million in 1340 and 22.5 million in 1450; population in all of eastern Europe numbered 13 million in 1340 and 9.5 million in 1450. Such figures clearly show the extremely sparse population of the third sector of the continent, where all of Russia had no more than 6 million inhabitants and Poland and Lithuania together 2 million. Even within central and western Europe and southern Europe, however, there undoubtedly were considerable differences in population. Still, at the same two dates of 1340 and 1450, the 10 million / 7.5 million inhabitants of Italy represent a much denser population than the 9 million / 7 million proposed for the entire Iberian peninsula; the 19 million / 12 million population estimated for France and the Low Countries suggest much thicker settlement than the 11.5 million / 7.5 million proposed for all of Germany and Scandinavia (where, furthermore, it is certain the Scandinavian countries had a lower population density than Germany). Furthermore, the agrarian population did not have identical relations everywhere with the cities and towns. Although some landed proprietors lived within the walls of urban areas (the number varied from one city to another but was generally fairly consistent within any one city), not all city populations included genuine agricultural laborers. The latter were often more numerous in smaller and less economically developed towns, for example in certain centers in southern Italy, and were largely unknown in larger manufacturing and mercantile centers like Florence, Pisa, Siena, or Ghent. The greater part of the farming population lived grouped in villages, unfortified or with protective walls or bulwarks, which they left in the morning to work in the surrounding fields, to gather fruit and nuts in the woods, to lead their animals to pasture, or to hunt and fish. A small portion of the population lived scattered through the countryside, at times in environments that differed and for different socioeconomic reasons. For example, some lived apart as they cleared land in areas of advancing colonization; others lived on scattered farms under sharecropping contracts in certain parts of central Italy. Contrary to past opinion, most peasant families were nuclear families or enlarged nuclear families—they were composed, that is, of parents, one, two, or three children, and one or more grandparents. Extended families seem to have been less frequent. In all cases, the peasant family was usually larger when material conditions were better, more land was available to it, and it owned more livestock (work animals in particular).

The peasants of Europe lived in agrarian landscapes that varied enormously, so their yearly agricultural tasks were naturally quite different. Mountainous zones—the Pyrenees, the Massif Central, the Alps, the Apennines, and the Balkans—usually had fields, planted with grains, that were proportionally smaller than their great stretches of woodland and pasture. Other areas of lower altitude but smaller population, where marshy land hosted malaria mosquitoes (such as the Tuscan Maremma or certain parts of Sardinia) were in many respects similar to the mountains. Other zones, such as the Meseta of Spain, central Sicily, and vast areas of central Europe were heavily planted in wheat and other grains. Elsewhere, as in the Tuscan hills and other regions of central and northern Italy, intensive farming of mixed crops of grains, grapes, and fruit increased during the final centuries of the Middle Ages. Other zones, Mediterranean lands in particular, came to have an agriculture based on a single crop or in which one product predominated. This was the case with olive trees around Seville or in Puglia, on the shores of the Italian subalpine lakes and in some areas of Liguria, or with grapes in the "gardens" of the Conca d'oro (where citrus fruits were only beginning to be cultivated) and around many villages of Calabria and Campania. Some areas, like the lands surrounding Valencia, Seville, and Palermo, benefited from Arabian agrarian technology, particularly irrigation systems. Elsewhere, where the climate precluded the cultivation of olive trees (and north of a certain latitude), walnut trees were widely cultivated, furnishing not only a precious "conservable" foodstuff (dried figs were commonest in this category), but also oil for both consumption and lighting fuel. Many agrarian landscapes—and not only in mountainous zones—bore the visible signs of transhumant herding, as in Provence, the Meseta, Puglia, and the coastal Maremma of Tuscany and Latium.

Systems of cultivation naturally dictated the rhythms and the seasons of agricultural labors. Everywhere and always the peasant's fundamental concern was to assure grain production in quantities sufficient for the needs of his own family and those who held rights over his land and its produce (seigneurial landowners, city proprietors, the local church). Grains were the prime staple in all diets, particularly at the lower levels of society. Even though it was the prime staple, however, bread was not of uniform quality, and whether one ate white bread, mixed-grain bread, or bread made of inferior grains such as spelt or even sorghum (common millet) was a first visible sign of place in the social hierarchy. In all rural communities from one end of the continent to the other, an unremitting pursuit of bread was the prime motivation for demands for political autonomy and economic self-sufficiency. It affected city-dwelling landowners and the upper levels of society as well, although other primary products, notably wine, entered into the picture to a certain extent. The underlying cause of such anxiety lay in the fragility of agriculture before the caprices of nature and an ever-present danger of shortages, combined with the arduous task of transporting agricultural products for any distance. This does not mean that agricultural products never traveled from one region to another. (I shall return later to wine.) Sicilian grain, to pick an example, was imported almost regularly by the more densely urbanized areas of central and northern Italy.

It should be added that although the cultivation of grains always required a large part of the peasant's time and labor—from plowing and sowing to harvesting and threshing—the work and the risks involved were not identical everywhere. At least four components entered into this picture: systems of crop rotation; the types of plows used, the work animals available, and the productivity of the soil. A fifth element, yield (as yet, unfortunately, insufficiently studied for all European rural areas), was related to soil quality, agrarian technology and practices, and to the number of plowings needed to prepare a field for sowing. By modern standards, the grain yield was extremely low all over Europe: at best it was four to one, with highs of seven, eight, or even ten to one and lows of two or three to one. In general, productivity was lower in the light soils of the Mediterranean basin than in the deep and compact soils of central and eastern Europe; lower on high ground than on the plains.

Not all peasants had draft animals to pull a plow, nor were conditions the same when they could hire them. Horses were occasionally used, but the typical plow animal was the ox, in pairs or even several pairs for the heavier soils. It is a telling detail that in peasant communities possession of one or more pairs of work animals was often decisive to social stratification. Furthermore, the peasants on farms that had the compact and deep soil of central and eastern Europe used a technically more advanced and heavier plow with a wheeled forecarriage, a coulter, and a share with a moldboard, which had become widespread during the Middle Ages; whereas Italian peasants south of the Apennines and peasants in all the arid Mediterranean zones still used the ancient scratch plow with a symmetrical plowshare that opened the soil without turning it over. In other areas like central Sicily and Sardinia the primitive "nail" plow or planting stick still persisted, at best with an iron-reinforced tip. Even systems of crop rotation differed: in the parts of Europe that had a more humid climate and deeper soils, rotation followed the three cycles of winter grains, spring-planted grains or legumes, and lying fallow, which meant that only one-third of arable land was untilled; in the areas of Europe that were drier and had lighter soils, rotation was two-cycle and the land was either planted with grains or left fallow.

Small sickles were used throughout Europe for harvesting grain, perhaps not always (as it was thought in the past) but often serrated (a common expression was "to saw the grain"). As we can see from the stupendous pictorial representations of the months in many churches of Western Europe, the stalks were topped and the shocks left on the fields, and after the gleaners had gone through in search of scattered grain, the remainder either provided modest fodder for animals or acted as a simple sort of fertilizer. When there were no trees or vines amid the grain plots, the straw was often burned, together with the grasses and weeds it contained, and the ashes were used to fertilize the soil. The pictorial cycles of the months also permit us to note, as scholars have pointed out, that artists were sensitive to actual environments and climates as well as to models and traditions, since the harvest was placed at a later date as the context moved north away from the Mediterranean. The same pictorial cycles, together with other artistic representations (as well as more specific documentation), show that threshing was often done by peasants working with flails in pairs or in groups or, in more southerly lands where the climate permitted working out of doors, by horses, oxen, or mules (in certain areas of the Mediterranean) that trampled the grain. To grind his grain (domestic hand-grinding may have persisted, but the question is not yet well documented), the peasant took it to a professional, the miller, who used hydraulic energy (exclusively or predominantly the case almost everywhere in Europe in the later Middle Ages) or wind in areas where water was scarce and the winds steady.

I shall limit my remarks on arboriculture to grapes for several reasons. First, because the cultivation of grapes tended to some extent to expand to all soils, besting the difficulties posed by altitude and climate. At a certain point grapes were even grown in England, apparently until the climate worsened during the thirteenth and the fourteenth centuries. Second, because the labor required by the vineyard and by wine-making was distributed throughout the seasons. Third, because wine, together with bread, was a prime staple in all diets (in some regions replaced by cider or beer), thus it was a product that was universally known, for liturgical reasons if for no other. Fourth and finally, because the search for quality wines (and, consequently, the encouragement of a particular sort of viticulture) was one of the distinctive marks of the upper levels of society, urban and nonurban, in the centuries that interest us here. We have evidence of the demand in the cities of central and northern Italy (and not only in Italy) for the sweet wines of southern Italy and Corsica, and for wine from Bordeaux in England and the Low Countries. Equally well known is the development of the wine trade in the valleys of the Rhône, the Saône, the Seine, the Moselle, and the Rhine, encouraged by external demand and easy river transport. Leaving aside the task of establishing vineyards and extending viticulture (constant replanting was necessary when war brought repeated destruction to the vineyards, along with the burning of villages and crops), vines required pruning, weeding, and fertilizing; branches had to be thinned; wine barrels needed to be prepared; after the harvest, the wine had to be processed. All this required manpower and, in the joyous season of the harvest, womanpower and childpower. This was not true of trees like the olive, which during the harvest and the pressing season gave their own unique stamp to certain rural areas, towns, and villages like those around Bari or on the Salentine peninsula. The only other regions in which one plant dominated the rural economy and gave it such a characteristic tone were areas of chestnut groves. In the days and the months of the harvest, the village poor searched the ground feverishly for scattered fruit before the village pigs were loosed among the trees to eat the last remaining nuts, while the chestnuts were husked, dried, and ground and the flour stored in great chests inside the villagers' houses.

Although self-sufficiency was the primary motivation for peasant labor, agriculture was increasingly conditioned and stimulated by other requirements. First of all, there was a demand for foodstuffs from the more densely populated urban areas; second, "industrial" products were needed to serve the needs of urban manufacturing. It has been suggested, concerning the cities' demand for foodstuffs, that in the interests of the crown and the baronial class, for example in Sicily, the island's production of grain was forced to the breaking point, with extremely negative consequences for the living conditions of the rural population. I might note, concerning "industrial" products, that the wool-processing industry in the cities of Italy and elsewhere encouraged the cultivation of a number of plants used as dyes such as woad or madder, and it appears to have contributed to an increase in transhumant sheepherding during the demographic recession between the mid-fourteenth and the mid-fifteenth centuries (also facilitated in many areas by a better balance between food production and population). All in all, however, the peasant family's participation in the market economy seems to have been modest. Rather than furnishing foodstuffs of prime importance such as grain or wine (which were traded by the lords, by ecclesiastical institutions, and by the large, city-based landowners), the peasants brought to village and town markets the products of the henhouse and the kitchen garden: fruit, fresh and dried, cheese and milk, fruits, nuts, and mushrooms from the woods, and small handcrafted objects.

The yearly routine of the transhumant shepherds was quite different from the life of either peasants or peasant shepherds of fixed residence. Between May and September the shepherds lived in huts in the mountains. In the autumn, before the first frosts, they descended toward the warmer plains with their flocks, often aided by younger shepherds (in many cases still boys), their horses loaded with their household goods. The shepherd's simple life was made up of cheese-making, caring for the sheep (the lambs in particular), shearing, defending his flock from wolves with the help of ever-present large dogs wearing iron-reinforced collars, learning to gauge the rivers and know the roads, watching over his flock to keep it from straying into cultivated fields. His nomadic life brought him greater contact with different environments and social situations than peasants usually had, in some instances giving him a richer psychological makeup and a greater store of knowledge, even in the solitude of the open countryside. Peasants of fixed residence raised comparatively fewer animals, first because formerly common pasturelands in more highly developed areas such as Tuscany or northern Italy had been transferred to private hands and put to cultivation, and pasturage rights to private lands had been reduced; second, because, in other areas, the lords' dominion over peasant communities also included priority for the lord's livestock in the use of pasturelands and fallow fields. Peasants seem to have kept more sheep, pigs, and goats than oxen or cows, as confirmed (at least in many southern regions) by the findings of a number of archeological studies of domestic refuse. Local and regional preferences introduced some variation in commonly shared customs, with the goat being more typical of the arid areas of southern Europe and the pig more particular to central Europe. There were also rural areas (Parma, Reggio Emilia, and Piacenza in Italy, for example) where the humid, rich pasturelands of the plains had given rise, toward the end of the Middle Ages, to real herds of milk cows that produced cheeses already well known and much appreciated.

The woodsman's life was still different. Often small landowners as well, or the owners of small herds of livestock, their chief occupation was cutting firewood and making charcoal, two activities that we can suppose were different specializations then as later. Forest work was inevitably seasonal, as it excluded the winter months. I should add that throughout the peasant world work was not limited to strictly agricultural labors; particularly in the dead of winter, it included some artisanal activities, such as making baskets and making or repairing implements and gear. Peasant women spun and weaved for the needs of the family, and in some country areas in which mercantile economy had penetrated, they also spun wool for the city wool merchants. All members of the family contributed to the family economy, even at a very early age, and children were often responsible for taking the animals to pasture. When family size outreached revenues from the land, various remedies were sought, such as sending quite young girls to work as domestic servants for city families or lodging sons with an artisan to learn his craft. The wife might find employment as a wet nurse for the children of well-off townsman or for the foundlings of a city hospice. In some Italian cities, these phenomena have left a rich and varied documentation that has been studied in depth.

In the greater part of the continent, midwinter brought the particularly exciting moment of hog butchering, once again represented in the pictorial cycles of the months that document the fusion of Christian spirituality and agriculture in medieval life. The monotony of peasant life was interrupted by rare moments of sociability. Opportunities for social exchange included attendance at Sunday Mass, frequentation of the village tavern (that counterchurch or "church of the Devil" condemned repeatedly but ineffectually by synods and preachers), trips to the markets, or going to the mill or the blacksmith's shop. Blacksmiths were present throughout rural Europe in this period, since the use of iron was growing in country areas, although it was still considered a "precious" metal and indeed peasants did not have a large number of iron implements. There were also more special occasions for social gatherings, annual events like the great religious feasts or the feast day of the patron saint of the local church, and there were truly exceptional occasions, celebrations such as weddings. All these moments broke the routine, primarily in diet and clothing. When they could, peasants displayed their finery at feasts involving enormous amounts of eating and drinking, invariably a counterweight to the poor diet of normal days.

*

The peasant was an individual with a specific life-style that set him apart from the artisan and the city-dweller; he was part of a family that for him was the first and natural social nucleus; he was a member of a parish that enrolled him in Christianity from his birth, independently of how deeply he understood its religious message as an adult. He was also a component of the local rural community. Even though, as we have seen, there were rural people who lived apart (not necessarily completely cut off from their communities of origin, however), and even though economic development uprooted increasing numbers of peasants who became vagabonds, beggars, brigands, and delinquents, it was the village that nevertheless made all European peasants similar, above and beyond differences (even notable ones) from one region and one period to another. Through Europe the power of a lord, lay or ecclesiastical, was superimposed upon the rural community, whether that lord held vast lands or ruled a tiny local domain; enjoyed sweeping powers or extracted a limited number of dues and services. The greater part of the peasant's social and political life was bounded by his relations with the community or with the lord and in the connections and conflicts between the two. The monarchy or other ruling powers must often have appeared remote to him, although they were endowed with powers of suggestion and coercion. In spite of this, in some parts of Europe new conditions appeared in this traditional world that greatly affected both the material and mental aspects of the life of rural folk. Precisely during the final centuries of the Middle Ages, change was particularly dramatic in the areas of Italy in which the development of the communes profoundly reshaped rural seigneurial rule. Municipal governments also brought a political, administrative, judicial, military, and economic reorganization to communal territories. Furthermore, urban proprietors penetrated deeply into rural areas and sweeping expropriation of the peasants provoked a serious crisis in many rural communities.

This situation was particular to Italy, but even elsewhere there were some localities not under the rule of a lord, hence there were peasant communities that enjoyed special conditions. This occurred in southern Italy wherever the monarchy declared lands *demaniali*—crown domains. The number of localities with this status varied considerably during the period, and although they were usually urban centers with only a narrow band of land around them, their economic makeup does not exclude the possibility that they included some genuine peasants among their population. Europe also included unique marginal regions such as Iceland, where the inhabitants lived in strong peasant communities not yet or not completely under the rule of lords, strictly speaking. I might add that even within lands under the seigneurial system not all the villagers had identical relations with the lord, particularly where landholding was concerned, and some peasants possessed land free of dues and services. Still, the situation commonest in Europe was the village dominated by one or more lords. Under the more common scheme, the land was divided into three overall portions. The first part was directly exploited by the local lord; the second was divided into plots conceded to peasant families, who had rights of inheritance, formal or de facto; the third, composed of woodlands and untilled lands, was left for collective use. The lord's own lands, the demesne or *pars dominica,* were worked by serfs attached to his household, by paid labor (temporary or permanent), or by days of labor required from his peasants, either alone or with their oxen. The exaction of days of labor tended to diminish during the course of the twelfth century, when the custom of labor service seems to have been dying out in France south of the Loire, in Burgundy, and in Brittany, and in central and northern Italy, remaining in widespread use in England until somewhat later. Such services continued to lighten during the following century as well, but in a number of areas (seigneurial domains in southern Italy, for instance) they did not completely disappear. For reduction or total abolition of day labor the peasants were obliged to pay a fixed sum to the lord or agree to pay higher rents for their land, in coin or in produce. The use of untilled lands for animal pasturage, the collection of firewood,and the gathering of wild fruits and nuts were also causes for dissension between lords and peasants, and we can often trace the lord's attempts to "privatize" nonarable land for his own benefit or to obtain priority for his own herds in its use. A similar trend toward the regulation of hunting excluded the peasants from enjoyment of that part of nature's bounty in favor of the baronial classes and the sovereign. De jure or de facto, however, peasants everywhere counted on fishing and hunting for a significant part of their diet and their earnings.

There was another way for the lords to draw revenue out of the land during this period—to draw increasing revenues, in fact, thanks to an increased dynamism and greater mobility in both the economy and in society, which implied greater freedom for land transfer as well. In addition to the sums that the lords demanded of their tenants for the "reinvestment" of their ancestral lands, they demanded ever-greater sums for the right to sell all or a part of their "holdings" (usually within the rural community, but on occasion to an outsider). It was not, however, from the concession of rights over the lands that their peasants exploited that many lords drew their highest revenues. With shrewd administration, greater earnings could be made from the exploitation of demesnial lands, even though the demesne tended everywhere, at least before the great demographic crisis, to be reduced by concession of ever larger portions of land to the peasants—a result of growing demographic pressure and the need for land, discussed above, and a tendency that led to a certain number of lords living only on dues and rents.

By this time, one of the largest sources of seigneurial revenue was the lord's monopoly of the use and industrial exploitation of water, to which a monopoly over the village bake oven and the tavern was added in some areas. The lord had exclusive rights to set up water-powered mills for grinding grain or fulling cloth, which he exploited either directly, through an appointed official, or leased to a concessionaire who charged a fee in coin or kind to grind grain. There are chronicles that describe the efforts of lords to oblige all the peasant families in the communities under their jurisdiction to cease milling grain by hand with domestic grindstones and to use the "banal" mill (from "*ban*," the overall right to command, constrain, and punish). To drive the point across, one landlord—a famous abbey on the outskirts of London—strewed the floor of the monastery parlatory with pieces of broken domestic grindstones to refresh the memories of peasants who came to pay their dues or request an audience.

Relations between the peasants and their lord were not based on a purely economic conditioning on the part of the landowner, to which the peasants might respond with an adjustment in the labor force needed to cultivate the earth, but on a political conditioning. The lords held varying but ample military, territorial, and jurisdictional powers. On the local level the lord served as judge over the inhabitants of the village, at least for minor infractions of justice, leaving capital punishment—the "right of blood" or "high justice"—to his hierarchical superiors or the monarchy. There were instances, however, of local lords who could sentence lawbreakers to death or corporal punishment. This was true of many lords in central and northern Italy, where the imperial power was weak and the cities' dominion over their territories not yet firm, or in parts of southern Italy in the fifteenth century, during the conflict between the monarchy and barons who were winning greater political power. For the lord, the administration of justice obviously meant not only power over the villagers but opportunities for revenues. His dominion was further reinforced by his military function as commander of an armed force, great or small, that saw service in skirmishes against other lords or in larger armies in support of higher-ranking lords or the monarchy. Exactly how the peasants collaborated in their lords' military functions still needs to be studied, case by case and place by place, to ascertain to what extent they financed his warlike undertakings and took part in his expeditions, or, to the contrary, whether, on the local level, the profession of arms was reserved to a particular group of inhabitants, perhaps even to those who bore the title of knight. The peasants cannot have liked war, both because it removed adult males from the community and, worse still, because of the damage and destruction it caused if the village was attacked and the livestock killed. This does not mean that peasant culture, like the rest of society, was not permeated with violence, tolerating the use of knives, bloody quarrels between individuals, and self-perpetuating vendettas. This was doubtless particularly true in marginal communities in contact with a harsher nature and often, like the communities of the northern Apennines, located in boundary areas. Thus an aversion to war combined with mental habits and actual behavior that included violence to demonstrate the complexity of a peasant attitude toward arms that is impossible to ascertain by a simple examination of political alignments and institutions. Peasants benefited from the lord's protection, from the defensive aspect of his military function, and from his professional outlook as a man of the sword. The fortification of villages or hamlets and the founding of new walled settlements has been studied, for example, for Italy in the eleventh and twelfth centuries, in its relation to the rural political and territorial hierarchies that it produced. Country people surely perceived fortification primarily as an opportunity for defense and refuge from external dangers for themselves, their families, their crops, their goods, and their livestock. Furthermore, just as towns and cities offered special protection to the peasants who inhabited or worked the lands immediately outside their walls, so the thick walls of abbeys and isolated baronial fortresses offered protection to peasants in the countryside.

The rural community was generally older than the seigneury, sometimes by many centuries if the village, as has been demonstrated for many Mediterranean regions, had origins reaching back to the Roman era or even to prehistoric times. Lay or ecclesiastical potentates claimed rights over such communities, either as the Middle Ages progressed or, on occasion, only during the central or final centuries of the Middle Ages. Other villages and communities developed from the villas of ancient Rome, the large landed estates of the late imperial era that gradually passed into the hands of the Germanic invaders and the Frankish aristocracy. This process was accompanied by a slow and gradual change in the personal condition of the former slaves, in the administration of the land, and in the rights of the titular owners of the "villas," and by an increasing shift from simple ownership of the land to dominion over men. Other villages and other communities arose, particularly in the phase of demographic rise in the eleventh and twelfth centuries, on unpopulated, wooded, or untilled lands that the great noble families or the sovereigns had conceded to the abbeys. Other villages, finally, had been founded under feudal rule—a rule perhaps less oppressive than in their inhabitants' communities of origin—as when groups of German peasants were encouraged to colonize the Slavic lands beyond the Elbe. In that particular case, the land also underwent internal colonization as well as the widespread clearing of vast wooded areas to create arable lands. Beginning with the twelfth century and peaking during the thirteenth century, masses of German colonists penetrated as far as Transylvania, encouraged by rulers, bishops, and religious orders of knighthood such as the Teutonic knights.

When we say that the rural community was in general older than the seigneury, we are appealing less to any concrete, abundant documentary evidence than to logical conclusions concerning the villagers' need to organize their life, to a few, isolated early medieval documents, and to what we know of earlier periods. In fact, the rural community appears in written documentation in Europe only in the final centuries of the Middle Ages (in a few cases as early as the eleventh century). It appears, in many regions of Europe, in hundreds of "charters of liberty" and "charters of enfranchisement"—*consuetudines, Weistümer,* and *statuti*—that communities managed to extract from their lords, constraining them to put into writing the peasants' obligations, the lord's own functions, and the terms of their agreement. Even when it directly regards the birth of a rural community, this written testimony seems more a demonstration of a return to writing than proof of the community's founding. Without in any way detracting from the political significance of this fact—which is more than a question of mere form—it should be added that already in the past the peasants had doubtless been obliged to collaborate at least minimally within the village and between villages to organize pasturage on tilled and fallow lands, to determine water use, to cooperate in plowing, sowing, and harvesting, to organize minimal surveillance of the fields to protect the crops from damages by men and livestock, and to arrange for constant defense against dangerous animals such as wolves, bears, and foxes. It seems difficult to imagine, particularly given the rudimentary conditions of administration of the age, that all questions could be entrusted to the relation between the peasants (who in any event could not have been dealt with singly, but must have been dealt with as a local collectivity) and the officers of the great landowner, the abbey, or the lord.

Complicating the entire picture during the centuries that interest us here, both for the men of the time and for modern scholars, was the relationship between the local community and the lord. Just as there were abbots, bishops, or barons who were lords of several villages, so there were sometimes villages divided between several seigneuries.

If, for all the reasons discussed, collaboration on the local level between the rural community and the lord was indispensable (we can even hold that the complete development of the system of seigneury stimulated community life by contributing to the peasants' deeper awareness of their own identity, both singly and collectively), conflicting interests were just as inevitable. The peasant reproached the lord for many things: an excessive fondness for warfare, the greed of his officials, an unjust sentence, and a variety of exactions, personal or pecuniary, that were unknown in the past. A lord's attempt to impose a monopoly of milling for his own water-powered mill could be viewed as abusive, as could tallage (which might be compared to the "aid" that a vassal owed his overlord in the feudal system). Tallage was paid in coin in amounts fixed arbitrarily by the lord (at least originally) to compensate him for the protection he provided. Conflict usually assumed the forms of grudging acceptance or silent resistance, but it repeatedly exploded into open rebellion, sometimes, when peasants had common interests and able local leaders emerged, even into regional or supraregional rebellions. Marc Bloch wrote that peasant rebellions were as congenital to rural seigneurial society as strikes are in capitalistic society. Their most widespread expressions during this period (though they had causes more complex than peasant discontent alone) were the Jacquerie of 1358 in France and the great peasant revolt of 1381 in England, during which the insurgents not only terrorized London but for a short time even had the person of the young king in their hands.

Points of dissension between lords and peasants varied according to the moment, the geographical environment, the differing levels of development of seigneurial institutions, and the degree to which the presence of superior powers was felt. Disputes arose over the juridical condition of persons and the juridical status of the lands, the exploitation of untilled lands, the administration of justice, seigneurial monopolies, and the arbitrariness or regularity of a wide variety of seigneurial rights. Statutes, charters of liberty, and written agreements for the most part concerned these questions, occasionally adding topics pertaining to the preservation of order and peace in rural life, such as the supervision of arable lands, the protection of crops, hay cutting, and protection against fires. Although there are notable differences from one end of the continent to the other (to begin with, in the abundance and the quality of available documentation), there was a common ground that lay in an attempt to ascertain what was owed the lord and in a struggle against what were or appeared to be new impositions. Holding the line against tallage and attempting to reduce if not eliminate the lords' monopoly of milling stand out everywhere. This seems particularly clear in agreements drawn up by certain rural communities in central Italy that rebelled against their lords and submitted to the nearest city, which in turn granted them not only the transfer of untilled lands to their exclusive administration and the elimination of the dues and services previously owed the lord, but also the transfer of the monopoly on milling to the village community.

Peasants also aspired to increased personal liberty from the lord through the commutation of labor service on seigneurial lands (or buying their way out of it), lower taxes and rents, greater liberty of choice in the selection of spouses, and so forth. Pressure for greater personal liberty was accompanied by—and to some extent, necessarily complemented by—a demand, sometimes backed by force, for broader rights to buy and sell land or pass it on to heirs. The communities' efforts to limit or at least gain a measure of control over the lords' juridical and political prerogatives is not always well documented (once again, central and northern Italy offer the most abundant sources). It evidently was possible for the late medieval peasant to accumulate some savings from the sale of produce in the rapidly growing cities and towns and the developing rural markets, and this and other factors not only enabled him to win greater personal liberty and a more ample opportunity to acquire land but brought greater social differentiation to peasant communities. This differentiation, which can be documented, in varying degree, throughout Western Europe, had other sources as well, such as the exercise of a function assigned to a peasant by the lord (a situation that leaves clear documentary evidence and one that opened up ample opportunities, legitimate and less legitimate, for making one's fortune) or the practice of usury. Instances of peasant "success" were more frequent near a large urban center, where the politics and interests of city-dwellers were more obvious. These groups of "rural bourgeois" often stood out from their fellow villagers by their exercise of an artisanal or mercantile activity (even more so when they destined their sons to be priests or even notaries). Their attitudes toward the city varied; in some regions they tended to move into the city, but in others they remained to dominate their villages of birth.

Scholars are still debating the influence of the demographic crisis on long-term trends in the seigneurial system and on rural society. Its effects appear to have differed greatly from one zone to another, and in many instances the specific political and economic decisions of the sovereigns, lords, and cities have to be taken into account. The ongoing trends in Western Europe were a weakening of seigneurial power, the reduction of the demesne, progressive gains in personal liberty for peasants, and a tendency to stratification in rural society. In France and England falling revenues obliged many great lords to rent out their entire estates. In Spain and southern Italy, where the king and the lords had no solid front of burghers to oppose them, a strong latifundium system developed. In eastern Germany demographic decline enabled the lords to take over abandoned peasant lands and build up vast holdings, giving rise, thanks to the weakness of the monarchy, to new sorts of *bans* and obliging the peasants to new labor services on the demesnial lands. Even in the West, however, a seigneurial revival accompanied the demographic revival of the late fifteenth century. It seems to have affected central and northern Italy as well, which in the preceding period had shown the highest degree of economic and social development on the continent. In England the revival of feudalism was represented above all by the phenomenon of enclosure. The lord took over the community's open fields, traditionally planted with grain, and lands that for centuries peasants had used as collective pasturage for their livestock. Joining these lands to his own, he then turned them over to a wool merchant or a stock raiser as pasturage. It has been said that in England "sheep ate men," but elsewhere as well, even earlier and in more strict connection with demographic decline, states encouraged the raising and transhumant pasturage of sheep, creating institutions to organize and supervise sheep raising such as the *Mesta* in Spain, the *Dogana delle pecore* in Puglia, the *Dogana dei paschi* of the commune of Siena in southern Tuscany, and the *Dogana delle pecore* in the nearby Papal States.

*

We still need to examine how men of the fields thought and what their sentiments and their aspirations were, but the paucity and the tendentiousness of the documentation remaining to us make this an almost impossible task. Except in extremely rare instances, peasants have left no direct testimony of themselves, and the reports from other levels of society—the clergy, nobles, merchants, artisans—often give a distorted or at best an indirect picture of them. Nonetheless, we can manage to find out something by gleaning bits here and there from a variety of sources, especially when documentation becomes more abundant and varied in the final centuries of the Middle Ages. For example, we often can find peasants, at times with their individual acts and their own words, in a broad range of judicial records, both secular and ecclesiastical. An example of the latter are the acts of a diocesan inquiry that have served Emmanuel Le Roy Ladurie for his description of a minuscule village in the Pyrenees that was still permeated with the Cathar heresy at the beginning of the fourteenth century. These documents provide a particularly eloquent demonstration that no matter how exceptional and abnormal court proceedings may be in comparison to the everyday life of the people involved, court records can reveal an entire mental and material universe. Not only has Le Roy Ladurie been able to study economic conditions in this village, the religious convictions of its inhabitants, and even the eating habits and the structure and conception of the family among its lords, its parish priest, and its transhumant shepherds; he also touches on more elusive topics, difficult to document, such as love, relations between the sexes, and the peasants' general conception of the universe.

Satire of the peasantry is an evident and easily identifiable current in European literature. It varies according to the environment from which it sprang, its author, and its public. For example, in more obviously feudal circles the peasant is satirized for his cowardice, whereas in bourgeois circles, as in Tuscany in the fourteenth and fifteenth centuries, where proprietors and sharecrop farmers had conflicting interests and peasants protested the injustice of a half-and-half division of crops, the most frequent accusation against the peasant was stealing from the landowner. Beyond these variants, however, satire often emphasized not only the peasant's filth, poor clothing, and minimal diet, but also a sort of bestiality that at times placed him almost at an intermediate level between beasts and humans. If we read these satires and other sources carefully, we can look beyond differences in levels of civilization from one region to another and the undeniable and widespread conditioning brought on by harsh living conditions, alimentary shortages, monotonous work, a daily struggle for existence, the great scourges of famine, recurrent epidemics, sickness, and the dangers of war—all of which determined the peasant's capacities and opportunities to feel and to think—to see that he was not totally devoid of ideas and aspirations. Although illiteracy was the rule in rural areas, there were some exceptions, in particular in more economically advanced territories dominated by cities, such as certain areas of Tuscany. There a few wealthier peasants and some small landholders, who perhaps had learned the rudiments from the village priest, could write, perhaps with difficulty, or at least read. The work of the parish priests was not limited to Tuscany alone, and there are instances (in central and northern Italy, for example) of communities—perhaps larger villages, with a small nucleus of rural bourgeois—that hired a schoolmaster, whose services might on occasion also be available to a peasant.

Furthermore, although country people were accustomed or constrained to live within the limited horizon of the village, this did not exclude opportunities for outside experiences. The peasant might easily have contacts with the nearby city; he might go on a pilgrimage, at least to the closest shrine; he might move away to find work (there is evidence everywhere, for example, of the temporary employment of peasants as unskilled workers in the building trades); he might migrate seasonally (migration was not limited to the shepherds of the poorest zones of agrarian economy like the Apennines). The more general problem of our knowledge of peasant self-awareness and mentality is closely connected to the problems of our knowledge of popular religious sentiment and of the relations between the peasant world, the ecclesiastical hierarchy, and the heretical sects. It is now known (and is universally applicable from one end of the continent to the other) that many peasant beliefs had their origins in the pre-Christian era or in non-Christian sources. Particularly on the parish level, the church was obliged to absorb many propitiatory rites, animistic practices, and forms of sympathetic magic. The parish priest himself on occasion was not loathe to practice magical arts, without eliciting scandal in the simple souls of his parishioners, who perceived such ministrations as part of his priestly function. Many church activities were connected in the peasants' minds with the returning cycles of agriculture. Even the peasant's relations with the saints was frankly contractual, savoring of magic, of *do ut des,* and offerings were made to the saints to assure good harvests, clement weather, and the health of men and animals. The peasants' attachment to the church, above all to the church of their own villages, was in general profound. The village church was not only a place of prayer but almost the heart of the community, as evidenced by the way the church building rose above the villagers' rooftops (in some cases sharing physical prominence with the towers and palaces of the lords). The community assembly met in or near the church, sometimes in the cemetery, until a special building was built; the parish priest announced matters of general interest from the pulpit; in moments of danger, people and goods found refuge in the church; many festivities—not always sacred in nature—took place in the church. The church, with its nearby cemetery, fed the collective memory of the community. Its bells, the word for which, in a fantastic etymology of the early thirteenth century, was traced to peasants—"a rusticis qui habitant in campo, qui nesciunt iudicare horas nisi per campanas"—not only called to prayer but tolled the hours of the day, since the peasants had not yet come to use the new "merchants' time." The bells also warded off thunderstorms, kept away wolves, signaled fires, and announced the perils of war. Like participation in the civil life of the community, participation in the life of the parish was part of the peasant's political education. He made it his business to observe the behavior of the parish priest and to collaborate in the upkeep of the church building and the care of liturgical vessels and vestments. The community set up organizations to do such tasks that bore different names in different places (*opera, fabbrica, luminaria, maramma*); in some places during the final centuries of the Middle Ages, on occasion at the suggestion of the mendicant orders, the villagers formed devotional confraternities for prayer, penitential exercises, and works of charity.

It was not pagan elements in their religion that enabled the peasants to give shape to their ideals and their political and social demands but Christian elements, orthodox or heterodox. The peasants understood well not only the consolation of the sacraments but the historical example of the primitive church, whose leaders appeared to all the subordinate classes to be a good deal closer to them than were the abbots or bishops of their own day, who differed from secular lords only in a shrewder, more demanding administration of their lands. This said, however, the relation between peasant discontent and evangelical heresies is not always clear. Among other reasons, the heresies often combined with an oriental dualism or with millenarian aspirations that had greater appeal for the destitute city poor than for peasants who held title to a farm, even a small one. For peasants, the golden age always lay in the imaginary realms of a remote past rather than in an undefined and undefinable future. In this respect peasant sensitivities were linked to a broader conviction that the world had declined through the centuries and was getting worse. For peasants, conflict with the lords, both muted and open, appeared in Christian guise as a struggle for liberty. One typical declaration states: "We demand that all serfs be liberated since God made everyone free with the shedding of his precious blood." As we have seen, aspirations for liberty took a more concrete form in demands for broader rights to buy and sell land, for a reduction of feudal exactions on persons and things, and for written agreements between the lords and the peasant village communities.

If the peasants' antagonism toward other social groups is both cause and proof of their (albeit elementary) political consciousness, we need to add to their aversion to the seigneurial class an aversion (in varying measure and different moments across Europe) to burghers and city-dwellers in general.

The most abundant evidence for this comes, once again, from central and northern Italy, where quite particular relations between country and city made relations between city-dwellers and peasants particularly tense, due to the many populous cities, the spread of communal city governments (that later blossomed into municipal seigneuries but inherited much from the communes), and the rise and establishment of a broad range of burgher strata. City-dwellers were well aware that underneath the peasant's obsequiousness and apparent placidity his soul was often exacerbated and filled with envy and hatred. This was demonstrated by occasional single acts of rebellion or by collective insurrections (which were, however, less frequent in zones where sharecropping was the rule and the peasant community was already in crisis, as we have seen). The peasants, for their part, reproached the city above all for its taxes and its restrictions on farm produce that disfavored the rural territory. They reproached city people for their contempt of country folk, and they reproached landowners in particular for their insensitivity toward the poverty and the drudgery of peasant life.

BIBLIOGRAPHY

A number of works give an overview of the economy and society of rural Europe, differing, however, in orientation. There is, first, *The Cambridge Economic History of Europe,* M. M. Postan and H. J. Habakkuk, eds., 2d. ed. (Cambridge: Cambridge University Press, 1966–), vol. 1, *The Agrarian Life of the Middle Ages,* which covers all Europe and the entire course of the Middle Ages. Another fundamental work (but which largely excludes Italy) is Georges Duby, *L'Economie rurale et la vie des campagnes dans l'occident médiéval: France, Angleterre, Empire, IXe-XVe siècles* (Paris: Flammarion, 1977) [*Country Life in the Medieval West,* trans. Cynthia Postan (Columbia: University of South Carolina Press, 1968)]. Useful for its abundant information on country life, particularly in France, is Roger Grand and Raymond Delatouche, *Storia agraria del Medioevo* (Milan: Il Saggiatore, 1968; 1981). A useful summary, above all for the relationship between population and resources, is B. H. Slicher van Bath, *De agrarische geschiedenis van West-Europa, 500–1850* (Utrecht: Spectrum, 1960) [*The Agrarian History of Western Europe, A.D. 500–1850),* trans. Olive Ordish (London: E. Arnold, 1963)], in which consideration of an extremely long time-span permits better placement in time of the centuries of interest to us here. For rural Italy during these centuries, see Giovanni Cherubini, *L'Italia rurale del basso Medioevo* (Rome and Bari: Laterza, 1984.)

R. Fossier, *Paysans d'Occident: XIe-XIVe siècle* (Paris: Presses Universitaires de France, 1984) treats the medieval peasant, even though the Italian scene is largely absent. Of great use, and not only for the conditions, aspirations, and struggles of English peasants, is R. H. Hilton, *The English Peasantry in the Later*

Middle Ages (Oxford: Clarendon Press, 1975). See also Werner Rösener, *Bauern im Mittelalter* (Munich: C. H. Beck, 1986).

Demographic questions can be followed up in J. C. Russel, "Population in Europe 500–1500," in Carlo M. Cipolla, ed., *The Fontana Economic History of Europe* (London: Fontana, 1972–76), vol. 1, *The Middle Ages*, pp. 25–70. Rural life as depicted in cycles of the months in cathedrals is studied in Perrine Mane, *Calendriers et techniques agricoles (France-Italie, XIIe-XIIIe siècles* (Paris: Le Sycomore, 1983). For the conception of time, see of course the first essay in Jacques Le Goff, *Tempo della Chiesa e tempo del mercante. E altri saggi sul lavoro e la cultura nel Medioevo* (Turin: Einaudi, 1977) [*Time, Work and Culture in the Middle Ages* (Chicago: University of Chicago Press, 1980)]. On peasant religious sentiment, see the rich and suggestive volume of Aron Ja. Gurevic, *Contadini e santi. Problemi della cultura popolare nel Medioevo* (Turin: Einaudi, 1986). On the Mesta of Spain, see the classical work of J. Klein, *La Mesta. Estudio de la historia economica española 1273–1836* (Madrid: Alianza Editorial, 1936; 1979) [*La Mesta: A Study in Spanish Economic History, 1273–1836*, Harvard Economic Studies, vol. 21 (Cambridge: Harvard University Press, 1920)]. The Pyrenees village referred to in the text is in Emmanuel Le Roy Ladurie, *Montaillou: village occitan de 1294 à 1324* (Paris: Gallimard, 1975; rev. and cor., 1982) [*Montaillou, the Promised Land of Error,* trans. Barbara Bray (New York: George Braziller, Vintage Books, 1979)].

SUGGESTED READINGS

Judith M. Bennett, *Women in the Medieval English Countryside: Gender and Household in Brigstock before the Plague* (New York: Oxford University Press, 1987).

Kathleen Biddick, *The Other Economy: Pastoral Husbandry on a Medieval Estate* (Berkeley: University of California Press, 1989).

Marc Bloch, *French Rural History: An Essay on Its Basic Characteristics* (Berkeley: University of California Press, 1966).

Wendy Davies, *Small Worlds: The Village Community in Early Medieval Brittany* (Berkeley: University of California Press, 1989).

Barbara Hanawalt, *The Ties That Bound: Peasant Families in Medieval England* (New York: Oxford University Press, 1986).

R. H. Hilton, *A Medieval Society: The West Midlands at the End of the Thirteenth Century* (New York: Cambridge University Press, 1983).

J. A. Raftis, *Warboys: Two Hundred Years in the Life of an English Medieval Village* (Toronto: Pontifical Institute of Mediaeval Studies, 1974).

J. A. Raftis, ed., *Pathways to Medieval Peasants* (Toronto: Pontifical Institute of Mediaeval Studies, 1981).

C. J. Wickham, *The Mountains and the City: The Tuscan Appennines in the Early Middle Ages* (Oxford: Clarendon Press, 1988).

FOUR

The City-Dweller and Life in Cities and Towns

Jacques Rossiaud

Toward the end of the twelfth century, Richard of Devizes, a monk at Winchester, spoke of Londoners and their city in these terms:

> I do not at all like that city. All sorts of men crowd together there from every country under the heavens. Each race brings its own vices and its own customs to the city. No one lives in it without falling into some sort of crime. Every quarter of it abounds in grave obscenities. The greater a rascal a man is, the better a man he is accounted. . . . Do not mingle with the throngs in eating-houses. . . . The number of parasites is infinite. Actors, jesters, smooth-skinned lads, Moors, flatterers, pretty boys, effeminates, pederasts, singing and dancing girls, quacks, belly-dancers, sorceresses, extortioners, night-wanderers, magicians, mimes, beggars, buffoons: all this tribe fill all the houses. Therefore, if you do not want to dwell with evildoers, do not live in London. I do not speak against learned or religious men, or against Jews: however, because of their living amidst evil people, I believe they are less perfect there than elsewhere. (Trans. Appleby)

William Fitzstephen, a contemporary of Father Richard, was of a different opinion:

> Among the noble cities of the world that are celebrated by Fame, the city of london, seat of the Monarchy of England, is one that spreads its fame wider, sends its wealth and wares further, and lifts its head higher than all others. It is blest in the wholesomeness of its air, in its reverence for the Christian faith, in the strength of its bulwarks, the nature of its situation, the honour of its citizens, and the chastity of its matrons. . . . The citizens of London are everywhere regarded as illustrious and renowned beyond those of all other cities for the elegance of their fine manners, raiment and table. The inhabitants of other towns are called citizens, but of this they are called barons. And with them a solemn oath ends all strife. The matrons of London are very Sabines. (Trans. Butler)[1]

Thus the city-dweller inhabited either Babylon or Jerusalem. These are old images, crystallized by two centuries of unrestrained urban

1. These two quotations are cited from Marie-Thérèse Lorcin *Société et cadre de vie en France, Angleterre et Bourgogne (1050–1250)* (Paris: SEDES, 1985), p. 318 [*The Chronicle of Richard of Devizes of the Time of King Richard the First,* ed. and trans., John T. Appleby (London: Thomas Nelson and Sons, 1963), pp. 65–66; F. M. Stenton, *Norman London, an Essay, with a Translation of William Fitz Stephen's Description by Professor H. E. Butler . . . (London: G. Bell and Sons, 1934), pp. 26–27*].

development; they show clearly that cities and towns were inhabited by a quite particular humanity, decried by some and praised by others. I need not insist on the obvious: by 1250 the urban network of preindustrial Europe was in place, or nearly so. By modern standards the result was modest: one city of monstrous proportions—Paris—with a population of more than 100,000; a good half-dozen metropolises (all Italian, with the exception of Ghent) of more than 50,000 souls; sixty to seventy towns and cities of more than 10,000 inhabitants; a few hundred towns of more than a thousand. Cities and towns were unevenly distributed in clusters of varying density. In areas of city expansion, one person out of three or four was a city-dweller; where growth was sluggish, only one out of ten.

Mere size was not of prime importance, however, and for at least two reasons. First, the cities and towns were vast necropolises for the rural world and consumed their rapidly replenished human raw material at an unprecedented rate. Second, their influence greatly surpassed their demographic weight: schools were established in cities, the mendicant orders operated there, princes made them their capitals, crafts and trades became diversified there and their markets reached out ever farther. A complex society was developed in the city that adapted to the seigneurial system and its ideology but that elaborated its own hierarchies.

Three questions inevitably arise: What did the beggar and the burgher, the canon and the prostitute, have in common? Or the inhabitants of Florence and Montbrison? Or the new townspeople of the first growth of cities and their descendants of the fifteenth century?

Although they differed in both social rank and mental outlook, the canon could not avoid encountering the prostitute, the beggar, and the burgher. They could not possibly have been unaware of one another. They were integrated into the same small, densely peopled universe, and it imposed forms of sociability unknown in the village, a specific way of life, daily familiarity with money, and, for some, an obligatory opening onto the world at large. The bishop of Paris, Guillaume d'Auvergne, noted as much in 1230. We need to guard, however, against falling into a mythology as old as urban history that exaggerates praise of the values of city-dwellers and contrasts them to the inertia of rustics. Between the peasant and the townsman there was only a difference of culture.

But was urban culture the same in Florence and Montbrison, in

Siena and in Saint-Flour? It was a question of degree, not of kind. The lexicons differed (and not always: clans in Metz had their festive "brigades" just like those of the Sienese and the Florentines), but the language was the same. There were no fortresses to isolate city-dwellers: The city cannot to be judged by itself, as Fernand Braudel reminds us. It was part of a series of relational networks (religious, commercial, artisanal, etc.) for the circulation of models that originated in the metropolises. In short, although no "urban system" existed, an urbanized West developed, the members of which were all somehow related; they belonged to a sort of clan that had its rich and its poor, but in which blood relationship was primordial.

As for the last question, urban culture—as an often pretentious self-satisfaction about urban activities and ways of living—took centuries to evolve. Each period of history had its type of city-dweller. Furthermore, most people did not grow up in the city; they came there in their early youth. Thus I will attempt to keep in mind the two time-spans, brief and long, of acculturation and a painful apprenticeship, and to insist upon the essential forms of sociability that produced ideologies and myths. To quote the words of an excellent specialist on urban life, the Franciscan Fra Paolino (1314), "fagli mestiere a vivere con molti" (teach him the skill of living among many).

Brief Glances at a Changing World

Around 1150, when a peasant entered the gates of a city to try to find work and perhaps to settle there, he was doubtless just as aware as his counterpart two centuries later of penetrating into "a universe protected by its privileges" (Fernand Braudel). Not that "city air makes men free," as the old German adage went—a verity that has been challenged only recently. Lille around 1200 refused bastards and deserters. Bologna and Assisi taxed nonfreemen more heavily, the lord everywhere had a year in which to recuperate a runaway serf, and in a multitude of rural towns living conditions differed little from in the big city. The fact remains that *Statgerichte,* though prestigious, was a mix of illusions and concrete advantages. Liberty depended primarily upon a progressive accumulation of rights and customs—extorted, acquired, negotiated, consented to, or extracted—much more than upon privileges granted by a charter or a law. A law was valid only by the strength of a community that could enforce its respect. The cities had on their side money, men in great number, and their formidable solidarities. The old cry of *Commune!* still had an emotional pull in Picardy or Flanders around 1300. This is why city freedoms were greater than freedoms in small towns.

City-dwellers (merchants first among them) had thus everywhere obtained the liberties necessary for their activities. From the late twelfth century, only the vestiges of oppressive or humiliating customs could be found here and there. An urban law was superimposed upon competing jurisdictions—the various *bans* that shared power over the city—and even when the right of justice remained entirely in the hands of the lord, the courts, peopled by the leading citizens, tended to impose unified conditions for both persons and goods. Businessmen had a law free of paralyzing formalities: they were free to recruit the manpower they needed for their workshops, to supervise weights and measures, markets and fairs, to regulate hiring and the trades, and to intervene to good effect in favor of their fellow citizens when they suffered thefts or arbitrary confiscation.

Benefiting from this collective solidarity supposed a citizenship that was in reality difficult to acquire. It implied admission, sponsorship, a time of residence of often more than one year, and inclusion in a trade or the purchase of property. Becoming a part of the people was not an easy matter, and most inhabitants without means proved incapable of penetrating the internal walls erected by jealous minorities. Nonetheless, even leaving aside dreams of steady work and social promotion, the simple fact of residing for a time in the city authorized several primary expectations: first, of living in relative security sheltered by walls that stopped marauding horsemen and pillagers; next, of not dying of hunger, for the city had food reserves, capital, and enough armed strength to assure that its grain convoys would reach their destination; finally, of surviving periods of unemployment and poverty thanks to the distribution of pittances—the crumbs left by plunder, power, and charity, the three sisters protected by the city ramparts.

*

The city began "at the limits of its suburbs like a dwelling at its garden gate" (Anne Lombard-Jourdan), and the city walls were a decisive frontier that separated two spaces. Except in England, every city in the West had its ramparts. Whether it symbolized hard-won unity or was the work of a ruler, the protecting circle of walls identified the city. German nobles concerned about the expansion of cities scornfully declared city-dwellers to be "peasants closed in by walls." All cities were enclosed out of political and military necessity, and as the city grew its defenses were rebuilt to include a larger space. This happened five times in Ghent between 1150 and 1300, three times in Florence. If a city neglected to enlarge its walls, war called it to order, as in the kingdom of France around 1350.

Considerable amounts of capital (from 100,000 to 150,000 *livres* for Reims in the fourteenth century) went into ringing the cities with stone. An object of pride but a devourer of city funds, the walls put their stamp on the whole of urban life: they gave structure to the permanent population who, divided into sectors, shared the duty of guarding the battlements and the gates; they defined the passage of time, as the gates closed at nightfall; they conferred sacred status on what they enclosed. Above all, however, they remodeled space and gave the cityscape a great part of its originality.

Not that everything was different once one passed through one of its gates and left the city. Nearby rural areas were dominated by city capital and city ownership and burghers' houses dotted the landscape. The peasants frequented the city market regularly, where they met farmers who lived in the city, even in the metropolises, in good number. As they made their way inside the walls the peasants would pass by gardens and vineyards and shoo away chickens or pigs just like the ones in their own villages, but born and fattened in the shadow of the city walls. There was one difference, however, and a sizable one: an agricultural town was more than an overgrown village, and the city in the West was not characterized by its agricultural production. Land in Milan in the twelfth century was worth thirty-six times more than in the surrounding countryside, and land speculation was responsible for making the fortune of a good many burgher families in Ghent, Genoa, or Pisa. The unusual concentration of people in a limited space inspired Bonvesin da la Riva to numerical lyricism, and it was certainly crowding—particularly in Mediterranean cities—that determined urban construction and the cityscape with its concentration of bell towers, the massive bulk of its cathedral, an abundance of nobles' towers, houses with common walls (at least in the central part of the city), and ever higher buildings (in Paris, Florence, Genoa, and Siena buildings four or five stories high were not unusual).

Constantly remodeled by expansion or destruction, the cityscape was also difficult to comprehend. It had no sweeping perspectives, and irregular blocks, a tangled network of tiny branching streets, courtyards, and alleys made the city a strange and fascinating world for the newcomer, a world he had to explore for some time before he understood it, perhaps never succeeding totally.

*

For the poor, living in a city or town meant occupying a windowless lair, two or three to an upper-story room, or a hovel in a back courtyard; it meant lodging at the tavern if some money was available, or having one or two rooms if one was married. It always meant having to share the use of a well and a kitchen. A craftsman usually lived in his own house and had his own cookfire, his cellar and his granary, but he shared space with his servants and his apprentices. Only a minority escaped the rule: one had to get used to living surrounded by neighbors of a great variety of conditions and occupations.

For two out of three city-dwellers, living in the city also meant dependence on the market either totally or for part of the year, buying one's bread, wine, and other foodstuffs. Finally, it also meant having to suffer the inconveniences of living behind walls: lacking safe drinking water at times because the wells were polluted; living surrounded by filth because in years of unrest many of the gates were walled up and piled high with rubbish that encouraged infection and endemic disease. The municipal government was able to relegate lepers to hospitals outside the walls and to pass sanitary regulations, but it was totally incapable of combating the plague, which, when climatic conditions were favorable for it, struck the central city and its industrial suburbs with lightning speed.

Contagion could also be mental in these crowded meeting-places. For months and even for years during a siege, a war, or a wave of plague, the city closed in upon itself, quick to react to rumors and anxieties that propagated just as fast as the diseases. "Terrors," "emotions," and collective atrocities often occurred when fear and claustrophobia seized the throng—which was just as quick to shout its joy at the announcement of a peace treaty as to wail in sorrow at the death of a king. The first condition of any urban culture was to learn to live in promiscuity and, above all, to be able to confront people of different customs and language.

*

It was of course the rural areas that fed the expansion of cities. It is probable that the first to be attracted to the cities (Amiens, Macon, Toulouse, Florence, and so forth), were prosperous countrymen drawn by the city's freedoms and opportunities to rise in society. This was still true of the Florentine *contado* in the early thirteenth century, where wealthy families set an example of success and offered a minoritarian model of urban immigration found everywhere and in all times.

It is equally certain, however, that as city expansion continued from the twelfth century on, the wealthier country people were preceded or followed by increasing numbers of fugitive serfs, paupers, and vagrants. Urban workshops drained the surplus population of the villages, the sons of peasant farmers with small plots of rented land, and even (around Pisa but also around Beaucaire and Saint-Gilles) farmer landowners ruined by the urban market's takeover of land and the conversion of wheat fields to pasturage. The city's zone of attraction (the size of which varied according to the city's dynamism) thus tended to extend to more distant villages, which nonetheless remained regional in the period of full population. Around 1300 Arles was still a Provençal city; Amiens was Picard and Lyons Franco-Provençal. Only the commercial, political, or university metropolises had sizable numbers of foreigners, but everywhere the newcomers outnumbered the original city population (immigrants accounted for 50 to 66 percent of the population of some parishes in Pisa around 1260).

These two characteristics, the enlargement of areas of migration and the imbalance of city populations in favor of newcomers, were further accentuated by the calamities of the fourteenth century. By 1450, in Florence as in the cities of the Rhône valley, newcomers came from farther away, the proportion of foreigners in the population had augmented constantly, and everywhere relatively lower wages in rural areas swelled the ranks of the poor—and of women—in search of a way to make a living. Immigrants did not always pose grave problems of assimilation—far from it. Assimilation depended on their numbers and their origin. Smaller cities, even in their periods of greatest expansion, were always able to control their new population without great difficulty, as the new arrivals spoke the same language and followed similar customs. It was another story when the annual influx was in the thousands. The bulk of newcomers to Florence around 1450 came from Piedmont or north of the Alps; in Avignon around 1370 people from throughout the West lived side by side in the same parishes; Dijon townspeople came from Franche-Comté, Picardy, Burgundy, and Lorraine. All these groups long retained their particularisms and maintained their alliances, solidarities, and contacts with their places of origin.

For the city fathers and the stablest and wealthiest segment of urban society, the newcomers were both a necessity and a danger. The interests of entrepreneurs and food retailers dictated openness toward immigrants, but within the artisan class, at the least recession, sentiments of hostility resurfaced and the gap widened between newcomers and older city-dwellers. Money of course facilitated integration, but it did not resolve all problems. Even with equal wealth, an immigrant did not have the relational networks, the employment opportunities, the admission into a trade, or the level of political participation that citizens enjoyed, and the latter did their best to raise ingenious juridical or social barriers before him.

For Dante, it was the "stench" of rapacious immigrants and a "mingled strain of men" (trans. Musa) that led to the moral decline of Florence. Filippo Villani mocked peasants who had hardly abandoned the plow when they presented themselves for civic offices. Two centuries later in Lyons, Symphorien Champier expressed his thoughts in similar fashion when he denounced a dull-witted *l'estrange populaire* as a source of vice and civic disorder.

This is why the merchants of the *gente nuova* invented their ancestors, founders of a *domus* of fabulous antiquity (as does Giovanni di Pagolo Morelli, in spite of his apparent prudence), and why chroniclers explained internal conflict by incompatible races inhabiting the city. The upheavals that followed arrivals and departures and a constant and at times considerable intermixture of the population marked all city-dwellers—members of an ancient lineage or recent arrivals, the latter more profoundly, however, since they lacked kin.

*

Not that great families were unknown in the city, nor that consciousness of lineage soon dissolved. Lineage dominated the social and political life of Mediterranean cities at least until the fourteenth century. In the eleventh and twelfth centuries it reinforced family solidity, revived genealogical memory, strengthened control over the family estates, and argued for transmission of the *domus magna* and the government of the family group to the eldest son. In Florence, Metz, Reims, Valenciennes, and Verdun power was identified with lineage: "the family secretes power just as power secretes the family" (Henri Bresc). When threatened or weakened, lineages produced vast artificial kinships unified under a totemic name.

Even when they did not live under one roof, family groups shared a number of common concerns (patrimony, marriage, daily or seasonal mutual aid). Thus the study of households must not be dissociated from family ties, which could prove quite strong, even among the affluent commoners, the *mediocres*. The fact remains, however, that large households were rare, that most humbler folk lacked awareness of lineage and had no family name, and that they never knew the joys of the extended, coresident family so dear to the moralists. The general tendency was to scattered families.

The mass of the city population appears to have lived in family cells of restricted size and households of low density. The urban family was smaller than the rural family, and its very structure made it fragile, at least among the middle and lower strata of society. Few fathers could marry their daughters at or near the age of puberty, between twelve and fifteen years of age: the average age at marriage rose to from sixteen to eighteen years (Florence and Siena, 1450) and from twenty to twenty-one (Dijon, 1450). The warnings of St. Bernardino of Siena (according to him, there were twenty thousand nubile girls in Milan in 1425) corresponded to those of the consuls of Rodez in 1450, who noted that there were sixty girls over twenty years of age, in a population of 265 households, whose poverty precluded marriage. We also know that men married very late—at over thirty years of age in Tuscany, at around twenty-five in Tours and Dijon—even at a time when standards of living and hopes for social promotion made settling down easier than a century or two earlier. Marriage in both town and village was thus a costly "social victory" (Pierre Toubert) that put an end to a long youth. Late marriage worried the notables, who saw in it the germ of unnameable sins and pretended to be unaware that it was the only way for the humble to avoid sinking into destitution. This structural aspect of urban families, already discernible in Genoa in the twelfth century, where artisans delayed marriage until their parents were dead, led to another: a high incidence of broken marriages. In Venice between 1350 and 1400 the average duration of a union was only twelve years among commoners and sixteen years among nobles. Late age at marriage and broken marriages explain the low birth rate, along with a decline in fertility in women, a high infant mortality rate that struck the poor hardest, frequent abortion (for all practical purposes legal in Dijon until the third month), and contraceptive practices (doubtless widespread in the Italian cities but unknown or rare in French cities). The age difference between husband and wife made the widow an even more familiar figure in the city than in rural areas.

Among craftsmen of modest status and journeymen, for whom family wealth or parental authority were lacking, marriage was often based on personal choice. The urban family thus seems to have been more flexible, more fragile, and less durable than the rural family.

Even *frérèches,* coresident households headed by brothers, were rarer in the city than in the villages, and the better part of such arrangements, agreed upon for a limited time-period, were dissolved by the will of one of the parties. The "reconstruction of lineage" so clearly discernible in rural areas shattered at the city walls, and among the lower classes such artificial families were contractual and of short duration.

City-dwellers had a clear awareness of family fragility, and they deplored the increased distance between kin separated by their activities, their life-style, and at times their residence. Fascination for the nobility came in part from this, as the modest burgher dreamed of solidarities based on lineage and on an active and generous kinship network. The authors of the *fabliaux* tell it clearly: when you need a cousin, he will let you down. Thus the city, by its economy, its environment, and its ethic was destructive of family ties among the masses. Epidemics struck hard, solidarity was stretched to the limit, moral dangers lay in wait, the authority of the head of the family was endangered. The city-dweller, often without ancestors and lacking wealth, could count little on his "friends of the flesh." This structural weakness was not only due to the number of men "without name or family" but to the very nature of urban wealth. It rested on money.

*

It would be both ridiculous and fruitless to claim to give a brief description of the diversity of urban activities and societies. Everyone knows that behind the city walls there lived side by side, in ever-changing proportion, canons and students, nobles and vintners, patricians and proletarians, wholesale merchants and used-clothes sellers, highly skilled craftsmen and ordinary workers (tossed, as their individual destinies and the economic situation dictated, from work to beggary). Everyone also knows that proletarians were more numerous than entrepreneurs, and that the patricians could be counted on the fingers of one hand. To take one example, around 1300 Saint-Omer counted from five to ten knights, three hundred wealthy men, three thousand property owners, and ten thousand heads of household, two thousand five hundred to three thousand of them poor (Alain Derville). Furthermore, differences in personal status, origin, profession, and social position—qualitative differences—introduced cleavages in addition to those created by wealth. No matter: the urban social model was the burgher and the essential criterion of differentiation was money. Everywhere the city-dweller divided the human mass that surrounded him into great and small—*majores* and *mediocres, gras* and *maigres, grossi* and *minuti.* The place of the individual within the hierarchy was determined by his revenues; by the price he commanded. Specialists in urban fiscal questions concentrate more on the product than on the nature of capital. This means that exceptions aside (Jews and foreigners), social condition always won over personal status, esteem over scorn; and, in spite of temporary obstructions, it meant that money made it possible to pass from a craft enterprise to business and to force entry into a hansa, a market hall, a wealthy circle—in sum, to join the "patriciate."

Even when city functions multiplied (diversifying more and more), the merchant mentality won out and modeled sensitivities and behavior. As Robert Lopez has emphasized, many craftsmen were part-time merchants: the waged artisan sold his *savoir-faire,* the proprietor a feudal tenure or a room, the jurist his knowledge of the law, the professor his learning, the day worker his physical strength, the minstrel his talent, the prostitute her body. Their *ministeria*—their trades—were organized according to a system of reciprocal exchanges that some (the theologians) called the common good and others (the burghers) the market, according to a just price, fixed daily, to the penny, posted in the market hall or the hiring place.

For money was the blood of the city, its vital fluid (Lester K. Little) and its organizing principle. When the burgher appears in a *chanson de geste,* a *fabliau,* or a proverb, he is a merchant, the natural representative of *dan denier* ("Sir Penny"). When they were not accusing him of usury, the clergy reproached him for his love of gain, his *avaritia.*

*

Burghers' fortunes almost always retained one quality that they had had from the start: mobility. Easily concealed or redeployed, placed in gold or silver ingots or vessels and later in credit instruments and contracts (work orders, partnership contracts, state-backed war loans, bank deposits, and so forth), their fortunes were dynamic and living entities. Even when success transformed their owners, fortunes remained relatively flexible: houses, workshops, retail shops, and land near the city were easily bought and sold. As for the patricians, although they held seigneuries and had crests, in the fourteenth century they never lived totally on their land revenues but often continued to operate as money-changers, or they farmed taxes, tolls, and rights of entry, as with the knights of Arles, Marseilles, or Pisa in the twelfth century, who built their power on their monopoly over collecting the excise taxes on salt, wheat, and textiles.

Liberal historiography, seduced by the abundant money in the period, the perfection of commercial techniques, and the immense possibilities offered to private initiative, were wont to see a happy artisan or a commercial success in every inhabitant of an Italian or Flemish metropolis. We must not be fooled by this golden legend. Many men could not or did not want to risk their meager savings in maritime ventures or the salvation of their souls in usurious ones. Nevertheless, all city-dwellers willy-nilly were sensitive to the stability of their money, to movements of the money market, and to events that affected supply and demand, wholesale and retail—Pisans and Genoese because they depended on wheat from Rumania, Sicily, or the Rhône valley; weavers and fullers because they feared unemployment when English wool no longer came through; workers in Paris and Lyons around 1430 because peace with Burgundy meant an easier life for them; and so forth.

The uprooted peasant recently settled within city walls thus discovered a world of far-reaching horizons, and he soon found himself constrained to reflect upon the value of labor and time. At the heart of the new economy, in the market hall or on the hiring place, he noted that prices changed just as constantly as fashions or social conditions.

*

The facades of twelfth-century cathedrals show the time-honored theme of the wheel of fortune ceaselessly carrying societies and individuals up to success or down to ruin. The image was a denunciation, bringing anguish to the rich and reassurance to the poor; it corresponded marvelously to the scandalized reaction of those who held to traditional ideology when they viewed the typically urban ferment of perpetual change in social status and condition.

Chronicles, histories, and songs overflow with parvenus, men who began with nothing and through usury, commerce, and even manual labor reached the summits of power. These were *exempla.* Even at the height of city growth, a prime condition for success was to have some money at the start, and we now know that a good many merchant-patricians of the twelfth century were the sons of rich men (*ministeriales* or knights) and that many "newly rich" were merely wealthy men from another city. The histories to some extent speak true, however: great merchants in Genoa around 1200 quadrupled their capital in five years, and in Venice in the fifteenth century profits from a far-flung commerce still permitted profits of 40 percent. Enrichment could thus be rapid, and ruin just as lightning-swift.

Adam de la Halle in the *Jeu de la feuillée* shows the *nouveaux riches* of Arras, but he also deplores the disgrace of Thomas de Bourriane, who had had to abandon textiles to become a simple ale brewer. Resounding failures were just as frequent as successes; "fortune worked by chance," wrote the Bourgeois of Paris around 1430, at a time when the *catasto* that had just been taken in Florence abounded with great names sunk into poverty.

In the long view, "old houses," patricians, entrepreneurs, victuallers, and jurists followed one another or mingled at the summit of society and in the municipal councils, while the ranks of the lesser were swelled with the respectful poor, some fallen from high places, but more often with wage-earners, who were permanently vulnerable in times of chronic high unemployment. Thus ostentatious wealth was counterbalanced by an anguishing and apparent poverty scandalous only when city people were its victims. Little pity was wasted on others. Was not a throng of beggars an indication of urban prosperity? The distance between rich and poor might occasionally be reduced (as between 1350 and 1450), but it remained enormous, just as changes in men and social conditions were always rapid, even in periods of relative stasis.

Social change was not the only phenomenon confronting the city-dweller, however. As Lester K. Little and Jacques Le Goff have emphasized, work specialization raised particular problems in the city unknown in the village. Individuals worked at highly differentiated tasks, hence they often had to confront problems of choice, thus of morality. (It should be unnecessary to cite the continual redeployment of industry and commerce in all economies between 1200 and 1500.) Urban activities thus multiplied moral dilemmas concerning the value of labor, profit, loans, wealth, and poverty. Similarly, when young men were obliged to an extremely long bachelorhood, women were easily available, and there were large numbers of clerics, it raised questions concerning a sexual morality poorly adapted to new conditions of existence. Several generations of intellectuals reflected on these anguishing questions and attempted to respond to them, for society possessed instruments for self-criticism. It had dialectic and the scholastic method, which forced the individual to take a stand, habituated him to an incessant questioning, and accustomed minds to the practice of discussion, to diversity of opinions, and to an exchange of ideas and experiences that for a time involved clergy, merchants, and manual laborers. Although the principal intellectual studia gradually closed or were transformed into routine-bound universities, nevertheless, the alliance had been lasting enough to modify a number of mental attitudes. Furthermore, room for contestation or for intellectual or moral confrontation still remained in many places—before the pulpit of the mendicant preacher taking his hearers to task, in the public squares, where public opinion was formed, in the taverns, on the platforms of secular theater, and in adolescent groups that tended to define their identity in opposition to well-established men. The author of the *Enfances Vivien* presents a burgher's son incapable of understanding the mind-set of his father, and Christine de Pisan indicates that in Paris in her day young and old were unable to "suffer one another."

Contestation was at times expressed by laughter, by Carnival rituals, or by scandal-provoking ruptures: Francis of Assisi publicly stripped himself of his cloak. Contestation added to the tensions prompted by unequal opportunities and by clan and family rivalries to make the city a world of incessant confrontation. It contributed to the slow forging of a new culture, but it caused anguish and encouraged violence.

*

The history of the cities of Western Europe is shot through with episodes of violence, fear, and revolution, episodes in which family honor, participation in the municipal council, or working conditions were at stake. Such conflicts opposed "magnate" and "popular" factions. In Italy they opposed actual political parties dominated by clans, and in the bigger cities of Flanders they turned into true class wars punctuated by massacres, exilings, and destruction. Such conflicts were frequent between 1250 and 1330, and they resulted everywhere in a defeat of the old rich and an enlargement of oligarchies. A second wave of unrest of a more clearly social character (the *ciompi* in Florence and Siena, the *maillotins* in Paris, and so forth) battered the urban world in the late fourteenth century. The defeat of the lower orders did not put an end to the tensions, which were transformed into an occasional brief terror, here and there, but were more usually expressed in continual but muted, "atomized" conflicts difficult to distinguish from common delinquency in the documentation. Stones thrown at night through a master's windows, a creditor brutalized, a brawl between two rival groups of workers were easily ascribed to ordinary violence by the judges.

In other words, many city-dwellers, even if they lived through long and difficult periods of tension, escaped the horrors of riots and repression, but they all had to face an atmosphere of violence on an almost daily basis. There is little need to accumulate examples: in Florence, Venice, Paris, Lille, Dijon, Avignon, Tours, or Foix, the judicial archives reveal an impressive series of cold-blooded vendettas, of *chaudes mêlées* between individuals or groups settled with knives or iron-tipped sticks, and of rapes, often collective, that marked for life poor girls beaten and dragged from their rooms at night.

These violent acts were for the most part committed by youths or adult men, often of modest social condition, but who were indistinguishable from law-abiding citizens. "The city drove men to crime," Bernard Chevalier has rightly said. Indeed, the cities of the Loire valley seem to have been twice as conducive to crime as their surrounding rural areas at the end of the fourteenth century, and in the Lyonnais and in Comtat sentences for violent acts are clearly fewer than in Lyons or Avignon themselves.

Wine—drunkenness was often an excuse—does not explain everything, nor do the arms that everyone carried in spite of municipal ordinances. The example came from on high: even in Reims at the beginning of the fourteenth century, the judges were incapable of keeping clans from resolving their quarrels by means of arms. However, civic violence (executions, torture, forcing a criminal to run through the city streets as the crowd jeered and struck him) was offered as a spectacle, and the domestic moral code allowed blows. Justice, what is more, did not inspire belief; it was more dreaded than appreciated, and it was inefficient and costly. When he was scoffed at, the individual turned to immediate vengeance. He did so to safeguard his honor: it was in the name of honor that young men punished girls who, to their minds, transgressed its canons. Like violence, honor was a value widespread in urban societies: prominent citizens were called "honorable." There was no reputation without honor and no honor without authority. The rich man's wealth and friends lent support to his honor; the working man without wealth held his reputation to be an essential capital. This is why in Lille or Avignon brawls usually opposed equals. Squares and streets—all public places—became stages on which honor could be won or lost. In taverns bordering on several wards of the city, it was a good idea to follow the advice of the spinning women in the *Evangiles des quenouilles:* "Two friends eating together should drink one after the other in order to come to the other's aid if need be."

Violence fostered anxiety. On occasion the notables denounced it, but they did not really seek to extirpate it (either in Venice or Dijon). For humble folk this fear added to other obsessions—of being abandoned amid general indifference, as with Dame Poverty, whom Jean de Meun described as covered with an old sack, "a bit apart from the others . . . crouched down and hunched over like a poor dog," sad, shamed, and unloved.

Opicinus de Canistris, the author of a work on the glory of Pavia (*Liber de laudibus civitatis ticinensis,* 1330) explains that in that city of a population of nearly fifty thousand,

> everyone knew one another, so that if someone requested an address, it was given to him immediately, even if the person he sought lived at the far end of the city, and this is so because the inhabitants assemble twice a day, either in the courtyard of the City Hall or on the cathedral square nearby.

Opicinus's Pavia was a fabulous city; clearly, the real city's inhabitants no longer knew one another. He was dreaming of an ideal city lost in the *inurbamento* of the twelfth and thirteenth centuries. Only the *majores* were in a position to take a turn through the town square twice a day. The other townspeople first had to reconstitute their universe and their village, make friends and perhaps kin in the city—in their neighborhoods and with their neighbors.

Among Neighbors and Friends

"When you have good company of your neighbors, you have no need to live with strangers" advised Paolo da Certaldo, and the Lyonnais, François Garin, echoed him: neighbors were friends or should behave as such.

Medieval urbanism expressed and facilitated life in the neighborhood. Cities often had more than one nucleus, the ancient *bourgs* keeping their individuality, on occasion their customs and their privileges as well. Noble family agglomerations segmented the cityscape into spaces that often turned inward, and in areas bristling with towers the households of one lineage were concentrated around a palace, a loggia, a courtyard, or a church, housing kin, allies, clients, and domestics.

Immigrants tended to group together in certain parishes. Access to lodgings and to a trade were difficult, the choice of an urban residence was largely determined by ties of friendship or kinship, and new city-dwellers felt the need to speak in familiar accents at home and in the street. Thus country neighbors often found themselves neighbors in the city. Ethnic dominance can be observed in Florence as in Lyons, in Paris as in the cities of Castile (where clustering was particularly strong and on occasion imposed by the authorities). The grouping of like people can often be explained by their common trade, as for butchers, tanners, or dyers.

Inside the neighborhood or the ward, the organization of the habitat and the need for defense and public security favored the particularism of one block (*quareel* in the dialect of Reims, *moulon* in Languedoc, *gache* in Provençal), one street, or one group of houses built around one or more courtyards. The neighborhood had fairly clear boundaries and a political center, tutelary sacred values, and a savor if its own.

For the newcomer in the city it constituted an easily mastered space whose outstanding features were also informal gathering places—the tavern, where the men gathered, the cemetery, where children and adolescents played and danced, the *trêve* (street intersection), a true village square where one could talk freely of city affairs, or the well and the bake oven, where the women gathered.

Everyone felt at home with people in the neighborhood, whom one met repeatedly and whose voice and figure were familiar. Near home—in France, at any event—one had less need to keep close rein on one's gestures and words, and people passed the better part of their time in the street, which belonged first to the inhabitants before being public domain and was indispensable when lodgings and shops were cramped. Children swarmed over the street freely and without great danger; girls could walk about, even when they reached marriageable age (in Italy they had to contemplate the spectacle of the street from their bedroom window). In Dijon in fine weather, women of a range of social conditions and ages sat before their houses and spun, by hand or with a wheel, commenting on neighborhood affairs. They were not forbidden to raise their eyes or to call to men by their names. As for the men, on hot days they served wine to their friends before their doors or gathered by the barrels in the wine cellar on the ground floor (in Avignon as in Tuscany, the ground-floor room was open to all). Women's society drew from the entire neighborhood and gathered almost daily in one house in another to help an engaged girl with her trousseau, dress a bride, attend a woman in childbirth, or keep a death vigil before making the solemn procession to the cemetery.

In Dijon in 1450, on the vigils of feast days Damoiselle Marie, the wife of the *bourgeois*, Pierre Damy, went to the parish baths with her female neighbors, on occasion accompanied by their husbands, one a vintner, the other a mason. As for the wealthy, they feasted well on *de bonnes et joyeuses chères:* the Berbiseys dined with the Molesmes in the company of the best society of the parish of Saint-Jean. In Florence around 1370, if Franco Sacchetti can be believed, the Bardis and the Rossis shared their table with their neighbor, a goldsmith. In the winter poorer folk joined for the *veillées* that from Burgundy to Brittany brought together men, women, and girls to chat and to work in someone's house, a hut constructed for the purpose, or, most frequently, in the church, where the parishioners felt quite at home. Young workingmen and youths were more likely to go to the tavern to drink and sing or to gamble in a gaming den before setting off on a nocturnal escapade such as girl-hunting or braving a rival band in another neighborhood.

An accident, a conjugal altercation more serious than usual, a call for help and the neighbors were there to intervene, pacify, or offer aid. Such were the minuscule facts of this dense sociability and this "daily mutuality" that, little by little, integrated youths and newcomers into city society and comforted sententious oldsters immobile on their benches. Or rather, this was how a milieu of good neighbors worked, for proximity did not always wear the seductive face so frequently portrayed by authors and moralists. Nonetheless, even in the poorest sections (with the exception of pockets of utter destitution), proximity assured some fundamental functions. It fostered and on occasion created identity by providing a nickname for the apprentice or the workman who arrived in the city bearing only a given name—a nickname that was usually the name of his village of origin and that later was changed into a patronymic. It bolstered the young, welded into a band by carousing, fighting, and gaming. It was also the neighborhood that recognized the conjugal status of an immigrant couple, legitimizing a union even if it had not been concluded in ritual fashion before a priest (the case in Italy) with noisy and bawdy manifestations at the nuptial procession and during the wedding night. It legitimized second marriages at the price of a distribution of small change to widowers' associations and to youth brotherhoods, or it punished with a cruel charivari (in Italy, the *mattinata*) the outsider who carried off a parish girl. It viewed concubinary couples with indulgence if they did not infringe upon "honesty." It even tolerated private bordellos if they did not threaten the tranquillity of the neighborhood by brawls or its salvation by dangerous transgressions. One example will suffice: in Avignon, as Jacques Chiffoleau has shown, judicial supervision was strict, and officers of the *cour temporelle* had the right to enter into citizens' houses on the pretext of confirming fornication, adultery, or concubinage. "Abuses" followed. Pope Paul II decreed (in 1465) that such incursions could henceforth take place only on formal and written request of the friends, kin, or neighbors of the suspected delinquents. This was neither an aberrant nor an extraordinary concession: the sovereign pontiff was ratifying a situation known to exist in many other cities. The right of the male population of territorial groups to define its own social practices was thus recognized.

Finally, it was the neighbors who, until the fourteenth century and often later, took charge of the body of the dead and accompanied it to the parish cemetery.

Documentation rarely permits exact measurement of the various social ties within the neighborhood or the parish, but they always appear to be of an extraordinary density. In Lyons in the early 1500s the boatsmen and day workers of the *quartier* Saint-Vincent married women from within the parish in four cases out of five. In Florence in the fifteenth century, the majority of marriages were contracted within the *gonfalone,* and even men of a level of wealth and political ambition that incited them to look beyond the neighborhood chose godparents for their children among their neighbors and friends. Burial in the parish was by far more attractive, especially among humbler folk, than in the cemeteries of the mendicant orders, and none forgot the parish council in their last wishes (Jacques Chiffoleau; Bernard Chevalier).

This cohesion was regularly reinforced (an apotheosis of "enlarged privacy," to use Charles de la Roncière's expression) by celebrations, above all within the family: baptisms, marriages, and funerals were grandiose affairs when the powerful were involved, whether they were named Baudoche or Gournay in Metz or Ruccellai in Florence. Guests were invited by the hundreds or by the thousands, but neighbors were treated well and seated at a table near the *loggia.* The circle was smaller when common people feasted, but companions and musicians escorted the hero of the day, be he an infant, a husband, or a corpse. During the annual Carnival and May Day festivities, neighbors collaborated to decorate wagons and plan a masquerade, and when the feast day of the parish's patron saint came around, families gathered after solemn Mass and a fine sermon in streets decorated with branches to banquet around a parish king and queen who shared the day with their children. Kin, friends, and neighbors: that day no distinctions were made and no one quarreled with the rulers of the feast.

Good religion was observation of community rites, secular and sacred. Under the common cloak of verities, fears, and hopes, there were a host of rituals proper to territorial groups. The true Catholic must first be faithful to collective customs; the good priest had to execute parish rites scrupulously. The major feast days—those great liturgies of neighborly fervor—recreated the spirit of neighborliness and made supportable a norm that was by no means always worked out in democratic fashion. The neighborhood had its leaders—patricians or minor notables—and very often had a confraternal association (*comitiva, aumône, charité,* etc.) to assure mutual aid, but also for surveillance and at times for exclusion.

Jacques Heers has given an excellent example of this: in the fifteenth century, the members of the *vicinia sancti Donati* in Genoa all came from the immediate neighborhood of the Porta Soprana. Only inhabitants of the ward had the right to join the society; should a member leave the neighborhood he was immediately excluded. A newcomer needed to be accepted by three-quarters of the members to be admitted. One can thus suppose that membership in the *vicinia* was obligatory for heads of household, but that the strict conditions for admission served as a powerful instrument for normalization and coercion. One can also suppose that the neighbor turned down by the *vicinia* would have little choice but to leave the neighborhood sooner or later. At best, he would find himself deprived of the collective solidarities, the works of charity, and the spiritual benefits of the parish. This must have been true of a good many confraternal organizations centered in parishes or political divisions of the city. Their leaders' power was all the more formidable because they were mediators: they represented their neighbors in the city councils and municipal authority in the ward. They could be "friends" (by arranging for a lower tax, getting someone exempted from the watch, etc.) or oppressors (by denouncing suspects); they could bolster neighborhood cohesion or weaken it. The very existence of ward confraternal organizations (exception made for the parish devotional confraternities, which were based on obligations of another order) shows that good relations among neighbors was not a natural phenomenon. Like any other community, the *quartier* or the *vicinanza* knew periods of calm but also times of unrest and upheaval. Calamities made incessant reconstruction inevitable, and fragility came not only from epidemics but from internal weaknesses. In four out of five cases in the *faubourgs* of Dijon, neighbors failed to intervene in nocturnal aggressions out of fear; in Venice adultery and rape usually occurred within the neighborhood (Guido Ruggiero).

For some, "the bliss of being included" (Michel Morineau) was accompanied by its inverse: a desire for independence. The burgher of the *Ménagier de Paris* hoped to live in tranquillity in his own house with his wife and "be away from others," but although the adage *Chacun chez soi est appelé roi* (Every man's home is his castle), was universally known as early as the thirteenth century, very few could enjoy that royalty. Franco Sacchetti narrates the maneuvers of a man who stirs up trouble between a couple whose lodging is separated from his own by only a thin wall: "The narrow alleys encouraged a widespread voyeurism [in which] nothing of importance long escaped the ferreting perspicacity of the neighbors" (Charles de la Roncière).

Renart le Novel presents a prominent burgher "rich in the world in all ways" who owned a country manor where he could breathe "better air than the town had." Was the urban air unhealthy? This man had all he needed to ensure a modicum of privacy in town. The seasonal migration of city-dwellers to their *granges* or their *poderi* certainly answered a combination of economic, hygienic, and (in Italy) climatic needs; it just as certainly fulfilled a need for isolation and recreation. It was in their country houses that the great burghers found the time for amusement, meditation, and reading. As early as the thirteenth century, city air was felt to be insufferable. In the early fourteenth century the burgher in the *Récits d'un Bourgeois de Valenciennes* grumbles about having to attend gatherings that suited neither his mind nor his mores: "No one on the block was talking about anything but coming to this banquet; indeed, everyone, poor or rich, was constrained to come to the dance of this populace under pain of heavy fines." In Valence in 1440, craftsmen took legal action to protest the violence and impropriety of the rites to which the workingmen of the Porte Tordéon subjected them when they married or remarried. *Mediocres* of the sort did not subscribe to the endogamy common in lower strata and found the community's customs restricting. The need to ally their families with others of the same social rank led the wealthier to seek alliances outside the neighborhood, on occasion even outside the city. Whereas his father chose neighbors to marry his sisters, the Florentine Lapo di Giovanni Niccolini expressed his own intention to marry outside the neighborhood, and in fact none of the men in his family married within the ward of Santa Croce but chose their wives from families across the city in the district of Santa Maria Novella (Christiane Klapisch-Zuber). Even in the *populo minuto* endogamy was less pronounced among families of some substance than among the true proletariat (Samuel K. Cohn).

When authors and moralists deliberately confused kinship, friendship, and neighborliness it shows that for many of them good relations were an ideal difficult to attain. This is why Carnival rituals portrayed the next-door neighbor as a key figure in domestic tranquillity and treated him to a mocking ride on ass-back when he faltered. They attempted to turn proximity into an obligation of friendship.

There was more to city life than the neighborhood, however. No one could spend his entire life with his neighbors, even if they were friends. Everyday needs would oblige the city-dweller of any means at all to frequent streets where luxury commodities were sold if he wanted to buy a good piece of meat at the central butchers' market or to sip a fine wine in a better tavern. The Parisian strolled across the Grand Pont, his counterpart in Arras or Siena went to the city square to see what was happening. Even if they did not frequent Sunday Mass regularly, everyone went now and then into a Franciscan or Dominican church to meditate, watch the priest elevate the consecrated host, or hear a sermon.

Work-related obligations sent the common people circulating around the city. The workplace and family life were not as inseparable as traditional imagery would have us think. In Florence, most craftsmen rented their shops and lived on another street, sometimes in another neighborhood. In Paris low-paid judicial functionaries and solicitors at the start of their careers could not afford to live near the Châtelet or the Palais de Justice. It is known that proletarians "with blue fingernails" of the Flemish textile centers often had to live in the *faubourgs* of the city since the city fathers wanted them outside the walls once their workday had ended.

Even if they had a shop a few steps from their bedroom, merchants and craftsmen had to frequent the central market hall or go to the center of the city to submit their work to the municipal inspectors, and others went from shop to shop with their team of journeymen and apprentices. Finally, the neediest went nearly every morning to the hiring squares and inevitably went from one temporary job to another without finding fixed employment. Instability was thus the common lot of a throng of modest to destitute city-dwellers, whether they lived in Paris, Arles, or Pisa. Poverty broke local solidarities among the working poor at just the point when they might have formed: it was an enemy of good feeling among neighbors.

*

One way to confront the dangers of city life with the aid of friends, to defend one's daily bread and one's life, and to assure a "good death," was to join a fraternal organization. The crises and calamities of the later Middle Ages made the need to associate even more imperious, which is why the confraternal movement transformed the structure of Western cities between 1250 and 1500.

It was long true that the only trades and guilds that were recognized were those of the powerful, whose association provided them with a security in shared responsibilities and mutual protection that they refused to others. Popular confraternal organizations seemed to such men dangerous hotbeds of revolt or heretical deviation, an attitude toward lesser tradespeople long held by members of the "trades" and "arts" once they had gained power. As late as 1400, in Florence as in Strasbourg, professional associations were subject to strict surveillance and were obliged to fit in with the clans and the guilds that gave the cities their sociopolitical organization.

Once they had achieved their conquest of the cities, the mendicant orders were quick to comprehend the advantages to be gained from these small consensual groups. They welcomed them and encouraged the creation of new associations, as did the municipal governments, who discovered their usefulness somewhat later and, except in times of social or political tension, gave them preferred treatment.

Still infrequent around 1300, fraternal organizations eventually proliferated. In the course of two centuries, more than one hundred organizations were founded in Avignon, close to sixty in Bordeaux, and seventy-five in Florence. Around 1500 in France, a mid-sized city would have thirty or more associations (as was the case in Arles, Aix, and Vienne), each with several dozen to several hundred members. A major part of the adult male population was enrolled in them—and young men had their own organizations in the "youth abbeys."

The movement was of course not exclusively urban. Still, fraternal organizations were never as numerous in rural areas, even when they drew their life largely from a city (as in Tuscany). In any event, the peasant had less choice than was available to the joiners' instincts of the city-dweller after 1450. Devotional or penitential, professional or civic, military or sporting, "joyous" youth groups or groups dedicated to hospital service, the fraternal associations covered the urban space with overlapping circles of membership and defined the city's structure. A head of household would belong to two, three, six, or ten such groups. Among the wealthy and the better-off, multiple affiliation had become the norm. Humbler folk were more economical (there were entry fees) but their attachment was all the stronger toward a group of their choice that might offer them human warmth and—who knows?—social promotion.

A fraternal organization gathered together men of different ethnic origins, almost always from several parts of the city, thus offering its members a broader social milieu. The professional brotherhoods even had a third order (masters and journeymen made up the first two) for kin and friends, who paid lower dues but had a right to the prayers of the group and to attend its banquets.

The newcomer could thus fraternize with people he did not know without risking his honor. They had solemnly sworn on the Holy Gospels at their admission, as he had, to respect the peace, to refrain from words or acts that might provoke discord or attract vengeance, human or divine. Maintaining harmony and mutual love was the principal task of the officers—bailiffs, priors, magistrates, captains, and so forth. They also weeded out drunkards, troublemakers, and the quarrelsome, arbitrated differences of opinion between members, and got rid of rebels. Joining the fraternal circle thus obliged a member to conduct himself according to freely accepted rules. This apprenticeship in social life was an essential part of the youth associations—"brigades" or "abbeys"—which were particularly numerous in the fifteenth century. They gathered together young men of varying ages and social status, and within them hierarchical, patriarchal, and ideological structures seem to have counted for somewhat less, as a journeyman could be elected prior or lieutenant. When the abbeys could temper the violence of their public manifestations they gave free rein to joy and spontaneity.

Fraternal organizations offered protection as well as peacekeeping. From a material point of view, their common cashbox allowed them to come to the aid of indigent brothers, making loans to them (reimbursable, of course, but at low rates of interest), or obtaining a hospital bed for them (sometimes in their own hospitals). In a society where recommendations and personal connections were of primary importance, such associations offered the support of new lines of patronage. They could mediate between the members and the powers that be with all the greater efficacy since the municipalization of assistance reserved the greater part of available resources for the city poor, leading to an urbanization of the economy of charity and transforming the hospitals into retirement homes monopolized by city-dwellers.

Solidarity operated vertically as well, and these associations counted on natural advocates in the courts of Paradise in their patron saints. Furthermore, if the masses and prayers sponsored by the brothers helped to save the souls of members who had passed to their reward, the dead in turn interceded for the living from Purgatory. This spiritual insurance system facilitated a "good death" with the aid of the bailiff and the brothers, who helped to ease the great voyage, visited the sick, exhorted to confession, escorted the dead (the coffin draped with the company's colors), and at times permitted burial in their chapel.

The chapels of fraternal organizations were for the most part in churches of the mendicant orders. In Florence in 1329 the churches that welcomed the *laudesi* were never strictly parish churches, and in Avignon in the fifteenth century fifty-five out of ninety-five of such groups' chapels were in the city's four mendicant churches. These centers for meetings and for prayer operated quite differently from the neighborhood solidarity groups, and the friars considered the entire city their parish; thus they worked to undermine the traditional ties of proximity and kinship.

Specialists in death and solicited for funerals by all during the fourteenth and fifteenth centuries, the mendicant orders, the Franciscans and the Dominicans, gave the city-dweller—and the member of a fraternal organization above all—a broader vision of the city. Thus they reinforced and paralleled the citywide vocation of the major fraternal organizations and youth abbeys, which paid little attention to internal divisions, and of the professional organizations, which claimed a monopoly of their trades and took possession of the entire city during their annual solemn processions.

The fraternal organizations did not limit their ambitions to giving their members a new sense of the city; they opened doors for them as well. Naturally, a member of modest status could not hope to sit on the municipal council. In the "good cities" of France as in the city-states of Italy and Germany, the municipal government designated the small segment of "the people" who in turn elected the government, which had little need of the people in the larger sense. Everywhere a refined system of co-option assured that an oligarchy of age, wealth, and social status remained in power.

Nonetheless, the fraternal organization was a commune in miniature. Its election rituals and governance reproduced municipal rituals (or inspired them, as in the west of France), and the arms of the "republic" graced their books, their candles, and their meeting rooms in a display of civic and religious piety, either commingled (in Italy and the Empire) or juxtaposed (in France). The fraternal organization was a microcosm of the city: the image illustrating the statutes of the Company of San Domenico in Florence (1478) shows "a hill supporting the mountain." The rapid turnover of officers (their terms of office ranged from several months to a year) and a systematic collegiality that ensured a broad distribution of authority gave a majority of the brothers an opportunity to play a leading role and to take responsibility. In short, the city "brother" was or could become a citizen within his organization.

Doubtless these organizations retained a sense of hierarchy and a sense of order. The officers were mature men, and in the professional organizations the journeymen hardly ever raised their voices. Still, the brotherhoods of the fifteenth century diffused a sense of equality. Their rituals, like those of the hansas, the guilds, the first communal associations, and the more or less clandestine understandings between journeymen accorded a place of honor to the mutual oath that engaged equals to work for the good of a collectivity organized according to a principle of the reduction of differences. The banquet was the main annual rite. Belonging to a fraternal organization primarily meant participating in the meal that followed a procession and a special Mass and to which the members devoted the better part of their funds. This was not a meal distributed to clients as in a patrician feast. It was shared among brothers, all of whom had paid their *droit d'écuelle* ("right to a bowl") and were seated side by side, often wearing a kerchief or a hood over their clothing or even a special robe as an expression of status and a symbol of equality.

In other words, within a city of hierarchical social divisions, the individual was led many times during his lifetime to swear an oath with equals or purported equals. Even if hierarchy soon reappeared, social dynamics encouraged the periodic and voluntary gathering together of people who for the moment believed in their equality. This is why urban upheavals were not always simple waves of emotion. Far from it. Before they rediscovered the joys of the primitive Christian community, the Age of Gold, or the millennium, many people (as with the common people in Damme in 1280 or the *ciompi* in Florence and Siena in the 1370s) wanted to live in a real but more just city. Above all, this is why upheavals were, in the last analysis, so infrequent. The city's sociability networks simultaneously integrated the individual into a territory, into chains of nonegalitarian solidarity, and into associations among equals. Such connections masked primordial contradictions, tempered clashes, contained great waves of unrest, and elaborated and diffused many values and styles of living—in short, they disseminated a culture that was becoming common to *mediocres* and humbler city folk. Thanks above all to their fraternal organizations, city-dwellers learned to live well before dying a good death.

The Ceremonial Citizen

Soon after 1550 the terms *urbanity* and *civility* made their appearance in language. First used in learned circles (Bishop Guillaume d'Auvergne knew them), the terms were soon widely used to designate an art of living proper to the urban world; a set of mental attitudes that over the course of two centuries had become distinct from "rusticity"—without, however, triumphing over traditional values. Even the Florentines had to import their ethos as well as their raw wool and silk. The refinements of urbanity were not the lot of all; the city never managed to polish the rough ways of all who came through its gates, but it did succeed in giving the majority "a vision of a unified and unifying world" (Bernard Chevalier). Civic rituals, sacred drama, and public preaching contributed to this vision, as did the fraternal organizations, but in reality urbanity came from ways of living that rigoristic preachers never ceased to denounce. Let us follow their example and examine the most obvious expressions of this "love of the world," for they are fundamental.

All authors of *fabliaux* and *chansons* insist on the burghers' passion for eating well, and they exaggerate only slightly. The city was privileged in its consumption of foodstuffs, both for the quantities consumed and the quality and variety of the products offered. Bread was of good quality. Just about everywhere bakers made three sorts of bread, which varied according to the type of flour used and how well it was sifted. The poor ate a brown loaf of mixed wheat and bran. The rich ate a kneaded bread made of pure wheat flour finely ground, but after 1400 white bread was accessible to workingmen. Black bread was used for trenchers and, when the meal was over, was given to animals to eat.

More importantly, beginning in the fourteenth century, bread represented a decreasing portion of the food budget (about 30 percent).

In bourgeois circles in Tuscany the man who ate bread with his spaghetti was laughed at. People no longer dreamed about the indispensable staple but about meat and fish, for city-dwellers were decidedly carnivores, as much by necessity as by taste, since workers in the textile industry required a diet high in calories. An inhabitant of Frankfurt on the Oder ate more than 100 kg (220 lbs) of butcher's meat per year in the early fourteenth century, and in the fifteenth century the citizen of Carpentras, with his 26 kg (57 lbs) of meat per year, still ate a good deal more meat than his descendant in the nineteenth century. Although the livestock often came from far away, the animals were fattened in fields close to the city rented by the butchers. Since peasants kept their animals until they were old, meat was of lower quality in the country, where, what is more, butcher shops were open only irregularly. The distribution of ocean and freshwater fish, eaten during the 160 fast days in the year, was even more unequal, since fish was in abundant supply in cities and unknown in the village.

It goes without saying that socio-alimentary levels varied. If the day worker was not fed on the job or at the master's table (like the journeyman or the apprentice), he had to be satisfied with bread, onions, and cheese at noon, and the evening meal, like the more modest craftsman's, was a soup containing a piece of well-boiled meat, since roasts appeared only on feast days. Among the wealthy, boiled and roast meats were eaten twice daily, flanked by meat pies and accompanied by piquant sauces (a sign of affluence, since spices were too costly for the common people). During Lent, a highly prized fish—trout, eel, lamprey, or sturgeon—contributed to the elegance of a meal, as did a capon or a leg of lamb on other days.

Burghers paid a good deal of attention to their table, since family honor was involved, but there were also professional cooks. All cities had their pastry cooks, their *rôtisseurs,* their innkeepers, and their renowned chefs who on occasion prepared dinners for private clients, wedding meals, and the banquets of fraternal organizations. A city could become famous for its cuisine: the *échevins* of the city council of Amiens made weekly inspection tours to make sure that the pastry cooks of their city sold "good meats, good cooking, and good meat pasties" and that the cream custards of the famous Gilles Castel were up to standard. Franco Sacchetti seldom lingers over the description of the taste of dishes (unlike the Sienese, Gentile Sermini), but could vie with the best once he got started telling a tale. The authors of the *fabliaux* were not mistaken: if the city-dweller did not eat at the tavern, he was at his best at a well-laid table at home or, on occasion, in female company at the baths.

*

In Sacchetti's day the city fathers considered prostitutes necessary: they helped to channel violence, thus protecting the honor of virgins and wives, and, equally important, they checked *le fol amour*—love's folly. It was thought that if sexual relations were commonplace it would reduce the errant affections that threatened family authority.

At first, prostitutes—*meretrices*—were subject to arbitrary justice and fornication was held a major sin. The *fabliaux* do not grant a *fille joyeuse* the right to found a family (Marie-Thérèse Lorcin), and in the thirteenth and fourteenth centuries the bordellos still closed at night during Lent and few cities administered public prostitution. After 1350 constraints began to relax, the wearing of distinctive signs became discreet or totally disappeared, and—above all—municipal governments institutionalized prostitution. About 1400 in Venice and Florence, a bit later in French cities, the authorities included prostitution among their civic values and made it an instrument of public well-being. And they acted with the assent of the clergy.

After the mid-thirteenth century, some more enlightened theologians considerably attenuated the gravity of the sin of simple fornication, and after 1300 the authors of treatises or confessors' manuals seem to place it almost with the venial sins. When they disputed the validity of a public prostitute's earnings, the quality of her work, and her price, churchmen introduced an element of measure and rationality into venal abandon. At the turn of the fifteenth century, the newer ideas won over the dominant orthodoxy and moralists taught that pleasures of the flesh were natural and should be part of marriage, but as moralists they also recommended late marriage based on careful reflection after asking the advice of kin. They denounced "crimes against nature" in no uncertain terms, and in practice they permitted bachelors fornication with *meretrices,* on the condition that they mend their ways with age and marriage.

It is no wonder, then, that Bernardino of Siena said not a word about the public brothels that had recently opened or been enlarged in Siena and Florence, or that Friar Richard in Paris did not speak about prostitution. Let the young men go gaily, alone or in groups with their "abbot" leading the way, to the city's "Good Street." Fathers gave their sons money for their sexual pleasures and for wine.

A flourishing prostitution organized primarily for young men cannot be explained by that clientele alone, however. Married men of the humbler sort went to the city house, and the wealthier had the baths, which offered the combined pleasures of the bath, the table, and the bed. The customs of trade associations, songs, costume, pantomimes and mummers' plays, and miniatures all display the same untroubled, bawdy sensuality.

Jacques Le Goff has demonstrated the triumph of Purgatory on the doctrinal level at the turn of the thirteenth century. This intermediate place between Heaven and Hell represented hope for a number of sinners who, either because of the gravity of their fault or simply because of their social function, had had little chance of escaping Hell. Henceforth, deathbed contrition gave entry to a place of suffering but of hope. To die a good death, thus to be saved through Purgatory, authorized living well. The organization of this passage required money, but denser networks of spiritual assistance and the "democratization" of masses made a good death accessible.

The new structure of the otherworld and the mechanisms of fraternal sociability thus fortified city-dwellers in their life-style. They were the rewards of the hard work that the teams of mendicant preachers exalted, along with the active life and a just distribution of wealth. A few preachers of the apocalypse ranted against the new Babylons and had set off pyres to burn vanities, but when the flames died down their censure was forgotten and merchants and craftsmen returned to their activities and their pleasures without shame.

*

As late as the mid-twelfth century, a few merchants in a troubled city, fearing for their salvation, would still abandon this world's goods and attempt to redeem themselves amid the poor. The accusation of usury weighed heavily on those who had money; the suspicion of venality threatened law practitioners and professors; many crafts and trades were looked down upon. For those who held to a traditional morality, money was an instrument of the Devil, the city was the daughter of Cain, and labor was simple penance. Fifty years later this morality was completely shattered.

Homobonus, a Cremona merchant, had always aided the poor, but he never stopped working and earning money. He was canonized as a merchant not long after 1200 and a statue of him was soon put up near that of the Virgin at the main entrance to the city's cathedral. In 1261, the archbishop of Pisa declared St. Francis the patron saint of merchants.

Cremona also had a craftsman saint—a goldsmith—who made with his own hands the great silver cross erected in the cathedral.

Other less illustrious workingmen offered a portion of their labor to God and had their patron saints and the tools of their trade represented in the stained-glass windows of the churches and on the altarpieces of their confraternal chapels. From the thirteenth century on, a long iconographic procession of urban trades unfolds in sacred buildings and on civic monuments, as on the portals of the basilica of San Marco in Venice, at the base of the campanile of Florence's Duomo, and in the communal palace in Siena. The patron saint of each profession was portrayed in the setting of the workshop, master works were put on display by the cathedral doors, and finished pieces were carried in procession for all to see. Merchants, carpenters, and masons appeared in secular and sacred drama using the language and imitating the gestures of their trades.

Working people entered into the theologians' reflections (most particularly in Paris in the group around Peter the Cantor) when it came to justifying all professions that worked for the common good. Thus a number of craftsmen whose activities had formerly been considered degrading found their place in the city, while a moral theology was elaborated to adapt to the difficulties and dangers of every category and profession. Doubtless the justifying ethic was above all that of the dominant groups, and men of the "mechanical arts" who worked with the sweat of their brow were scorned, first by the wealthy, then by the intellectuals: "I do not work with my hands," Rutebeuf exclaims. But, more important, labor was no longer an obstruction to salvation, and craftsmen and merchants no longer need doubt their dignity or their social utility. Within the city, the most important moral frontier separated those who labored for the *respublica* and those who did not. Cardinal Robert de Courçon proposed to bar men of leisure from city government; Dante reserved the most ignominious place in the otherworld for "those sad souls who lived a life . . . with no blame and no praise" (trans. Musa); François Garin of Lyon exalted the active life; Paolo da Certaldo declared, "It is better to act in vain that be idle in vain." Why let capital lie idle? No treasure slumbered in the city: even sacred objects were put to work, and the bodies of the saints, which usually nestled in the shadows of the crypt, came out of the churches at times of danger or of festivity and took part in the defense of the city just as much as its walls.

This explains the clergy's vilification of usurers (idle men who got fat earning money while they slept). It explains the hostility that all the *mediocres* shared toward the old orders of society, the reluctance of the French bourgeoisie of the fifteenth century to have their daughters devote their lives to virginity and prayer, the increasingly open mistrust of begging, especially when poverty was voluntary, the preference, even after attaining wealth, for standing apart from the nobles by remaining in commerce or banking or by taking public office, and, finally, an interest in not wasting a wealth that by then only fools and millenarians condemned.

In 1260 in Augsburg Albertus Magnus praised the city, stable and powerful thanks to the wealthy, who alone assured its defense in times of crisis and furnished arms and rations to the workers, who otherwise would not survive. All means of acquiring wealth were not acceptable, of course, but wealth and the wealthy were glorified, while people slowly acquired a better conscience regarding the means to earning wealth. With the aid of casuistical arguments of risk and loss, many ended up believing (as in Florence around 1340) that usury was only a venial sin. "It is a fine thing and a great science to know how to earn money," Paolo da Certaldo taught. It was also a grace of God, added the Dominican Giovanni Dominici not long before 1400. Not only was wealth legitimate, it facilitated self-realization, virtue, salvation. Popular preachers condemned only its excesses, burned women's tall conical headgear, and denounced luxurious clothing. However, they portrayed the apostles as honest craftsmen with a bourgeois life-style and the Virgin as a lady receiving her friends in an opulently furnished house.

The city-dweller thus did not need to hide his wealth. It could be figured in minute detail on the altar painting offered to the donor's saintly protector, displayed on the façade of his house, and flaunted in the city. Wealth could at times be wiped out by the poor in revolt, but in normal times it was ritualized and portrayed during holidays, as in the public display of St. John's Day in Florence, the feast day of Santa Maria Formosa in Venice, and Carnival parades or May processions in Metz. Wealth was a civic virtue as much as a personal virtue, so it was not to be wasted. It was good to show one's generosity, but with measure. All city-dwellers learned to put order into their earnings, their expenditures, their time, their words, and their acts. Good upbringing advised it; instruction often made it possible.

"Have your sons learn at school with a master who knows [his material] well," François Garin recommended. His aim was not to prepare the young to read romances or histories that would lead them into dreaming—worse, into love—but to learn how to "number" and to "know and understand sooner the counting of gold and moneys." Garin's concern was just as practical as that of twelfth-century merchants, but in his time it had revolutionary results, for such preoccupations resulted, as Henri Pirenne pointed out in 1929, in the appearance of the first lay schools in the West since classical antiquity. Not that clerical schools had not been marked by the city's needs: in Laon there is a manuscript of the twelfth century containing eighty practical problems concerning moneys and measures. It was not the schools' principal concern, however. Students in clerical schools did a good deal of singing and Latin was spoken.

Private or municipal elementary schools well-adapted to the needs of merchants' and craftsmen's sons arose everywhere (first in Flanders and in Italy), complemented, at least in the metropolises, by technical or "abacus" schools. School systems were often inadequate during the entire Middle Ages, however. They were vulnerable to pressures from the church, to competition from preceptors, to the instability of the schoolmasters, and to the irregular frequentation of students who alternated between the shop and the school, even in Florence. These deficiencies should not prevent us from seeing an essential fact, however: the burgher had the opportunity to give his sons enough instruction (in school, at home, or with a notary) to conduct private business or, when the occasion arose, to participate in public affairs. What proportion of the city population had access to the world of the written word? We will perhaps never know. Still, schooling gave urban society its unique character and immense powers, and it marked all cultural and festive occasions. More concretely, the urban schools adopted the vernacular, proposed practical reading matter, and taught a rapid and legible hand that cared little for elegance (the *scrittura mercantesca* diffused in Tuscan cities at the beginning of the fourteenth century gives testimony to this, as do notarial records). At times the schools proposed courses in modern languages (as in Bruges around 1370), but above all they taught students to "number." Errors are rare in private or municipal financial records, and although it rarely reached the virtuosity achieved in Venice and Tuscany, manipulation of figures was mastered throughout Europe.

The chroniclers' passion for counting—counting everything—reflects this familiarity with figures, and a poetics of numbers that was at first a part of this passion slowly gave way to a preoccupation with precision, intensified by the calamities of the fourteenth century. The demand for precision appears in equal measure in the evaluation of a city's resources and in family chronicles (the Florentine Lapo di Giovanni Niccolini gives an exact count—sixty-seven years, two months, twenty-six days—of the time that his mother had lived in the house of her husband's lineage). The training in numbers that permeated the mind of city-dwellers transformed their rites of social control and justice just as much as their vision of the otherworld and religious practice did. Everything was *ratio* in a merchant city: after totting up his sums and making his logical deductions, the townsperson was expected to act "rationally." "Reason," however—the ability to understand the past, analyze the present, and predict the future—also implied an order of the universe, thus a measurement of time.

*

"Campane dicuntur a rusticis qui habitant in campo qui nesciunt judicare horas nisi per campanas" (They are called bells by the peasants who live in the field and who are unable to judge the hours except by means of the bells) declared John Garland in the early thirteenth century. This does not mean that city-dwellers of the time were already accustomed to mechanical clocks and automatons, but they had had their own bells for at least two generations. Hung at the highest point of a church or a belfry, their tolling punctuated the workday, signaled the opening and closing of the gates, ordered curfew, or called the citizenry to council. In short, they gave a rhythm to a secular, municipal time.

After 1300, bells served only to reinforce clocks, whose revolving face, then moving hands indicated the ongoing hours, and they rang them out with their carillons or the blows struck by mechanical figures. As for astronomical clocks, such marvels dictated the most favorable moment for praying to the saints, starting off on a voyage, or organizing a city-wide procession. Despite their uncertain accuracy, their winding down, and negligence on the part of the "governor" charged with their maintenance—and despite the specificity of individual urban time-schemes—the clock was fundamental to collective life. Thanks to mechanical clocks the entrepreneur could keep track of hours worked (which his workmen were quick to contest), and clerics and princes saw them as a means of disciplining the throng. "The machine that so justly divides the twelve hours of the day teaches observance of justice and the laws" proclaims an inscription, written soon after 1500, over the clock of the Palais de la Cité in Paris; in 1481 the canons of the city church of Saint Nizier in Lyons, who wanted a clock, declared to the consuls of the city that "if such a clock were made, more merchants would come to the fairs, the citizens would be greatly consoled, joyful and happy, and would want to live a more orderly life." The clock permitted better regulation of the hours for meals, prayer, and leisure, and it enabled the faithful to relive the hours of the Passion more accurately. As a measure for actions and behavior, it was an important part of *ratio* in the city.

*

"Honesty" in mores, a fundamental value of urban living, was immediately revealed by one's attitudes and acts, and all the authors of songs or praises of the city insist on the "civility" of their fellow city-dwellers. In *Guillaume de Dole* the *citains* of Mainz are of a perfect courtesy; according to Bonvesin, the women of Milan had a regal bearing; for Opicinus, all the citizens of Pavia "show themselves to be affable and familiar in their relations with one another; sociable, polite, they rise when someone enters into a room." Beggars and paupers, always portrayed as disorderly, defined the inverse of urban codes of "honesty."

The city was an extraordinary school of behavior in this regard. We must not exaggerate, however: in manners as in other domains, everyone spoke two languages. Each socio-professional group had its own code (formalism existed in all milieus) as well as adopting the common language. As the exemplary civility of the great filtered down the social scale it either became diluted, mixing with the standards of behavior proper to each group, or was juxtaposed to those standards. Family upbringing was of course fundamental in this process, as all contemporary authors of personal journals insist. Still, confrères, preachers, actors in mystery plays, image-makers, and municipalities had a role to play in the disciplining of the body. Control did not come only from festive games or from patricians dancing the *carole*, but also from constraints in the workplace, from the police, from the market hall, and from the town square.

"Civility" was not simple imitation. The acquisition of a code of behavior was nowhere more valuable than in the city. One's honor and on occasion one's life could be at stake. It was dangerous to indulge in unacceptable behavior on consecrated ground, to express one's sorrow too noisily in plague times, or to attack the good name of one's confrères in a procession. Moreover, sincerity did not exist without formalism, nor religion without "civility." *Savoir-vivre* did not only concern the living, but determined one's attitude toward the saints and toward God. Thus God was at the mercy of the behavior of the faithful, of their manners (Francesco da Barberino compares people who fail to display good manners to their fellow dinner guests with people who bother others during Communion), and of their ways of honoring the powerful (Richard C. Trexler).

The city-dweller thus learned to eat with moderation and without excessive noise, to share his dishes, to enter a church and approach the altar circumspectly, to address an unknown person according to his rank, to modulate his voice when he prayed, to control expressions of pain and sorrow, and to behave appropriately before a holy image, in a market hall, or on the town square. Above all, he learned how to express friendship, to express his sentiments or his love, to show courtesy. Urban standards of courtesy were different from those of the courts, however. Patricians preferred refinement, but the elite of Metz knew how to lace their jousts with burlesque episodes or dance to the bagpipe with an earthiness that came right from the city streets. Elsewhere in society, there was a form of courtesy that was even more necessary, for marriage, as has been pointed out, often involved individual ambitions and personal choice. Preconjugal acquaintance permitted the husband-to-be to gauge the moral or physical qualities of a possible bride, and visits, serenades, and dances enabled the couple to get to know one another better.

"Joyous brotherhoods" and other associations contributed to the ritualization of social relations, purging them of violence and dramatizing manners and speech. They succeeded only partially, and the "courtesy" of the city workingmen was a mixture of brutality and consideration. On occasion it resulted in shared pleasures, but love, at the end of the fifteenth century, came to be considered a disease worse than smallpox; it was an urban malady propagated by "honest courtesans."

*

Measure, order, courtesy: city-dwellers adhered slowly and in unequal measure to these standards of urbanity, thanks to rituals that forced them to live in peace, to dominate their violence or their fear, to free themselves from their follies, and to express their loyalties and their obedience.

Laughter and contestation counterbalanced the gravity of civic processions. In December, during Carnival, or in May, folly and gravity walked hand in hand in periods set aside for festivities that appeared free, but in which the participants' spontaneity was channeled by their membership in fraternal organizations. The townsman could give free rein to his high spirits several times during the year, however. If he was young he could dizzy himself with celebration, gesticulate under cover of a foolscap with his companions, the town musicians, and girl-chasers; he could laugh with the master fool, jester's bauble in hand, who declaimed choice couplets and absurd satirical poems drawing on public affairs, the schools, or the law courts;

he could render burlesque justice in which social values were turned upside down; under the shadow of an effigy of Goodman Carnival he could lose himself in the cacophony of countermusic and use his sovereign powers of satirical contestation of power and hypocrisy.

He might on occasion vie with a rival neighborhood for possession of a bridge at Venice or control of the Rhône at Beaucaire, but in an atmosphere of joy and amid all the citizenry. He might combine folly and epic dreams by donning the livery of the archers, who invented a wild and forested space for themselves just outside the city walls, where they indulged in the pleasures of the hunt and in shooting matches (like the young men riding behind their king evoked by Galbert de Bruges or, in a later period, the yeomen/youngmen of the cities and the towns of England behind Robin Hood, the May King). After such contests, the archer companies would parade in good order and feast on their hard-won reward in the company of victims forced to drink the wine that they had paid for.

Also in ritual manner, the city-dweller, young or old, could be moved and dazed listening to a holy man and miracle worker in the public squares who could make the crowd laugh or cry for hours at a time (like the actors in mystery plays), mixing bawdy stories and terrifying descriptions, denouncing the predators of the people, debauched clerics, and female wiles—but also teaching obedience to the father, the master, and the city magistrates.

These regenerative or purifying rites favored unanimity. They were an integral part of a civic religion whose essential liturgies took place on the main streets, which led to a ceremonial gate, the city square, or the seat of the municipal government.

The city fathers soon understood that a politics of prestige constituted an excellent means to domination. In Flanders and the Artois the most powerful guilds built proud market halls flanked by belfries. In Italy after the victory of the people and in Alsace after that of the trade organizations new palaces to welcome the new communal institutions were built (in Italy, higher than the nobles' towers) to proclaim the glory of the city over vast and slowly filled spaces. Such efforts came much later in the "good cities" of France, where often the bell tower of a collegiate church served cities with no municipal belfry and a church of the mendicant orders made do as an assembly hall.

Although civic monuments were by no means always situated in the topographical center of the city, they formed the heart of a social, historical, or sacred space that ceremonial and dramatic practice helped to magnify. The street that led from the gate to the cathedral or the city palace may have been sinuous, but thanks to magnificent decorations it became a grandiose artery when every loggia, entry, and balcony of the palaces along the way transformed it into a majestic scene of collective power.

Processions and corteges formed or ended in these streets. Dramatic, narrative, or symbolic elements might be grafted onto it, but the procession constituted the essential feature of civic celebration. Behind the crosses they carried and under the protection of the saints, the male citizen body displayed its strength to the onlookers. The cortege, like a long narrative silhouette, clearly expressed political rules that only much later were formulated in theoretical writings. Processions made the order of dignities immediately comprehensible to the mass of spectators. If conflicts of precedence arose at times, they were expressed within the ceremonial system, not outside it. No Venetian Sensa, the blessing of the Adriatic on the Feast of the Ascension; no Florentine San Giovanni in celebration of the city's patron saint; no Schwoertag in Strasbourg was the occasion for disorder or revolt. The citizens knew that their periodical ceremonial gatherings (thirteen general processions annually in Bruges, sixteen ducal processions a year in Venice, several in even the smallest towns, in particular the Corpus Christi procession that had become a civic celebration everywhere) were indispensable to the maintenance of community. The liturgical context in which the processions were formed sanctified the hierarchic arrangement in which all took their places behind the banners in an order established by municipal decree. The cortege ostensibly expressed the rallying of territorial powers and the authority of the fraternal organization around the city government. It ignored old intra-urban boundaries and, in the tableaux vivants that punctuated it or were scattered through the time schedule of the festivities a repertory of popular traditions mingled with inventions of the cultivated elites.

As it floats and its "triumphs" showed, the procession was an efficacious way to recall that citizens united behind their magistrates and their crosses had put an end to an epidemic, had discouraged an enemy, had effected a victory. In other words, the procession, by its order, its symbolic "stations," the hymns it raised, and the decor that framed it, illustrated the ideational forces of urban theology. It persuaded the participants that the city was indeed, according to Guillaume d'Auvergne's metaphor, an edifice common to free and united citizens living peaceably in a marvelous setting. As civic history taught, the city, a place of physical and social harmony, triumphed in the end over disorders and enemies. It crushed monsters (as the legends told); it propagated peace (as the frescoes of the communal palace showed). More ancient than Rome, at times shattered but always reconstructed, the city was reborn, steadfast thanks to its tutelary powers, to its own virtue, and to the valor of its inhabitants. The city was portrayed as beautiful, holy, and courteous in the living form of pantomimes or in immobile form, sculpted in stone, in Pisa and, two centuries later, in Toulouse.

All evidence indicates that city "triumphs" remained until the sixteenth century efficacious instruments for enlisting popular support for civic values. Because periods of public celebration were also times of pardon, the banished had their share in the largesse, and festive princes distributed tokens that gave a right to alms. The city councils knew how to reward the crowd: wine flowed in profusion and the poor had their part (when they had not been thrown out of town before such pleasures began) in an urban setting transformed by flowers strewn on the streets, canopies, and hangings in every window and door.

*

Let us leave the medieval city-dweller with this festive image. Somewhere in urban Europe in the 1500s a man, a craftsman perhaps, contemplates men marching with the other citizens in the thick of the procession, behind the royal officials or the prince's men—men whose thoughts and ambitions were nevertheless far from the city. Some of these men lived in their manor houses rather than within the city walls; other had built sumptuous city houses that turned their backs to the street, isolating themselves in their magnificence and no longer treating their peers with the same familiarity as their forebears.

But this same observer mocks the countrymen's crosses when they converge on the cathedral. He plays the shepherd in his country house, but he is intransigent toward his herdsmen or toward rustics recently arrived in the city. He acts just as "honorable men" had acted toward him thirty years before. Now he is well established, even though modestly. He eats his fill, no longer fears poverty, thanks to his circle of friends and confreres, stands in awe of God but no longer dreads death (his dues are fully paid), and he lives in peace behind the city walls. He may be the most prominent man in his urban village, and he cares little if the great raise their voices or if paupers are chased out of the city one fine morning because an epidemic threatens. Thirty years of urban life and of constraints well handled have left him with a clear conscience, and he believes in the city. He has his share of the common good, the result of four centuries of successes. This is his strength and that of his merchant neighbors. It launched their sons on the highways of the world.

BIBLIOGRAPHY

Ariès, Philippe, and Georges Duby, eds. *Histoire de la vie privée.* 5 vols. (Paris: Editions du Seuil, 1985–87). Vol. 2, Georges Duby, ed. *De l'Europe féodale à la Renaissance* [*A History of Private Life,* 3 vols. (Cambridge: Belknap Press, 1987–89). Vol. 2, *Revelations of the Medieval World*].

Burguière, André, Christiane Klapisch-Zuber, Martine Segalen, Françoise Zonabend. *Histoire de la famille.* 2 vols. (Paris: Armand Colin, 1986).

Chevalier, Bernard. *Les bonnes villes de France du XIVe au XVIe siècle* (Paris: Aubier Montaigne, 1982).

Cohn, Samuel Kline, Jr. *The Laboring Classes in Renaissance Florence* (New York: Academic Press, 1980).

Duby, Georges, ed. *Histoire de la France urbaine.* 5 vols. (Paris: Le Seuil, 1980–85). Vol. 2, Jacques Le Goff, ed. *La ville médiévale des Carolingiens à la Renaissance.*

Le Goff, Jacques. *Pour un autre Moyen age: Temps, travail et culture en Occident* (Paris: Gallimard, 1977) [*Time, Work and Culture in the Middle Ages.* Trans. Arthur Goldhammer (Chicago: University of Chicago Press, 1980].

———. *L'Imaginaire médiévale* (Paris: Gallimard, 1985) [The Medieval Imagination. Trans. Arthur Goldhammer (Chicago: University of Chicago Press, 1985)].

———. *La Bourse et la vie. Economie et religion au Moyen age.* (Paris: Hachette, 1986) [*Your Money or Your Life: Economy and Religion in the Middle Ages.* Trans. Patricia Ranum (New York: Zone Books, 1988)].

Little, Lester K. *Religious Poverty and the Profit Economy in Medieval Europe* (Ithaca: Cornell University Press, 1978).

Muir, Edward. *Civic Ritual in Renaissance Venice* (Princeton: Princeton University Press, 1981).

Rossiaud, Jacques. *La prostituzione nel medioevo* (Rome and Bari: Laterza, 1984) [*Medieval Prostitution.* Trans. Lydia G. Cochrane (Oxford: Basil Blackwell, 1988)].

Ruggiero, Guido. *The Boundaries of Eros: Sex, Crime and Sexuality in Renaissance Venice* (New York: Oxford University Press, 1985).

Trexler, Richard C. *Public Life in Renaissance Florence* (New York: Academic Press, 1980).

Weissman, Ronald F. E. *Ritual Brotherhood in Renaissance Florence* (New York: Academic Press, 1982).

SUGGESTED READINGS

William M. Bowsky, *A Medieval Italian Commune: Siena Under the Nine, 1287–1355* (Berkeley: University of California Press, 1981).

Christopher N. L. Brooke and Gillian Keir, *London, 800–1216: The Shaping of a City* (Berkeley: University of California Press, 1975).

Richard A. Goldthwaite, *The Building of Renaissance Florence: An Economic and Social History* (Baltimore: John Hopkins University Press, 1980).

J. K. Hyde, *Padua in the Age of Dante* (Manchester: Manchester University Press, 1966).

———, *Society and Politics in Medieval Italy: The Evolution of the Civil Life, 1000–1350* (New York: St. Martin's, 1973).

D. V. Kent and F. W. Kent, *Neighbours and Neighbourhood in Renaissance Florence* (Locust Valley: J. J. Augustin, 1982).

Frederic C. Lane, *Venice: A Maritime Republic* (Baltimore: Johns Hopkins University Press, 1973).

Lauro Martines, *Power and Imagination: City-States in Renaissance Italy* (New York: Knopf, 1979).

Lauro Martines, ed., *Violence and Disorder in Italian Cities, 1200–1500* (Berkeley: University of California Press, 1972).

John H. Mundy, *Liberty and Political Power in Toulouse, 1050–1230* (New York: Columbia University Press, 1954).

David Nicholas, *The Metamorphosis of a Medieval City: Ghent in the Age of the Arteveldes, 1302–1390* (Lincoln: University of Nebraska Press, 1987).

Iris Origo, *The World of San Bernardino* (New York: Harcourt, Brace and World, 1962).

Leah L. Otis, *Prostitution in Medieval Society: The History of an Urban Institution in Languedoc* (Chicago: University of Chicago Press, 1987).

Susan Reynolds, *An Introduction to the History of English Medieval Towns* (Oxford: Clarendon Press, 1977).

Dennis Romano, *Patricians and Popolani: The Social Foundations of the Venetian Renaissance State* (Baltimore: Johns Hopkins University Press, 1987).

Daniel P. Waley, *The Italian City-Republics* (New York: McGraw-Hill, 1969).

FIVE

The Intellectual

Mariateresa Fumagalli Beonio
Brocchieri

ANYONE BORN BETWEEN THE YEARS 1000 AND 1400 WOULD HAVE UNDERSTOOD THE TERMS "WOMAN" (*MULIER*), "KNIGHT" (*MILES*), "city-dweller" (*urbanus*), "merchant" (*mercator*), "poor man" (*pauper*). He would have not understood the meaning of the word "intellectual" (*intellectualis*) attributed to a person. For anyone who had frequented the schools, man was to some extent rational (*animal rationale* and, alas, *mortale*), but this was a definition that had come down from Aristotle covering the entire human species. The adjective "intellectual" accompanied various nouns with some variety in meaning. "Intellectual substance" (opposed to "material substance") was the mind or the soul; "intellectual knowledge" (opposed to "knowledge of the senses") was the sort of knowing that reached beyond the instrument of the senses to grasp forms. The Aristotelians also spoke of "intellectual pleasure" (reserved to the elect and quite distinct from "sensual pleasure") and "intellectual virtue" (different from "moral virtue") following the time-honored analysis of the *Nicomachean Ethics*.

Does this preamble have a meaningful connection with the theme of "the intellectual in the Middle Ages"? Most certainly. The modern term "intellectual," which indicates a category of person rather than a quality, entered into use very recently—in late nineteenth-century France with the *Manifesto des intellectuels*, where it designated a group of writers proclaiming their solidarity with Zola in connection with the Dreyfus affair. This recent term lends itself splendidly to our purpose, however, which is to delineate a category of men who "worked with words and with the mind" during the Middle Ages; men who did not live on revenues from land nor were constrained to "work with their hands" and who were conscious (in varying measure) of being different in this from the other categories of humankind.

A further reason for adapting the term "intellectual" to a group of medieval men lies also in a specific if implicit meaning of the adjective form of the word, used by contemporaries in connection with virtue, knowledge, and pleasure. In all the contexts cited, in fact, "intellectual" signified something held to be more valuable and elevated than its contrary and indicated something indisputably positive. The self-esteem of medieval intellectuals and their judgment of themselves had a common denominator: their profession and their activities were, in their eyes, more prestigious (a quality often contested by others) than other professions and activities. From our modern point of view, then, it seems fully legitimate to speak of the "medieval intellectual." Analysis of the typology should offer further confirmation of this.

Medieval men, of course, used other terms to indicate the persons we call intellectuals. It is interesting to recall them, as they give a first indication of different types of intellectuals. "Master" and "professor" referred to the same "substance": persons who taught after having studied. It is curious, however, that while *magister* always indicated a quality of moral superiority and indisputable dignity, *professor* often bore a trace of irony directed at the arrogance and presumption of some "who trust too much in their knowledge." We find this negative connotation in Abelard, for example, when he speaks of "professors of dialectics" and in John of Salisbury's ironical perplexity at their "verbosity."

Eruditus and *doctus*, used nominatively, were more neutral terms, indicating someone who had studied and accumulated knowledge from books. The term "philosopher" was in a certain sense less meaningful: the slight suspicion of secularity it conveyed in contradistinction to someone who studied the *pagina sacra* made it less frequently used. "Philosophers" were still understood to be the ancient philosophers, even if some men quite consciously made the term their own—Abelard, for example, who declared himself a "philosopher of the world" and on another occasion "philosopher of God," or Siger of Brabant and his fellow Averroists, who called themselves philosophers with a quite precise meaning in mind. Some of these learned men (such as Bradwardine in the fourteenth century) considered themselves *viri scientifici;* many declared themselves *speculativi,* dedicated to the highest human activity according to the Platonic and Aristotelian vision. All felt themselves to be and were indeed called *litterati*.

Litterati was the broadest category, hence the least precise. All who knew how to read and write were *litterati,* and they dominated the world of discourse, oral or written in sermons, lessons, and treatises. In those centuries they made up an extremely small minority in comparison with the vast group of the illiterate (also called *idioti, simplices,* or *rudes*). "Illiterate" was also a term of broad meaning, including those who could neither read nor write (the modern meaning of the term), but also those who did not know Latin, the "language" par excellence, who knew it imperfectly, like English lords in the fourteenth century, or were unable to write it but understood something of it.

One thing is certain: the "lettered" man was almost always a cleric—especially in the first two centuries after the year 1000. In practice the two terms coincided. Isidore of Seville (seventh century) gave a precise definition but a vague delimitation of the term: "The cleric is one who dedicates himself to the religious life and searches for moral perfection." When we pass to the centuries after the year 1000, however, we find Jacobus de Viterbo declaring (in the 1200s): "sometimes any lettered person is improperly called a cleric for the fact that clerics must be lettered." A century later, Konrad von Megenberg, describing the scholastic system, calls all schoolmen "clerics" without distinguishing the level of studies or the discipline taught. In spite of these variations in meaning—or, better, thanks to the singular process of secularization of the figure in question—clerics emerge as a discernible group and a force in society guiding both organization and dissent during those centuries.

It may be useful to distinguish between a strong and a weak sense of the term "intellectual" by describing two types, between which there was of course a wide range of activities that could well be called intellectual. I will call a "strong intellectual" a man who not only was involved in intellectual activities but also in transmitting his capacities for investigation, along with his instruments for inquiry, his course of development, and well-defined goals. It is natural that he was above all a teacher—a *magister*—in the schools of the time. We can see a weaker sense of "intellectual," on the other hand, when the term is applied to men who used their intelligence and the spoken or written word, but who changed their roles (even often) and the context of their activities in a way that at times reveals a certain indifference to the purpose of their labors. These men were diplomats, men in the curia, bishops, "free-lance" writers, and tutors, like John of Salisbury and Vincent of Beauvais. In such men we sense a lesser awareness of their "diversity," connected, it seems to me, to their not being teachers interested in transmitting their working tools to their disciples (just as craftsmen did in their workshops). But since we already have introduced the intellectual in the full and the strong sense of the word into this examination and in a context that is, quite rightly, clearly identifiable—the city and the school—it seems useful to begin our story with Europe after the year 1000 and with its great transformation.

*

The revival of city life, an inverse movement to the decline that characterized the period beginning in the third century of the Common Era, was undeniably a slow phenomenon, but in the twelfth century it had taken on a clear enough profile to be evident not only to modern historians, who look from afar, but also to men of the time, who noticed it and saluted it, doubtless with a variety of sentiments (satisfaction, pride, horror), but who always took it as an unequivocal fact.

In the Europe of the eleventh century, urban centers were still few and relatively unpopulated, and cultural initiative remained in the hands of the abbeys and the few cathedrals able to organize and supervise a teaching program. The parallel careers of Lanfranc of Pavia and the great Anselm of Canterbury, born in Aosta, can serve as examples for this period of few and scattered intellectual centers. Lanfranc, who was born soon after the year 1000, studied law and the liberal arts in Bologna and founded a school in France at Avranches. After he entered the monastery of Bec in Normandy, he directed its school, which became increasingly famous in the cultural world of the time (it was here that the great canonist Yves de Chartres studied). In 1070 he became archbishop of Canterbury, and he died in that city twenty years later. This typically medieval career seems odd to our modern eyes: it was an international career that took Lanfranc to regions of quite different spoken languages in an age in which communications were neither easy nor frequent. Nonetheless, we can suppose that the Latin language and monastic institutions offered a comforting uniformity of context essential for an intellectual who was also an organizer.

Lanfranc tells us, "When the object of the dispute can be explained more clearly through the rules of the art of logic, I conceal the logical rules as much as I can within the formulas of faith, because I do not wish to seem to place more trust in this art that in the truth and authority of the Holy Fathers." In this attitude, which it would be ungenerous to define as merely prudent, we can grasp early and timid signs of a substantial trust in logic, but also a profound and living substratum of monastic life. This life was quite different, even on a theoretical level, from the one that was soon to make its appearance—the culture of the city school. The problem the city school posed itself was to *certificare fidem:* the monks seem absorbed in the task of *clarificare fidem*.

One cannot avoid the impression that Lanfranc's career—which is interesting in itself—prefigures the more famous and prestigious career of Anselm. Anselm became prior in 1063 and abbot in 1078 of the same monastery of Bec, founded by the Norman knight, Herluin. Anselm also became archbishop of Canterbury (in 1093), in the midst of the investiture controversy between the English king, Henry Beauclerc (Henry I) and the Roman pope, Paschal II. It would be difficult to call Anselm an intellectual: in him the serene climate of the cloister and its atmosphere of meditation prevail over investigation. But what a great quantity of "intellectual" traits this saint, monk and archbishop possessed! First of all, the need to find "an intelligence" in faith; then the desire to communicate to his fellow monks and his disciples working tools that were undeniably intellectual and cultural. Furthermore, the form of one of his major works, the *Monologion,* was structured like a *disputatio.* Finally, he possessed the intellectual honesty to seek tightly argued and deeply involving confrontations, as in the exchange with a less knowledgeable interlocutor in the *Proslogion*.

Faith, however, was an individual affair not transmissible in itself: the essential quality of Anselm's teaching, the one that distinguished it from that of the masters of the city schools that were just beginning to appear, was connected to this aspect of his thought. In the protected tranquility of the monastery Anselm taught disciples who were also fellow monks. Between the teacher and the student the economic relationship found outside the cloister—a "real" relationship between the giver and the receiver—did not exist. For Anselm, investigation still much resembled prayer; it was an example of tacit meditation, carried on internally, then written down for his fellow monks.

Roscelin was a younger contemporary of Anselm, but from what we know of his relationship with his students (he taught at Compiègne, Tours, and Loches) it must have been quite unlike Anselm's. First bishop of Soissons and later archbishop of Reims and a city "master," Roscelin's relations with his most gifted pupil, Abelard, were far from familiar, as we learn from a harsh and distant letter. Abelard was for him simply a paying student, probably disliked.

The cathedral school of Tours was one of the schools that give positive evidence of the dynamism of the French episcopate in the late eleventh century. Compared to a nearly unpopulated Germany and to the various regions of Italy, still relatively undeveloped, the schools of Laon, Reims, Chartres, Orléans, Tours, and Paris presented a quite different picture, to which the peace guaranteed by the Capetians and the extraordinary economic development of the "sweet region of Gaul" contributed. Each of these centers shone through the study of a particular discipline: students went to Laon to study theology (unless, like the restless Abelard, they found their studies there disappointing); in Chartres they learned *physica*—a combination of natural philosophy and the *pagina sacra;* in Orléans they studied the poets; in Paris, rhetoric, dialectic, and theology.

The structure and the life of cities were by this time supported by specialization and division of labor: teaching became one profession among others, on a par with artisanal and commercial activities. Thus it needed a precise definition indicating the tasks, the advantages, and the areas in which this activity could be exercised and specifying the work loads for both teacher and student. To give one example: during one of his first sojourns in Paris, Abelard, in order to avoid further *querelles,* went to teach just beyond the jurisdiction of the *scolasticus* at the Mont Sainte-Geneviève (to which he was to return, years later, as a mature man, famous and unhappy). The *scolasticus* was charged by the bishop with assigning the *licentia docendi* (which was free, it is true, but given on the basis of requisites held to be indispensable).

The university was born of a similar context, a context that changed with the growth of the new centers, with new concessions of social and juridical status to masters and students, but also with the increasing rigidity in structures. The first signs of the disciplining of this growth were the dictates of the Lateran Council of 1179 stating that it was the duty of every cathedral chapter to keep a school. Other "charters" were to come, in the various centers, to mark the development of this new institution. Some of these reveal the church's intention of maintaining its monopoly of schooling; others show resistance on the part of the teachers and the students. This generated tensions. In 1200, when the pope and the king agreed to give students a status equal to clerics, the tumults that had bloodied the streets and the taverns between the church of Saint-Germain-des-Prés and the Seine died down. As was often the case, as "charters" and laws regulated this spontaneous phenomenon they extinguished its vital thrust, and later some, realizing what had happened, regretted the passing of this first disorderly but vital phase. Fifty years later, Chancellor Philippe de Grève wrote, "Once, when every master taught on his own account and the very name of university was unknown . . . there was love of studies. Now . . . the lessons have become infrequent, teaching is reduced to very little indeed, and time taken from the lessons is frittered away in vain discussions."

If we examine the doctrinal context in which intellectuals operated from the mid-twelfth century to the thirteenth century, we note that although the physical aspects of their milieu differed according to the school's connections with the various political powers (the king of France in Paris, the emperor in Bologna, the pope everywhere), doctrine developed more homogeneously, showing more uniform tendencies in the various universities. This development closely paralleled the evolution of both the figure of the master and his attainments.

The various disciplines were organized according to the ancient structure of the seven liberal arts: the trivium (grammar, logic, rhetoric) and the quadrivium (arithmetic, geometry, music, and astronomy). This "road to wisdom" was felt to be preliminary training for the study of the highest expression of human knowledge, theology, the doctrine of the salvation of the soul. The relation with theology, however, was never as linear as it was presented in the classical division of disciplines into *domina* (theology) and *ancillae* (the others). In every case, although learning and teaching theology was considered the goal of doctrine and the crowning of the intellectual's career, in practice (and in some cases quite soon) when the disciplines of the preparatory courses (the arts, medicine, and jurisprudence) were freed from their propaedeutic status they became autonomous. The broadening and the "liberation" of these disciplines was accomplished in two ways. On the one hand, the contents of every branch of the trivium and the quadrivium proliferated as sources multiplied; on the other, the seven-fold structure broke up into new fields of investigation.

*

At the dawn of this epoch in the first half of the twelfth century, one figure—Abelard—fulfills nearly all the requisites of the "strong" intellectual. His declaration in his autobiography, the *Historia calamitatum mearum,* remains exemplary (and let us note in passing that even the fact of writing an autobiography was a rare, if not a unique, phenomenon). He says, "It was sheer pressure of poverty at the time which determined me to open a school . . . so I returned to the skill which I knew, and made use of my tongue instead of working with my hands" (trans. Radice). Abelard is speaking here of the school of the Paraclete, founded near Troyes, where he taught logic and theology, the two disciplines he loved most.

This stubborn Breton made a name for himself quite young. Renouncing his right of primogeniture (and with it a life as a knight), he threw himself with an already polemical passion into the study of logic, which he called, after Augustine, *disciplina disciplinarum.* His early career was typical, thus exemplary for the study of the figure of the intellectual in the twelfth century, an epoch of "rebirth." Since it also illustrates his tenacity and the originality of his positions, we find ourselves in the fortunate situation of being able to study both an individual and a type. The language of the autobiography is military, as has been noted. Abelard declares his intention to "storm the citadel of studies, Paris"; he prepares himself for continual "sieges" of schools and chairs; he contemplates and puts into effect "various strategies" such as an indirect approach to Paris, the goal he yearns for and the "new Athens"—via Melun and Corbeil. But if the language of his narrative was often that of the knight, his actions, as can be seen from his statement about teaching at the Paraclete, were rather those of the merchant. As the merchant sold his time (and we are all aware of the struggle to gain recognition of commercial ethics), Abelard sold his knowledge. But time and knowledge were gifts of God; better, they belonged to God. The city "master" had to fight to establish the prestige of his teaching, combating mistrust of doctrine imparted without the silent but high protection of the institution of monasticism.

Many episodes in Abelard's dramatic life could serve to illustrate characteristics of the "full-time" intellectual. First, there was his bent and his talent for criticism, which he exercised in various fields, from the dispute over the nature of universals with his former master, Guillaume de Champeaux, to textual criticism that at times involved him in extremely acrimonious disputes (for example, with the monks of Saint-Denis over the person of their patron saint). More often, though, this talent led him to masterly analyses, such as in the prologue of the *Sic et non,* where he lists rules for the interpretation of "discordances." The same method guided him to a delicate but stable accord between the Christian and the philosopher in the *Dialogus,* his last work.

An impassioned and unremitting involvement in teaching and in communicating his ideas and his readings accompanied this gift for criticism. To recall only one example, the most touching: Peter the Venerable tells us that when Abelard was at Cluny, ill, weary, and disillusioned, "he continued to teach, to write, and to dictate" just as he had done in his younger and happier years in Paris and in the fervid and exhausting years at the Paraclete. Abelard possessed another gift characteristic of the true intellectual, however. In all the areas he touched and at all the stages of his teaching career, he cared more for the method of investigation than its object; more for the theoretical process of analysis than for the topic itself. An enormous faith in his method (which was rational and, in theology, analogical) distinguished him just as much as his awareness that he could never arrive at the truth "but only at its shadow, at verisimilitude." "In all the things that I expose," he states, "I do not claim to define the truth but only my opinion."

There are some traits that unite and others that divide Abelard and John of Salisbury, whom we can define as the prototype of the "weak" or "incomplete" intellectual. The two men were linked by John's great devotion to his master and by the influence of Abelard's ideas and language that permeates the pages of that disenchanted Englishman. The latter half of the twelfth century had seen a great change, however: the library of mankind had been broadened by the "return of Aristotle" (through translations first from Arabic and then from Greek) and Moslem scientific and philosophic texts had begun to reach Europe. It was already possible to imagine what knowledge would come to be (and the problems it would bring) at the end of the vast process of enrichment and transformation. Even the Paris of 1136 visited by Abelard's pupil John, "verily thirsting for knowledge," was no longer the Paris that the twenty-year-old Abelard had known. The "cloister" of the Île Saint-Louis and the *rive gauche* was now thick with schools whose luminaries were men like Adam du Petit Pont and Abelard at the Mont Sainte-Geneviève, the monks of Saint-Victor at their abbey. There were other great names at the school that John frequented: Otto of Freising and Arnold of Brescia; there were many future bishops and one future pope, Orlando Bandinelli. Political life was calling our Englishman, however, and his brief later return to the Athens of the North was a disappointment. His declaration is telling: "I had the pleasure of seeing again old friends and fellow students still occupied in the study of logic . . . and of measuring our reciprocal progress . . . but it was immediately clear that they had not progressed even by the slightest proposition."

Were these the same people whom John cites elsewhere as "professors who disdain and repay poorly the devotion of a lover of philosophy"—that is, of a dilettante like himself? In any event, there is an obvious break between the intellectual who teaches and the man who leaves off his studies to involve himself in real life and politics. In spite of his "devotion" John's judgment is harsh, and it expresses well his sense of discomfort with a culture that seemed to him predominantly made of words, unverified analyses, and abstractions. As secretary to Thomas Becket and witness to dramatic events, John found little time to cultivate his beloved *litterae*, an ideal of culture that took inspiration from Cicero's, and despite himself he plunged dutifully into curial and political responsibilities. The ultimate unifying goal of his "two lives" lay in the idea of "service," which gave meaning to the daily practice of politics (at times demeaning, John confesses), and which raised politics to the level of philosophic reflection. Ciceronian *otium*, for this gifted pupil who never became a master, was equivalent to the peace that others sought in the cloister.

Before we abandon the twelfth century we need to add a word (or rather a question) concerning another great personage, necessarily in the shadow, since we know so little about him: Arnold of Brescia, also a pupil of Abelard's and a man to whose intellectual honesty John of Salisbury gives clear testimony. Was Arnold an intellectual? The sources tell us little about his teaching at the Mont Sainte-Geneviève and permit only suppositions. Certainly he was a man who "said things that were entirely consistent with the law accepted by Christian people, but not at all with the life they led" (John of Salisbury, *Historia pontificalis*). His activities as a reformer cannot easily be separated from his teaching of poor students "who publicly begged their bread from door to door."

*

The great masters of the thirteenth-century university were seen as officiants of culture more like ministers of the cult than the intellectual combatants and tenacious men of both thought and action that they really were.

We do not know as much as we would like about the universities of the thirteenth and fourteenth centuries. We do know enough, however, to define them as ambivalent and richly contradictory contexts for work, a characteristic that perhaps did not harm the masters' activities. University corporations were "short-term" affairs, modeled on crafts guilds but quite different in substance, as the students belonged to the corporation only temporarily and came from all regions of Europe (in fact, the various *nationes* were obliged to speak Latin in order to understand one another).

One of the men in this sphere most aware of what we might call "intellectual difference" was Bonaventure, born in Bagnoregio, the leader of the conservative wing of theologians who opposed both the masters of the Faculty of the Arts and Thomas Aquinas. Although in his day the term "philosopher" was reserved for Aristotle, a man whom Bonaventure considered dangerous for Christian culture, he acknowledged that intellectual, philosophical, and scientific investigation was legitimate (in the measure, of course, in which they could be "reduced" to theological truth). Responding to questions on the work of the Franciscans he declared:

> If we had to live by manual labor alone, we would be so preoccupied by the work to be done that we could not attend to others' affairs, nor celebrate divine office in worthy fashion, nor dedicate ourselves as freely to prayer. . . . In reality, except for the infirm, all among us labor: some by studying in order to instruct the faithful, others by reciting the divine office and praise of God, others by collecting alms for [our] common sustenance, still others by taking on domestic tasks in free obedience.

Bonaventure's attitude about an awkward problem for intellectuals of all ages—should one lend books?—is curious but significant. With a pedantry not without shrewdness he observes:

> Since we do not know the secrets of the human heart, it is a sign of rashness to interpret in the worst fashion what at times might be done even with good intentions and without blame. . . . Thus not lending one's own writings to others might be an action as condemnable as it is irreproachable. . . . It is a sign of prudence not to lend to others a text of which one has continual and frequent need, because no one is held to furnish to others things not of the first necessity, neglecting one's own interests. Not to give books on loan is not subject to condemnation when one has frequent though not constant need of a volume one owns and cannot long remain without it. For it happens that many are most zealous to ask but slow to return. . . . He who has a book on loan passes it to another without asking permission of the owner, and this one to a third, so that at the end the proprietor no longer knows who to ask for it, and the chain of loans is at that point so distant that no one is personally responsible for the book received.

The contrast of manual and intellectual labor returns in the pages of Bonaventure's great contemporary Thomas Aquinas, also a master in Paris (indeed, twice). For Thomas, who operated within the Dominican order to which he belonged, "working with one's intelligence" was above all "teaching and preaching." Keeping this in mind, we need to make a few observations on the difference between the two activities and the implicit hierarchy governing them as those questions relate to our theme of the pure intellectual and his relations with society. Thomas says, "Those who find [a way] to live otherwise than by means of manual labor are not obliged to work with their hands; otherwise all the wealthy, clerics and laity, who do not work with their hands would be in a state of damnation, which is absurd." Furthermore, Thomas observes:

> At times it is better to work with one's hands; at times no. When, in fact, manual labor does not take one away from some more useful work it is better to work with the hands. . . . When instead manual labor prevents one from accomplishing some more useful piece of work it is better to abstain from it, as results from the gloss of Luke 9:60: "Leave the dead to bury their own dead" . . . and as it results from the example of the apostles who ceased to work when they had the opportunity to preach. And manual labor certainly represents a greater impediment to modern preachers than to the apostles, whose science of predication was given by inspiration: modern preachers must instead prepare themselves for predication with continual study. . . . Some have a public responsibility to dedicate themselves to letters by teaching or learning in the schools, as do masters and students, religious and secular. . . . In analogical fashion, some have a public responsibility to occupy themselves with the word of God, preaching publicly to the people. . . . These [men] carry on these spiritual activities as a public charge, legitimately accepting the food that they receive from the faithful in exchange for their work because they serve the common good.

In spite of their cautious phraseology, the writings of both Bonaventure and Thomas give an implicit sense of the distance separating the two human activities. We know that in reality there were two distinct groups of men, those who worked and those who studied. The separation was emphasized by the learned in a vast range of attitudes from the most explicit and contemptuous, as in William of Conches, who, as early as the twelfth century labeled anyone incapable of studying a "cook," or Albertus Magnus, who called those incapable of comprehension "brutes," to Roger Bacon, who spoke of the *ventosa plebs*, or the good-humored condescension of Bartholomaeus Anglicus, who claimed he wrote also for the *rudes ac simplices*. The fundamental conviction was expressed with joking brutality by the students in the *Carmina Burana:* "The unlettered man is like a brute, being to art deaf and mute." The theoretical foundation for this attitude lay in the widely accepted definition of man: "rationality" was among his attributes; it expressed his difference from the other animal species, hence it was to be cultivated.

We owe to Thomas an intellectual operation of great historical importance; a masterly analysis that nonetheless came from a master with a clear perception of the world outside the schools. Thomas's faith in reason and in the Aristotelian model of knowledge led him to a paradoxical attempt to shape theology—which was *domina,* the queen of the sciences—according to the structure that Aristotle had described as typical of *knowledge in itself,* which was a rigorous process, constructed according to unequivocal norms that began from self-evident principles to arrive at conclusions that extended knowledge. This operation, at first sight theoretical and scholastic, belonged instead to a broader and more "real" project that affected all of society. Affirming that theology was a science (or a quasi-science) meant affirming that it could be taught even to people who did not believe in the *sacra pagina.* Thus there was hope of using reason to convert the infidel (the Moslems in particular, since their lands were contiguous to Christian lands).

The historical climate and the university context in which Thomas lived were feverish. The mendicant orders were not part of the birth of the university, but they had created a place for themselves there with a strongly partial solidarity directed against the established corporation. This explains their opposition to strikes, their refusal to accept honoraria, and their greater respect for the superiors of their orders than for the decisions of the university. All this can be found in a letter written by the "secular" masters (that is, those who were neither Dominicans nor Franciscans) in 1254 to complain of the outcomes of the great increase in "regular" masters (subject to a monastic rule). In spite of attempts at a compromise sponsored by the pope himself, matters worsened to the point that the "secular" masters refused obedience and were excommunicated and for some years the university was fettered.

Roger Bacon, who differed from Thomas in many ways, also lived in this climate of institutional and cultural contestation. In fact, the targets of his polemics were Alexander of Hales, a Franciscan, and Albertus Magnus, a fellow Dominican and Thomas's master. He criticized them sharply for their "ignorance of natural philosophy and because their books are full of infinite falsities and nonsense." These were not accusations simply dictated by academic spite: it is difficult to find a clearer and more operative idea of the social function of "Christian knowledge" in the Middle Ages. For Bacon the "republic of the faithful" was an organic whole and a unified society in expansion even physically "until the Greeks and the Tartars are converted and the Saracens destroyed." Bacon's utopia was a forceful return to the idea of power and knowledge working together in a direction imposed by the pope and in realization of divine purpose. This quite traditional concept contained powerful new elements, however: the primacy of knowledge, which was to establish a new morality and to rectify the corrupt times; knowledge of languages, needed to follow the progress of the divine revelation of wisdom, first to the Hebrew people, then to the Greek and Arabian philosophers; the central position of mathematics rather than logic (which Bacon found "fragile and equivocal"); and the importance of the *scientia experimentalis*, the science that "makes things certain, not with verbal arguments, and without which one cannot even arrive at philosophical perfection." This solitary and persecuted intellectual possessed, unlike many of his contemporaries, a lively interest in the world of things and of men. He judged it important that "the community of the faithful be guided in things earthly and useful to the person . . . in order to conserve the health of the body, a long life, and material goods," and he dreamed of fast-moving vehicles, better conservation of foodstuffs, and increased agricultural production, often with impressive foresight.

Bonaventure and Thomas, two saints of the church, and Bacon, a persecuted friar, are three examples of the thirteenth-century *intelligentsia*. They were united by their awareness of laboring in ways different from those of the greater part of humanity; they differed in their programs for the transformation of religious, political, and cultural reality, which all three men entrusted above all to the force of knowledge and speech. "Strong" intellectuals, they always aimed at the transmission of their theories. With the *Summa* that he never completed, Bacon dreamed of extending his ideas beyond the limits of university lectures.

*

In 1255 the works of Aristotle officially entered the Faculty of Arts of Paris. Soon after, the study of the commentary of the Arab, Averroës, grafted a new and, to most, a suspect process onto the themes of Christian philosophy. This happened for two principal reasons. The first lay in the transformation of the Arts from a preparatory faculty that taught the dialectical method necessary to the further study of philosophy and law into an autonomous faculty oriented toward philosophical investigation (and into a faculty ever more conscious of its academic independence). The second lay in the nature of the Averroistic system, which seemed extraneous to the Christian tradition that derived from Augustine.

From this system a new figure of the intellectual emerged whose theoretical profile and whose function in the practice of teaching contrasted strikingly with the traditional image of the master, even with the image of the three great figures discussed above.

The most notable difference consisted, in my opinion, in a singular moment of professional self-awareness. Siger of Brabant and Boethius of Dacia, the "Averroists" (a debatable but useful term), attempted, for the first time, both to fulfill the ideal role of the philosopher and to teach daily in the Faculty of Arts. Siger wrote, "The philosopher's task is exposition of the teachings of Aristotle, not correction or concealment of his thought, even when it is contrary to [theological] truth." This simple affirmation distinguishes in the clearest possible manner (and the most modern, the one closest to our own point of view) the difference between professorial and scholarly aims. It was a conception unacceptable to anyone who shared the traditional idea of Christian culture as a unified whole.

The difference of opinion became manifest in the condemnation of 1277, when many theses from the Faculty of Arts congenial to the Aristotelian/Averroistic teachings (for example, the eternity of the universe and the unity of human intellect) were censured by Bishop Tempier. Ideas that found support in the Faculty of Theology were included in his censure, and even Thomas Aquinas was involved. All this would belong more to the history of ideas than to the history of the intellectual if the condemned theses had not included propositions such as: "There is no more excellent state than to study philosophy" or "The only wise men in the world are the philosophers" (trans. Fortin and O'Neill). A new figure of the intellectual was born, founded on meditation of the *Nicomachean Ethics:* "And because there is pleasure in speculative knowledge, and all the more so the nobler the objects known, the philosopher leads a life of very great delight" (Boethius of Dacia, trans. Wippel). The philosopher was the true aristocrat: "According to the perfection of human nature, the philosophers who contemplate the truth are nobler than kings and princes." Traditionalists and the majority brought strong pressures to bear on this new type of professor to whom "knowledge of what is true gives delight." These men appeared strange and dangerous. There is bitterness in the words of Jacques de Douai:

> Many believe that the philosophers, who give themselves over to study and philosophical contemplation, are malicious, unbelieving men not subject to laws, and that for that reason they should legitimately be expelled from the com-

> munity. This is what they say, and because of this everyone who gives himself to study and philosophical contemplation is defamed and suspected.

"True felicity that by contemplation of the truth is acquired" was the goal of philosophy in the pure "Averroist" style of Dante's *Convivio.* Dante was far from sharing the metaphysical theses of this current of thought, however. Can we find in him the essential characteristics that define the intellectual?

In many ways the great figure of Dante appears to fit the description of what I have called the "weak" intellectual—a man who labored with his intellect and with the spoken or written word but not in a setting conceived for the purpose, nor in a context in which he could transmit not only his ideas but also his methods and sources, as could a master to his students in the school situation. Significantly, for our purposes, Dante was continually and painfully aware of not being in his "natural seat"—of being elsewhere, "out of place," where he was not permitted fullest expression of his intelligence. As he put it:

> After it was the pleasure of the citizens of that fairest and most famous daughter of Rome, Florence, to cast me out of her dearest bosom, . . . I have wandered through almost every region to which this tongue of ours extends, almost a beggar. . . . Truly I have been a ship without sail and without rudder, wafted to divers havens and inlets and shores by the parching wind which woeful poverty exhales. (trans. Jackson)

This aspect of Dante's persona is confirmed in his enrollment in the corporation of the doctors and druggists. The participation in political life that for the intellectual found expression *naturaliter* in his teaching activities was made possible for Dante only through the conventional act of signing the register of a professional organization in which he was essentially an outsider.

The relationship between intellectuals and politics requires looking at, while we keep in mind, however, that for the medieval intellectual, involvement in politics often meant making a choice between the two greatest contemporary expressions of power, the papacy and the empire.

*

One of the greatest intellectuals of the fourteenth century, the Englishman William of Ockham, was never a *magister.* He studied in the Franciscan friary in Oxford, where he earned his university bachelor's degree, the first step in his career. As custom dictated, he composed a commentary on the *Sentences* of Peter Lombard. In 1324, when he was called to the papal seat in Avignon to defend himself regarding some theses contained in this commentary, he was already the author of great works of logic consolidating and organizing the nominalist doctrine, which had arisen in the twelfth century. This was obviously not the object of the accusations, however. Logic was a discipline of the Arts, and as such did not directly touch on any position concerning faith or religious discipline. Still, it is difficult to rid oneself of the impression that there was a connection between the two fields of knowledge that Ockham so amply cultivated in his lifetime. Nominalism had led to the abolition of the universal *res,* general structures that conditioned even the divine plan of creation. For Ockham, God was once more omnipotent, creator not according to preestablished plans, but by absolute and free will. This inspiration, which also found its roots in a mystical and individualistic Franciscanism, runs throughout the work of the English philosopher. His political writings belong to the second half of his life, following his flight from Avignon in the entourage of the emperor Louis IV ("the Bavarian"), first to Italy and then to Bavaria. A key idea in these writings presents the church as a "congregation of the faithful" without power or wealth and inspired only by evangelical values. The work doubtless could also be read as a demand for the autonomy of the empire.

Secular power, for Ockham, concerned bodies and earthly goods, and its aim—a negative aim, to some extent—was to prevent conflict among individuals. In order to achieve this aim it needed recourse to preventive and repressive means of a political and physical nature. Political ideals had no place in this vision: the act of Ockham's that gives the measure of his political involvement is his flight from Avignon rather than his dedication to the imperial cause. The dominant themes, however, in the thought of this great Franciscan who used Scripture to demonstrate that "empire does not derive from the papacy" and that "every argument aimed at sustaining the dependency of civil power on the pontiff is sophistical" were a religious utopia, a church without wealth, and a pontiff who was a father of the faithful rather than a sovereign.

Theology and political fervor combined into a clearly-defined and conscious stand:

> Against the pontiff [John XXII] "I have set my face as a most hard rock" (Isaiah 50:7) so that as long as I have hands, paper, inkwell and ink, nothing can detach me from assiduous criti-

> cism of his errors, neither the falsity and infamy thrown against me, nor any type of persecution that might strike my body but not my person, nor the great number of the pontiff's supporters.

His *Epistola ad fratres minores* concluded in this fashion:

> I think I have contributed in these last years to changing the customs of my contemporaries much more than if I had conversed with them for years on the same question. . . . This is a time of trial in which the thoughts of many will become manifest.

I might add that it was also a time for choice, something of which the intellectual Ockham was well aware.

Some decades later another intellectual, John Wycliffe, also chose an awkward political stance. His career is worth scanning. A professor of logic and theology at Oxford, in 1372 he entered the service of the crown of England, changing literary genres with his two great works on dominion, divine and civil, in which by sustaining the autonomy of civil from ecclesiastical dominion he in fact sided with his sovereign. It is thus understandable that the pope, condemning the two texts with a bull, should refer to a resemblance "to the perverse theses of Marsilius of Padua." Not long after, Wycliffe began his active reforming work, organizing a group of "poor priests" who circulated English-language versions of texts that he had written in Latin on the "poverty of Christ and of his church." The revolt of 1381 made Wycliffe suspect in the eyes of the wealthy laity who previously had supported him against the papacy, and the lords found the program of the "poor priests" too similar to the demands of the rebels. Wycliffe's last years were solitary. Though he lived under suspicion and was ostracized, the tacit protection of the University of Oxford nonetheless saved him from active persecution.

Not only was Wycliffe's career exemplary, his is one of the few medieval lives to which we seem to have the key, since the chief theoretical aspects of his philosophy soon became operative in reality. His philosophical realism dictated the concept of the "church invisible" (as opposed to the visible and corrupt Church of Rome), and his analysis of divine dominion (the only truly complete and "full" dominion) was used as a "measure" for inquiry into the various sorts of human dominion. Wycliffe declared, significantly, in a deduction at once logical and theological, that the only human dominion that was legitimate (because it most resembled divine dominion) was the one realized through "participation in wealth"—the communitarian state. The corollary to this belief lay in the active participation of this master of logic in the revolt of peasants who sang, "When Adam tilled and Eve span, who was then the gentleman?"

Wycliffe was persuaded that theory must pass into political practice and that all analysis—even of the contemporary world—must be founded philosophically with the use of rigorous conceptual instruments. "My analysis is valid even for rough politicians," he declares, "since the principles of the knowledge of divine dominion and possession are useful even in application to the world of the created beings." Unlike most scholastic writers, Wycliffe, concerned about the efficacy of his discourse, did not neglect the rhetorical and persuasive aspects of his style: "What reason is there for maintaining a fat, worldly priest in pomp and in pride, for giving him handsome horses, elegant saddles, ornate bridles that jingle along his way, and gaudy clothing? What reason is there, I say, for the poor to bear hunger and cold instead?"

The year of the Peasants' Revolt was also the year of a magnificent royal wedding when Richard II of England wed Anne of Bohemia. Many Czechs, students at Oxford, were present at the wedding, and when they returned home they brought with them Wycliffe's texts and his ideas. At the end of the century, Jan Hus annotated the manuscript of Wycliffe's *De dominio* with enthusiastic comments, and Jerome of Prague declared that the *Dialogus*, another of Wycliffe's works, was "the root of true knowledge."

The Bohemia of the early fifteenth century in which both Hus and Jerome lived was a land of extreme social and cultural tensions. After the schism of 1378 serious breaches had opened up. The king and the Czech population remained neutral in the conflict between the popes, supporting the cardinals who had worked for the reform of the church, while the archbishop and the German population took sides with the Roman pope, Gregory XII. This opposition was intensely felt within the University of Prague, which was divided into *nationes* among which the Germans, now in the minority, were still powerful. The citizenry of Prague practiced their religion with a deep sense of involvement and tended toward radical renewal. The "Bethlehem Chapel" was to be the center of this movement, and when Hus became its rector in 1402 he preached there on a nearly daily basis.

An important aspect of the intellectual activity of both Hus and Wycliffe was the use of the national language—Czech in the case of Hus. For Hus the use of Czech signaled his awareness of a social opposition (to the wealthy), a political opposition (to the Germans), and a religious opposition (to the Roman Church). When Wycliffe and Hus opted to abandon Latin, the language that defined them and distinguished them as intellectuals, they reached the true point of arrival in the career of the intellectual who, in the turbulent climate of the late Middle Ages, chose political involvement and sided with dissent and reform against tradition. Both men felt that translation of the Bible and preaching in the vernacular were desirable "in order to change things," not simply to make themselves understood by a larger audience.

Events in Prague were reaching a crisis and the Reformation broke out in a mixture of demands for religious reform, a refusal of the internal hierarchy of the church (particularly of the distinction between laity and clergy), and a violent denunciation of luxury as a social injustice. Hus continued to maintain his doctrinal objectives, and he defended the university's right to use texts written by heretics (Wycliffe had been declared a heretic and his books had been condemned to be burned). The archbishop placed the city of Prague under interdict, but King Wenceslas prohibited the application of the decree. Hus defended the king's right in this move on the basis of arguments that went back to his master at Oxford. The king, he declared, is the minister of God, and as such he exercises God's power, which consists in protecting the good and combating the wicked, whether they are lay or ecclesiastical. King Wenceslas' intervention thus appeared motivated by the good end and the "superior" nonpolitical nature of his act, whereas the archbishop was impeding the apostolic mission of priests. Reform of the Church thus passed, for Hus and Wycliffe alike, through the sacred power of the sovereign, founded on passages in the Bible in the Book of Kings.

The day before he was led to the stake Hus wrote "to all the Czech faithful" in these terms: "You must know that the council that sentences me has neither listened [to me] nor read my books in Czech. Even if they had listened they would not have understood, because at the council there were only Italians, English, French, Spanish, and Germans." Not only had the natural element of the medieval intellectual—the Latin language—dissolved, but writing and preaching in the national language had become a sign of option for a particular social and political side.

Europe was still one great common stage, however, even with the centrifugal tensions that had by this time become apparent. Echoes of the sermons from the chapel in Prague and of Wycliffe's discourses to the English peasants had reached as far as the University of Paris, where Chancellor Gerson had the responsibility of gathering, evaluating, and judging the various sentences and declarations. It was a task that contrasted with his own nature, which was mystical and contemplative, but that he carried out with great zeal, urged on by the obligation of "service."

Jean Gerson's politico-cultural program was to restore the University of Paris to the splendor and primacy it had in the thirteenth century. He wrote to the students of the College of Navarre: "We will follow the beaten path (*tritum iter*) that is the most convenient, straight, and distant from the confines separating us from error and scandal." This seems to have been his ruling preoccupation. Questioning Jerome of Prague, Gerson observed, "Jerome, when you were in Paris you believed yourself an angel, strong and powerful in your eloquence, but you have disturbed the university by sustaining erroneous theses."

It is understandable that as rector in an epoch of great cultural *querelles* Gerson had to aim at peace within the university rather than freedom of investigation. Internal peace seemed to him threatened by polemical amplification of "scientific" doctrines carried on in the world outside the university by people not "scientifically" prepared: "If an affirmation has a meaning erroneous, scandalous, and offensive for pious ears, it can reasonably be condemned even if on the grammatical or logical plane it has a sense judged to be true."

It would be unfair, however, not to remark that this most prudent administrator was also a sharp-minded intellectual. His choices of field in the areas of philosophy and theology were certainly not the usual ones. He recommended to his theology students the works of Durand de Saint-Pourçain, a Dominican who had opposed the "way" of Thomas, thus arousing sharp criticism and censure; he saw realism (the most "official" philosophical tradition) as the source of all heretical movements; indeed, he had condemned Wycliffe and Hus, realism's champions. He cited Aristotle's *Ethics* to affirm that the contemplative life was nobler than involvement in practical life, even of the most virtuous sort.

Wycliffe, Hus, and Gerson: three clear examples of intellectuals involved in guiding (following the purest "medieval" style) dissent and programs for reform, but also the organization and conservation of society. By the force of things (first among them, because the church was congruent with Christian society), the intellectual of the Middle Ages had often found it natural and desirable to be involved in an activity with a collective dimension, but the extinction of many ideals, the fall of universalism, and the crisis of faith in the incisiveness of reason as a practical and political instrument had changed the climate little by little.

It is doubtless more difficult to trace a common and unified portrait of the humanist intellectual and to pinpoint any one characteristic such men shared. The passage from the "medieval" intellectual to the "new" sort seems to have been marked by proliferation in the typology of the intellectual.

*

The historical milieu of those who "labored with the mind and the tongue" had now changed. Various signals from the university world tell us as much: the involvement of several universities in national politics (in Prague, as we have seen, or in Paris, which took the side of the English in the Hundred Years Wars and took charge of the trial of Joan of Arc); the political usefulness of the Italian universities, which furnished councilors and administrators to their communes; but also the universities' economic dependence on the city, which nearly always reserved to itself the right to control recruitment of the professors in its pay. A stratum (almost a hereditary caste) of great professors began to take shape, and several of these men, who taught in the most prestigious universities, enjoyed an excellent economic position, thanks to their city stipend, the students' honoraria, and interest on loans they made to needy students. Moreover, the student population was itself fast becoming a socioeconomic elite.

The *magistri* had waged a two-pronged battle right from the start of the universities: downward, against the *rustici* and the plebians; upward, against the landed proprietors and the nobles. In the first case their chief weapon was verbal disdain; in the second, it was equating nobility with virtue. Let us look at two examples. Guillaume d'Auvergne wrote in the thirteenth century, "The plebs, for their multitude and little genius, live like brute animals [and] are led to commit robberies and assassinations in the same manner as wolves. . . . The wise, instead, dominate their passions and the virtuous use of free will." He concludes that the definition of "rational man" only applies to the stratum of the learned. Comments on the upper classes range from the picturesque declaration of Jean de Meun ("The learned are more noble than those who spend their lives hunting hares or attending to the properties and the dungheaps they have inherited") to the lengthy treatises of Dante or Coluccio Salutati.

This dual polemic was comprehensible when the learned were nearly all masters and professors who transmitted knowledge, but at the end of the fourteenth century the situation became more fluid and more problematical. Variety was introduced into the panorama of the intellectual citadel, and a new intellectual stratum began to emerge that included jurists and, in Italy, notaries, flanked by the new figure of the artist. Dürer's evolution is a case in point. After his trips to Italy, where he frequented humanists' discussions, he changed from a goldsmith and a craftsman into an intellectual, writing treatises and illustrating the books of author friends. (Significantly, he was reproached for this by his wife, who urged him "to return to his workshop and not mix with superior people.")

The jurist Coluccio Salutati began as a notary and ended up as chancellor of Todi and of Florence. It was his life that dictated the theoretical model implicit in his writings. "Speculation is not the final end of man," he declared, and

> The active life is to be placed before the speculative life that is so greatly exalted. . . . Will you really call wise one who has known celestial and divine things as much as a human intellect can, without for all that having provided for himself? If he has not been able to be of use to his friends, his family, his colleagues, his homeland? I, to tell the truth, will courageously affirm and candidly confess that willingly, without envy and without quarrel, I leave to you and to whoever raises pure speculation to the heavens all the other truths, as long as I am left knowledge of human things.

His polemic against the Aristotelian ideal of felicity through speculation led him to exclaim: "Do not believe . . . that fleeing the throng, avoiding the sight of beautiful things, closing oneself up in a cloister or segregating oneself in a hermitage is the way to perfection."

When Salutati judged the previous epoch, few of the intellectuals whom we have examined here seemed "good." Among them were Abelard and above all John of Salisbury, whose political work, the *Policraticus,* he knew. It is significant that these authors both lived before the rise of the university, loved the classics, and were deeply involved in the active life.

The Italian universities of the Po valley became centers of diffusion for the new humanistic culture, and the Roman, Lorenzo Valla, who had lived in the Florentine milieu, wrote his most important works in Piacenza and Pavia, where he was a professor. Many aspects of Valla's thought differed from and opposed the intellectual tradition that had prevailed during the centuries of the Middle Ages and its universities. First among these new orientations was the revived Epicureanism of Valla's *De voluptate,* written in Pavia, a defense of human desires and human works against an ascetic morality that had become a moralism. Affirmation of earthly happiness and virtue, understood as a just and balanced order among pleasures, dominates his thought: "The arts, and not only the liberal ones, tend to satisfy fundamental needs, and they aim at rendering life decorative and elegant. Such are agriculture, architecture, the arts of weaving, of painting, of dyeing with purple, of sculpting, of fitting ships." Connected with this theme were a distaste for vain attempts to penetrate the inaccessible divine secret ("learning that makes one witless"), for metaphysics that excites the more abstract sort of debates, and for the desiccated logic of the last disputations of the nominalists—a logic that seemed to Valla useless, since it was uprooted from its vital, practical context and removed from the concrete concerns of grammar and the efficacy of rhetoric. Rather than simply typifying a certain sort of philosophical or erudite polemics, such themes in reality are useful to portray the new man of culture: the professor primarily concerned with attaching the schools to the functional reality of men's daily lives.

Next to lay intellectuals such as Salutati and Valla, there were illustrious humanists in the "ecclesiastical area," men like Enea Silvio Piccolomini, secretary to Pope Calixtus III, bishop of Trieste and Siena, and cardinal before he himself became pope; Marsilio Ficino, who became a priest at forty years of age; Angelo Poliziano, proposed for the cardinalate by Lorenzo the Magnificent. In practice the relationship between the church and humanistic culture was closer and more complex than it might first seem. Many intellectuals came to view the institution of the church not only as the most powerful organization known but, paradoxically, the most tolerant protector (above all regarding one's private life).

When the intellectual's environment shattered, toward the end of the fourteenth century, other milieus substituted for the university and became centers of culture—the circle and the academy, later the library, above all the court. With the concentration of power at the court, the intellectual lost his relationship with political life and with the larger social sphere. It is not by chance that Latin, which had already been abandoned in favor of the vernacular, should return as the language of literature, clearly distinct from the language of daily life.

Was it true that the court intellectual was freer than the University of Paris professor, who ran the risk of having his theses condemned (like Siger, Boethius of Dacia, Durand de Saint Pourçain, and others), and that he participated in an exchange that resembled open political debate without predetermined winners? I do not think so. There was a rapid, discernible change, during the fifteenth century, toward a definition of liberty as an increasingly private area limited to the confines of the family and of *otium*. Great choices of camp (reform or conservatism, pope or emperor, pope or sovereign) were no longer available to the intellectual who was a guest at the court of great lords like the Gonzagas, the Malatestas, the Medicis, the Rucellais, and their ilk. The intellectual soon developed the "two-faced" nature—public and private—for which he was known in the early modern era. The public figure supported the rationale of power, at times halfheartedly, never ardently; the private figure, skeptical, took refuge in inner reflection and melancholy.

*

A long and learned tradition burdened the theme of melancholy. Aristotle had elevated it to a "heroic" attitude proper to the man of genius, but the church Fathers saw it as one of the worst enemies of the soul. Melancholy generated sloth, "smallness of soul," a myopic view of things, restless and disordered wanderings of the imagination, rambling loquaciousness or its opposite, mutism. Thomas Aquinas gives a good summary of the judgment passed on this dangerous mood: it threw man into "true desperation" and persuaded him that salvation of the soul was unreachable or, worse, useless.

Melancholy took on other hues in the pages of Petrarch. It was a new attitude combining depression with "a certain voluptuousness in sorrow" and a preference for solitude. It was a way of feeling and of being that reflected certain modes of the medieval intellectual, but it anticipated others typical of the man of letters and the philosopher of the early modern period:

> I rise at midnight; I go outdoors with the first light; and whether in the fields or in the house I am busy thinking, reading, writing. . . . I have all my friends, present and past, not only those who have been tested by life in common, but those who died many centuries ago, known to me by benefit of letters. . . . I assemble them from every place, from every time, into my narrow valley. I converse with them more eagerly than with those who presume that they are alive by discharging rank words and catching sight of their vapor exhaled on the cold air. Thus I wander, free and secure, alone with my chosen companions. (Trans. Bishop)

City or country? Involvement in political life and in work or studious solitude, serene and protected *otium*? This was a clear opposition that divided intellectuals in the centuries of the Middle Ages not so much according to their historical contexts or their activities as by their cultural models. Petrarch comments irascibly:

> Let us leave the city with no idea of returning to it. . . . We must tear up the roots of our troubles, break the chains which hold us confined, destroy the bridges behind us. . . . Arise, come, hasten, let us abandon the city to merchants, attorneys, brokers, usurers, tax-gatherers, scriveners, doctors, perfumers, cooks, bakers and tailors, alchemists, fullers, artisans, weavers, architects, statuaries, painters, mimes, dancers, lute-players, quacks, panderers, thieves, criminals, adulterers, parasites, foreigners, swindlers, and jesters, gluttons who with scent alert catch the odor of the market-place, for whom that is the only bliss. (Trans. Zeitlin)

He adds haughtily, "They are not of our kind."

For Petrarch (as for the monk Bernard of Clairvaux, two centuries earlier) the city was a corrupt Babylon. Worse: Petrarch's return to older positions and judgments concerning the dignity of manual labor isolated him—dramatically—from the trades and the human activities of his time. He seems to have forgotten the word of Hugh of St. Victor, who defined architecture, the art of navigation, weaving, and the other "mechanical arts" as "the fourth part of philosophy" because "these human actions that alleviate the disadvantages of our mortal condition . . . possess in themselves regulatory wisdom."

Bonaventure, in the thirteenth century, justified his choice of the city for religious reasons that fitted in with the way society was developing: "In country places the inhabitants are so dispersed that it is difficult to gather them all together for sermons. . . . In the city, though, where foodstuffs abound, a great number of persons gather and live. There we can legitimately hope to reap better results."

Francisco Ximenez, a Franciscan who lived in the fourteenth century in Valencia and was counselor to the king, gave a vivacious version of what was by then the dominant attitude:

> When you come into the city you meet people, your heart is calmed and you can stroll about with joy. . . . The city is an excellent place, where a man can free himself from ignorance. In the city it is difficult to be sad, and sadness dries out the bones and annihilates life. . . . In thickly inhabited and well-governed cities, a man can find many reasons for serenity: he

> lives in security, he is better satisfied in his material needs, he sees others and speaks with them.

The intellectual's attitudes concerning another lively and much-debated theme—marriage and the family—continued along more traditional lines. A veritable dossier against marriage, which chose its arguments from St. Jerome (*Adversus Jovinianum*), circulated during the twelfth century. We possess an interesting documentation of it in the pages of a woman intellectual, Héloïse, the lover and later the wife of the philosopher Abelard. (Two centuries later it was praised for its tone by Petrarch, a great reader of Abelard's autobiography.) We can distinguish various threads in the thick tissue of arguments Héloïse weaves together to argue against matrimony. First, there is the influence of the classical philosophical repertory, which paints marriage as the quintessence of the life of the senses, a concentration of mundane and annoying necessities and material needs, hence a fatal removal from the ideal realm of philosophy. Next come the "reasons of the saints," which describe matrimony as a remedy for lust, a remedy, however, that could easily slide toward the evil it is intended to avoid. Finally, Héloïse expresses a subtle and profound sense of malaise about an institution that can add nothing to true and "disinterested" love. This last aspect was connected to the influence of Cicero's *De Amicitia,* and it seems to have been shared by goliardic and courtly literature as well ("Do not usurp the word love to indicate the conjugal affection that binds in matrimony"). The arguments against matrimony were obviously complex, multiple, and shared by most intellectuals. Some writers emphasized ascetico-religious reasons for their disapproval of marriage, others stressed more clearly moral arguments, but certainly it would have been difficult for them to feel enthusiasm for an institution so discredited philosophically or to plead in its favor.

Even Siger of Brabant, the "Averroist" of the Arts faculty, asks "what state is the better adapted to the philosopher, the virginal or the conjugal?" He responds that "the philosopher must lean toward the condition that least hinders him in the search for the truth," concluding that matrimony involved "too many worldly occupations" and was thus doubtless not advisable for anyone seeking "intellectual pleasure."

To our modern eyes the figure of the medieval intellectual is often blurred and diminished by his relationship with his *auctoritates.* We should keep in mind, however, that the notions of supremacy and compulsion now inherent in the term "authority" emerged in the early modern era. *Auctoritates* were for medieval men simply the authors, the texts, and the set of works on which they were working. Their library contained both saints and philosophers. The philosophers' library, as one scholar of the twelfth century astutely remarked, was made of authors who "in life had never agreed with one another [so] it was useless to wear oneself out searching for the same opinions in them." On the one hand, there stood the enormous production of commentaries and glosses—on Plato, on Aristotle, on the Evangelists, and even on recent writers who immediately emerged as "authorities" (Peter Lombard, for example). On the other hand, however, the variety of the commentaries, the number of their differing stands, the acrid debates and bitter quarrels all document for us a labor that was concrete, often personal, and occasionally courageous. Let us leave this survey of the medieval intellectual with a few statements that testify to the critical awareness of both reason and authority in these men.

Adelardus of Bath, in the first decade of the twelfth century, criticized "the vice of this generation, which considers acceptable only the discoveries made by the ancients or by others." He adds, "I know well what is the destiny of those who teach the truth; for that reason in exposing a theory I will indicate it as a theory of my Arabic masters." Following the *auctoritas* rather than the *ratio* was for him "abandoning oneself to the most bestial credulity and allowing oneself to be lured into a perilous trap." Albertus Magnus, the great Dominican master, warned: "Whoever believes that Aristotle was a god must believe that he never erred. But if he thinks that he was a man, then without doubt he could err like us." Siger, in agreement on this point, observed, "Authority alone is not sufficient for the investigation of the truth of this thesis. All those who sustained it were moved by one reason or another. But we are men exactly as they were. Why then should we not, like them, occupy ourselves in rational investigation?"

BIBLIOGRAPHY

Bianchi, Luca. "La felicità intellettuale come professione nella Parigi del Duecento." *Rivista di Filosofia* 78, 2 (1987): 181–99.

Dionisotti, Carlo. "Chierici e laici." In Dionisotti, Carlo. *Geografia e storia della letteratura italiana*. Turin: Einaudi, 1977–).

Le Goff, Jacques. *Les intellectuels au Moyen Age*. Paris: Editions du Seuil, 1957.

Murray, Alexander. *Reason and Society in the Middle Ages*. Oxford: Clarendon Press; New York: Oxford University Press, 1978.

Smalley, Beryl. *The Becket Conflict and the Schools: A Study of Intellectuals in Politics.* Oxford: Blackwell; Totowa, N.J.: Rowan and Littlefield, 1973.

Verger, Jacques. *Les universités au Moyen Age.* Paris: Presses Universitaires de France, 1973.

SUGGESTED READINGS

Robert L. Benson and Giles Constable, eds., *Renaissance and Renewal in the Twelfth Century* (Cambridge: Harvard University Press, 1982).

Marie Dominique Chenu, *Nature, Man, and Society in the Twelfth Century* (Chicago: University of Chicago Press, 1968).

William J. Courtenay, *Schools and Scholars in Fourteenth-Century England* (Princeton: Princeton University Press, 1987).

S. G. Kuttner, *Harmony from Dissonance: An Interpretation of Medieval Canon Law* (Latrobe, Pa.: Archabbey Press, 1960).

Gordon Leff, *Paris and Oxford Universities in the Thirteenth and Fourteenth Centuries* (New York: Wiley, 1968).

Colin Morris, *The Discovery of the Individual, 1050–1200* (New York: Harper & Row, 1973).

Charles M. Radding, *The Origins of Medieval Jurisprudence: Pavia and Bologna, 850–1150* (New Haven: Yale University Press, 1988).

Beryl Smalley, *The Study of the Bible in the Middle Ages* (Oxford: B. Blackwell, 1983).

Richard William Southern, *Medieval Humanism and Other Studies* (New York: Harper and Row, 1970).

———, *Robert Grossteste: The Growth of an English Mind in Medieval Europe* (Oxford: Oxford University Press, 1986).

———, *St. Anselm and His Biographer* (Cambridge: Cambridge University Press, 1963).

John Van Engen, *Rupert of Deutz* (Berkeley: University of California Press, 1983).

Helen Jane Waddell, *The Wandering Scholars* (New York: Barnes & Noble, 1966).

SIX

The Artist

Enrico Castelnuovo

WHO BUILT THEBES WITH ITS SEVEN GATES? BRECHT'S FAMOUS QUESTION CONTRASTS THE ANONYMITY OF THE MANY WHO MADE HISTORY far from the spotlight with the renown of the few who are presented as history's protagonists. One could ask the same about the artists in the Middle Ages. Who designed the mosaics of San Vitale? Who painted the frescoes of Castelseprio? Who sculpted the capitals of Cluny? Who built the cathedral of Chartres?

Works of art have an important role when we seek to imagine and to visualize the Middle Ages. Among all the images that monuments, chronicles, and documents give us of the epoch, one in particular stands out: more than any other age, the Middle Ages appears to us in pale churches teeming with sculptures, in mosaics and multicolored stained-glass windows, in scintillating jewels, in brightly illuminated books, in sculptured ivories, in immense bronze doors, in enamels, in mural paintings, in heraldic banners, embroideries, stuffs and weavings of iridescent color and singular design, in paintings on golden backgrounds. But in comparison with the profusion and the variety of the works of art that solicit our admiration and set our imaginations to work, we can bring together only a handful of artists' names—often isolated names, linked to one work alone. Even the creator of a monument as important as the Palatine chapel in Aix-la-Chapelle, a milestone of medieval architecture, remains elusive and unascertainable. Who was Odo of Metz? How can we define him or situate him?

It was once the fashion to lament the egocentricity of modern artists, their vanity, and their need to play the hero, by praising the dedication, modesty, and virtue of the medieval craftsman, whose only reward was divine recognition, who sought no glory in his own name but was humbly content with anonymity, asking only to participate in the great collective effort for the greater glory of the faith.

This view was a product of Romantic culture and it corresponds poorly to reality. Even though a great many works remain anonymous, some names and signatures of medieval artists have come down to us and a wealth of documents tell us about them and help us to grasp just how different the situation was from the way it has been described—how pride substituted for humility and fame and notoriety for anonymity. Nonetheless—and this we find disconcerting—the undeniable evidence of the artists' pride and high self-esteem in no way excluded widespread and well-documented attitudes of humility, just as the fame of a few does not contradict the anonymity of many. In many ways the behavior of medieval artists seems to us very different from that of those who preceded them and those who followed them. It is almost as if the space in which they moved and in which they manifested an extraordinary and unequaled creativity was totally different from the operating space of other artists before and after them.

How, then, did artists of the Middle Ages work? What were their roles, and what awareness did they have of their own activity? How did their contemporaries view them? What was their image and their position in society? To answer these questions, we need to look first at the situation of the artists who worked before them in classical antiquity. Only by comparison can we state whether, when, and how a change occurred (and of what type) in their status as artists, their working methods, the techniques they favored, their relations with their clients and with the public, their contemporaries' image of them, and the function attributed to their works.

It is unlikely that questions such as these will receive a precise answer. Scholars do not agree on the status of the artist in classical antiquity, on whether and how he differed from the artisan, on the position he occupied in society, on his economic situation, or on the image society had of him. To what degree did the artist enjoy widespread appreciation? Was he instead considered a *banausos*—a person of inferior, even of the lowest social status? We have many artists' signatures from the classical period, but what do they mean? Among ceramicists, for example, do they testify to artistic pride or are they simply a maker's mark, a sort of copyright?

Many ancient sources mention artists' names, establishing a hierarchy among them and praising some of them in particularly admiring terms. What meaning should we give, then, to Plutarch's famous phrase in his *Life* of Pericles, "No generous youth, from seeing the Zeus at Pisa [Olympia], or the Hera at Argos, longs to be Pheidias or Polycleitus" (trans. Perrin)? Was the profession of the artist depreciated or appreciated? Or, were works of art the object of an admiration that did not extend to their creator or to his profession? Historians and archaeologists have long discussed these problems, throwing light on a quantity of data and questions, but failing to come to any agreement. It seems clear, in any event, that it would be difficult to reach a satisfactory definition of the artist valid for all periods and places during the long time-span that goes under the name of classical antiquity. The situation of an artist who worked in Athens in the fifth century was very different from someone active in the fourth century at the court of Alexander, not to speak of the differences between the complex Hellenic situation and the Roman, or of the contradictory attitudes in the texts arising from the social, cultural, and political position of their author.

If we are uncertain about the precise position of the artist in the classical world, we are even more uncertain concerning the medieval world, first, because what is known as the Middle Ages covers a millennium of extreme diversity, but also because there has been less research on this period than for classical antiquity.

When crisis struck the ancient world it brought a dramatic reshuffling of the cards: the entire field of the arts was restructured and the positions of its components shifted, thus transforming roles and attitudes. Rich and refined collectors disappeared; production in what had been important artistic centers declined to the point of ceasing; in other places it continued, though on a highly limited scale. Clients and typology shifted, and both the functions and conceptions of the work of art were profoundly altered. Images began to appear suspect and they even aroused hostility, since they were traditionally linked to the world and the culture of the gentile nations and might conceal idolatry. In increasing measure the figurative arts were put at the service of the church, its mission, and its programs for redemption and salvation. They even came to be considered as a substitute for reading among the illiterate. Pope Gregory the Great wrote to the bishop of Marseilles in the year 600, "Indeed, what writing is for those who know how to read, painting is for the illiterate who look at it, because those who do not know letters can read in it, for which [reason] painting serves principally as a lesson for the people."

As a general rule, the classical world's stigma marking anyone who did manual rather than intellectual work continued during the many centuries of the Middle Ages. This is evident in Pope Gregory's view of painting as a surrogate for writing good enough for people who could not read. If reading was a higher and more noble exercise than looking at a painted scene, it followed that those who wrote were to be esteemed as more worthy than those who painted.

The system that Martianus Capella and Cassiodorus imposed on ancient pedagogical method, which privileged the liberal arts grouped in the trivium and the quadrivium over manual activities, which they considered servile, marked the artist's social status for centuries. At least until the cultural structure of the ancient world reached a crisis during the twelfth century and was swept aside by the impetuous growth of the cities and the social and mental changes that accompanied their growth, the artist was considered a manual laborer.

In contrast, the *Enneads* of Plotinus, written in the third century, provided a defense of the artist's activity that was to have consequences in the Middle Ages. Plotinus praises Phidias for having represented Zeus, not "from any model perceived by the senses, but [he] understood what Zeus would look like if he wanted to make himself visible" (trans. Armstrong), thus he granted the artist the privileged ability to attain a reality beyond what our senses can perceive. Even though the hierarchy imposed by a division among the arts was to hold firm over the long time-span, the Plotinian current that surfaces at times in medieval culture worked—perhaps not always explicitly—toward particular consideration for the activity of the artist.

Medieval texts have no term to designate the people we today call artists. The term *artifices* was commonly used to designate artisans and, with them, artists: "Obiit Berengarius huius matris ecclesiae artifex bonus" notes a necrologist of the cathedral of Chartres in 1050, without further explanation, leaving us to wonder in vain what art Berengarius may have exercised (he probably was the architect who directed the reconstruction of the cathedral after the fire in 1020). As for the term *artista,* when it is found it indicates a person who studies or practices the liberal arts. Only at the end of the thirteenth century, in the chronicle of Salimbene, did it indicate a person gifted with a particular technical skill.

Hierarchical value judgments became apparent within the arts. The architect was particularly esteemed, as his work involved planning and organization, thus had an intellectual component. People's conception of the architect varied enormously during the Middle Ages, however. One image inherited from classical antiquity that was to survive to the Carolingian era saw him as a professional who planned projects and organized their construction. For Isidore of Seville, the early seventeenth-century author of the most widely read encyclopedia of the Middle Ages (until the thirteenth century, when it was supplanted by the scholastic *Summae*), the architect was a combination of a mason (*caementarius*) and a designer, and his definition was repeated by Raban Maur in the Carolingian era. Traces of Vitruvius still remain in this view of the architect's activities; later, when he was identified with the constructor, practical activity prevailed over theory and planning; still later the emphasis shifted once more.

There is an improbable anecdote related by Ordericus Vitalis in his *Historia Ecclesiastica,* written around 1135, that testifies to the capacities and the technical secrets attributed to the architect. According to him, an architect named Lanfredus, "who was then famous above all other architects in France for his skill" (trans. Chibnall), was decapitated after he had constructed the tower of the castle of Ivry, in Normandy, so that he could never build another one like it. Another anecdote from the *Gesta* of the abbots of Saint-Trond is significant for the architect's new awareness of his work. A famous *lamotus* (stonecutter) had answered the abbot (who criticized one of his proposals), "If you do not like what I have well designed, I prefer that you seek another artificer." We get very different impressions from the architect-sorcerer of Ordericus Vitalis and the haughty interlocutor of the abbot of Saint-Trond.

Goldsmiths, who worked in the most precious materials, and master glassworkers, experts in a difficult technique, enjoyed esteem, as we shall see. The sources also contain high praise for some Italian painters much sought after for their skill, like the Johannes that Otto III called to Aix-la-Chapelle or the Lombard Nivardus, the most talented of the painters called to work in the monastery of Fleury (later Saint-Benoît-sur-Loire) by the abbot, Gauzlin, the illegitimate son of Hugh Capet and a munificent client. Moreover, the boundaries between techniques were not inviolable, and the sources frequently refer to artists capable of working in several fields.

Our principal sources for medieval artists and their image in contemporary eyes are monastic and episcopal chronicles, the necrologies of the abbeys and the cathedrals, and episcopal and abbatial letters. Many names have come down to us in this manner; others—fewer, at least in the earlier ages—through signatures and inscriptions placed on the works themselves. To this we can add information from payment documents, contracts, and corporative statutes.

After the turn of the fourteenth century in Tuscany, the artist appears as a literary personage as well and poets and writers mention his name. This was an advanced and isolated case, limited, at first, to one specific cultural milieu.

A preliminary remark to be made concerning the early Middle Ages is that artists' signatures disappeared (except on coins, where the designer's mark was a sign of authenticity). Signatures reappear, not coincidentally, in Italy, where traditions had remained alive. In 712 one "Ursus Magister" and his disciples Joventino and Joviano are cited in contemporary documents as signing a ciborium in the church of San Giorgio of Valpolicella, while an inscription with a similar name ("Ursus magester fecit") can be found on an altar front of the abbey at Ferentillo, near Terni, that can be dated by the mention of the client, Hildericus Dagileopa (probably Hilderic, duke of Spoleto in 739). The artist has chosen to depict himself in an elementary and schematic style, standing beside his client with a chisel and a mallet in either hand. That the two signatures and their accompanying qualification of "magister" should be found in areas under Lombard domination is significant. In 643 two articles of the edict of King Rothari established norms for the exercise of architecture within the Lombard state, and later the *memoratorium de mercedibus commacinorum* mentions the hierarchic structure of the *commacina* mastership system. The origin of this term is unclear: it may indicate geographical provenance, like the later *magistri antelami,* or it may refer to a certain type of equipment, *cum machina*. In any event, the "teams" under this system were composed of apprentices, workmen, and collaborators of various sorts under the direction, precisely, of "magisters."

One of the first artist's biographies after those of classical antiquity was the life of St. Eloi, the great Limousin goldsmith and medal and coin designer who became a highly important person in the Merovingian court, ended his life as bishop of Noyon, and was later canonized. His biographer is not particularly interested in Eloi's artistic activities, which entered into his personality and his story along with other qualities that the biographer considered just as important if not more so. More than the biography of an artist, this is the life of a saint who, among other things, was also an artist. The biographer speaks with enthusiasm of Eloi's extraordinary skill as a goldsmith and in other arts ("aurifex peritissimus atque in omni fabricandi arte doctissimus"), of his religious fervor and his compassion, of his familiarity with monarchs, but also of his aspect, of his long aristocratic fingers, and of the precious vestments he wore. In this portrait we can see a desire to emphasize Eloi's high social status as well as his artistic capacities and profoundly religious nature. One episode, however, illustrates the superiority of mental over physical labor. The biographer tells how Eloi, while working intently on a piece, kept an open codex within sight so that he could carry on two tasks, the manual one for men and the mental one for God ("manus usibus hominum, mentem usui mancipabat divino").

The high social status of the medieval goldsmith finds confirmation in the golden altar-frontal in the cathedral of Sant'Ambrogio in Milan (c. 840), whose creator, "Vuolvinus magister phaber," signs his piece and represents himself being crowned by St. Ambrose along with the client, Archbishop Angilbert II. There is a significant difference between the two crowned figures, however. The client, "Angilibertus Dominus," is shown with his head framed by a square nimbus and preparing to kneel to the saint to offer him the altar; Vuolvinus, with no nimbus and empty-handed, is more evidently kneeling. The artist's signature, self-portrait, and his near equality with the patron are significant facts, revelatory of the high social rank of the goldsmith and of society's image of him. In the Middle Ages the relation between the artist and the client was an unequal one; hierarchical position, economic resources, and, often, the culture of the client humbled the artist. "Ars auro gemmisque prior. Prior omnibus autor" (Art is superior to gold and to gems, but the client is first of all) warns an inscription on an enamel with the image of Henry of Blois, archbishop of Winchester (c. 1150).

Another goldsmith who enjoyed social prestige was the Adelelmus mentioned in a written sermon of the very end of the tenth century narrating the vision of Robert, abbot of Mozac, and the construction of the cathedral of Clermont. The cathedral was designed by Adelelmus, a cleric of noble origin, who was highly skilled in working in stone and in gold, was known by all, and whose ability no artist of the past had equaled ("Nam sililem ei, multis retroactis temporibus, in auro et lapide omnique artificio nequimus assimilare"). He was also responsible for the famous reliquary statue of the Virgin of Clermont that became a model for the revival of sculpture. Adelelmus was, like St. Eloi before him, a churchman and an artist, which was also the case of another great personality of the tenth century, St. Dunstan, a reforming monk and statesman expert in singing and playing the harp, a sculptor and goldsmith who also worked in bronze ("in cera, ligno, vel ossa sculpenti et in auro, argento, vel aere fabricando"), a painter and calligrapher. At his death he was archbishop of Canterbury.

For centuries, the goldsmith's craft was one of the great pilot techniques of medieval art, a technique in which the best artists tested their mettle and in which the newest and most significant works were executed and the most modern experiments attempted. The value of the materials used, their price and their rarity were taken as a challenge by the artist, and frequently (as in a twelfth-century text of Suger of Saint-Denis or in another of the thirteenth century of the Englishman Matthew Paris) we can find the ancient Ovidian *topos* "materiam superabat opus": the artist's work surpasses the value of the material. This affirmation could be contradicted, however. One cross of the Ottonian period in the cathedral of Mainz bears an inscription specifying that six hundred pounds of gold went into its making; another inscription on the altar of St. Remaclus, commissioned in 1148 by Wilbaldus, abbot of Stavelot, details the cost of the silver, the gold, and the entire piece. Whatever the worth of the artist who executed it, it often happened that in case of need the work was melted down for its raw materials, which made it a fatally provisional form of hoarding wealth. At the same time, thanks to the economic sacrifice they entailed, their splendor, and the innumerable biblical references that could be read into them, works of the goldsmith's craft represented the highest homage that the client could offer to God, to the Virgin, or to the patron saint. Hence they required the collaboration of the best craftsmen available.

In the region of the Meuse the growth of great commercial centers in the early twelfth century was accompanied by flourishing artistic activity, particularly in the goldsmiths' art and in metal casting. Leading craftsmen in these fields occupied important and responsible public positions. Rénier of Huy, who made a bronze baptismal font for the church of Saint-Barthélemy in Liège, a monument of extraordinary importance both for its iconography (it adapted the "molten sea of bronze" described in the Old Testament to New Testament subjects) and for its precocious (1118) and thoroughgoing classicism, belonged to the urban patriciate and was probably the *ministeriale* of the bishop of Liège. During these same years goldsmiths appear as the protagonists of extraordinary legends, like the one narrated in the *Gesta Sancti Servatii* written around 1126. The reliquary for the head of St. Servatius commissioned by Emperor Henry III aroused the anger of the illustrious client, who threw the goldsmiths in prison because the precious stones used for the eyes of the saint made him look cross-eyed. During the night the saint appeared to the emperor, showing him his face and stating that the artists' hands had rendered him as God had made him. The miraculous intervention freed the two goldsmiths capable—and this was a significant homage—of rendering human features as God had made them.

The Mosan goldsmiths enjoyed extraordinary celebrity. Suger of Saint-Denis, one of the most outstanding and enlightened patrons of the Middle Ages, called six or seven of their number to work at the abbey, under partial reconstruction around 1140, which he was furnishing with sumptuous new ornaments—stained-glass windows, gold and silver pieces, sculptures, and bronze doors. Although Suger goes on at some length enumerating and describing the works of art, their aspect and their iconography, the high quality of the rich gold and silver pieces, the brilliant stained-glass windows, and the luminous architecture, he never once names an artist. The only name that returns in all the inscriptions he so assiduously notes on windows, gold objects, and doors is his own.

During the same years in which Suger was demonstrating how little importance he gave to craftsmen as individuals by showing his unwillingness to pass on their names to history, another goldsmith and his client enjoyed a particularly strong bond. We have singular testimony to this relationship in an exchange of letters in 1148 between Abbot Wibaldus of Stavelot and a goldsmith whose name began with G., probably the great Godefroid de Claire of Huy. The abbot-bishop writes:

> Men of your art often have the habit of not keeping their promises because they accept more jobs than they can carry out. Greed is at the root of every evil, but your noble genius, your eager and industrious hands are safe from every suspicion of falsity. May trust accompany your art, and may your art be accompanied by truth. . . . What is the purpose of this letter? Simply so that you will apply yourself exclusively to the labors that we have commissioned from you, putting aside every other task that could come in their way until they are completed. Know then that we are ready in our desires and that what we want we want without delay. "He gives twice who gives in haste" writes Seneca in his treatise, *De Beneficiis.* We propose to write to you at greater length later concerning the conduct of your house, the rule and the care of your family, the manner of directing your wife. Adieu.

The goldsmith answers him:

> With joy and obedience I have received the communications inspired by your great beneficence and your wisdom. They merit my attention both for their necessary insistence and for the prestige of he who has sent them to me. I have therefore engraved them in my memory and have taken note of the fact that trust should recommend my art, truth mark my work, and that my promises should be crowned with effect. Who promises, however, not always succeeds in keeping his promises, especially when the one to whom the promise was made makes it impossible or delays its fulfillment. For that reason, if, as you say, you conceive your desires rapidly and want immediately what you want, make haste on your side so that I can put myself rapidly to your works. For I am making haste,

> and always will make haste, if necessity does not put obstacles on my path. My purse is empty and none of those whom I have served pays me. . . . Therefore, . . . come to my aid in my difficulties, make use of the remedy, give in haste in such a way as to give doubly, and you will find me faithful, constant, and totally dedicated to your work. Adieu.

The letter ends with an ironic, allusive postscript: "Consider how much time there is from the beginning of May to the feast of St. Margaret, and from then to that of St. Lambert. *Sapienti sat dictum est!*" (roughly, "A word to the wise is sufficient").

If this exchange of letters illustrates the relations between a famous goldsmith of the twelfth century and his client and shows the artist's economic difficulties and precarious situation, it also shows his refined literary culture, his irony, and the rhetorical artifices he could employ to respond to the exhortations of a powerful abbot. This attitude seems in harmony with the portrayal of Godefroid recorded on the day of his death by the necrologist of the abbey of Neufmoutier (where he had become an honorary canon) as a "vir in aurifabricatura suo tempore nulli secondus," the author of famous works, and the donor of a precious reliquary to the same abbey. Gilles d'Orval, the thirteenth-century historian of the bishops of Liège, insists at length on the abilities, the merits, the voyages, and the works of "Godefroid . . . master goldsmith, the best and the most expert and subtle workman known in the world in that day, and who had sought out all regions."

After the goldsmiths, those who worked, founded, and cast metals had a place of honor. The *Life* of Gauzlin, abbot of Fleury, records as active in the abbey and responsible for important works one "Rodulfus, in every art of founding most expert" and a second Bezaleel. Einhard, who had charge of the imperial constructions in the age of Charlemagne, had already been compared to the mythical maker of the Ark of the Covenant, whom the Book of Exodus (31:2–5; 35:30–33) calls capable of working, with God's help, in gold, silver, bronze, marble, precious stones, and woods of all sorts. The comparison was to be used again in the future to indicate artists skilled in many techniques. It is possible that behind the prodigious polyvalence that medieval sources attributed to certain artists there lay the biblical model, become a *topos*.

The names of the makers of great bronze doors, those extraordinary undertakings regarded with admiration throughout the Middle Ages, are often recorded, and in some cases their faces as well. The man who modeled the doors of the church of San Zeno in Verona is shown on them, but his name is not given. On the doors of the cathedral of St. Sophia in Novgorod, the work of Saxon metalworkers, we see the founder, Riquin, carrying a scales to weigh metals, young Waimuth, who is using tongs to hold a cauldron full of boiling metal, and a third master, Abraham, also with a cauldron and carrying a mallet in his other hand.

We also know the names and faces of a certain number of illuminators of the Romanesque period. Some of them have left their signature and, less often, their image on a text; contemporary documents speak of others. The most important post in the scriptorium, however, and the one that brought the most social prestige, was that of the *scriptor,* the copyist. We have many names and portraits of these men. Their work was considered more elevated and more intellectual than the manual work of the painter, and as copyists of divine utterances and writers on the saints, they basked in the reflected light of the Word. A splendid portrait of the monk Eadwin, seated at his desk intent on his work, is surrounded with an inscription recommending him and his creatures, the letters, to the reader. The *scriptor* proclaims himself the prince of copyists, of imperishable fame and glory, and he invites us to ask the letters who he was. One letter proclaims the everlasting fame of Eadwin, represented in the image, whose skill can be seen in the beauty of the volume offered to God. The form of this high eulogy suggests that the work is a posthumous homage that the Canterbury scriptorium wanted to render to the most famous and skillful of its copyists, rather than a portrait made during Eadwin's lifetime.

One of the first self-portraits of a miniaturist depicts a monk named Hugh on a late eleventh-century text of St. Jerome (Oxford, Bodleian MS 717). Hugh is shown with pen and erasing knife in hand, according to the scheme of the portrait of the scribe, but is identified as the painter and illuminator of the work. Hugh was probably a monk in the great Norman abbey of Jumièges, and his image is found on another codex (Paris, Bibliothèque Nationale) with the legend "Hugo levita." Another illuminator of the same period, Robertus Benjamin, paints himself kneeling and signs his name to an initial in a commentary on the Psalms by St. Augustine now in the library of the cathedral of Durham (MS B ii 13). A small genre scene drawn on the last page of a manuscript of St. Augustine's *City of God,* copied around 1140 and now in the chapter library in Prague, introduces us into the intimacy of the scriptorium. A book is propped up on a reading stand held up by a lion. Facing it, on an impressive throne, is seated a person with a splendid long garment (an elaborately bordered tunic or mantle) indicated as Hildebertus. He is represented as a *scriptor,* a copyist, with a pen perched behind his ear and other pens, two inkhorns, minium, and an erasing knife laid out on a reading desk. By means of the throne and the lion, symbol of St. Mark, that holds up the reading stand, the image deliberately recalls depictions of the evangelists. Everwinus, a helper, is shown at the foot of the picture, seated on a low stool painting a frieze of leaves on a parchment folio. Not far off a table set for a meal is being reduced to confusion by a rat who has tumbled a roast chicken and a large bowl to the floor and is about to carry off a piece of cheese. Distracted from his work, Hildebertus turns in fury, his hand raised to throw a sponge at the rat. The book on the stand gives us his angry exclamation: "May God send you to perdition, miserable rat, who so many times have made me angry!" We find the same Hildebertus (who signs himself "H pictor"), again with Everwinus, in an illumination on another codex known as the *Horologion of Olumuc,* a collective volume now in the Royal Library in Stockholm. At the foot of one page, under a great illumination representing St. Gregory amid a throng of people, Hildebertus shows himself painting one side of a scroll while a scribe-monk works on the other side. Beneath them a disciple hands them the paint pots.

The *scriptor* might be an illuminator as well, or the illuminator might practice other techniques. The signature of Savalo, a monk at Saint-Amand, is found on six manuscripts from the abbey's scriptorium approximately between 1160 and 1170, always in the same form: "Sawalo monachus me fecit." His mark is also engraved in a small ivory knife, now in the museum of Lille. The mastery of many techniques for which the sources praise many medieval artists must have been more true to fact than simple use of the *topos* of the biblical Bezaleel would indicate.

There is one way to enter the workshop of a twelfth-century artist, to know what he thought of his own work, his role in society, and his relations with religion and the gifts of the Holy Spirit, to hear his enthusiasm for his own activities, to learn about his aesthetic preferences and his literary and technical culture, and, at the same time, to discover the methods, procedures, and secrets of his trade. There is the *De diversis artibus* written under the pseudonym of Theophilus by an artist monk named Roger who worked in a German monastery at the beginning of the twelfth century, possibly Roger of Helmarshausen, a monk and master of metalworking techniques active around 1100, some of whose works are extant.

Theophilus's text is divided into three books. The first is on painting, its techniques and its materials from miniatures to mural painting and painting on wood; the second speaks of glass, the various ways of working glass and its uses from vessels to stained-glass windows; the third treats ways of working metals. This third part of the treatise, which is the longest, discusses various ways to work iron, copper, silver, and gold, various types of objects, enamels, sculpture in ivory and in bone, and how to work precious stones.

The work is not a "how to do it" book like other medieval technical treatises such as the *De coloribus et artibus Romanorum* of Eraclius, the *Mappae clavicula,* and other writings on painting and sculpture, but a sort of autobiography in which the author speaks of his work, his intentions, his faith, and his convictions in a personal, engrossing, and impassioned manner. The treatise makes tangible the Romanesque artist's multiform skills and the different areas in which he could apply his talents. Along with the letter of the goldsmith "G." to the abbot of Stavelot, it confirms the high grade of literary culture that an artist of the twelfth century could attain.

The hierarchical system among the arts was by this time in crisis. In the *Didascalicon* of Hugh of St. Victor, in the works of Honorius of Autun, in the *Polycraticus* of John of Salisbury, the mechanical arts, although repeatedly called inferior, began to find a place for themselves, even if Hugh of St. Victor, writing in praise of them, considered them appropriate only for *plebei et ignobilium filii.* The situation had progressed somewhat in Italy, where Otto of Freising, Barbarossa's biographer, declared that even persons active in the fields of the mechanical arts—bothersome as they were—could obtain high military and civil positions. During this period we find a great number of artists' signatures, particularly in Italy.

Contradictory data and many problems arise from what has been said thus far. The first problem regards the position of the artist: was he free or serf, lay or cleric? The second concerns whether great persons—bishops, archbishops, and abbots—were directly involved in artistic production, not just by commissioning works. The third is that of the hierarchy of techniques and the versatility of the artists active in more than one technique. The fourth involves the first biographies of the artists and an evaluation of their work.

The artist first. We have seen artist-clerics who had splendid careers, such as St. Eloi and St. Dunstan, or Johannes, the famous Italian painter called to the court of Otto III and made bishop, but there was no lack of lay artists in the cities (a capitulary of Charles the Bald in 846 confirms privileges to Parisian goldsmiths) or in the courts (two master glassworkers, Baldricus and Ragerulfus, laymen with wives and children, worked in the court of Charles the Bald in 862). There were even lay craftsmen working in the monasteries. The plan of the monastery of Saint Gall in the ninth century shows that two buildings within the monastery walls lodged lay artisans and artists, and an informal census of the *familia ecclesiae* of the monastery of Corvey gives the number and the qualifications of the laymen who worked there, goldsmiths, master metal-casters, parchment-makers, and so forth. One of the greatest artists of the Carolingian age, the goldsmith Vuolvinus, must have been a layman, to judge by the clothes he is wearing in the representation of him on the altar of Sant'Ambrogio. Moreover, the boundary between the two was somewhat permeable, and a layman working for monasteries and episcopal seats might be made an honorary canon, as happened in the cases of a master glassworker who worked for Bishop Godefroy of Auxerre in the eleventh century, of Godefroid de Claire of Huy in the twelfth century, or of one Daniel, *pauper vitri tractor et fere laicus,* who replaced the abbot of Ramsey Abbey in the middle of the century, was then named abbot of Saint-Benet-at-Holme, and nearly succeeded, with the support of the king, in becoming archbishop of Canterbury. For a long period, until the end of the eleventh century, many of the artists of whom specific trace remains were ecclesiastics, but this may be because the sources tend to be diocesan or abbatial chronicles. In any event, the situation changed with the rapid growth of the cities at the end of the eleventh century.

One contemporary document tells us much about the social condition and the payment of an artist. It is an agreement between Girard, the abbot of Saint-Aubin in Angers, and a certain Fulco, *pictoris arte imbutus,* who agreed to decorate the entire monastery, using the subjects indicated to him, and to make its stained-glass windows. If he did so, Fulco was to become a lay brother in the monastery and a freeman of the abbot. Further, the abbot and the monastery would concede to him as a fief a vineyard and a house, on the condition that he maintain them during his lifetime and that they return to the monastery at his death, unless he had a son who practiced his art and thus would serve Saint-Aubin.

The conditions proposed to Fulco do not seem particularly generous, but this type of compensation, which permitted binding an artist for his entire natural life, were not rare at the time. A document of 1095, thus nearly contemporary, in fact seals the restitution to the bishop of Grenoble of a vineyard that had been conceded to the ancestors of the donor, masons employed by the bishops for the construction of churches. Better treatment was promised to the Lombard, Raymond, who agreed with the bishop of Urgel that he would finish the Church of the Virgin within seven years and would receive as personal compensation an annual revenue equal to that of a canon's prebend. After seven years, if he had finished his job, Raymond would be free to do what he wanted with the honor and the money that he had earned in the undertaking. Nearly a century had passed (we are in 1175) since the episode involving Fulco, and Raymond was a better technician, capable of constructing a church and leading a team of five of his compatriots.

In some cases the artists could earn enough to become donors of works of art themselves. During the twelfth century, we can find artists who gave valuable works to monasteries, Godefroid de Claire of Huy, for example, who presented the church of Neufmoustier with a highly valuable reliquary containing a relic of John the Baptist that had been given to him by the bishop of Sidon; or Gerlachus, a painter of stained-glass windows, who, around the mid-twelfth century, gave the Premonstratensian abbey of Arstein on the Lahn a splendid stained-glass window with scenes of the life of Moses. At the bottom he represented himself in one of the most extraordinary self-portraits of the Middle Ages, intent on painting with the brush in his hand. An inscription ringing the picture recommends the artist to the Lord: "Rex regum clare Gherlaco propiciare" (O illustrious king of kings, be propitious to Gerlachus).

The problem of clerical artists is closely tied to that of the bishops, abbots, and other high personages of the religious hierarchies who not only commissioned works of art but were directly involved in their production. Doubts are always admissible concerning the various formulas encountered in the sources, in which *fecit, accomplevit,* and the like can be used either for the artist or the patron. The same is true of terms like *aedificator, fabricator,* or even *architectus.* Nicolaus Pevsner has stressed the fact that the creative personality did not interest the Middle Ages enough to make it worthwhile to insist on a terminological distinction between client and artist. The sources do not permit us to doubt the existence of great ecclesiastical personages who intervened personally, even professionally, in artistic activity. The most famous case is that of Bernward, the bishop of Hildesheim at the beginning of the eleventh century, whose competence in both the liberal arts and the mechanical arts is emphasized from the first chapter of his biography. His biographer states, "And although his soul burned with the liveliest fire for every liberal science, still he dedicated himself to the study of those arts of minor weight which are called mechanical. He first shone in writing, but he practiced painting, the blacksmith's techniques, and those of foundry." The bishop's many skills are underscored in the biography written by Thangmar, dean of the chapter at Hildesheim and rector of the cathedral school, who had been Bernward's teacher. He describes Bernward's skills in sculpting in semiprecious stones and rock crystal, in chasing gold and silver objects—coffers, treasure boxes, reliquaries, chalices, and codex bindings—and he insists on the bishop's abilities as a painter, a builder, and an architect. Bernward's name appears on a number of works, in particular on the superb bronze doors at Hildesheim. Aside from Thangmar's written biography, we have a few autobiographical passages from Bernward himself that are interesting for a clearer idea of the intentions behind the works he commissioned. He was so active, determined, and engrossed that the thought is inescapable that he must have given more than simple direction to the artists working for him and was in many ways directly involved in their work. There are biographies of other ecclesiastical personalities that also emphasize their personal interest in art. At the beginning of the eleventh century, thus contemporary to Bernward, the abbot Ekkehard IV of Saint Gall, writing the history of the abbey, traces a rapid profile of one artist-monk, Tuotilo, who lived during the ninth century. Tuotilo's innumerable virtues made the emperor regret that such a man should have become a monk, and Ekkehard praises the beauty and nobility of his looks, his athletic build, his clear and eloquent voice, as well as his knowledge of music, his culture, and his linguistic talents. Instructor to the young nobles in the monastery, Tuotilo's activities were above all artistic. A painter, an ivory sculptor, and a goldsmith, he made many precious objects for the cathedral of Constance—altars, relic boxes, and a gold cross studded with gems. He made admirable sculpted ivory scenes for his abbey, a valuable antependium for the church of Saint Castor in Mainz, an image of the Madonna and Child for Metz for which the Virgin herself was reputed to have appeared miraculously to pose for him and advise him.

Another artist's biography is the *Vita* of the painter Johannes, who was called from his native Italy by Otto III to paint the Palatine

Chapel in Aix-la-Chapelle. The *Life,* written around 1050, thus fifty years or so later, by Baldericus, bishop of Liège, invites the reader to admire the paintings, even though they have been damaged by time, and it notes that others existed in Liège, the city where Johannes wanted to be buried. Baldericus also tells how, to reward his merits, the emperor named Johannes bishop of a vacant Italian diocese, but he refused the honor and chose to live far from home at the court, where he had become part of the "family" of the emperor, who showed him signs of particular friendship. The reason given is that he did not want to violate the church's rule of celibacy by marrying the daughter of the duke of the region in which his diocese lay.

One biography that testifies to a bishop's interest in architecture is that of Benno of Osnabrück (c.1028–84), superintendent of construction for the emperors Henry III and Henry IV. According to his biographer, Benno was an "architectus praecipuus caementariae operis solertissimus erat dispositor" (first among architects, and a most skillful constructor of walled structures). He took charge of both the planning and actual construction, directing the work force of the cathedral of Speyer, and he took on important construction projects in Goslar and Hildesheim, where he was provost of the cathedral.

In the early twelfth century a new attitude toward the artist was making headway in Italy. In Pisa and in Modena, highly laudatory inscriptions placed on the walls of the new cathedrals celebrated the artists who had worked there. In Modena a stone inscription dictated by Aimo, master of the cathedral school, is posted on the apse of the cathedral to commemorate the founding of the building. It praises the church, last resting place of the body of St. Geminiano, for the brilliance of its sculpted marbles, and it lauds the architect, Lanfranc, famous for his talent, learning, and skill, who was head of the building commission, rector, and master ("Est operis princeps huius rectorque magister"). Lanfranc is also mentioned in a contemporary account of the translation of the body of St. Geminiano that speaks about the first phases of construction of the church. The account stresses the search to find an architect capable of drawing up the plans for a building of the sort and constructing it ("tanti operis designator, talis structure edificator") and boasts the extraordinary talents of Lanfranc, "mirabilis artifex, mirificus edificator." Lanfranc is shown in the miniatures that accompany and illustrate the text giving orders to the workers excavating for the foundations and the masons ("operarii, artifices") and participating in solemn events and ceremonies in the company of the bishop or Countess Matilda. His long clothing, his hat, the staff in his hand, his isolated position, and his attitude of command distinguish his figure from others in the pictures that illustrate the early phases of construction. The miniatures belong, however, to the early thirteenth century, and nothing says that they reproduce older images; indeed it is probable that the picture they give of Lanfranc responds better to the thirteenth-century conception of the architect.

On the facade of the same church in Modena another stone tablet, also commemorating the church's founding, bears at its foot the name of the sculptor Wiligelmo and singles him out for praise: "Inter scultores quanto sis dignus onore claret scultura nunc Wiligelme tua" (How worthy you are of honor among sculptors is now evident, O Wiligelmo, by your sculpture). The new cathedral was thus marked in its most significant parts—the apse and the facade—with the names of the artists who worked in it.

The tomb of the first architect of the Duomo of Pisa, Buscheto, is prominently placed on the facade of the church. Over the ancient sarcophagus is a laudatory epigraph in verse showing Buscheto as superior to Ulysses because his genius was dedicated to construction and not, like the Greek hero, to destruction, and to Daedalus, the builder of the dark labyrinth in Crete, because the architect's new marble temple was white as the snow: "Non habet exemplum niveo de marmore templum" (a church of marble white as snow has no peer). The comparison of the architect to Daedalus was not a novelty. As early as the Carolingian era a labyrinth was planned for the abbey of Saint Gall, and a text referring to the architect who worked there in the time of Louis the Pious states, "quid est Winihardus nisi ipse Daedalus?" The Pisan inscription even affirms the superiority of the cathedral's architect to the mythical Greek, however. Buscheto's technical skills and ingenuity are praised by evoking salient episodes in the building process, such as the invention of devices that made it possible for ten young girls to move weights that a thousand oxen had been unable to budge, or the sea transport of immense columns and their recovery when the ship sank.

Since the present facade of the Pisa cathedral was not part of Buscheto's original construction, his tomb had to be moved, and it was placed in the new wall, which demonstrates a desire to keep alive the memory of the great architect. When the building was enlarged and the facade redone, the name and qualities of the new architect were proclaimed in a high-sounding inscription: "Hoc opus eximium tam mirum tam pretiosum Rainaldus prudens operator et ipse magister constituit mire sollerter et ingeniose" (This distinguished work, as marvelous as it is precious, was erected by Rainaldo, master and prudent constructor, in admirable, able, and ingenious fashion).

A propitiatory inscription runs under the text that sings Rainaldo's praises, framing a marble intarsia plaque on which a figure with a cross in his hand is shown between two ferocious monsters: "De ore leonis libera me domine et a cornibus unicornium humilitatem meam" (Save me, O Lord, from the claws of the lion and protect my humility from the horn of the unicorns), an apotropaic formula to be taken as the prayer of the same "prudens operator et ipse magister." Pisa and Modena, then, are privileged places for following the evolution of the social status of the artist in the early twelfth century, and it is not by coincidence that they were both important communes. The outcropping of artists' signatures should be seen as related to the communes' great artistic and building projects. To have procured the best workmen and to have realized, thanks to their collaboration, the most extraordinary constructions redounded to the eternal glory of the collectivity and added to the city's prestige. The artist saw his own social position and his role improve through his connections with this new collective client.

Inscriptions bearing artists' signatures abound during the course of the twelfth century, particularly in Italy but also, with differences in emphasis and nature, in France and Germany.

In Italy it was architects, stonemasons, and sculptors who put their names to their works. A monumental inscription running across the facade of the Duomo of Foligno recalls how in 1133, under Bishop Marco, the church was reconstructed by Atto, who was a stonecutter (*lathomus*), an important man (*magnus vir*), and an excise tax collector ("Extitit vir magnus lathomus Acto chomarcus quos [Bishop Marco and the stonecutter Atto] Christus salvet benedicat, adiuvet. Amen"). This same Atto put his name on the facade of the church of San Pietro in Bovara, not far from Foligno, stating that he had made the church and the rose window with his own hands: ("Atto sua dextra templum fecit atque fenestram cui deus eternam vitam tribuat atque supernam"). Atto is extremely interesting for our purposes, since he was a stonemason who was also a notable personage in the city (*magnus vir, chomarcus*), yet he states that he has put his own hands to the job, not just directed it (*sua dextra templum fecit*).

The distinction between the functions of inventor and director of construction, on the one hand, and stonemason and/or sculptor, on the other, was already present in the Modenese and Pisan inscriptions referring to Lanfranc (on the commemorative tablet, "operis princeps huius rectorque magister"; in the chronicle, "operis designator, structure edificator" and "mirabilis artifex, mirificus edificator") and to Rainaldo ("prudens operator et ipse magister"). They permit us a closer look at the division and superposition of tasks. There were architects who drew up plans and directed construction; there were constructors who were able stonemasons personally involved in stonecutting (the superb masonry of the cathedral of Foligno justified Atto's pride), master masons, and carpenters; there were craftsmen who were primarily sculptors and who sign their names as such, but who may also have had a personal and direct responsibility for construction. According to the circumstances, one qualification was weighted more strongly than the other.

In Italy in the twelfth century the figure of the sculptor emerged to join that of the architect. Wiligelmo was a sculptor, as was Niccolò da Ferrara, who invited viewers to admire the intertwined botanical motifs concealing beasts and monsters ("flores cum beluis comixti cernitis") that he had made for the portal of the Zodiac in the abbey of San Michele della Chiusa. He also invited them to comprehend the meaning of his work ("hoc opus intendat quisquis bonus exit et intrat") by scrutinizing the images and reading the inscriptions ("vos legite versus quos descripsit Nicolaus"). An inscription on the cathedral of Ferrara affirms Niccolò's skill and predicts his long-lasting glory ("artificem gnarum qui sculpserit haec Nicolaum hic concurrentes laudent per secula gentes").

In Tuscany, Guglielmo proclaimed the priority of his art among the "moderns" ("prestantior in arte modernis") on the pulpit he sculpted for the cathedral of Pisa between 1159 and 1162 (sent to Cagliari a century and a half later when Giovanni Pisano sculpted a new pulpit). Guglielmo's tomb, like that of Buscheto, was set into the facade of the cathedral, and it is marked by an inscription ("sepolcro di maestro Guglielmo che fece il pergamo della cattedrale"). In Pisa, Lucca, and Pistoia the use of artists' names became more frequent and more widespread during the rest of the century. On several occasions Biduinus put a refined and classical signature to his works: the architrave of San Cassiano in Settimo bears the inscription, "Hoc opus quod cernis Biduinus docte perfecit" (The work that you see Biduinus has learnedly completed). Gruamons, who worked with his brother Adeodatus, signs himself "Magister bonus" on the architrave of the church of Sant'Andrea in Pistoia; Roberto declares himself "in arte peritus" on the font in San Frediano in Lucca and in the same city

Guidetto leaves his name on the facade of the cathedral; in Milan the architect Anselmus, "Dedalus alter," and the sculptor Girardus, "pollice docto," leave their names, with full classical trimmings, on the Porta Romana gate, which was rebuilt after it had been destroyed by Barbarossa.

Signatures of sculptors and architects in the eleventh and twelfth centuries are a good deal rarer outside Italy. One Umbertus left his name on a capital of the tower that Abbot Gauzlin wanted to offer as an example to all the Gauls, and he was probably among the artists that the abbot had brought to Fleury. Later, toward the end of the twelfth century, Bernardus Gelduinus—probably a goldsmith who also worked in ivory and in marble, a more valuable material than stone—signed the altar slab of the high altar in the church of Saint-Sernin in Toulouse. One of the most spectacular creations of French Romanesque art, the tympanum of the Last Judgment in the cathedral of Autun, is signed by one Gislebertus, to whom, for stylistic reasons, a great many of the capitals inside the church can also be attributed. Also in Autun, Martin, a monk, signs the tomb of St. Lazarus in more elaborate fashion; a certain Brunus leaves his name in Saint-Gilles; one Gilabertus proclaims himself "vir non incertus" in Toulouse; a Robertus signs the handsome capitals of Notre Dame du Port in Clermont. The list could continue, but we have no names for the most spectacular monuments of French Romanesque sculpture—the cloister and portal of Moissac, the portals of Souillac, Conques, Vezelay, and many more. It is as if the role of the sculptor were very different in France and in Italy, which explains why sculptors' names disappeared completely in the great Gothic cathedrals.

Germany also provides many names of Romanesque sculptors. At Goslar an inscription on the surviving facade of the cathedral tells us that "Hartmannus statuam fecit basisque figuram," while a relief on the east side of the choir of the cathedral of Worms is signed "Otto me fecit" and in the crypt of the cathedral of Freising the name of one Liuptpreht appears. In the church of Larrelt in eastern Frisia both the iconography and the inscriptions of the tympanum are more singular. Here in this frontier march, this missionary land, the center of the tympanum is occupied by the image of the priest who commissioned the church, one Ippo, and Meinhard, who constructed it. The name of the sculptor of the relief, Menulfus, also appears. An inscription states: "Ippo non parcus fuit / Artifici mihi largus" (Ippo was not parsimonious but generous toward me, the artist). The appearance of the names and images of this singular trio breaks with the traditional iconographic scheme of a saint's image in the tympanum; in this peripheral zone the influence of tradition was weaker.

All over Europe during the course of the twelfth century names and signatures of sculptors appeared, unevenly distributed but following a growing trend, thus testifying to the renewed importance of monumental sculpture and to a more precise role for the sculptor. This common tendency had different outcomes, however. In Italy the role of the sculptor-architect was to become sharply defined and take on increasing importance; in France the figure of the architect was to dominate the scene.

One great artist working in northern Italy at the end of the twelfth century was a sculptor who belonged to the group of the "Magistri Antelami," Lombard stonecarvers from the Val d'Intelvi. On a tombstone in the Duomo of Parma showing the Deposition from the Cross (1178) he signs himself "Benedictus" ("Antelami dictus sculptor fuit hic Benedictus"). Although he proclaimed himself a sculptor, Benedictus Antelami was an imaginative and talented architect open to experiment who built the Baptistery in Parma. He was arguably the first Gothic artist in Italy. This dual level of activities was common to many artists who called themselves sculptors but who were capable of directing the construction of a great edifice—of a cathedral in the cases of Niccolò in Ferrara, Benedictus Antelami, Nicola Pisano and Giovanni Pisano, and many others (in even greater number in the fourteenth century). That they proclaim themselves and indeed were primarily sculptors shows the prestige in Italy of a technique felt to be closely connected with classical culture. It also reveals a particular conception of architecture in which plastic and decorative aspects were extremely important. This was not the case elsewhere.

In France the figure of the architect assumed great importance during the course of the thirteenth century. His role in a great construction project was distinct from that of the stonecutter or the mason. The architect designed the edifice and coordinated the activities of various groups of workers, craftsmen, and artists—sculptors, painters, master glassworkers, goldsmiths, ironworkers, carpenters, and more. A sermon of Nicolas de Biart (1261) shows the architect arriving at the workplace, wearing gloves, staff in hand, showing the stonecutter how to cut a block of stone, for which, without ever putting his hand to the job, he received higher wages than the others. The Dominican preacher disapproved of this behavior and he uses the architect as an example in his criticism of contemporary prelates. In reality, however, Nicolas's case showed modernity and an advanced division of labor. Beginning in the first decades of the thirteenth century, we know the names of many of the architects who directed work on the great Gothic constructions. There was Robert de Luzarches, followed by Thomas de Cormont and Renault de Cormont in Amiens; Jean and Pierre Deschamps in Clermont-Ferrand; Jean le Loup, Jean d'Orbais, Gaucher de Reims, Bernard de Soissons in Reims, Gauthier and Pierre de Varinfroy and Nicolas de Chaumes in Meaux and Sens; Jean and Pierre de Chelles, Pierre, Eudes, and Raoul de Montreuil, Jean Ravy, and Jean le Boutellier in Paris (Notre-Dame, Saint-Denis, and the Sainte-Chapelle); Jean d'Andely in Rouen.

Their names are sculpted on the buildings (on the south transept of Notre-Dame in Paris an inscription recalls that that part of the cathedral was begun in February of 1257 by Master Jean de Chelles), or they are recorded in tombstone epigraphs or in the meanders of the labyrinths plotted in the church pavement. The labyrinth (the house of Daedalus, the mythical progenitor of all architects) was represented in the cathedrals of Amiens and Reims with the figures of the various architects who had directed construction placed at the center and at the four corners. We have seen Daedalus associated with the title of architect in the early twelfth century in the inscription on Buscheto's tomb in the cathedral of Pisa. That image, along with an early labyrinth on the porch of the cathedral of San Martino in Lucca, implies that Italy had a role in diffusing the comparison. The images and the memorial inscriptions exalt the figure of the architect. On his tomb in the choir Guillaume, the architect of Saint-Etienne in Caen is called "petrarum summus in arte"; Pierre de Montreuil, the architect of the abbey church of Saint-Denis, Saint-Germain-des-Prés and of the Sainte Chapelle in Paris, was called "doctor lathomorum" on his tombstone in the chapel of the Virgin in Saint-Germain-des-Prés, implicitly putting him on the same plane as a university professor, as if to turn the weapons of the scholastic offensive against the mechanical arts back against their inventors. Hugues Libergier, architect of the church of Saint-Nicaise in Reims (now destroyed) is represented on his tombstone dressed in a formal gown like an academic toga, holding a model of the church he constructed—a privilege that to that point had been granted only to the client.

The new and spectacular characteristics of French Gothic architecture were much in demand, and French architects were sought after throughout Europe. William of Sens chose the new style rather early, when he began construction on the chancel of the cathedral of Canterbury; Etienne de Bonneuil was called from Paris to Sweden in 1287 to work on the cathedral of Uppsala; around 1270 the reconstruction in *opera francigeno,* following the dictates of the Gothic style, of the church of Wimpfen im Tal, on the edge of the Black Forest, was entrusted to a *peritissimo architectoriae artis latomo* who came from Paris; toward the middle of the century Villard de Honnecourt went to Hungary. Villard's model book is extant, and in it sketches of floor plans and elevations, projections and particulars of buildings from Meaux to Laon, Reims, and Lausanne alternate with drawings of sculptures, ancient monuments, and machinery. The variety of the subjects in Villard's sketches confirms that the man at the head of a great work-project in thirteenth-century France coordinated and directed the activities of various specialists, furnishing all of them with requirements, ideas, and suggestions. It is probably for that reason that in France we find not one signature of a sculptor in the thirteenth century, even though they had been numerous in the preceding century, and only one signature of a master glassworker, the Clément de Chartres who left his name on a window in the cathedral of Rouen. It is possible that some of the men who headed the great Gothic construction projects had previously been sculptors, as were Gaucher de Reims, master-in-chief of the cathedral of Reims between 1247 and 1255 (who, we are told, "worked on the voussoirs and the portals," in all probability executing many of the sculptures) and Etienne de Bonneuil, called to Uppsala to "work on cutting stone." Besides the architects, it seems that the only artists who had the right to a name in the thirteenth century were the goldsmiths. They too were much sought after in all Europe—and beyond, if one thinks of the adventure of Etienne Boucher. Like Villard de Honnecourt, Etienne went to Hungary. He was taken prisoner there by the Tartars, and in China he became goldsmith to the Great Khan, as Willem van Ruysbroeck tells us in his account of his voyage to the Orient.

In the French court at the turn of the fourteenth century and in other courts that took the French as a model a new phenomenon arose: the ennoblement of the artist. For the moment we have too little data on this question and we need further research before we can grasp its full implications. The fact remains, however, that in 1270 King Philip IV of France (Philippe le Bel) granted a noble title to his court goldsmith, one Raoul, and in 1289 the name of Pierre d'Agincourt, architect to the Angevin court of Naples, appears in a document followed by the title of *miles.* Unless it is a case of homonymy, this may also have happened to Simone Martini during his stay in Naples. One might well ask whether the artists who entered the "family" of the sovereign were rewarded and ennobled for their art, or whether these were special cases in which the functionary was honored more than the artist. It is certain that in France, in England, and in Naples, the reorganization of the court more and more frequently gave rise to a new personage, the court artist. This undeniably opened the way to a new social position and a new recognition of the artist. The situation that would prompt Albrecht Dürer to exclaim in Venice, "Hier bin ich ein Herr" (here I am a lord) was to become clearer and to promise well for the future of artists in Italy.

The situation was completely different in Italy and in France. Italy did not have the overwhelming hegemony of a center like Paris. To the contrary, the communes were arriving at the height of their economic strength and marking the landscape with signs of their irrepressible polycentrism. Furthermore, there was not the absolute supremacy of the architect that there was in France.

Painters developed and extended their activities in Italy, particularly in the cities of Tuscany. Pisa, Lucca, Florence, Siena, Arezzo, and Pistoia were important centers, for which we have a great many painters' signatures: Giunta Pisano, Bonaventura Berlinghieri, Coppo di Marcovaldo, Meliore, Guido da Siena, Margaritone d'Arezzo, and Manfredino da Pistoia, to cite only a few for whom documentation and evidence exists. We also have the earliest contracts for painted works, such as the contract for the Rucellai Madonna by Duccio or those covering Coppo di Marcovaldo's activities in Pistoia. Commissions from the popes and the cardinals called artists to Rome in that luminous Saint Martin's summer that the city enjoyed in the last decades of the thirteenth century; the decoration of the basilica of Saint Francis in Assisi employed artists from various regions, while the courts of southern Italy, first the Swabian court of Frederick II, then the Angevin court in Naples, provided other centers of attraction and points of convergence for artists.

Even in this dynamic, polycentric, promise-filled situation, it was once more a sculptor, Giovanni Pisano, who most fully and significantly revealed the artist's new ambitions and his view of himself and his work. One of the greatest names in medieval art but also an exception that tests the rule, Giovanni was an artist with an enormous sense of the importance of his own work and a boundless pride. He never avoided conflict or feared breaking with his clients and was an artist who, by his behavior, seems to have tried to break out of the limitations shackling and humbling the medieval artist.

Giovanni had dramatic confrontations with clients in Siena, where he abandoned his charge as master-in-chief of the cathedral and left the city without further ado. The same thing occurred in Pisa, though with a less definitive conclusion. His pride and his awareness of his own worth show not only in his actions but in the inscriptions he left on his works. On the pulpit of Sant'Andrea in Pistoia he both stresses his family tie and affirms his own superiority when he proclaims himself better than his father (something that simply was not done): "Giovanni sculpted this, who never did unworthy works [*qui res non egit inanes*], born of Nicola, but gifted with greater knowledge [*Nicoli natus sientia meliore beatus*], learned beyond anything ever seen [*doctum super omnia visa*]." This was behavior quite different from that of Tino di Camaino, who, twenty years or so later, in his inscription for the tomb he designed for the bishop, Antonio d'Orso, in the cathedral in Florence, declared his unwillingness to be called "master" as long as his father, Camaino di Crescentino, was alive ("Hunc pro patre genitivo decet inclinari / ut magister illo vivo nolit appellari").

In the two inscriptions on the pulpit of the cathedral in Pisa Giovanni consigns to posterity a dramatic autobiography. In the first he expresses his ideas on art and on creativity, which he considers a gift from God ("Laudo deum verum per quem sunt optima rerum / Qui dedit has puras hominem formare figuras"). By creating splendid works in various techniques and materials ("sculpens i petra, ligno, auro splendida"), and incapable, even if he wanted to do so, of sculpting ugly pieces ("tetra sculpere nescisset vel turpia si voluisset"), he shows himself gifted to the highest degree with this God-given talent ("Criste miserere / cui talia dona fuere"). Sculptors are many, but among them all, honors and praise go to him for the excellent sculptures and varied figures he has made ("Plures sculptores: remanet sibi laudes honores. / Claras sculpturas fecit variasque figuras. / Quisquis miraris tunc recto iure probaris").

Giovanni's second inscription is a sort of personal apologia listing the unjustified criticisms that he has had to bear. It begins with the cosmogonic significance of his work and with himself: "Circuit hic amnes mundi partesque Johannes" (Giovanni has here inscribed the rivers and the parts of the world). This refers to the sculptures of the Evangelists and personifications of the theological virtues that hold up the pulpit, which Giovanni identifies allegorically with the rivers of Paradise and the parts of the world. The work and its author are inseparably bound together, and the justificatory and biographical tone immediately prevails in his insistence on his efforts and experiments ("plurima temptando gratis discenda, parando / queque labore gravi"), in particular when he speaks of the accusations and the calumnies he suffered and his own lack of caution ("non bene cavi"). He concludes by affirming his own absolute superiority, challenging calumniators and critics: "Se probat indignum reprobans diademate dignum / Sit hunc quem reprobat se reprobando probat" (He who criticizes one worthy of a crown shows himself to be unworthy; he who reproaches proves that in his turn he is reproachable).

Giovanni Pisano's work, his acts, and his dramatic autobiographical remarks prefigured those of the Renaissance artist (if they are not that already), but for the moment his was to remain an isolated case without immediate imitators. The figurative arts would later find another way to break out of their still subordinate situation by means of what might be called an alliance between artists and intellectuals, men of letters, and the custodians and legislators of the privileged field to which for centuries only those who cultivated the liberal arts had had access.

The university title of "doctor" awarded to Pierre de Montreuil on his tombstone had already been used for an artist. Solsternus, who in 1207 designed the great mosaic for the facade of the cathedral of Spoleto, proclaimed himself in it "Doctor Solsternus—hac summus in arte modernus." Terms like *doctus* and *doctissimus* had on occasion been used to refer to sculptors and stonecarvers during the twelfth and thirteenth centuries, as we have seen. The "learned thumb" of the sculptor Girardus in Milan and the "learned hand" of Nicola Pisano were rhetorical expressions with which the artists sought to escape the ghetto of the mechanical arts. An authentic rupture occurs, however, in the passage in the eleventh canto of Dante's *Purgatorio* in which he mentions two illuminators, Oderisi of Gubbio and Franco of Bologna, and two painters, Cimabue and Giotto, and compares them with men of letters. The bracketing of painters' names with those of men of letters is important in itself; it was of even greater importance that these names should appear in a text destined for such rapid and widespread success as the *Divine Comedy.* This was in fact the high point in the artists' partial liberation from a subordination imposed on them by their connections with the "mechanical arts."

Artists achieved this liberation in Florentine culture thanks to the weight of Dante's words and the profoundly innovative work of Giotto. A network of complicity and admiration was quick to grow up around Giotto. The way in which his name and his works are evoked in contemporary documents is an indication of his extraordinary fame: one testament of 1312 mentions the Crucifix in Santa Maria Novella painted by "the most worthy painter, Giotto di Bondone," while in 1313 Francesco da Barberino, a man of letters interested in painting, cited the Envy that Giotto had portrayed on the base of the walls of the Arena Chapel in Padua. In 1330, while he was working in Naples, we find Giotto mentioned as being on familiar terms with the king, Charles II, and called *protopictor* and *protomagister.* When Giotto was called to Florence three years before his death, the Florentines solemnly declared that no one more able than "Maestro Giotto fiorentino" could be found, and that thanks to his settling in the city his knowledge and his teaching would profit many artists, and many beautiful works would be made in Florence. He was in fact called to Florence to be offered the charge of Architect of the Commune. This was the highest office that the commune could offer him but it also meant that his talent for drawing and design could be applied in other fields.

The familiar passage from Dante was enlarged upon, repeated, and variously interpreted by the commentators of the *Divine Comedy,* and some expressed surprise that the poet had cited persons of such humble condition. During the course of the century, men of letters took over the figure of Giotto to the point of making him one of their own, an artist who belonged to an elite and was understood by that elite. Boccaccio uses Giotto as the protagonist of one of the stories on the *Decameron.* He states:

> By virtue of the fact that he brought back to light an art which had been buried for centuries beneath the blunders of those who, in their paintings, aimed to bring visual delight to the ignorant rather than intellectual satisfaction to the wise, his work may justly be regarded as a shining monument to the glory of Florence. (Trans. McWilliam).

In 1370, when Petrarch bequeathed a painting by Giotto to the lord of Padua, he noted in his testament that its beauty, incomprehensible to the ignorant, stupefied the masters ("cuius pulchritudinem ignoranti non intelligunt, magistri autem stupent").

This distinction between a learned and an ignorant public (which operates on the terrain of reception) was to do excellent service as an evaluative instrument. The figurative arts used the distinction to come closer to the dignity of the liberal arts at the end of the artists' long struggle to establish their legitimacy by signing their works, thus insisting on how learned, cultivated, and intellectual they were and how far from the "mechanical." Petrarch juxtaposed the names of Virgil and Simone Martini in the Virgilian allegory that he asked Simone to paint on the first folio of a codex of Virgil rediscovered by a lucky series of events, saying that Mantua gave birth to Virgil "qui talia carmina finxit" and Siena Simone, "digito qui talia pinxit." Even though the play on words between *finxit* and *pinxit* and the mention of working with one's fingers subtly allude to the old distinction, the capital fact of the pairing remains. Toward the end of the century Filippo Villani included Giotto and other Florentine painters in his praise of the famous men of his city, "many thinking, not wrongly, that certain painters were not inferior in genius to those who were masters in the liberal arts." The mention of artists as intellectuals (who by definition exercised liberal activities) was to do much to further an early development of the arts in Florence and to give them a new and more complex structure.

BIBLIOGRAPHY

Armandi, Marina, ed. *Lanfranco e Wiligelmo. Il Duomo di Modena.* Modena: Panini, 1984.

Barral, Xavier, ed. *Artistes, artisans et production artistique au Moyen-Age.* Actes du Colloque de Rennes. Paris: Picard, 1987.

Binding, Günther and Norbert, Nussbaum. *Der mittelalterliche Baubetrieb nördlich der Alpen in zeitgenossischen Darstellungen.* Darmstadt: Wissenschaftliche Buchgesellschaft, 1978.

Camesasca, Ettore. *Artisti in bottega.* Milan: Feltrinelli, 1966.

Clausberg, Karl, ed. *Bauwerk und Bildwerk im Hochmittelalter.* Giessen: Anabas, 1981.

Claussen, Peter Cornelius. *Magistri Doctissimi Romani.* Corpus Cosmatorum, 1. Stuttgart: F. Steiner Verlag, Wiesbaden, 1987.

Du Colombier, Pierre. *Les Chantiers des cathédrales:ouvriers architectes, sculpteurs.* Rev. ed. Paris: A. J. Picard, 1973; originally published 1953.

Egbert, Virginia Wylie. *The Medieval Artist at Work.* Princeton: Princeton University Press, 1967.

Gimpel, Jean. *Les Batisseurs des cathédrales.* Paris: Le Seuil, 1958 [*The Cathedral Builders.* Trans. Teresa Waugh. New York: Grove Press, 1983].

Huth, Hans. *Künstler und Werkstatt der Spätgotik.* Augsburg: Dr. Filser Verlag, 1923; Rev. ed., Darmstadt: Wissenschaftliche Buchgesellschaft, 1967.

Knoop, Douglas, and G. P. Jones. *The Medieval Mason: An Economic History of English Stone Building in the Later Middle Ages and Early Modern Times.* Manchester: Manchester University Press, 1933; 3d ed., rev. and reset, New York: Barnes and Noble, 1967.

Kosegarten, Antje Middeldorf. "The Origins of the Artistic Competition." In *Lorenzo Ghiberti nel suo tempo.* Atti del Convegno internazionale di studi (Firenze, 18–21 ottobre 1978). 2 vols. Florence: L. S. Olschki, 1980, 1:167–86.

Larner, John. "The Artist and the Intellectual in Fourteenth Century Italy." *History* 54 (1969): 13–30.

Legner, Anton, ed. *Ornamenta Ecclesiae. Kunst und Künstler der Romanik: Katalog zur Ausstellung des Schnutgen-Museums in der Josef-Haubrich-Kunsthalle.* 3 vols. Cologne: Stadt Köln, 1985. Vol. 1.

Martindale, Andrew. *The Rise of the Artist in the Middle Ages and Early Renaissance.* New York: McGraw-Hill, 1972.

Mortet, Victor, and Paul Deschamps. *Recueil de textes relatifs à l'histoire de l'architecture et à la condition des architectes en France au Moyen-Age.* 2 vols. Paris: A. Picard, 1911–29.

Pevsner, Nicolaus. "The Term 'Architect' in the Middle Ages." *Speculum* 14, 4 (1942): 549–62.

Stein, Henri. *Les Architectes des cathédrales gothiques: Etude critique.* Paris: H. Lauren, 1909; 1929.

Wentzel, Hans. "Glasmaler und Maler im Mittelalter." *Zeitschrift für Kunstwissenschaft* 3 (1949): 53–62.

Warnke, Martin. *Bau und Uberbau. Soziologie der mittelalterlichen Architektur nach den Schriftquellen.* Frankfurt: Syndikat, 1976.

SUGGESTED READINGS

Frederick Antal, *Florentine Painting and Its Social Background: The Bourgeois Republic Before Cosimo de'Medici's Advent to Power: XIV and Early XV Centuries* (Cambridge, Ma.: Belknap, 1986).

John Harvey, *The Master Builders: Architecture in the Middle Ages* (New York: McGraw-Hill, 1971).

George Henderson, *Early Medieval* (Harmondsworth: Penguin, 1972).

———, *Gothic* (Harmondsworth: Penguin, 1967).

Spiro Kostof, ed., *The Architect: Chapters in the History of the Profession* (New York: Oxford University Press, 1986).

Wendy Slatkin, *Woman Artists in History: From Antiquity to the 20th Century* (Englewood Cliffs, N.J.: Prentice-Hall, 1985).

John White, *Art and Architecture in Italy, 1250–1400* (Baltimore: Penguin, 1966).

Rudolf Wittkower, *The Artist and the Liberal Arts* (London: H. K. Lewis, 1952).

Rudolf Wittkower and Margot Wittkower, *Born Under Saturn* (New York: W. W. Norton, 1969).

SEVEN

The Merchant

Aron Ja. Gurevich

THE ADVANCES MADE BY MEN IN THE MERCANTILE SECTOR IN WESTERN EUROPEAN SOCIETY BETWEEN THE ELEVENTH AND THE FIFTEENTH CENTURIES reflected changes of extraordinary importance for the economy of the age, the structure of society, and culture. The merchant at the beginning of the Middle Ages, a notable but nevertheless secondary element in a prevalently agrarian society, gradually became a figure of primary importance who embodied new relationships that sapped the traditional foundations of feudalism. Here, however, our interests lie not so much in the merchants' economic activity per se as in the merchant as a human type. The merchants' mentality was in many ways substantially different from that of knights, the clergy, or the peasantry. The worldview that formed gradually in the consciousness of the developing merchant class conflicted with the vision of the world in the other strata and levels of feudal society. The profession and the way of life of men of affairs favored the formation of new ethical orientations and a different sort of conduct.

*

At the beginning of the eleventh century, when the overwhelming majority of the population of Europe lived in the country, towns and cities existed, and merchants were one component in society. Indeed, their role was far from negligible. Sovereigns, prelates, the aristocracy, and, to some extent, the wealthier strata of the population required various sorts of articles and merchandise that could not be produced locally and thus had to be imported from other and at times distant places. Not only luxurious garments and stuffs, fine tableware, and other rarities to satisfy the governing elite's need for prestige, but also more ordinary merchandise was often furnished by merchants who plied the waterways and the land routes. The seas of southern and northern Europe, the great rivers, and, on occasion, the roads inherited from Roman times were used as commercial arteries.

The merchant of the early Middle Ages was a personage radically different from his counterpart in the more fully developed later Middle Ages. The traders who operated in northern Europe during the age of the Vikings offer an excellent paradigm. The Viking was a warrior, a conqueror, a plunderer, a bold navigator, and a colonizer. The inhabitants of France and England, ancient Russia, and the Mediterranean suffered attacks by Vikings from Scandinavia. Where their banners appeared villages and cities burned, monasteries fell to ruins, men and domestic animals died. The Vikings took rich booty, including church treasures and slaves. Throughout Europe prayers were raised to God for protection from the assaults of the Northmen. We should not forget, however, that Viking expeditions were closely connected with commerce. Often the voyage of a Norwegian or a Swede into a nearby territory was something of a mixed enterprise. He brought with him merchandise—products of the hunt or craft articles—and exchanged them for his daily necessities. In the many finds from the Viking era, archaeologists have found not only weapons but pairs of scales with weights that were used by the Scandinavian navigators, and certainly pillage was not responsible for all the many hoards of silver and gold coins found in the North. Some of the money came from peaceful mercantile exchange. As the Icelandic Sagas tell us, however, the Scandinavians' commercial voyages often ended with an assault on the local inhabitants, and what they could not get by exchange they took by force. Commerce and pillage went hand in hand.

During the early Middle Ages, however, even the merchants who were not involved in banditry needed a certain aggressivity. They had to take their caravans into far-off lands, make their way among alien races and populations, and confront all imaginable dangers, from marauders to local lords more like brigands who did their best to get their hands on the merchants' wealth either by charging them exorbitant customs duties or simply relieving them of their merchandise and their earnings. The merchants had to withstand storms at sea and all the trials of land transport over nearly impassable roads. Profit could be high when the merchandise was precious, but the risks involved were just as high. In his *Colloquy,* the English churchman and abbot, Aelfric (early eleventh century), describes the various professions, citing the merchant along with the monk, the farmer, the shepherd, the weaver, the salter, the fisherman, the hunter, and the smith. The merchant is quoted as saying,

> I am useful to the king, the noble, the wealthy man, and the whole population. I board a ship with my goods and I navigate to the lands beyond the sea; I sell merchandise and acquire precious things that are not found here in our land. I transport them at great risk and sometimes I am shipwrecked, losing all I have and only barely escaping with my life.

According to Aelfric, the merchant carried costly clothing and fine stuffs, precious stones and gold, wine and oil, ivory, iron and other metals, glass, and many other commodities. His interlocutor asks him: "Do you sell these goods at the price at which you have bought them?" to which the merchant answers, "No. What then would I get for my trouble? I sell more dear than I have bought precisely in order to earn a profit and to keep my wife and children."

Still, Aelfric considers the labor of the plowman, who provides food for everyone, more important to society than that of the merchant. "Economic thought" in the early Middle Ages did not reach beyond the horizon traced by natural economy. Following the same logic, theoreticians of nascent feudalism represented society as a three-part system that was headed by the monarch and included only the clergy ("those who pray"), the knightly class ("those who fight"), and the peasantry ("those who plow the land"). The urban population, the craftsmen, and the merchants escaped their notice, not because their roles were totally insignificant but because in the society of the eleventh and twelfth centuries, dominated by tradition, the old conceptual schemata retained so much of their ancient vigor that the vital complexity of concrete reality could be ignored. From the point of view of the dominant ethic, agricultural labor, the prayers of the monks and the clerics, and the bellicose acts of the warriors were equally necessary for the functioning of the social organism; but urban occupations, commerce in particular, remained dubious and invited circumspection. The peasants' mistrust of the merchant and the noble's contemptuous haughtiness found a parallel and a justification on the ideological plane in the teaching of the church.

Society's attitude toward the merchant was extremely contradictory. On the one hand, it was difficult to do without him. In the Norwegian *Speculum regale* (The King's Mirror), a father gives instructions to his son. He describes the various levels and categories of society from the point of view of a cultivated Norwegian of the first third of the thirteenth century, beginning with a description of the activities of the merchant:

> A man who is to be a trader will have to brave many perils, sometimes at sea and sometimes in heathen lands, but nearly always among alien peoples; and it must be his constant purpose to act discreetly wherever he happens to be. On the sea he must be alert and fearless. When you are in a market town, or wherever you are, be polite and agreeable; then you will secure the friendship of all good men. (Trans. Larson, as for following quotations)

The merchant must study carefully the commercial customs of the places he visits. In particular, he must know commercial law thoroughly. To be successful in his commerce, the merchant must know languages, Latin and French above all, since they were the most widely diffused. The merchant-navigator must know how to orient himself by the stars, to observe the "grouping of the hours," and to know "the points of the Horizon." Furthermore, the father advises, "you ought never to let a day pass without learning something that will profit you. . . . A man must regard it as great an honor to learn as to teach, if he wishes to be considered thoroughly informed." The merchant should keep his temper and maintain reserve, but avoid being thought a coward: "Though necessity may force you into strife, be not in a hurry to take revenge; first make sure that your effort will succeed and strike where it ought." Particular caution should be exercised in the choice of business associates, and "always let Almighty God, the holy Virgin Mary, and the saint to whom you have most frequently called upon to intercede for you be counted among your partners."

By observing all these counsels one might become rich. The author of the *Speculum regale*, recognizing the great risk connected with overseas commerce, advises the young merchant:

> If you find that the profits of trade bring a decided increase to your funds, draw out the two-thirds and invest them in good farm land, for such property is generally thought the most secure, whether the enjoyment of it falls to one's self or to one's kinsmen.

The most curious aspect of this advice is that it was given in Norway, a country without much agricultural land. Investments in farmland from the capital created by mercantile activities can be found in the lands of continental Europe from Germany to Italy. Commercial occupations were important, but the dangers of all sorts that beleaguered them and the social and economic risks of the profession prompted merchants to turn back to the higher guarantees of landownership.

Moreover, the merchant's social prestige was fairly modest. The wealthy man aroused envy and ill will, and people entertained serious doubts about his honesty and conscientiousness. In general, the merchant remained a "pariah" in early medieval society. Precisely how could his profits be justified? He acquired merchandise at a certain price and resold it at a higher price. That was where the possibilities for deceit and unjust gain were concealed, and the theologians were fond of repeating that "the merchant's possession is not pleasing to God." According to the Fathers of the church, it was difficult to avoid having sin creep into the relations of buying and selling. Commerce almost always figured on the lists drawn up by theologians of professions qualified as "dishonest" and "impure." When the clergy rejected things of this world in favor of the celestial realms, they could not fail to condemn commerce, an occupation that pursued the objective of profit.

This was the position of the church, at least until it was forced to give greater consideration to the changing conditions in real life that had become noticeable in the thirteenth century. One indication of this change is that the church was constrained to shift the focus of its efforts to impose and reinforce its ethical and religious doctrine from the countryside to the city. The new mendicant orders of the Franciscans and the Dominicans were primarily based in the cities, and although their preaching did not neglect the other segments of society, it was primarily directed at the urban population. According to one representative of the church, Humbert of Romans, since the mass of the population was concentrated in the towns and cities, that was where the inhabitants of rural areas were drawn and where—this was the most important point—the heresy that had to be eradicated best took root. Even in this period, however, attitudes toward the merchant's profession were highly contradictory. Even though the church recognized the importance of commerce for the existence of the body social, and even though from time to time it assured its protection to commerce and drew profit from it, it retained all its prejudices against trade. "There is something disgraceful about trade, something sordid and shameful," wrote Thomas Aquinas, though he fully recognized its necessity for society.

This contradictory attitude toward the medieval merchant is perfectly displayed in the sermons of the mendicant friars. We must not forget that the founder of the Order of the Friars Minor came from a family of wealthy cloth merchants. Imbued with the idea of evangelical poverty, Francis of Assisi rejected his inheritance and broke with his family, founding a confraternity of followers that soon became a monastic order. Faced with the people's growing discontent at the wealth of the church, of the nobility, and of the higher levels of urban society—a discontent that bred heresy—the church found it opportune to take the mendicant friars under its protection and incorporate the movement into its official structure. It wanted them to "follow naked the naked Christ" under its aegis, not be swept along by a heretical current. The new orders' preaching confronted the wealthy with an acute moral dilemma. The kingdom of heaven was reserved to those who had repudiated earthly goods and greed—the source of wealth and one of the gravest of the deadly sins. Preachers thundered tirelessly against the avaricious and the wealthy.

*

Wealthy men who lent money at interest inspired particular scorn, and it was the merchants who most often used this system for increasing their capital. Rather than themselves undertaking commercial voyages to distant lands, which involved notable risks, many wealthy merchants preferred to lend money to others who needed it—and everyone from sovereigns and nobles to small-scale businessmen, artisans, and peasants needed money. Christian authors had always condemned usury and predicted that usurers would suffer the tortures of hell in the other world, and in 1179 the church officially prohibited usury to Christians. The role of the Jews in the economic life of the West can be explained above all by prohibitions of this sort: since they were "infidels," Jews could take on an activity necessary in practice but decisively condemned by the church as a non-Christian profession. In spite of church prohibitions, many Christians were moneylenders as well.

Preaching during and following the thirteenth century contains decided elements of social criticism. The friars started from the principles of Christian ethics, and they mercilessly stigmatized everyone who strayed from those principles, which was practically the entire population: sovereigns, the knightly class, city-dwellers, peasants, even the clergy; no one was without sin. Their most menacing invective was reserved for usurers, however. In their *exempla*—brief anecdotes borrowed from folklore or from traditional literature that they used in their sermons to illustrate a point—the usurer was portrayed as a moral monster. The *exempla* regarding usurers play continually on the idea that the usurer is the enemy of God, of nature, and of man. When the usurers' money swelled the friars' coffers, it corrupted honest alms. During a sea voyage, one *exemplum* ran, a monkey escaped to the top of the ship's mast after snatching the usurer's purse. He sniffed at the coins and flung into the sea all the money gotten from usurious operations. The usurer's soul was judged at the moment of his death, and terrifying demons dragged him directly to hell while forcing red-hot coins into his mouth. The usurer was the most faithful servant of the Devil, who appeared at his deathbed to collect his soul, refusing the unhappy man any pause to remedy the harm he had caused or to seek forgiveness for his sins by dint of prayer. Dante's *Inferno* vividly portrays the infernal torment inflicted upon the usurers. Nothing could save the soul of the man who lent money for interest except the total distribution to all whom he had exploited of all his unjustly acquired wealth. No partial restitution could help him.

The usurer was repugnant in the eyes of God and of humankind, the preachers insisted, because his was a sin that knew no respite: adulterers, libertines, assassins, perjurers, and blasphemers tired of their sins, but the usurer's profits continued without interruption, denying the normal rhythm of work and rest. Usury destroyed the connection between the person and his labor because interest continued to accumulate while he ate, slept, or even listened to a sermon. The Lord commanded all men to earn their daily bread by the sweat of their brow, but the usurer got rich without toil. By buying and selling the expectation of money he was selling time; worse, he was robbing from time, the patrimony of all created beings. By that token, whoever sold the light of day and the quiet of night had sold eternal light and eternal rest, which he then had no right to possess.

Malediction weighed so heavily on the soul of the usurer, the preachers state, that at one usurer's funeral his neighbors were unable to lift his body. Since the priests refused to bury profiteers in consecrated ground, the usurer's body was hoisted onto an ass's back and the animal carried it outside the city, where it was thrown on a rubbish heap by the gallows. There was one *exemplum* in which the rich usurer at death's door attempts to persuade his soul not to leave him, promising it gold and silver. When he fails, he indignantly sends his soul off to hell. A usurer aware of the sinfulness of his profession could be visited with terrible visions. One of them, lying in his bed, suddenly saw himself at the Last Judgment and heard the sentence that turned him over to the devils. When he awoke, he ran out of the house in a fit of madness, crying out his refusal to repent and to repair the harm he had done. Just at that moment a ship with no helmsman appeared on the river, progressing rapidly upstream against the current. The usurer cried out that the ship was full of devils, and they forthwith grabbed him and bore him off.

Usury inspired the preachers to an incommensurable wrath. How can we explain their furious accusations? Why did they feel it so necessary to return ceaselessly in their sermons to attacks on usury? It is doubtful that all their reasons derived from doctrine. On the contrary, we need to suppose that the theologians' arguments against usury that instructed the faithful on its sinfulness were derived from and provided some sort of learned justification for the hatred that the preachers' audiences bore usurers. It is improbable that all the stories about usurers that fill the sermons came from the authors of *exempla*. Could they not, at least partially, have originated in public opinion? Some of the *exempla* clearly portray the hostility of city-dwellers toward those who lent money at interest. One priest, who wanted to demonstrate that lending money was such a shameful occupation that no one would dare be recognized publicly as a moneylender, declared during his sermon: "I want to give you absolution of your sins according to your trades and occupations. May the blacksmiths rise." The blacksmiths rose from their benches and received absolution. After them, he gave absolution to other crafts groups. Finally the preacher proclaimed: "Let the usurers rise to receive absolution." Even though there were more of them than in the other professions, no one rose to his feet; all ducked down to hide themselves, then left in shame amid general laughter. The *exempla* often describe the unmasking of a usurer as a public scandal taking place at the center of city life. Thus, during a wedding ceremony in Dijon in 1240, a usurer is reported to have died at the doors of the church, his head split open when it was struck by the stone purse from the statue of a usurer above the east portal, the scene of the Last Judgment.

Hatred for usurers was total. One chronicler of the early thirteenth century, Matthew Paris, wrote of the Lombards (as Italian bankers and moneylenders were called in countries north of the Alps) in these terms:

> The Lombards, great rogues, . . . are traitors and impostors. . . . They devour not only men and domestic animals, but also mills, castles, farmlands, meadows, heath, and woods. . . . They hold a sheet of paper in one hand and a pen in the other; with their help they fleece the local people and with their money they fill their purses. . . . They wax fat on others' needs, and they themselves are like wolves who devour men.

The persecution and slaughter of Italian usurers, in particular in France during the late thirteenth and the fourteenth centuries, were phenomena as frequent and widespread as pogroms against the Jews, with the one difference that the pogroms were prompted by religious motives as well as by hatred of wealthy moneylenders of a different faith. In the *Strasbourg Chronicles* (late fourteenth and early fifteenth centuries) we read: "If the Jews were poor and the lords were not indebted to them, we would not burn them."

Usury not only damned the souls of the profiteers, but of their children, should they inherit ill-gotten gains and fail to pay reparations for the harm their fathers had done. One son had a vision in which a great tree grew out of the stomach of a man lying among the flames of hell, and from its branches hung men being devoured by flames. What did this mean? The supine man was the progenitor of several generations of men who had risen in society through usury, and his descendants were suffering because they had followed in his footsteps. One priest mentioned by Jacques de Vitry declared in his sermon, "Do not pray for the soul of my father, who was a usurer and refused to return the riches he accumulated through usury. May his soul be damned and suffer in Hell for eternity so that he will never see the face of God or escape from the clutches of the demons."

In a hierarchical, stratified society, inherited nobility and the knightly courage connected with it were valued over all other qualities. Nobles regarded the city-dweller with scorn, even if he was a wealthy merchant, and no chivalric virtue was expected of him. For the knights and noble ladies he was on a par with a villein or worse. Nonetheless, the wealthy of the cities—merchants and moneylenders—sought to improve their social position through their wealth. The anecdote told by one French preacher of the thirteenth century illustrates the rise in the estimation of others of the nonaristocratic newly rich. An urchin covered with scabs from a fungal infection begged his way to the city, where he became known as "Scabby." But as he gradually became richer from usurious moneylending, his social prestige changed. First he was called *Martinus scabiosus,* then *domnus Martinus,* and when he became one of the wealthiest men in the city he became *dominus Martinus,* soon followed by *meus dominus Martinus.* The French equivalents of these titles are even more resounding: *maître, seigneur, Monseigneur.* In the *exemplum,* the usurer's rise on the social scale was expected to end with his fall into Hell.

Greed was the most abominable of the vices. "You can receive the cross from the pope's hands, cross the sea, combat the pagans, conquer the Holy Sepulcher, and die for the cause of God and even be buried in the Holy Sepulchre," the German Franciscan Berthold von Regensburg told a terrified usurer listening to him preach, "but in spite of all your sanctity, your soul is lost." Nothing could save the usurer but complete restitution, to the last penny, for the damage he had inflicted.

The church retained its negative attitude toward usury in the following centuries as well. Although the theoretical treatises of Antoninus, archbishop of Florence, make some concessions to financial activities (which had reached their point of highest development in the

Italian cities of the fourteenth and fifteenth centuries), the sermons of Bernardino of Siena paint an impressive picture, bringing all the forces of the entire universe, sacred and natural, to bear on the condemnation of the usurer:

> All the saints, the blessed, and the angels in Paradise exclaim, "To the inferno, go to the inferno!"; the Heavens howl, with all their stars, "Into the fire, go into the fire!"; the planets proclaim, "to the depths of hell, to the depths of hell!" and the elements rise up against him to cry out, "to the executioner, to the executioner!" And the house in which the dying man lies, and its walls and its beams, call out ceaselessly for his punishment.

Preaching against usury and condemnation of the profession of moneylending could do little to limit such activities, even though lenders were constrained to seek expedients to avoid public ignominy. Nonetheless, it would be a profound mistake to imagine that such accusations had no importance. Their influence was largely psychological and social. The contradiction between a lucrative economic practice and its extremely low evaluation on a moral scale could not help but bring a certain schizophrenia to the spiritual world of the moneylender whose religious faith remained strong.

Not only was the ethics of accumulation in conflict with religious doctrine; it also was in clear contradiction with the fundamental orientations of the aristocracy, among whom the frank and ostentatious possession of wealth and expenditures for public display were considered virtues. Spending money with no thought to actual income was taken as a sign of nobility and generosity. The merchant, on the contrary, could not be anything but parsimonious and economical; he had to accumulate his money and spend his resources wisely if he hoped to make a profit. An anonymous poem appeared in England in the mid-fourteenth century entitled *Wynnere and Wastoure* (*A Good Short Debate Between Winner and Waster*). The first debater represents the merchant and the jurist; the second personifies the knight or the aristocrat. The Winner takes pleasure in contemplating his accumulated wealth and praises men who spend little, boasting that he knows how to live thriftily and prosper in business. He views with incomprehension and indignation the Waster's unconcerned extravagance, evident in his clothing and his table. The list of the dishes served at a banquet in the Waster's house resembles a culinary treatise. People who have not a penny in their pockets and nevertheless acquire rare furs, precious stuffs, and other costly luxury items arouse the Winner's suspicion and distaste. He reproaches the idle Waster for not tilling his lands and for selling working tools to pay for his military adventures and the pleasures of the hunt. Intemperance in food and drink, he states, bring on the dissipation of wealth from inherited lands. He invites the Waster, in vain, to limit his expenditures in order to avoid bankruptcy and to persuade his friends and family to work. The Winner's view is that overweening pride moves the Waster to dissipate his wealth.

The Waster, for his part, charges that the treasures that the Winner gathers are of no use to anyone. "What should wax of that wealth, if no waste were to come? Some would rot, some would rust, some rats would feed" (trans. Gollancz). He urges the Winner, in the name of Christ, to stop cramming his coffers and to give the poor a part of his money. The Waster insists on the vanity of wealth and speaks of the harm it can cause: the more wealthy a man is, the more vile he is. Is it not preferable to lead a short life but a merry one?

The dispute between the Winner and the Waster, brought before the king of England for judgment, remains unresolved. The Waster and the Winner are not so much socially defined types as they are personifications of differing principles of life and opposed systems of values. There is no doubt, however, on which side of this argument the merchant stood.

*

As we have seen, clerical authors of the eleventh and twelfth centuries characterized society by the trifunctional scheme of "prayers-warriors-plowmen." By the thirteenth century, however, this archaic scheme was in obvious contradiction with social reality. The mendicant preachers recognized a greater variety of trades and social strata in their sermons. The loss of the older comprehension of social structure was tied above all to the increase in the urban population and, in particular, to the rise of its merchant class. The most interesting and consistent attempt at a new understanding of the complexities and the multiformity of the social system came from Berthold von Regensburg, whom we have already met.

Berthold saw the orders and levels of society as a sort of analogy of the celestial hierarchy on which the earthly social organization was founded and by which it was justified. Nine orders of humans providing various services corresponded to the nine angelic choirs described earlier by Dionysius the Areopagite. As the inferior choirs of angels served the superior ones, the inferior orders of men were subject to the superior ones. If in the angelic hierarchy there were three upper choirs, in exactly the same way three orders of men were raised above all the others, and the Creator himself had selected them so that all the other orders would obey them. Those three orders were, first, the priests, with the pope at their head; second, the monks; and third, lay judges, which included the emperor, kings, dukes, counts, and all secular lords. The first two groups had the cure of the souls of Christians, the third, of their earthly well-being, including the defense of widows and orphans.

What, then, were the other six orders whose representatives were to carry out their assigned duties and faithfully serve the superior orders? We should note first that Berthold refuses to view them in hierarchical order but places them side by side "horizontally." The hierarchy that pertained in the celestial world lost all meaning for the human world, which in his sermon turns out to be the urban universe. The first of these six lower "orders" or "choirs" was made up of those who make clothing and footwear. Artisans who work with iron tools (jewelers, coin minters, blacksmiths, carpenters, masons) made up the second "choir." The third was merchants who transport goods from one kingdom to the other, who ply the seas, and who bring one thing from Hungary, another from France. The fourth "choir" and fourth function was those sellers of provisions who furnish food and drink to the population. The fifth "choir" was the peasants, the sixth the physicians. These, along with the three upper echelons, were the nine "choirs." Furthermore, just as a tenth choir of angels had abandoned God to follow Satan, there was a tenth "choir" of men, including mimes and actors, whose entire life was directed to evil and whose souls were predestined to perdition. It is easy to see that when he mentions specific professional categories such as craftsmen, great merchants, and small shopkeepers Berthold is speaking of the various occupations practiced, for the most part, in cities. He was addressing the many categories of townspeople, not just the peasantry, exhorting them to work and to serve honestly without deceit. The distinction he makes between great merchants who practiced commerce over great distances and small shopkeepers is typical of the medieval city. Urban professions are central in Berthold's thought, and although he incessantly condemns the "avid" and the wealthy, he nevertheless fully justifies the existence of trade and of the merchants. Merchants were necessary to the functioning of the whole, and Berthold interprets their occupation as a vocation predetermined by the Creator, exactly like the vocation of the plowman, the judge, or the monk. Honest commerce was the ideal of both

Berthold von Regensburg and the other preachers of the thirteenth century.

Just as interesting as this Franciscan friar's "sociological" turn of mind in his description of the urban population within the structure of society is his interpretation of the Gospel parable of the talents (or the pounds) entrusted by the Lord to his servants (Luke 19:12–28). In Berthold's sermon on this text we can see how real life induced the preacher to introduce a new content into the traditional form of the exegesis of a sacred text. What are these "pounds" or "talents" that have been given by the Creator to man? The first of them is "our person," which the Lord created in his own image and likeness and ennobled by conceding us free will. The second was "the vocation to which God, who has given every man his service, has predestined you." Society was made up of people who carried out the social functions assigned to them, and every task, great or small, was important and necessary for the existence of the whole. It is interesting to note that whereas the old trifunctional system presumed anonymous "orders" taken in the collective, mass sense, Berthold von Regensburg refers to individuals rendering specific services. His point of departure is the person, not the group. Functions have been distributed with wisdom, in accordance with the will of God, and no one can abandon his "service" to pass from one social order to another. Certain activities, however, are not callings established by God. They are usury, hoarding and monopolistic trade practices, deceit, and theft. At this point Berthold berates shopkeepers who water their wine, sell "air instead of bread," adulterate beer or beeswax, or use false weights and measures. In this manner, if God's first gift to man is his person, his second gift is the social function of the individual and his calling to a certain level of society and a profession. In Berthold's conception, "person" is socially defined, and the individual's virtues are closely coordinated with the class, level, or social group to which he belongs. Instead of arguing for the contemplative or ascetic life and retirement from the world, Berthold insists upon the necessity for socially useful activity as the basis for society's existence.

The third "pound" that God entrusted to man was the time assigned to him to live, and God, Berthold insists, wants to know how we are spending it. Time is given to us for our tasks and should not be consumed in vain pursuits. We will answer for the time we spend to no purpose, and we must use time for our salvation, not for increasing the torments of this world.

The fourth "pound" that God granted humankind is earthly

goods. They must be exploited with good sense and administered with integrity. Ownership is acquired legitimately with honest labor. When Berthold rages at the "greedy people," "thieves," and the "deceivers," his ire is not provoked by unequal distribution of property but by its poor use. What the Lord has created is sufficient to nourish everyone. Inequality in possessions and the presence of rich and poor are of secondary importance in comparison with the absolute equality of all humankind before the Creator. Everything comes of him and will return to him. For this reason, Berthold does not recognize full and absolute right of ownership. God entrusts goods in accordance with the person of the owner and his allotted task and time on this earth. That person is the sole administrator of his wealth, and he must answer for its use.

The fifth gift, finally, is love of one's neighbor, who is to be loved as oneself. We shall soon see in what manner.

Thus the five gifts entrusted to man and the principal valuables for the use of which he must respond to the Almighty were person, vocation, time (lifetime), terrestrial goods, and relations with other people. And the soul? Berthold does not mention it, but in his reasoning it is present as the invisible center at which all the gifts of the Creator converge. The important point lies elsewhere, however: "service" fits into the conceptual sequence established in this sermon as a human quality inseparable from the person. Person cannot be reduced to the unity of soul and body because it includes social function. Furthermore, in a totally logical fashion, the third of the Creator's gifts—time—turns out to be the time-span of human life. Obviously, time is not secularized in this sermon; it is not completely transformed from "church's time" into "merchant's time." It is the time of the Lord, and man is obliged to answer to him for how he has spent the time allotted to him. For Berthold, the time of this earthly life, the time to work for salvation, has not yet taken on an autonomous terrestrial value; it leads into otherworldly life and clearly disintegrates when the discourse turns to eternity. Nonetheless, it is highly significant, promising important consequences, that the *Sermon On the Five Talents* inserts time into the series of values central to human life as a condition of the fulfillment of "service" or vocation. It considers time an inseparable parameter of the person.

Evidently, for the preachers who belonged to the mendicant orders and worked in close contact with burghers, time began to take on a new value, and although they continued to interpret this new value in traditional theological terms, the very fact of uniting the category of the time of human life with the categories of person and vocation was highly symptomatic. We can suppose that the high value normally given to time (along with membership in a corporation) in mercantile and artisanal circles of the cities and towns of the early Middle Ages exerted an influence on preaching, which in turn transferred time, appointed tasks, and wealth to the moral and religious plane.

Interestingly, when Berthold von Regensburg addressed the faithful of the cities, he could no longer speak of wealth in exclusively negative terms, like preachers of the preceding period. Goods served to satisfy men's needs and those of their families. Certainly, one must aid the poor and the unfortunate and do good works, but without forgetting oneself. Berthold returns on several occasions and in various sermons to the notion that wealth is distributed unequally, some having much, others little or nothing. What practical conclusions does he derive from this observation, however? That he who owns several suits of clothing should share them with the indigent? When an imaginary interlocutor poses this question, Berthold answers:

> Yes, I have a handsome garment and I am not going to give it to you; but I would like you to have nothing less and even more than what I have. Love for one's neighbor consists in desiring for him what you desire for yourself. You yearn for the celestial kingdom: yearn for it for him as well.

In Berthold's day, the doctrine that he who has two shirts should share them with the poor was already considered heretical. In the minds of merchants and city-dwellers wealth was so solidly connected to the person and to his "service"—his predestined role—that loving one's neighbor had a much more anemic, passive meaning than in earlier times.

There is little doubt that this reevaluation of Christian values shows the subterranean influence of the new ethic of work and property forged in the city. Berthold's ideals, which stemmed in great part from his activities in the urban environment, were radically different from traditional monastic ideals. The sermon on the talents contains an undeniable internal contradiction, a sort of tension between the traditional theocentric vision of the world and the vision of the world centered on man, his aspirations, and his earthly interests, that had gradually taken form in the social consciousness of the burgher class. The new picture of the world did not in any way negate the role of the Creator (in this sense it too was theological), but it already included new potentials. It would have been difficult for Berthold von

Regensburg not to have perceived impulses of the sort from burgher and merchant groups. I might also recall that the cities of southern Germany in which he preached (Augsburg, Regensburg, and others) were in the thirteenth century large commercial centers with a wealthy merchant class.

During this period Christianity, according to Georges Duby, changed from a "religion of the churchmen" to a "religion of the masses." Berthold von Regensburg, a theologian and a preacher, kept rigorously to the medieval meaning of Christianity. This same meaning, however, was shifting its accents and changing in ways imperceptible to contemporaries. "New wine" was beginning to flow into the "old wineskins." These changes were increasingly noticeable in the fourteenth century, but we find presentiments and traces of presuppositions of them in that German preacher of the mid-thirteenth century. Berthold developed ideas that gave an ethical and religious formulation to the hopes and aspirations of men who were not yet ready to express them themselves. That his discourses gave these demands a theological basis stamped them with particular force and significance. Earthly preoccupations and material interests received sanction from on high and were elevated to the rank of fulfillment of divine commands. The human person began to be a consciously perceived entity, and people started to see their social and professional vocation, their property and their time, as gifts of God, "talents" that must be returned to the Creator intact or multiplied. Personhood could not yet be autonomously based, but its submission to the Creator justified the belief that the values it possessed were absolute. By defending those values, the individual took a personal and direct part in the universal conflict between the supreme good and metaphysical evil.

With their preaching, their confessors' manuals, and their theological *summae,* the theologians and friars of the mendicant orders made a notable contribution to the ethical and religious justification of commerce and the merchants.

*

The full flowering of the commercial segment of society came in the thirteenth century and the first third of the fourteenth century. In many cities and towns in Europe the highest echelon of merchants, who concentrated vast wealth in their hands, formed the cities' governing class—the patriciate—and exerted a decisive influence on civic government. Even though numerically they made up an insignificant proportion of the urban population, these merchants and entrepreneurs held all power in the city. They filled the city councils, turned tax policies to their advantage, and controlled justice and local legislation. Masses of wage-workers, serfs, small-scale artisans, and shopkeepers were dependent upon them. In Florence this oligarchy bore the expressive name of *popolo grasso,* as opposed to the *popolo minuto.* According to one Italian chronicler, the "people" (*populus*) was "that part of the population that lives on buying and selling"; he did not consider anyone who "lived with the labor of his hands" to be of the "people." One German chronicler, relating the revolt of Mainz, called the plebeian population a "pestiferous mass" (*pestilens multitudo*) and a "dangerous mob."

The knight's nobility was based primarily on his origins. In specific cases even a merchant could appeal to hardworking and fortunate ancestors or parents (and there were also merchants of aristocratic extraction), but in general he had to depend upon his own enterprise. One Lübeck merchant, Bertold Ruzenberg, wrote with pride in his will (1364) that he had not inherited anything from his parents and had obtained all his wealth with hard work. In the spirit of the age, a successful merchant was of course apt to explain his rising revenues by God's benevolence. His own capabilities and their intelligent use, not his origins, were the merchant's principal virtues. He was a self-made man.

What can we know about this newly rich merchant who had slipped into the patriciate? As is known, the noble landowners' exploitation of their peasants could be extremely harsh, and the lords often considered their serfs with ill-concealed contempt, even with hatred, denying them all human dignity. Nevertheless, relationships in the feudal system could on occasion be personal—true face-to-face relations, not impersonal, not anonymous. Were relations between wealthy men in commerce and industry and the small producers dependent upon them organized on the feudal model? I would have to say no. The "small people"—artisans, manual laborers, and preproletarian elements in the medieval city—were treated with brazen and unbridled exploitation. In the agrarian world the very structure of seigneurial relations presumed a certain paternalism; in the medieval city the pursuit of hard cash excluded it.

One typical example of the city merchant is a Flemish draper named Jehan Boinebroke, who died around 1286. This Douai patrician stopped at nothing to increase his cash intake. The craftsmen and workers whom he exploited mercilessly were, in his eyes, simply instruments for making a profit. Not only did Boinebroke fleece them and bankrupt them, he also humiliated them in all possible ways, insulted and mocked them, recognizing no human qualities in them and exploiting their total dependence upon him. Georges Espinas, who has studied the Boinebroke archive, describes him as a man single-mindedly dedicated to money, for whom enrichment was the only goal in life, and who subordinated his every thought, word, and action to this objective. He appears totally unconcerned by the amorality and cynicism of his methods, which included fraud, theft, and blackmail. His guiding principles were to leave debts unpaid and to appropriate what did not belong to him. Persons and circumstances did not interest him. Boinebroke behaved like a lawless tyrant, a "true industrial bandit," Espinas concludes, emphasizing that his evaluation is by no means an exaggeration. Nonetheless, this cloth merchant could not avoid the realization that punishment awaited his soul in the otherworld, and his heirs, following the stipulations of his will, repaid those whom he had robbed during his lifetime.

Sweeping generalizations should always be avoided, but to judge by the explosions of hatred that shook the cities of Western Europe during the course of the thirteenth and the fourteenth centuries, Boinebroke's case was not exceptional. Bertran Mornewech, who started life poor but grew rich with dizzying rapidity and became a member of the city council of Lübeck, is an example of an equally immoderate profiteer. He died in the same year as Boinebroke, and his widow found that many a wealthy family owed her money.

Godric of Finchale, a merchant who lived at the turn of the twelfth century, was something of an exception, not because his life did not follow the usual story line of a small merchant rapidly becoming a great trader who plied the Baltic and reaped enormous profits by selling rare merchandise, but because after he had made his fortune he renounced his profitable commerce and retired to a religious life to save his soul. After his death he was proclaimed a saint. Even Godric was not unique. A century later Homobonus of Cremona was declared a saint for having bequeathed to the poor all the wealth he had accumulated during a lifetime in commerce, and in 1360 the Sienese merchant Giovanni Colombini founded the mendicant order of the Gesuati (The Apostolic Clerics of St. Jerome, or Jeronymites). A character in the first *novella* of the first day of Boccaccio's *Decameron,* ser Ciappelletto of Prato, noted for breaking his sworn promises and a great blasphemer, springs immediately to mind. His false deathbed confession so thoroughly deceives the friar attending him that after his death he is proclaimed a saint. Still, we should not forget that, before he dies, his sense of solidarity with his hosts, who are Florentine moneylenders, leads Ciappelletto to charge his soul with that final sin.

The "new men" whose commercial and financial activities brought them to the forefront stood out for their energy, their initiative, and their readiness to seize the occasion, but also for their insolence, their egotism, and their nonchalance toward the paternalistic norms of their times. The possession of movable goods alone did not assure them esteem and prestige in feudal society, however. In a characteristic case that illustrates the contempt that the nobles felt for those on the summit of wealthy urban society, when in one German city a member of the city council permitted himself critical observations on an influential knight, the latter exclaimed, "Even if the master and the pigs share the same roof, they still have nothing in common." Similarly, when a Ravensburg burgher attempted in a letter to use the familiar form of address to a knight (as the knight had done addressing him), he was promptly put in his place by the knight's reply which recalled his own ancient nobility and reminded his correspondent that he was merely a burgher and a merchant. Let him take himself to the beer hall to seek information on his cargoes arriving from Alexandria or Barcelona; he would do well not to flaunt his origins! In Italy the confines between the nobility and the patriciate had been eroded if not obliterated, but in Germany this was not yet the case.

It is understandable, then, that the urban patriciate should hope to attenuate the barrier that separated it from the aristocracy. For some of the merchants the "way up" lay through the acquisition of vast landed properties or through a "mixed" marriage in which an impoverished knight sought to put his affairs in better order by marrying the daughter of a wealthy merchant. A few city-dwellers even succeeded in acquiring knighthood. One characteristic of merchant patricians was an aspiration to live in luxury, and, in order to raise their prestige and impress others, they built themselves stone houses and palaces crowned with towers. The late Gothic buildings of the southern German patriciate and the Renaissance palaces of the Italian merchants might easily have aroused the envy of the aristocracy. Glass appeared at the windows of patrician houses, the rooms were richly furnished, and the walls were hung with tapestries. Following the example of the nobility, the merchants took up hunting, the "sport of the nobles." They rivaled the aristocracy in their clothing and their ornaments. Funeral ceremonies among the patriciate were carried out all possible pomp, and they adorned their tombs with costly monuments to immortalize their own glory. Some might be taxed with eccentricity. In 1415, a detailed inventory of expenses for the wedding of one patrician in Pistoia lists such items as payment for an escort of eight pages on horseback, the acquisition of six gowns decorated with fur and silver for the fiancée, the purchase of chests, gems, bed linen, and more. All this cost a fortune—nearly six hundred *fiorini.*

The royal power was also obliged to have dealings with leading members of the mercantile and entrepreneurial class, as rulers needed financial aid and political support from them. Some of the richest merchants were close to the court. The banker Jacques Coeur, "the first financial magnate in Europe" (c. 1395–1456), invested his capital in all possible sorts of lucrative ventures and had interests throughout Europe. He became the treasurer and minister of the king of France, Charles VII, and he had a hand in state reforms and in military and diplomatic policies. Jacques Coeur's unprecedented rise and fall (he was forced to flee France in disgrace and he died in exile) produced an indelible impression on his contemporaries, and François Villon expressed serious doubts that the soul of this royal merchant had a comfortable place reserved for it in the next world.

Jacques Coeur's life was full of adventures and vicissitudes, but so was that of merchants of incomparably more modest scope, such as Buonaccorso Pitti, a slightly older contemporary (1354–1430). Pitti took an active part in public affairs in Florence. Considering himself equal to the highest aristocracy, he participated in wars and political intrigues and lived in the thick of factional struggles in his city. He traveled from Florence to Nice and Avignon; to The Hague and Brussels, to Augsburg and to Zagreb in search of "fortune." He was charged with diplomatic missions to London and Paris and to the court of the Holy Roman emperor, and he occupied high office in the Florentine republic. A shrewd merchant, he was also an avid dice player who won and lost sums of money that he then noted down with scrupulous care. Pitti was an adventurer, a man of affairs, and a writer who left remembrance of himself in a *Cronaca* that he filled with notes on all the events of his adventurous life, on the members of his immediate family and his kin, on the duels and intrigues in which he had participated, and also on the political conflicts that he happened to have witnessed.

In no other part of Europe did the mercantile class reach as great economic and political power as in the Italian cities. In no other place was there such a large segment of the population involved in commercial activities. One voyager who passed through Venice shortly before the Great Plague of 1348 reached the conclusion that "all the people are merchants." People said of the Genoese, "Genoese, hence a merchant." Judgments of this sort were correct in the sense that the large commercial community set the tone for all of economic, social, and political life in these Italian cities. There the merchant's profession was rehabilitated morally, and Jacobus de Voragine, bishop of Genoa and author of the famous *Legenda aurea,* compared the merchant to Christ himself (as did Federico Visconti, bishop of Pisa): Christ arrives on the ship of the cross to offer men the opportunity to exchange transient terrestrial things for eternal ones. Wealth no longer had a negative connotation since, Jacobus de Voragine asserts, the biblical patriarchs and even Christ himself were wealthy men.

In the thirteenth and succeeding centuries many merchants undertook long and perilous sea voyages—the famous Marco Polo, for one. In 1291 two brothers from Genoa, Ugolino and Vadino Vivaldi, undertook a voyage that, according to a contemporary witness, "no one before them had attempted." Sailing off beyond Gibraltar, they headed west to discover the fabulous wealth of India. Whether they reached the western waters of the Atlantic or circumnavigated Africa, they had neither predecessors nor bearings to guide them. It was India, China, Africa, and the Near East that attracted courageous discoverers and voyagers for whom the quest for lucre combined with a curiosity for knowing more and a spirit of adventure. The merchant was easily transformed into a corsair. The fourth *novella* of the second day of the *Decameron* gives an example of this: after being attacked and robbed, a merchant takes up piracy and returns home a rich man. Merchants were armed when they left on commercial voyages, and in 1344 a law was approved in Genoa that forbade them to venture beyond Sicily or Majorca unarmed.

The merchant who undertook long peregrinations in search of merchandise and who subjected his wealth to risk and his very life to dangers is the hero of many *fabliaux.* Their authors describe the merchant's profits, but they also point out his qualities: ability, energy, courage, and a fondness for dangerous ventures. According to *Le dit des Marchéants,* merchants deserved much consideration, since their services were important for the church, for the knightly caste, and for all of society. Confronting dangers, they transported rare merchandise from land to land and province to province. In the *fabliaux* as in other sources, merchants, an errant, restless lot, are usually contrasted with other wealthy city-dwellers who lead a more sedentary life. One wealthy late-fourteenth-century Parisian merchant of advanced age left a book of instructions for his young wife in which he advised her to remarry a merchant when she was left a widow. He counsels her to take care to make her husband comfortable, as he would be obliged to travel in rain, storm, and snow and would experience all the perils and inconveniences of the road. He also suggests that she remember to rid the bedchamber of fleas.

The merchant must be ready to confront danger. Danger was inseparable from his profession, which means that awareness of risk and the threat of ruin never left his mind. Danger lurked particularly in long sea voyages, in shipwrecks, and in attacks by pirates or rival merchants. It was inherent in market fluctuations but also in the people with whom the merchant had relations. This is why there are so many insistent warnings about rival merchants, fellow citizens, friends, and even relatives in the notes and the instructions penned by merchant writers. The merchant had to be constantly on the alert. As old age approached, one wealthy Prato merchant, Francesco di Marco Datini, warned his second-in-command, "You are young, but when you are my age and have had dealings with as many people as I have, you will understand that in himself man represents a danger, and that it is risky to have dealings with him." One merchant in Kiel states that he had spent his entire life in toil, danger, and anxiety. The formation of commercial companies in which the merchant who provided the working capital shared risk with the merchant navigator, in case of loss, was prompted, to a large extent, by an awareness of the imminence of danger. In the Venetian *colleganza,* the Genoese *commenda,* and the north German *Widerlegunge* the first risked his money and his merchandise and the second his life and the more modest means that he had invested in the enterprise.

Gradually, however, a change took place in the dominant type of great merchant. Rather than an entrepreneur who traveled by land and by sea vulnerable to all sorts of danger, he became a merchant manager who stayed home and took care of his business through agents by correspondence. This transformation had far-reaching consequences for the figure of the merchant, for his psyche, and for his culture.

*

Up to this point we have heard about men of affairs occupied with trade and moneylending only from those who were not merchants. This is quite natural, given that the ability to read and write was long the privilege, if not the monopoly, of the clergy. With the thirteenth century, the situation began to change everywhere, from Flanders to Italy. Commercial activity demanded a preparation that included some learning. An illiterate merchant would have had difficulty in carrying on his affairs successfully. In cities great and small lay schools made their appearance, and in them the children of the well-to-do learned to read, write, and figure. In religious schools the pupils studied sacred texts, and arithmetic was needed primarily in order to observe the church calendar, but in the new urban schools knowledge had practical goals. Consequently, teaching methods changed, and the schools' focus shifted from the classical to the applied "sciences." The needs of the mercantile class contributed to the change from Roman to Arabic numerals, which were better adapted for commercial accounting, and to the introduction of the zero. Gradually there came into being an "arithmetical mentality" (as Alexander Murray has put it)—that is, a penchant for calculation and for precision, qualities less characteristic of the preceding period of the Middle Ages. Arithmetic developed not only in the studies of learned men and in the offices of the kings' exchequers, but also at the merchants' counting tables. One wag of the thirteenth century altered the word "arithmetic" into *aerismetica*, or the art of money. A Venetian merchant stipulated in his will in 1420 that his sons had to frequent the "abacus" school "in order to learn commerce." Guides for commercial accounting, sometimes in rhyme to make their lessons easier to commit to memory, began to be written in the thirteenth century. The merchant, banker, and chronicler of early fourteenth-century Florence, Giovanni Villani, the first author to show an interest in statistics, calculated that from eight to ten thousand students in that city frequented six city schools, where mathematics was taught. In London a special statute obliged goldsmiths' apprentices to frequent the schools. Latin was taught in city schools, but letters and documents were often written in the vernacular. The oldest known text in the Italian language is a fragment of a commercial account book from Siena (1211). The change in written letters of the alphabet from Caroline minuscule to cursive was directly connected with the development of business correspondence, commercial correspondence in particular.

The sons of men of affairs often entered the universities. One city councilman in Hamburg set up scholarships in the University of Rostock for burghers' sons. Eighteen young men from three generations of the family of one city council member in a small north German city went to the university. Not all merchants' sons returned to take up their fathers' occupations when they had finished their course of studies. Some became churchmen, physicians, or jurists: in 1360 the son of one cloth merchant in Lyons earned his doctorate in Roman law. Others remained in commerce and became members of the city council or burgermasters. Approximately one-half of the members of the city councils of some German cities had had university instruction.

The study of foreign languages was considered important. The sons of Italian merchants learned English and German; the Germans of the Hansa learned Russian (needed for the profitable Novgorod trade) and Estonian (in order to communicate with agents in the nearby territories of the Baltic). Vocabularies and phrase books were compiled for the needs of merchants, including manuals for the study of oriental languages. The languages most frequently used for international communication were Italian in the Mediterranean and Middle Low German in the Baltic.

The book, once owned exclusively by churchmen, made its appearance in the houses of merchants and wealthy burghers. Although in the late Middle Ages books remained luxury items and were not widely present in these circles, still, in Sicily (to pick one example), out of the one hundred twenty-three libraries of the fourteenth and fifteenth centuries known to historians, more than one hundred were owned by lay city-dwellers. What books were in the merchant's library? First of all, lives of the saints, the Bible, and the Psalter, but also the works of Boethius, Cicero, the Roman poets, the *Divine Comedy,* and even Boccaccio. Solid libraries, by the standards of the times, were available to members of municipal councils in Germany.

In his registers the merchant noted, along with his entries of debits and credits, a great variety of events that seemed to him noteworthy. His mental horizon had been enlarged not only by travels to other lands and other cities but also by his schooling. By studying the markets of Europe and the East he became aware of the customs and institutions of different peoples and could compare them with the history and the culture of his own city and his own state.

There also appeared practical guides for commercial activities listing types of merchandise, giving local weights and measures, indicating exchange rates, customs duties, and ways to get around the various authorities who collected taxes and fees from the merchants. These guides described commercial routes, provided models for accounts and calendars, and even offered advice on making a variety of articles. The authors of these guides for merchants and entrepreneurs were not interested in abstract, academic knowledge scornful of daily practice but in concrete information applicable to measurable things.

The man of affairs kept up a vast correspondence. He wrote letters in his own hand or had a secretary write them under his dictation. Knowing how to read and write was a precondition for the successful conduct of business, and merchant ships usually carried commercial correspondence along with their usual cargoes. More than 150,000 business letters have been conserved in the archive of Francesco Datini, the great merchant of Prato who died in 1410. In the set of instructions mixing pious admonitions with purely practical advice compiled in the 1460s by the Florentine, Paolo da Certaldo, Paolo attributes great importance to business correspondence. Read your letters as soon as you receive them, Paolo warns, and if necessary, arrange for a courier immediately, particularly if they involve a purchase or a sale. Do not forward letters sent through you to a third party before you have taken care of your own affairs, for they may contain information that works against your interests, and you should not serve others while you are taking care of your own concerns.

Paolo spells out the mercantile ethic: it is important to know how to earn money but even more important to know how to spend it in a just and sensible manner. The key words in his book are *amante del lavoro* (a lover of work), *operoso* (assiduous), *tenace* (tenacious), and *solerte* (diligent, painstaking). Paolo was convinced that wealth earned by one's own efforts was preferable to inherited wealth. Like other merchants who wrote in the fourteenth century, he was a religious man, but what was his view of religion? Hell beckoned the incautious, and since it was impossible not to fear death, one must hold oneself constantly ready—that is, always keep one's affairs in perfect order and pay one's debts to God and to one's associates before death. In Paolo da Certaldo's mind, the merchant's debt to God was on exactly the same plane as his other obligations. Paolo was aware of the contradictions between the demands of daily life and ethical and religious ideals, however; without making a fuss about it, he wavers between those two poles but implicitly resolves the conflict in favor of the mercantile ethic.

It is hardly surprising that merchant circles produced authors of "family chronicles." What is not clear, however, is whether these chronicles arose under the influence of works of history, often compiled (in Florence in particular) by men of the same mercantile extraction and reflecting the interest of men of affairs in economics, statistics, and factual precision, or whether history on the grander scale developed parallel to the "small-scale" histories of businessmen's families. Be that as it may, such chronicles represent a unified intellectual movement found in all the larger cities of Europe and tied to the development of self-awareness, individual and collective, on the part of men of affairs, the most evolved, prosperous, and active segment of the urban population. The essential point is that family chronicles, which contained notations of births, marriages, and deaths in the family along with the registration of lucrative commercial transactions and remarks on elections to city office, also contained information of a purely historical nature. The title of one of these works is characteristic: *Libro di Giovenco Bastari di tutti i suoi fatti, creditori, debitori e ricordanze notabili* (Book of Giovenco Bastari of all his affairs, creditors, debtors, and noteworthy memoranda). The affairs of the merchant authors were often directly dependent upon the political situation in the city and in the land and upon any disturbances that were taking place.

Buonaccorso Pitti's journal, which he kept to his dying day, fits poorly under the definition of family chronicle because his persona is always at the center of his remarks. His egotistic "I" speaks from every page of his memoirs, making his book more of an autobiography.

The personality and the principle values of the Italian merchant of the late fourteenth and early fifteenth centuries emerge more clearly from the pages of the *Ricordi* of Giovanni di Pagolo Morelli (1371–1444) covering the period between 1393 and 1421. This descendant of dyers and cloth merchants did not belong to one of the leading families of the Florentine oligarchy, nor did he possess great wealth. A merchant of middling status who had put together a certain amount of capital through hard work and parsimony, Morelli expresses fairly openly in memoirs not destined for publication principles that doubtlessly were also those of many fellow citizens of his class.

Unlike Pitti, who lived at the summit of political events in Florence and in Europe and was involved in the most extraordinary intrigues, Morelli was an extremely cautious and prudent man. He teaches his reader how to get rich without risk and without pursuing profits too closely when that proves dangerous. He is perhaps more representative of the late medieval mercantile class in his loyalty to the principle of *moderatezza*. Patriotism for Morelli comes second to love of his own "house" and his immediate family. His *Memorie* abound in advice: you should seek to conceal your total revenues from the communal government in order to avoid paying taxes and should use every possible means to show only half of what you really own. (This recalls the character in a Franco Sacchetti *novella* who pretends that he is bankrupt so that he will not have to pay his taxes.) You must always be friends with whoever is in power and belong to the strongest party; you should trust no one, not servants, nor kin, nor friends, because men are full of vice and imbued with deceit and betrayal; when money or any other possession is in question, there is no friend or acquaintance who can take better care of your interests than you can yourself; if you are rich, be happy to buy friends with money if you cannot gain their friendship by other means. Morelli gives advice on the need to refuse to grant loans or stand surety for others, on how to prevent relatives from eating too much at your table, and on keeping an eye on the domestic help. In his opinion, moneylending is not so much blameworthy in itself as it is dangerous because of the reputation for usury that the moneylender acquires. Morelli outlines the egotistical morality of the cynical profit-taker with extreme clarity.

For Morelli, good was identified with profit, virtue was represented by balanced books, and evil by losses. Leonid Batkin remarks that Morelli cannot remember how many children his daughter-in-law has had, but the sums paid for dowries are noted with precision.

Like merchants of the modern period, Morelli considers rigorous bookkeeping of prime importance, but he does not reduce knowledge to practical matters alone. Aside from bookkeeping and grammar, he says, it is good to know Virgil and Boethius, Seneca and Cicero, Aristotle and Dante, not to speak of the Holy Writ. It is useful to travel and know the world. This mercantile individualist, who put the art of becoming wealthy at the top of his value system, lived in an age of a vast cultural movement to which he was far from indifferent. Even though he favored development of the capacities needed for entrepreneurial activities, culture brought him even spiritual pleasure. In reality, Morelli transfers the standard of the merchant to that part of his life as well: "In studying Virgil," he writes, "you can remain in his society as long as it seems to you opportune and he . . . will teach you without demanding payment in money or any other form."

Morelli's faith reconciled God and a yearning for wealth. He remembers his father as never wasting even one minute of time, working always to merit the love of the Creator and attract the friendship of good, wealthy, and powerful persons. God helps the wise and they help themselves. Morelli takes successful commerce as a service to God. Even in this respect he is not totally original, as in many business documents establishing commercial transactions we find invocations to the Creator, the Madonna, and the saints: "In the name of our Lord Jesus Christ and of the Holy Virgin Mary and of all the saints in Paradise, may they grant us possessions and health, by sea and by land, multiply our sons and our wealth, and save our souls and our bodies!" In the aim of insuring their own souls against disagreeable surprises in the other world, merchants kept an account in their books (as did commercial companies) for *"Messer Domeneddio"* in which the sums given to the poor and to charitable institutions were reported. The Creator was treated as a partner in the commercial company, and since his share depended on the amount of profit received by the company as a whole, God had a personal interest in granting the entrepreneurs maximum income! This was a totally rational method of inducing the Creator to lend an ear to the prayers of the merchants and bankers. The merchants' piety was imbued with the commercial spirit and they understood their pursuit of this world's goods as a divine undertaking. Upright conduct of commercial affairs not only did not hinder but, on the contrary, smoothed the way for the soul's salvation. This, in any event, was the conviction of the author of an inscription on a building erected by a commercial company in Valencia in the fifteenth century: the merchant who does not sin with his tongue, who keeps his sworn promises to his fellow men, and who does not lend money at usurious rates "will become wealthy and merit eternal life." The seals of English merchants bore such mottos as "The Right Hand of the Lord Has Raised Me up" or "O God, Help This Better Man." In their testaments they speak of the estate "that God has granted to them."

To return to Giovanni di Pagolo Morelli, like many of his contemporaries he was profoundly pessimistic. Men were evil by nature, life was hard, destiny cruel, now more than ever before. For the Italian merchants of his time, the "Golden Age" was a bygone age, and they viewed society and business as ruled by deceit and treachery. Batkin speaks of Morelli's "commercial pessimism," pointing out that Morelli counted more on keeping what one had than on earning profits and increasing one's wealth. Under such conditions, life was a drama, an uninterrupted and merciless struggle, and the family was one's only refuge. Morelli's pessimism clearly reflects the perception of the world of men of the Renaissance. There is an image that persists even today of Renaissance optimism and faith in the omnipotence of man, who supposedly discovered his own inner world and the world in which he lived for the first time in this epoch. Today there is increasing support for the opposite view: men of the Renaissance, who were intimately acquainted with death and every adversity, were in no way permeated with sentiments of joy or visited by festive states of mind. An awareness of the instability and the vulnerability of human life and a desolate vision of the nature of man are spontaneously present in many humanists, as they are in merchant writers like Giovanni Morelli.

Morelli's "mercantile epic" arose within the complex economic and social crisis that struck Italy in the mid-fifteenth century—the crisis that provided a background for the Italian Renaissance. There was a vast gap separating the mercantile utilitarianism of the *popolo grasso* and humanism. The humanists were closed up within an artificial cultural universe, whereas the merchants pursued purely worldly interests. The first humanists' world of ideal values was only weakly correlated with the exclusively practical and business-oriented world of the merchants; the culture that the poets, artists, and thinkers created was profoundly different from the civilization built with the active participation of men of affairs. Nonetheless, between these very different and even opposed worlds there existed one tie, which had little to do with the fact that many humanists were involved in commercial affairs and banking. The interpretation of the world that the humanists formulated was basically an expression—sublimated and transformed into art and literature—of the demands that the bourgeoisie was making when in its private enthusiasms it revealed an ideal vision, not idealized and utopian like the humanists' ideal, but uniquely terrestrial and prosaic. In the paintings and the portraits of Italian and Flemish masters, the rich merchants appear to us as solemnly elegant and pious men, munificent donors, founders of hospitals and patrons for the decoration of churches and other public buildings, but in their personal journals and the "family chronicles" their merciless egotism and their cynical use of their fellow citizens and the people with whom they had commercial dealings are obvious. The Renaissance man of affairs possessed both of these natures. He combined culture with commerce, piety with rationality, devotion with amorality. Freeing politics from morality was indeed a "Machiavellianism before Machiavelli." The Renaissance man of affairs sought to reorganize the relations between morality and religion so that faith in God would not be an obstacle to his not overly clean operations.

In reality, this did not always prove possible, and there were a number of merchants and bankers so frightened by the fires of Hell that they were moved—even if it was at the very end of their lives—to give their wealth to the poor and to the church. The "melancholy" so often encountered in philosophical treatises and in the art of the Renaissance is not a sentimental sadness but, as is clear from a reading of the family chronicles and the wills of merchants, a much more painful and inextinguishable fear of eternal malediction, a terror founded in doubt that salvation was possible. Toward the end of the period that interests us here, the term "melancholy" was widely used to designate prevailing states of mind in mercantile circles. Scholars (for example, Jean Delumeau) define the Renaissance as the "golden age of melancholy," and they stress that the word "desperation," used rarely in texts of the preceding period, becomes much more frequent in Renaissance texts. The "guilty conscience" of the man of affairs, his anxieties about the heights and the depths of human destiny, exaggerated by fear of punishments in the otherworld, were the symptoms that accompanied the development of individualism.

Preoccupation with the salvation of the soul, however, did not stop Mediterranean merchants from engaging in commerce with the enemies of Christianity, the Moslems. It cost Spanish and Italian merchants nothing to violate the prohibition against exporting arms to the Arabs and the Turks. Trade in Christian slaves earned fabulous profits, and Petrarch speaks with distaste of the "filthy mob" of slaves who crowded the narrow streets of Venice and profaned that stupendous city.

Did the pursuit of profit put the merchant and the financier in a difficult moral contradiction? The many condemnations for usurious operations led city authorities in Florence to set limits for the allowable interest rates, and rates greater than 15 or 20 percent were considered usurious. Citizens of Constance could not, under municipal law, charge more than 11 percent on loans. Many men of affairs provide a glimpse of their afflicted consciences and their fears of punishment after death when in their wills they bequeath a notable portion of their goods to the poor. Francesco Datini dedicated himself to repentance in his old age. He went on pilgrimages, fasted, and at the end left nearly all his enormous estate (75,000 *fiorini*) to works of charity—all of which still did not free him from a sense of guilt and "melancholy." Some of the doges of Venice abandoned their office for moral reasons, and there were wealthy men who retired to monasteries when they shut up shop.

Naturally, not all merchants were equally sensitive to arguments against the unbridled accumulation of wealth. It has been noted that the Italians in particular were more active in seeking ways to elude the ecclesiastical prohibitions on usury than the men of the Hanseatic Leagues.

The Middle Ages borrowed from antiquity the image of Fortune, an incarnation of blind destiny ceaselessly turning the wheel that first raises up and then dashes down the success-seekers who cling to it. In medieval society this image perhaps fitted no one better than the merchant. The word itself—*fortuna*—continued to have two meanings: that of destiny or the ineluctable succession of events, and that of a large sum of money or wealth. Naturally, the sense of risk, always present in the merchant, was tied to the thought of a destiny that toys with humankind. The medieval idea of a fate with a will of its own that dispenses successes and failures to men became more frequent and more intensely felt, both among the merchants, who had practical experience with rapid enrichment and even more rapid ruin (as with the failures of the greatest banking companies of Florence, those of the Bardi and the Peruzzi families), and among thinkers of the Renaissance. Naturally, they no longer thought in terms of the ancient Fortuna, but of a chance sent by God. One merchant in Augsburg wrote that God had granted his ancestor "mercy, success, and profit" (*Gnade, Glück, Gewinn*). Under conditions of growing crisis, however, the concept of "fortune" assumed a more and more unilateral sense of a destructive, baleful force freighted with mortal peril and denying destiny.

The merchants needed protection from the instability of destiny, and they found it in Nicholas of Myra, the patron saint of commerce and navigation. From the late eleventh century St. Nicholas's relics were conserved in Bari, and they attracted masses of pilgrims. Venetian merchants, however, claimed that St. Nicholas's true remains were in their city: commercial rivalry found an echo even in the cult of the saint. Nicholas was venerated as the patron saint of merchants even in the north of Europe and throughout the Baltic. It has been noted that, as economic insecurity intensified, there was an increasing tendency among Italian city-dwellers to give their children saints' names in an attempt to assure the saint's protection in life's adversities, and saints' names began to appear with a certain frequency in the names of merchant ships as a form of "insurance" against shipwreck.

When the commercial climate became less favorable, some merchants attempted to avoid the risks connected with wide-ranging commerce by turning to a system of investment of their money that offered better guarantees. The history of the Venetian Barbarigo family is perhaps paradigmatic in this connection. Andrea Barbarigo the Elder, a merchant, preferred to buy land at the end of his life, and his son Niccolò left instructions in his will for his son, Andrea the Younger, telling him not to invest capital in commerce. In like fashion, Matteo Palmieri, the author of *Della vita civile* (1438–39), praised mercantile commerce, but he put agricultural occupations above all others for guaranteeing a tranquil life.

When Italian men of affairs gave up trade in favor of finance and landownership, it diverted them from participation in discoveries beyond the Atlantic Ocean. The geographical discoveries of the turn of the sixteenth century placed Italy out of the new major commercial routes and coincided with the beginning of Italy's economic decline.

A decrease in economic activity and the colossal population decline that followed the Great Plague of 1348–49 (which was understood by contemporaries as a manifestation of divine wrath for the sins of humankind) prompted a serious psychological, social, and moral crisis that struck the merchant class along with the rest of society. Death became a close acquaintance and a permanent threat. The amusing tales narrated in the *Decameron*—a "mercantile epic" (Christian Bec)—cannot be fully understood without the perspective in which Boccaccio set them. The first day of the *Decameron* opens with a sinister panorama of devastation and human savagery brought on by the plague that includes the disintegration of all human relations, including family bonds. This is the background for the tales about curious cases and frivolous adventures told by ten young men and women who have abandoned Florence while the pest rages. The stories they tell are an artistic transformation of reality, but it would be a mistake to lose sight of the horrifying defeat of life present both in Boccaccio's narrative and in the consciousness of his contemporaries and which can be defined as the triumph of death. In the preface to his *novelle* Franco Sacchetti writes openly that people wanted to hear stories that brought them ease and consolation amid so many disasters, the plague, and death. To grasp the degree to which people of the Renaissance were obsessed with the idea of death and castigation after death we need only recall the work of a friend of Boccaccio, the cloth merchant Agnolo Bencivenni Torini, describing the calamitous and precarious nature of human existence.

The urban governing class also took part in the mass demonstrations of penitence and the waves of frenetic piety and fanaticism, accompanied by public processions of flagellants, that suddenly spread throughout Europe in the "waning of the Middle Ages." From time to time, that class also displayed heretical tendencies, although the role and the specific weight of the mercantile class in heretical movements is far from clear. Moreover, wealthy burghers were invariably detested by the poor, whom they exploited, as seen in the revolt of the *ciompi* in Florence (1378), which in certain ways prefigured class struggle between the proletariat and the bourgeoisie. A century later Florence, freshly liberated from the tyranny of the Medicis, became the arena in which Savonarola, a reformer and apostle of asceticism, attacked the rich and the clergy. Savonarola's ideal was to transform the city into one great monastery from which luxury, wealth, and usury would be banished, along with art and profane letters. These were exceptional cases, however, and extreme instances of open display of hatred toward the rich. In general, the ideal of the Middle Ages, as far as commerce was concerned, was small-scale production destined for a circumscribed market and moderate commercial exchange responding to the demands of a "just price" and a "moderate profit" not to surpass repayment of the merchant's losses and the satisfaction of his family's needs. Nonetheless, ideal demands of the sort were in acute contradiction with reality. The merchant's religious impulses were intertwined with his thirst for lucre and his eagerness to possess wealth. In the last analysis, his entire ethic was determined by this thirst.

I have already cited the words of the priest who asked his parishioners not to pray for the soul of his father who had been a usurer and hence should be damned for all eternity. These words are contained in an edifying *exemplum*, and we have no reason to believe them invented. Neither should we take them as an accurate reflection of actual practice, however. We find a nearly literal repetition of this parental malediction in the will of Simone di Rinieri Peruzzi, directed this time not from the son to the father but from father to son: "May my son be damned for eternity, by me and by God! May it be so, if after my death he is still in life and I cannot punish him as he merits; may the castigations of God fall upon him as a disloyal traitor." What had provoked such terrible paternal ire, which Armando Sapori has called the most fearful malediction ever written during the Middle

Ages? The son had stolen a handful of silver coins from his father's strongbox.

It would be a mistake, however, to conclude from evidence such as this that the merchant family did not have a solid affective base. On the contrary, it was precisely in these circles that the profile of the modern family began to take shape. The profession of the head of the family was passed on to his sons, which meant that in recognition of the father's domination the nuclear family began to center on the child who would eventually carry on his father's profession. The family was the principal structural element in the organization of widespread commercial enterprises and credit networks, and the companies that dominated the economic life of the fourteenth and fifteenth centuries were above all family associations. The wealthy families in a city held title, by birthright, to the most important responsibilities in the municipal government. For example, in Cologne in the thirteenth and fourteenth centuries, members of the Overstolz family occupied the position of *Bürgermeister* twenty-five times. The family chronicles in German cities such as Nuremberg, Augsburg, and Frankfurt (as well as in Italy) are among the clearest indications of a high "family self-awareness." They stood as confirmation of the family's merits and celebrated its honor, and they often present the family and the individual, the city and the state, history and the contemporary scene with a lively historical awareness. Leon Battista Alberti's treatise *Della famiglia* (1432–41) is only one of many testimonies to an increased attention to family life and to an intensification of the centripetal forces within the family. It is perhaps not coincidental that in the late Middle Ages religious painting more frequently represents family scenes from sacred history. In painting of precisely this period, the action takes place more and more inside the home, and the hearth begins to emerge as a center of attraction. The burgher family became a subject for group portraiture, increasingly popular in the art of the time. In a desire to have themselves immortalized, merchants and financiers commissioned portraits of themselves, and artists painted them in concrete situations inside their houses or their places of business and with their wives and children.

*

The activities of men of affairs had made a new system of values necessary and had brought it into being, but that system was slow to gain recognition in literature. Dante regarded the merchants coldly, with lofty aristocratic contempt. Petrarch simply paid them little heed. Urban commercial life overflows, however, from the pages of the authors of the Italian *novelle* of the fourteenth and the fifteenth centuries. Vittore Branca, a great specialist of Italian literature, quite rightly defines the *Decameron* as "a true Odyssey of commerce." A new hero came to take the place of the knight and the warrior: the enterprising and energetic merchant, the "authentic pioneer of the late Middle Ages." These "knights of commerce" founded the new world, and Boccaccio was the first to give them their due in literature.

The circulation of money transformed the traditional medieval mentality, little inclined to the mercantile approach to humankind that was gaining ground. In Italy and in France in the fifteenth century it was common to express a person's worth in terms of his wealth: "he's a man worth thousands of *fiorini* (francs, etc.)." A mercantile cast of mind and a tendency to view the full range of life through the prism of the calculation of individual interest were widely shared characteristics. Jacopo Loredano of Venice noted in his account book, "The doge, Foscari, owes me for the death of my father and my uncle." After his adversary and his son had been eliminated from public life, the merchant noted with satisfaction on the facing page, "Paid."

Calculation and self-interest penetrated to the afterworld as well, however. The thirteenth century was the age in which a new kingdom appeared in the Catholic geography of the other world—Purgatory. If in earlier centuries of the Middle Ages the souls of the dead were thought to go (either immediately or after the Last Judgment) to Heaven or—much more probably—to Hell, henceforth there was the new possibility of reaching the heavenly abode after undergoing torments of varying duration in Purgatory. One's sojourn among the flames of Purgatory could be shortened by the celebration of funeral masses, by making generous donations to the church, and by offering aid to the poor. In fourteenth- and fifteenth-century testaments the wealthy often stipulate that immediately after their death their executors and their heirs were to have an enormous number (hundreds of thousands) of masses celebrated for the earliest possible liberation of their souls from the torments of Purgatory and their admission to Paradise. Testators were literally obsessed with the need to put pressure on the heavenly forces with the greatest possible number of masses. Fear of the torments beyond the tomb was one of the motivations for the spread of the practice of testaments in the late Middle Ages. The idea of some sort of equilibrium between "good works" in this world and reward in the other began to take root. The wealthy man, the merchant, made every effort to assure his comfort in the netherworld.

The new vision of the world found expression in painting in the triumph of a linear perspective that organized space from the individual's viewpoint. The base from which the disappearing point was calculated in the new perspective painting was the position of the spectator, whose sight actively penetrated deep into a pluridimensional space, an urban space for the most part.

Portulans—guides to and descriptions of ports and maritime routes—and maps of Europe and the world answered the needs of the merchant navigators, and in turn the voyages and navigational enterprises of the fourteenth and fifteenth centuries encouraged both the development of cartography and a more rational domination of space.

Frequentation of merchant fairs and the exploitation of favorable economic fluctuations required a high degree of attention to time if commercial and financial operations and speculations were to be successful. The merchant thought in terms of days, not centuries, and changes in the perception of time quite naturally accompanied the reorganization of space. As we have seen, historical time penetrated the family chronicles. A patrician merchant of Nuremberg, Ulmann Stromer, wrote the history of his family at the end of the fourteenth century, beginning with what was remembered of a knightly ancestor who had lived in the beginning of the thirteenth century. The portrait, which was gaining ground in painting, was an expression of an interest in halting the passing moment in the life of an individual and keeping it forever. "Merchant's time" declared its autonomy from "church's time" (Jacques Le Goff), and the church began to lose track of its own control over time. Men of affairs found the ecclesiastical calendar, with its movable feasts and its year that began somewhere between March 22 and April 25 no longer suited to their needs. A better sort of subdivision was needed for a more exact calculation of time, and under pressure from merchants' needs, the beginning of the year came to be fixed at the Feast of the Circumcision of Christ, on January 1.

Merchants also needed a precise and uniform way to measure smaller time-intervals, however; they needed clocks and the equal division of the day into equal hours. Mechanical clocks, invented in the late thirteenth century, were installed in the towers of city halls and cathedrals throughout Europe: in Paris in 1300, in Milan in 1309, in Caen in 1314, in Florence in 1325, between 1326 and 1335 in London, in 1344 in Padua, in 1354 in Strasbourg and Genoa, in 1356 in Bologna, in 1359 in Siena, in 1362 in Ferrara, and so forth. Henceforth, the days were divided into twenty-four hours signaled by the striking of the clock or, as in Strasbourg, by the crowing of a mechanical rooster. This new invention had practical advantages, but above all it symbolized the transfer of time to the service of the *bürger,* the patricians, and the secular authorities. In the fifteenth century mechanical clocks for personal use appeared. "Theological" time was replaced by "technological" time. Sensitivity to the passage of time increased. Genoese notaries registered not only the day but also the hour at which their documents were signed.

Time was more highly valued, and if time had been viewed before as the patrimony of God (this is the sense in which we should understand Bernardino of Siena when he says, "There is nothing more precious than time"), henceforth it was perceived as belonging to human beings. Seneca was quoted as saying, "Nothing belongs to us as fully as time; all other things are extraneous to us; only time is ours," and Leon Battista Alberti wrote, "There are three things which a man may call his own personal property." These things are gifts of nature that can "never be separated from you." The first is the soul; the second is the body, the "instrument of the soul"; the third is "the most valuable of all things. It is more mine than these hands and these eyes. . . . It is time." Alberti adds that all losses can be compensated except lost time. The elderly Parisian burgher who wrote instructions for his young wife reminds her that in the next world everyone will answer for the time he or she has wasted in this world. In the same fashion, Giannozzo Manetti, a member of the Florentine city government, declared that everyone has to render an account, at the end of his or her life, of how the time allotted by God has been spent. According to Manetti, the Lord will ask each of us to account not only for years and months but also for days, hours, and instants. This was a humanist's judgment. The banker and entrepreneur, Francesco di Marco Datini, warned that "he who knows how to spend his time better will outstrip the others." In his *Libro di buoni costumi,* Boccaccio's friend Paolo da Certaldo recommends specific moments for the buying and selling of various products. Heaven and Hell share space in Paolo's work with prices for wheat, oil, and wine; eternity rubs elbows with the annual business cycle. A century later, a Venetian merchant noted the months of the year in which the demand for money increased and money could thus be invested with maximum profit: demand was highest in Genoa in September, January, and April, when ships took to sea; in Valencia in July and August, following the wheat harvest; in Montpellier when fairs were held there three times a year, and so forth. In calculating their resources and ways to make them multiply, the merchants had one eye fixed on the calendar. Time was money!

Naturally, "merchant's time" was not the same as "humanist's time," and men of affairs valued time for incomparably more prosaic reasons than poets and philosophers. Still, the spirit that imbues both the merchants' and the humanists' pronouncements on time is, in the last analysis, the same. Time became subjective, "humanized," and the need to "make it one's own" and to possess it was felt in equal measure by men of affairs and by scholars, poets, and artists who valued time for attaining knowledge in order to "become day by day what one had not been before (Morelli).

Men of affairs in Florence and in the other Italian cities provided humanism with its principal social foundation. Their sponsorship of cultural enterprises and their commissions, along with those of popes, the rulers of cities, and other aristocratic lords, assured a living to the artists, architects, sculptors, and painters who built cathedrals and palaces and decorated them with frescoes and statues. The wealthy, in an effort to imitate the aristocracy and join its ranks, spent money generously for the glorification of their native cities, hence of themselves. Initiation into the world of the arts increased their social prestige and contributed to a considerable amplification of their spiritual horizon. The mythologized, utopian worldview typical of the culture created by the masters of the Renaissance cast its glow on the merchants and the entrepreneurs, ennobling their lives. These men who knew so well how to calculate costs and accumulate money also knew how to spend it generously to cultivate a world of high spiritual values around themselves. The merchant's instruction was not limited to strictly utilitarian needs, and he found personal satisfaction in contemplating works of art and reading literature. The relations of men of affairs with artists and poets varied enormously, ranging from veneration to the simple utilization of artists as wage-earners on a par with all the other craftsmen whom the merchants employed as manual workers. They must have recognized, however, that art gave festivity and animation to their practical lives and imbued them with greater meaning. A new comprehension of nature; an ability to observe it in its intimacy; an assimilation of spatial perspective and a taste for realistic detail; a profoundly changed sense of time and an understanding of history; the "humanization" of Christianity; and the new value given to human individuality—all this responded to a more rationalistic vision of the world and to profound needs in the new class of the protobourgeoisie. The merchants' practice and the creative activity of the geniuses of the Renaissance were worlds apart, and humanists and men of affairs differed equally widely in their comprehension of the principles of the individual, of worth, and of virtue. Both groups contributed to a common cause, however, and participated in the creation of the new world.

*

The position of men of affairs in medieval society was extremely contradictory. By lending money to the nobles and the monarchs (whose insolvency or refusal to pay often caused the failure of great banks), and by acquiring landed property, concluding marriages with knightly families, and pursuing noble titles and crests, the mercantile patriciate became deeply entrenched in feudal society, to the point of being an inevitable and fundamental element of it. Crafts, commerce, the city, and finance were all organic parts of fully developed feudalism. At the same time, however, money was sapping the traditional bases of aristocratic domination—land and warfare—and pauperizing the artisan class and the peasants, since the great enterprises launched by merchants employed wage-workers. When in the late Middle Ages money became a powerful social force, large-scale international commerce and the spirit of gain that moved the merchants became the heralds of a new economic and social order: capitalism.

In spite of all his efforts to "root himself" in the structure of feudalism and adapt himself to it, the great merchant was a totally different psychological and social type from the feudal lord. He was a knight of profit who risked his life not on the battlefield but in his office or his shop, on board a merchant ship, or in his bank. To the warlike virtues and the impulsive emotivity of the nobles he opposed careful calculation and cause-and-effect thinking; to irrationality, he opposed rationality. In the milieu of men of affairs a new type of religious sentiment came to be elaborated in a paradoxical combination of faith in God and fear of castigation in the otherworld, on the one hand, and, on the other, a mercantile approach to "good works" that expected indemnification and compensation, which were to be expressed as material prosperity.

If in the late Middle Ages Europe was separated from the other civilizations of the world by its discovery of how to break through the barriers of traditionalism and archaism, launching the expansion throughout the globe that eventually changed the face of our planet and inaugurated a new era of true world history, the merchants deserve to be remembered as first among those who most contributed to the realization of this extraordinary and unprecedented venture.

BIBLIOGRAPHY

Bec, Christian. *Les Marchands écrivains. Affaires et humanisme à Florence, 1375–1434.* Paris and The Hague: Mouton, 1967.

Branca, Vittore, ed. *Mercanti scrittori, Ricordi nella Firenze tra Medioevo e Rinascimento.* Milan: Rusconi, 1986.

Espinas, Georges. *Les Origines du capitalisme.* Vol. 1, *Sire Jehan Boinebroke, patricien et drapier douaisien (?-1286 environ).* Lille: Emile Raoust, 1933.

Herlihy, David. *Medieval and Renaissance Pistoia: The Social History of an Italian Town, 1200–1430.* New Haven: Yale University Press, 1967.

Kedar, Benjamin Z. *Merchants in Crisis. Genoese and Venetian Men of Affairs and the Fourteenth-Century Depression.* New Haven and London: Yale University Press, 1976.

Le Goff, Jacques. *La Bourse et la vie. Economie et religion au Moyen Age.* Paris: Hachette, 1986 [*Your Money or Your Life: Economy and Religion in the Middle Ages.* Trans. Patricia Ranum. New York: Zone Books, 1988].

———. *Marchands et banquiers du Moyen Age.* Paris: Presses Universitaires Françaises, 1956; 5th edition rev., 1972.

———. "The Usurer and Purgatory." In *The Dawn of Modern Banking.* New Haven and London: Yale University Press, 1979, pp. 22–52.

Maschke, Erich. "La Mentalité des marchands européens au Moyen Age." *Revue d'histoire économique et sociale* 42, 4 (1964): 457–84.

Renouard, Yves. *Les hommes d'affaires italiens du Moyen Age.* Paris: A. Colin, 1949; new edition, Bernard Guillemain, ed., Paris: A. Colin, 1968.

Sapori, Armando. *Le Marchand italien au Moyen Age: conférences et bibliographie.* Paris: A. Colin, 1952 [*The Italian Merchant in the Middle Ages.* Trans. Patricia Anne Kennen. New York: Norton, 1970].

SUGGESTED READINGS

Raymond de Roover, *Money, Banking and Credit in Medieval Bruges; Italian Merchant-Bankers and Money-Changers, A Study in the Origins of Banking* (Cambridge, Mass.: Medieval Academy of America, 1948).

Edward D. English, *Enterprise and Liability in Sienese Banking, 1230–1350* (Cambridge, Mass.: Medieval Academy of America, 1988).

Richard W. Kaeuper, *Bankers to the Crown: The Riccardi of Lucca and Edward I* (Princeton: Princeton University Press, 1973).

Frederic C. Lane, *Andrea Barbarigo, Merchant of Venice, 1418–1449* (New York: Octagon Books, 1967).

Robert S. Lopez, *The Commercial Revolution of the Middle Ages, 950–1350* (Cambridge: Cambridge University Press, 1976).

Iris Origo, *The Merchant of Prato* (Boston: David R. Godine, 1986).

M. M. Postan, *Medieval Trade and Finance* (Cambridge: Cambridge University Press, 1973).

Kathryn L. Reyerson, *Business, Banking, and Finance in Medieval Montpellier* (Toronto: Pontifical Institute of Mediaeval Studies, 1985).

Sylvia L. Thrupp, *The Merchant Class of Medieval London, 1300–1500* (Ann Arbor: University of Michigan Press, 1976).

EIGHT

Women and the Family

Christiane Klapisch-Zuber

In the eleventh century, at the beginning of the period that interests us here, the three-part scheme dominating people's concepts of Christian society granted no specific place to women. It placed "orders" or "conditions"—knights, clerics, and villeins—into hierarchical relation, but the resulting pyramid (with those who prayed and those who fought and rendered justice competing for the first position) made no provision for a "feminine condition."

Men of the Middle Ages long conceived of "the woman" as a category, but only late in the period did they distinguish variations in the behavior expected of women by applying criteria such as professional activities to their model. Before she was seen as a peasant, the lady of a castle, or a saint, "the" woman was defined by her body, her gender, and her relations with family groups. Wife, widow, or maid, her juridical persona and the ethic by which she lived her daily life were portrayed in relation to a man or a group of man.

I have no intention of composing a gallery of portraits, juxtaposing the various roles that women played as pawns on the social chessboard during the course of half a millennium. Instead, I will attempt to situate women within the framework that contemporaries automatically assigned to them and within the sets of constraints that kinship and family imposed upon the emergence of women as individuals possessing full enjoyment of juridical, moral, and economic personality. Limiting my remarks to the context of the family, I shall consider gender-based relationships where they were most obviously at work on a daily basis—in the division of domestic tasks and responsibilities that expressed the aims and ambitions of the family unit and the kinship group.

A project of this sort might seem to be overly influenced by the blind spots and the prejudices of both the Middle Ages and latter-day medievalists. After all, it evokes the homemaker and relies on a time-honored normative tradition that ineluctably imprisoned women within domestic routine, stifling them in a lackluster round of humble activities. By refusing to base my arguments on the brilliant role conferred on a few women by monastic culture, inherited feudal functions, royal birth, or a rich spiritual or mystical life, I could be accused of once more relegating "the" woman to a place on the side of the body and of nature; to condemning her all over again to a colorless routine of housekeeping and maternal preoccupations that brought no glory and was not even a profession. In short, I could be charged with deliberately choosing the gloomiest picture, one that neglects a good part of the facts and, in the last analysis, supports a reductionist view of the "feminine condition."

There are obvious risks involved in the approach I have chosen. I will first invite the reader to see the family as a kinship group that exceeded the limits of domesticity, for not all questions pertaining to women were resolved in that narrow space. Solicitations and injunctions involving them developed in a larger and more fluid sphere where bonds were founded on friendship, economic cooperation, or political aims as well as on blood and marriage. Social anthropology has made important contributions (which need not be listed here) to the full range of problems, tools, and ideas at the disposal of historians of the family and of the feminine condition whose traditional grounding was in the history of the law. This new perspective has permitted them to investigate further the modalities and aims of alliance and to revise their interpretation of the control of alliance through time. The first question to be investigated here will thus concern the place of women within kinship and alliance groups.

Next, I shall seek to evoke the hopes and fears aroused in men by the women in their families, using the heterogeneous and often ambiguous raw material that historians of population have amassed for those still-obscure centuries. Although uncertain and dispersed, the information furnished by historical demography nevertheless gives new insights, for example into sexual and conjugal practices, into the couple's relations and relations between generations, or about people's sense of intimacy or of what was honorable. Our sources for the earlier ages are necessarily limited to normative or repressive measures. In the later Middle Ages, however, our vision can be based on an infinitely richer choice of administrative, judicial, or familial documents.

Few of these texts, however, and few images of the woman and the family bring us the voices of the women themselves. The echoes of daily pleasures and pains and domestic joys or skirmishes come to us—tinged with condescension, malice, or frank hostility—much more often from men than from women. This first and capital limitation is accompanied by a second one, which applies to all investigations of the family and of women's roles. All that we know about these topics is informed (and distorted) by a predominance of sources from the upper levels of society—the knightly class for the earlier period and the urban burgher class for the later Middle Ages. Unfortunately, seigneurial *courtoisie* and bourgeois derision circumscribe banal sentiments and daily behavior no better than the admonitions and penances of the churchmen of the early Middle Ages. The picture we paint can never be a totally faithful likeness, since our observations are necessarily dependent upon the wealth, culture, and gender of our informants.

*

In the Middle Ages alliance was primarily a "peace pact." Marriage put an end to a process of rivalry—at times of open warfare—between two families, initiating and sealing a truce. Giving a woman to the lineage with which a family was becoming reconciled placed the bride at the center of the entente. As a gage of peace and an instrument of concord, her role went beyond her individual destiny or her personal aspirations.

Even more than for fulfilling her wifely duties toward her husband, she was responsible for maintaining the alliance between the two clans by her blameless conduct, for working to perpetuate the lineage into which she entered by procreating for it, and for faithfully assuring it the use of her body and of the goods that she had brought it. Ecclesiastical circles needed to reflect on the foundation of the conjugal bond for quite some time, and very profound economic and social upheavals needed to take place before the couple began to take shape within this network of constraints and before the "good wife" became a discernible figure within the couple.

There are abundant examples of matrimonial alliances that used women to establish or restore amicable relations between two lineages. The most important figures to seek out such unions were of course the heads of Christendom: one eleventh-century king of France, Henry I, sought a bride in the far-off principality of Kiev in Russia. Georges Duby has shown that this conception of alliance extended to a somewhat lower social level in the diplomatic exchanges of wives practiced by feudal dynasties of the eleventh and twelfth centuries in pursuit of their territorial ambitions and their political goals.

Still lower on the social scale, ancient hatreds and prolonged vendettas among the urban patriciates of the thirteenth to the fifteenth centuries were also terminated by a spectacular exchange of women, and private or public wars occasionally flared up when a projected union came to naught. In Florence around 1300 the party of the "Whites" coalesced thanks to an alliance concluded in 1288 to join a man of the Cerchi family to an Adimari bride, thus ending their long enmity, while unhappy marital relations between the leader of the "Blacks" and his first wife (as it happens, a Cerchi), followed by his remarriage with a cousin, a wealthy heiress taken from the opposing faction, stirred up passions and civil war anew. Several years later (in 1312) another Florentine, Giotto Peruzzi, noted in his *Libro segreto* the amounts to be paid by each male member of his lineage as contributions to the enormous dowry his daughter was to bring to the Adimari family, with whom the Peruzzis had just drawn up a solemn promise of peace "with assembly of friends from the one side and the other in the Piazza de' Priori." Moved like a pawn on the familial chessboard, the woman guaranteed respect of the pact. She was the embodiment of peace, that great aspiration of the Middle Ages.

Although strategies of alliance were described abundantly in chronicles and documents, they were less often a topic for theoretical discussion. The one exception is a literature inspired or written by churchmen, in great part based on the propositions of St. Augustine that equated the injunction to exogamy—the obligation to wed outside the kinship group—with a need to guarantee social bonds and to found social cohesion on the "charity" and love that allies owed one another. Blood-based solidarities, to the contrary, risked setting too tightly defined family groups against one another.

Exogamy was not contradictory to family practices aimed at peace and social equilibrium. The church, however, turned to exogamy to justify its proscription—which intensified between the sixth century and the early thirteenth century—of marriage between blood relations. In doing so it frustrated one of the most ardently held obligations of lineage: to conserve for one's descendants the patrimony received from one's ancestors. The laity was prepared to wink at kinship bonds to marry their sons and daughters to one another when the family fortunes required it, even if the churchmen declared the projected marriage incestuous.

Thus the aspiration for peace and its corollary, the obligation to exchange women, did not have the same implications for churchmen and for secular society. Where for the churchmen such aspirations excluded all marriage between too-close cousins, for families they could encourage unions within the kinship group. The conflict between these two attitudes became acute in royal and princely marriages about 1100. As years went by the church became more flexible. In 1215 the Fourth Lateran Council lowered the requirements for exogamy from the seventh degree of kinship to the fourth, which meant that descendants of a common great-great grandparent could marry. In exchange, not even the humblest Christian could continue to feign ignorance of kinship. The church reinforced its control over the legitimacy of unions by instituting the publication of marriage banns preceding the wedding in order to make sure that engaged couples poorly informed of their cousinship could avoid "incest."

*

Alliance was an oath or promise of peace; it also involved the social status and the honor of the families. Both in giving and in receiving a bride, families quite naturally evaluated the consideration and the material advantages that the union would bring them. What is important for our purposes is that a woman given in marriage moved in two directions: laterally, when she went to her husband's house, but also vertically, either upward into a family situated higher on the social scale than her own, or downward. It has been shown that the matrimonial strategy most current among the knightly class in the eleventh and twelfth centuries and among aristocratic and burgher circles in the fourteenth and fifteenth centuries led fathers to choose daughters-in-law of higher birth. Many women, perhaps the majority, thus found themselves degraded socially by their marriages, given to husbands of inferior blood or rank to whom they nonetheless owed obedience.

The embittered, quarrelsome wife who incessantly reminds her husband of his lower birth is a constant theme in medieval literature, as is the companion theme of male fear of affronting such a dragon bristling with family crests and genealogies. Boccaccio gives a savory caricature of this figure in the remarried widow of his *Corbaccio,* who constantly vaunts "the nobility and magnificence of her family" as if she were "of the House of Swabia" (trans. Cassell) or of royal lineage. A contemporary of Boccaccio, Paolo da Certaldo, also discourages taking a second wife "who is better born than the first, so that she cannot tell you, 'More is owed to me than to her, because I am born of a greater house and more honorable kin.' "

When a woman passed from one lineage to another it involved not only her physical transfer but also a transfer of wealth. The honor of both families was at stake in both contexts. In order to be recognized socially—irrespective of the milieu, the epoch, and the juridical system in effect—marriage demanded that goods (even of minimal worth) be "given" by one group to the other as the cession of the woman was prepared and then carried out. During the early Middle Ages these goods were given by the husband or his family to the family of the bride in "compensation" for its loss of a daughter. Later they were given to the bride herself, who in return continued to bring her husband effects, properties, and sums of money that she either "gave" to him or retained in her own possession. This way she was assured maintenance after her husband's death. The deeper intention of such exchanges of gift and countergift lay elsewhere: they worked to establish a solid bond between two families involved in a carefully calculated game of gift and countergift to signify both the friendship between the two families and their respective social positions.

Beginning in the twelfth century, the dowry brought by the wife increased and gradually surpassed the marital dowry or the gifts and contributions of the husband. Some marital gifts were even prohibited by law, such as the Genoese *tertia* of Frankish origin, abolished in 1143, which gave the widow a right to one-third of her husband's estate. On the margins of the chronicle relating the promulgation of this decree the scribe has sketched two lamenting women. The dowry became the central contribution in exchanges, particularly in lands under revived Roman law, and the pivot around which all law concerning patrimonial relations between spouses in the later Middle Ages revolved. Without ever eliminating all trace of the older marital contributions, the dowry henceforth held the center stage. Its evolution was complete in the fourteenth and fifteenth centuries when the married woman in southern France and in Italy (later in Spain as well) was defined by the dowry her family had provided. In the north the widow's portion funded by the husband persisted until the early modern era. I should add that in both cases the woman usually lost the right to full disposition of both what she had brought and what her husband had "given" her, whereas earlier she had had free use of such properties at her widowhood and often during her conjugal life. Henceforth the husband administered her holdings and disposed of the revenue during her lifetime; at his death his widow had little more than lifetime interest on her properties and could not transmit them by testament to persons of her choice.

The reasons for this sort of "dispossession" of women are complex. One that is often suggested is that the feudalization of landholding excluded women from the transmission of goods, castles, and fiefs. In urban circles dependent upon commerce and crafts, professional corporations were closed to women and reserved their activities and responsibilities to males. Dowering permitted the elimination of women from the inheritance of family wealth: they renounced their rights in their brothers' favor, and once they were married they abandoned active control of holdings that were theoretically theirs. With many variations from region to region and from one set of customs to another, women everywhere had less control over wealth (their own in particular) at the end of the Middle Ages than in earlier times.

The deterioration in both women's economic role and their ability to administer their own wealth led ineluctably to a decline in their "worth." The misogyny that imbues so many texts from the last three centuries of the Middle Ages had, of course, other sources than women's shrinking financial worth and juridical rights—among them, the persistent anxiety of churchmen regarding the fair but forbidden sex. Nonetheless, both as cause and effect of this hostile atmosphere, the refusal to allow women the freedom to manage properties placed in their names and even the limitations on the amounts they could receive played a role both in establishing platitudes unfavorable to women and in the widespread diffusion of mistrustful and negative attitudes.

In much of urbanized Europe, families let themselves be drawn into a veritable inflationary spiral of dowries, which provided a new source of male recriminations. Dante was one of the first to deplore the passing of the "good old days":

> In those days fathers had no cause to fear
> a daughter's birth: the marriageable age
> was not too low, the dowry not too high.
> (Trans. Musa)

If families yielded to this practice, which they blamed on female cupidity and vanity, it was because the dowry and the other marriage contributions allowed them to affirm their social position and to obtain recognition of their status in the eyes of the collectivity—in short, to maintain and increase their "honor." For women, who went to a husband bearing a dowry, often with no hope of receiving a marital counterpart, the consequence of this new development was, in mercantile terms, that it was extremely expensive to marry them off. This investment with no return did little to improve the regard in which they were held by the family males who had to provide for their future. Family honor was paid for at every union, but we could say without exaggeration that the men pursuing that honor made their womenfolk pay dearly for it.

Honor did not rest merely on the material power and prestige of the lineage, however. It had a strong gender component, also depending upon the actions of the women who were the agents of alliance. The principle of succession in the male line was becoming firmly established, and there was renewed discussion of medical theories inherited from classical antiquity on whether the woman was active or passive in conception. For many writers, paternal "blood" kept all its purity in the gravid woman, who did nothing but "bake" or "form" the child. All "good lineages" dreaded the unwitting admixture of undesirable blood. A man's offspring born out of wedlock of course strained the delicate mechanism of inheritance, but they were easy to spot. The adulterous children of a wife were more dangerous, since their mother had a better chance of concealing her crime. They were born of fraud and, when they survived, they risked dual reprobation for their birth from a sin of the flesh and for their mother's betrayal of the family into which she had entered. The sexual fidelity of women was solidly at the heart of family structure, and women's bodies required unflagging surveillance to guard against fraudulent changelings who might discredit the great body of the lineage.

*

Placed in the uncomfortable situation of a union that was often unequal, married women owed loyalty and devotion to the interests of both families allied through her. Such demands could conflict with the affection and the obedience they also owed their husbands, particularly since the churchmen's conceptions of conjugal duties entered into the picture. Toward the end of the period that interests us here lay people's awareness of these questions worked against obedience to the lineage.

The young girl was expected to show unhesitating obedience to her father, her brother, or her guardian, keeping silent about her own inner aspirations and accepting the man they had chosen for her. But the church, which, as we have seen, intervened to dissuade cousins from marrying, also insisted (with increasing firmness from the late eleventh century on) on the need to obtain, in due and proper form, the consent of both spouses, also insisting that young people not be given in marriage at an age at which their consent was meaningless. For the church, the founding of a new family could take place only when the liberty of the contracting parties was respected, and those parties were not the representatives of the lineages but the future spouses. This shift prompted a considerable revolution, at least in theory, by according to the woman a place equal to that of the man in the administration of the sacrament of marriage. We need, however, to gauge the practical effects of that upheaval.

The appropriation of women by violence, frequent during the early Middle Ages, later became rare, and it seldom met with social and religious approval. Still, both the practice of kidnapping the bride (often to force the families to come to an agreement) and the habit of leading theologians of taking the silence of the woman as modest acquiescence should put us on guard against an overly optimistic interpretation of the conditions under which women acquired a voice in the matter. As late as the height of the Renaissance, texts abound with sinister stories of girls given to husbands or sent to convents against their will. The very rites that the church created or set up to guarantee freedom of consent were on occasion twisted to other ends.

Between the eleventh century and the fourteenth century, the rituals of marriage concentrated on several crucial stages—sometimes brief, sometimes protracted—in the process of the formation of a couple. In Normandy, for example, the traditional ceremony of transfer of the bride from her father or her guardian to her husband, a ceremony that was normally carried out in private during all the early Middle Ages, was invested by the church with complementary rites and moved from the home to the porch of the parish church, where the priest welcomed the engaged couple and they exchanged their statements of consent. The public nature of the place, the presence of witnesses, and the solemnity conferred by the presence of the priest certainly gave unusual weight to the woman's voice—a voice not always heard in all places or in all social circles under such protected conditions. The rich and powerful, in Italy, for example, continued to the mid-sixteenth century to celebrate this moment in a totally familial setting and before only the notary. By its very formality, the religious ritual that surrounded the exchange of consent reveals the limits of the practical influence of the church in a domain in which families fought inch by inch to keep their freedom of action and their control. Centuries of pastoral teaching would be needed before the idea of a union not only accepted without any pressure but founded on individual impulse and reciprocal attraction could become an integral part of people's thinking.

As it happened, the ends that the church of the period assigned to marriage prevented it from envisaging the affective and sensual basis of marriage with much confidence. "It is better to marry than to burn," St. Paul had said, justifying the conjugal state but establishing the idea that marriage was a lesser evil. In the eyes of a medieval churchman, to "burn" within marriage was hardly more acceptable than pursuing one's carnal passions outside it. Only a concern to procreate a legitimate descendance justified entry into that inferior state.

Its conception of the sacrament of marriage nonetheless led the church to declare valid and thus indissoluble any union founded on a true accord of the spouses expressed before witnesses, even when the couple's motivations were purely carnal and the ritual forms of the marriage short-circuited the forms the church was attempting to impose. In the eyes of the church, promises of marriage publicly pronounced, sealed by the sharing of a glass of wine or a piece of fruit or by the exchange of small presents between the young couple, constituted vows of engagement just as binding as the religious engagement ceremonies the church was doing its best to establish. Suits brought before the episcopal courts (which had jurisdiction in such matters) show the sincerity of many of these young lovers, who gave themselves to one another by popular rites of alliance and often consummated their union without further ado. They also show that some people utilized such rites to marry their offspring by taking them by surprise. The churchmen, who disapproved of passions of the flesh just as much as they abominated the abuse of familial power, were caught in their own trap: they often found themselves legitimizing the union of couples united by such rituals even though they condemned the motivations behind them. In the sixteenth century, the Council of Trent was to clarify the ambiguity of the church's positions, bringing them closer to the families' positions and putting an end to the relative liberality that characterized the use of ritual in the late Middle Ages.

Obligatory consent—including the woman's—thus bore an explosive charge for family relations and relations between the sexes. As René Nelli has insisted, however, it was not the churchmen who invented marriage by inclination. Even though young people sufficiently audacious to take the initiative forced recognition of their personal aspirations by their conscious recourse to ritual gestures and words; even though the carnal passion so mistrusted by the churchmen slipped almost unnoticed through the cracks in the nuptial procedures, nonetheless, their mistrust of sexuality prevented the churchmen from accepting all the implications of their doctrine of the bases of the sacrament of marriage.

Did the church, as the anthropologist, Jack Goody, has recently sustained, want the smallest possible number of conjugal unions concluded, viewing marriage as a lesser evil justified by assuring the survival of humanity to the end of time? and did it want most marriages to be of limited fecundity so as to increase the chances of wealth devolving to the church? These somewhat Machiavellian aims reinforced the churchmen's fear of sexuality and of the female body and led them to accumulate obstacles to conjugal life. They set themselves up as judges of sexual practices even within the bonds of marriage and claimed that only they could pronounce on the legitimacy of sexuality. Were the laity so easily persuaded?

From the very earliest Middle Ages, as Jean-Louis Flandrin has shown, churchmen established a calendar, in theory very limited, of the times when a couple could have sexual relations without arousing clerical objections. To verify the effect of these prohibitions, which we know above all by the repressive literature of the penitentials stipulating the punishment appropriate for each possible infraction, is quite another affair. In the later centuries that interest us here, confessors' instructions call for a less meticulous count of forbidden days, but they show continuing vigilance concerning the legitimacy of the practices, the postures, and the times for conjugal relations. From the thirteenth century on, the faithful had to explain their deviations from the norm to a confessor at least once a year. Thus the judge of the faults of married people was necessarily a celibate, and a celibate who, from the eleventh century on, was ceaselessly reminded by the Gregorian reformers of his vows of chastity and of sexual purity—a man who had renounced founding a family and given up all sensual pleasures. Nonetheless, a number of priests still kept concubines and maintained their progeny in the thirteenth century, and the *Lamentations de Mahieu,* the work of a priest from Boulogne forced by the Council of Lyons in 1274 to decide between his woman and his sinecure, speak to the difficulty of choosing between secular aspirations and the obligations of the ecclesiastical state. There is no doubt that the presence of so many clerics living in a pseudomarital state (without mentioning the priests skilled at seducing their beautiful parishioners, the archetype of which is the curé of Montaillou) led the laity to judge priestly incursions onto the quicksands of sexual and conjugal morality *cum grano salis* or even, like the *fabliaux* and the tales, to salute them with joyous mockery.

As for the laity, family order adjusted to a sexual apprenticeship and to trial sex but to later generations of churchmen and more "scientific" observers they seemed rather much to ask of the young people's self-restraint. How can we reconcile the severity that families showed where the marriage and the "establishment" of their children was concerned with the permissiveness of certain forms of amorous courtship? How was it admissible that the young vassal learning the exercise of arms with his lord also be initiated into the delights and torments of love by the lady of the castle? Or for the maid of courtly romances to welcome the knight fleeing hot pursuit into her dwelling in the depths of the forest, admitting him into her bed and offering her body for all the games of love except one—*fors un*? Or for young peasants in many regions to couple up, sharing a warm spot in the stable, without having pregnancies result? In all these amorous relations governed by self-restraint, it was the women who guided the proceedings and set the uncrossable threshold between dream, desire, and possession. The fact remains that their families tolerated adventures of the sort, which are not all pure literature. This obliges us to look closely at our evaluation of familial matrimonial strategies. They did not exclude inclination, nor apprenticeship and sexual play, as long as the group kept ultimate control when the body and the wealth of the woman was invested in another family. The rest, after all, was the affair of the churchmen or the poets.

*

Engendering valid heirs was the great challenge that faced families in an epoch in which death struck hard and often. At the heart of the medieval house was the bedchamber. It was there that the woman lived—where she worked, conceived, gave birth, and died. We still know little about the biological life of the married woman or about the effects on her body and her behavior of the functions assigned to her. Documentary sources are heterogeneous, scattered, and often contradictory. We can at least see that everywhere her role in the reproduction of the group was what most frequently prompted discussions and admonitions, the greatest precautions and the highest praise.

The key to this role was thus marriage. During the early Middle Ages, barbaric law and synodal statutes, hagiographic tales and descriptions of great domains give the impression that young people at their first marriages (outside of the aristocracy, where girls were married at a very early age) married at roughly the same age and at a relatively mature age. In the central Middle Ages a clear change took place, and from one end of Europe to the other, barely adolescent girls were given to husbands markedly older than they. In Flanders, in England, in Italy, and in France in 1200 the aristocracy and the urban patriciate married their daughters when they were barely pubescent. An age of twelve or thirteen—the age at which canon law permitted engagement for marriage or the taking of religious vows—returns constantly in the lives of female saints (who, it is true, were in the very great majority born into good families). Information on marriages in the rural and popular classes before the fourteenth century is much more scarce. Still, the average age of girls at their first marriage in those milieus seldom seems greater than seventeen or eighteen in spite of demographic pressure for somewhat deferred marriage.

From the late twelfth century on, men seem to have entered into "the trammels of marriage" at a later age than had previously been the case. Scions of knightly families set the example by waiting to be installed in a fief, to have inherited, or to have found the heiress that would permit them a proper establishment. Information is just as scanty on customs among other classes of men before the fourteenth century, although the literature of the *fabliaux* widely exploits the theme of unequal ages in marriage between a graybeard and a tender young thing.

There is more information for the second half of the fourteenth century and for the fifteenth century, after the Black Death. More frequent censuses, although they too seldom display the wealth of data and the homogeneity of the Florentine *catasti* of the fifteenth century, nonetheless enable us to estimate the average age at marriage. For women it was under eighteen, with a tendency in the peasantry and the urban proletariat to delay marriage one or two years and among the rich to advance it to fifteen. A familial literature of journals, *livres de raison,* and *ricordanze* (especially in Tuscany) finally permit more accurate calculation of female age at marriage. In the Florentine bourgeoisie between 1340 and 1530 some 136 young brides were married at an average age of 17.2 years. Variations over this long period are slight, although there is a noticeable tendency to delay weddings somewhat, as around 1500 Florentine women married at an average of one year later than before 1400. The stability of the whole is nonetheless more noteworthy than this late rise.

Analogous calculations taken from a similar group of young men coming from the same families of the mercantile bourgeoisie show an average age of over twenty-seven at the celebration of their first marriages. This age shows stronger variation than the age at marriage for women, dropping, for example, after lethal epidemics; it declines discernibly during the latter third of the fifteenth century in a movement opposite to the rise in the curve for females. Still, the important fact is that ten years or so always separated male age at marriage from female.

A man nearing thirty, an adult, thus brought an adolescent into his house. This unsymmetrical situation in the later Middle Ages strangely recalls Roman customs of the classical age. Should we be astonished, then, that the resurgence of moralizing literature and treatises on domestic economy during the later Middle Ages included admonitions directly inspired by Aristotle's *Politics* or Xenophon's *Economics*? Rationalizing the practices of their own milieu and their times, men like Leon Battista Alberti (in his *Libri della famiglia*), or like Giovanni Morelli, took their model from real life: the man should wait to marry until he has reached the fullness of the "perfect age"; the woman, to the contrary, should be given to a husband young—*fanciulla*—in order to avoid perversion before marriage, since women "become full of vices when they do not have what nature requires." Some writers deplored an evolution, which they judged recent, that led their contemporaries to give their daughters at an increasingly early age. All agreed that in order to establish his authority over the household and to engender the handsomest children, a man would do well to put off marriage. Late age at marriage—which was to continue to be characteristic of the population of Western Europe in the modern age—thus seems both the practice and the norm for the male partner alone from the thirteenth to the fifteenth centuries.

The nearly negligible proportion of first births in Florentine families occurring before the eighth month after the marriage is a good indication of the rigorous surveillance that their families exercised over these young women, who on occasion saw their intended husbands only on the day they received his nuptial ring. Similarly, the relatively large interval between marriage and the first birth shows that these adolescent girls certainly had not all attained the physiological maturity required for bearing a child immediately, although that did not stop their husbands from initiating them immediately into conjugal relations. After the first child, however, pregnancies and births followed one another at a rapid pace. In 1461, one burgher's wife from Arras became a widow at twenty-nine after having brought twelve children into the world in thirteen years of marriage. There is nothing extraordinary in this: the few French *livres de raison* and the many Italian *ricordanze* bring us many examples between the fourteenth and the fifteenth centuries of the high fertility rate characteristic at least of the women of wealthier urban milieux. A Florentine woman of good family who had married at seventeen and had not lost her husband before she reached the age of the menopause could hope to give birth to an average of ten children before she reached thirty-seven years of age, or one child more than French peasant women of the modern era, who married from seven to ten years later than Italian city women. Systematically marrying off daughters very young thus had a noticeable effect on the overall fertility rate and on the total number of births. By lowering female age at marriage, families sought, with varying degrees of awareness, to fill the terrible gaps made by the age's fearful death rate.

Their hopes were fragile, however, for even in families as protected as those of the bourgeoisie of one of the wealthiest cities of Europe, many unions ended prematurely, and the number of children they procreated was lower than the ten or so indicated for couples that enjoyed a long conjugal life. The total number of children brought into the world by all Florentine couples (whether their life together was interrupted by the premature death of one of the spouses or not) fell to an average of seven. This is still a considerable figure, but, as we shall see, few of this rapidly decimated progeny survived their parents.

For the moment, we might note that pregnancies occupied close to one-half of the lives of married women under the age of forty. In several families of notables from the French Limousin (also known by means of their journals), the average intergenetic interval was close to twenty-one months, which was also the average for seven hundred Florentine births occurring in families of comparable wealth. This figure even falls to less than eighteen months if we eliminate exceptional intervals evidently due to the husband's absence on business or if we restrict consideration to couples who remained united throughout their natural fertility span. In Florence, as near Limoges, conceptions followed one another more rapidly than two or three centuries later. In practical terms, this meant that a woman was pregnant or had just given birth and was newly "churched" for nine months out of every eighteen.

Another consequence of closely spaced pregnancies was that during half of their conjugal life a couple was theoretically supposed to abstain from marital relations for fear of "spoiling" the fetus, in particular after quickening. Infringing this prohibition was perhaps only a venial sin after the time of Albertus Magnus, toward the middle of the thirteenth century, but it was a sin all the same. The couple was also held to abstinence if the mother breast-fed her infant, for the birth of a younger child risked shortening the nursing period, hence the life, of its elder sibling. Did the couples in our French and Italian examples continue to respect these ancient prohibitions? It is difficult to tell. Contemporaries at times repeat the ancient taboos, which seem still in force, but which are more likely to concern the danger of sexual relations during the woman's menstrual period. The great preacher Bernardino da Siena told women, and the merchant Paolo da Certaldo reminded men, that "if children are generated at such a time, they will be born monstrous or leprous"; that one risks sick children or children with ringworm; and that "never is the creature generated at such a time born without some great and notable defect." Disgrace would fall on the father who had failed to respect the prohibition "and [the child] could also bring you enormous harm."

The degree to which people heeded submission to religious prohibitions is more obvious, and observance of "prohibited times"—Advent and Lent—when the church forbade the celebration of marriages and recommended continence (though without making it obligatory) is more directly measurable. It is a standard exercise to ascertain the effect of these prohibitions by checking the number of marriages and of conceptions. As it happens, in both the Limousin and in Tuscany, we can see significant dips in the marriage curve in December and in March and a lowering of conceptions during Lent. At least among city people, the preachers' target of choice, the church's injunctions were heeded.

Study of our French and Tuscan samplings suggests, finally, that couples did not seek to avoid conception by recourse to the various contraceptive means—abortive potions, salves, condoms, and charms—that their clients and their judges claimed were used by prostitutes and by women accused of magic and sorcery. All councils from the early Middle Ages to the twelfth century ceaselessly reiterated the prohibition and the punishment of actions aimed at preventing a birth or doing away with the infant. From the thirteenth century on, acquaintance with Arab medical treatises and the vogue for Ovid may have diffused contraceptive practices in certain milieux. In any event, discussion of them led the theologians to mitigate their prohibitions somewhat. Some of them no longer forbade copulation between barren partners or they allowed *coitus reservatus*, which meant that a couple could seek pleasure, not procreation. Others no longer equated contraception with infanticide. Up to the end of the period that concerns us, however, the preachers constantly returned to the mortal sin of a sexual union "against nature" that went against "the form of matrimony." Bernardino told his women listeners:

> Listen: every time that you use together in such a way as to prevent generation, every time it is a mortal sin. Have I told you clearly enough? . . . It is worse for a man to use in such a

> way than with his own mother in the usual way. . . . And yet—O Woman! learn this this morning, and tie it to your finger—if your husband asks of you something that is a sin against nature, do not ever consent to it.

The only occasion on which the woman could and must contravene her duty to obey her husband, even at peril of her life, was thus if he should impose upon her a position in sexual relations that "breaks the order of God," changes the woman "into a beast or into a male," and prevents conception.

Sodomitic or not, practices "against nature" between Christian spouses were combated by directors of conscience because they attributed contraceptive aims to them. It does not seem, however, that such procedures had any perceptible effect on the fertility rate of couples of the time. The average interval between births remained quite stable until the next to last birth, which shows that couples did not massively use any sort of artifice to avoid their duty to reproduce. It is true that Limousin notables and Florentine merchants had the means to provide for the upbringing of their progeny. Here again, we cannot generalize from their example to all provinces and all social milieus in medieval Europe.

There was one perfectly natural and legitimate way to slow the rhythm of births, which was to allow the mother to breast-feed her infant. The wet nurse, however, a familiar character in *chansons de geste* and courtly romances, was no longer the exclusive privilege of the nobility during the latter centuries of the Middle Ages. To cite Florence once more, in the fourteenth century patrician families frequently included a nurse in their households, and recourse to the services of a country woman was widespread throughout all the middle level of the bourgeoisie during the following century. This had two consequences: poor women, who nursed their own children for many months, rented out their milk if a child died, thus earning not only a wage but a chance to put off a new pregnancy. On the other hand, sending a child out to a wet nurse offered an opportunity for more closely spaced children, thus for more children, to wealthy families in search of heirs, who valued fertile women and large numbers of offspring. One can find the highest number of children per couple under the roofs of the wealthiest families listed by the census in Tuscany at the beginning of the fifteenth century. The bed of the poor was then less fecund than that of the powerful.

The childbearing life of an adult female married before she was eighteen years of age, as we have seen, was punctuated with births and ended some twenty years later. Few of all the children whom she had brought into the world were present at the same time under the paternal roof. Maternity was fitful in the Middle Ages. Mothers who gave their infants to a wet nurse outside the house immediately after baptism got them back—if they survived—only a year and a half or two years later. In the meantime some of the child's siblings might have succumbed to the diseases and plagues that periodically bled the population. This means that the enormous families of ten, even fifteen children remain theoretical, the result of a reconstitution on paper by historians of demography. In the everyday flux of births and deaths, medieval households included an average of barely more than two living children, as shown in the census documents, and the survivors mentioned in the father's or the mother's testaments rarely exceed this meager total.

Private journals show that in the merchant class at least one-fourth of the tiny Florentines sent out to nurse died there. Worse: 45 percent of the children born to wealthy families failed to reach the age of twenty. Death stalked the new life and lay in wait for its mother. Women died perhaps less often in childbirth than is said; nonetheless, even wealthy women went through one of the most perilous moments of their life. One out of three Florentine women who died before their husbands did so bringing a child into the world or as an immediate consequence of childbirth. To those who died we should add those who suffered for years from various postnatal disorders, like one unfortunate wife, who had borne her husband fifteen children in twenty-three years and was diagnosed by him in 1512 as having a *mal della matricha*. Overall, one mother out of seven or eight in these otherwise well-protected families fell victim to her procreative duties. Obviously, she usually carried her newborn child to death as well.

The burden of pregnancies and childbirths thus meant that a child had only one chance out of two of reaching adulthood. We can understand the Christian resignation to which parents clung when once again they lost a child—a resignation that somewhat hastily leads us to tax them with insensitivity. Certainly, sending a newborn infant to a far-away nurse did little to favor the blossoming of maternal sentiments or paternal interest, and the news of the child's death did not provoke the rending anguish that follows daily observation of the child's development and that can be seen in expressions of the father's grief at the death of a child who lived at home. It is impossible not to believe in the sincerity of the father of Falchetta Rinuccini, who died at the age of three in 1509, when he writes "I am certain that she has flown to heaven" and prays that "this saintly little dove will pray Divine Goodness and his sweet Mother for us." Nor can we doubt Giovanni Morelli, who exclaims after his ten-year-old son's death in 1406, "I could never have thought that God having divided from me my said son, [and having him] pass from this life to another could have been for me and is such a grievous knife." Even the dryly conventional phrases that accompany notation of the death of a child at the wet nurse's do not completely veil the profound disappointment and frustration that parents so frequently experienced in their desire at least to perpetuate the family and the family name: "It pleased God to call to himself the said Lucha on the eleventh day of August 1390; let us hope he has received him with his blessing and with my own," and so forth. Another father notes, "And on the fourteenth day of the said month and year he was brought back dead from Pian di Ripoli by the nurse: we think she smothered him. He was buried in [the church of] San Jacopo tra le Fosse: may God bless him and our other dead."

Outside these favored milieus in which parents knew how to express their hopes and their suffering, direct testimony on the relations between parents and children is rare. In the immense majority of the population mothers nursed their newborns. Still, many mothers were constrained by destitution, sickness, or public reprobation to abandon their child fairly soon after his or her birth. How can we measure the true extent of abandonment during the Middle Ages and how can we distinguish it from infanticide? There has been much discussion about whether infanticide was practiced differentially, to weed out female babies judged to be undesirable in the great domains of the Carolingian age, and some have sought to account in this manner for an observable gender imbalance among children. Later, in the central Middle Ages, the problems of infanticide and abandonment (which were often confused by censorious writers) are still very poorly documented. Both infanticide and abandonment are attested, and beginning with the thirteenth century hospices in certain cities received the new mission of providing an alternative to infanticide, the more serious crime since it barred access to heaven for all eternity to a child who died unbaptized. Such institutions henceforth accepted orphans and foundlings as well as the poor, pilgrims, and women in childbirth. We have to wait for the last centuries of the Middle Ages, however, to have any clear idea of the extent or the consequences of the abandonment of newborn infants, as reflected in hospital archives, censuses, and the first fragmentary birth registers.

Without ever reaching the massive proportions of the early modern epoch, the rejection of newborn infants seems to have been a widespread practice, at least in the cities. It was fed by the pregnancies of domestic servants, free or slave, and by poverty, both chronic and related to times of scarcity, when poverty-stricken families left their legitimate children with the city hospice, on occasion consoling themselves with the hope of taking them back at a later date and with the belief that the hospice could save them from death better than they themselves. However, the mortality rate was terrifying in the first specialized hospices such as the Innocenti in Florence. To abandon a child meant increasing its chances of dying soon. In short, it was a delayed infanticide in which the parents who abandoned the earthly salvation of their baby to God and to charitable souls hoped both to prolong its life a bit and assure it eternal life. Among the foundlings, female infants were more numerous than male. There was in fact a discrimination that from birth slightly favored boys, but it is difficult to discern the unconscious motives, never clearly expressed in the notes attached to the child's ragged clothing, that led the mothers or the parents of the babies to show preference to males.

If unwelcome births incited a number of parents to renounce their duty to bring up their children, breast-feeding also tested their sense of responsibility toward the nursling. As we have seen, the Doctors of the church exhorted parents to remain continent as long as the wife was nursing the child. This appeal to foresight and temperance stubbornly focused parental attention on the destiny of their offspring, slowly preparing families to consider with less fatalism the fate of their individual children. The clergy emphasized another aspect of parental responsibility: when parish priests and confessors relentlessly (after the fifteenth century) combated the "oppression" of infants suffocated in their parents' or their nurse's bed, and when they reiterated that parents were guilty of a crime of negligence and could even be suspected of premeditation, they obviously aroused a salutary concern for the baby's survival in the laity, which had considered these accidents with indulgence or nonchalance.

In brief, the later Middle Ages saw the slow maturation of an awareness that paved the way, much later, for the first genuinely contraceptive practices. The paradox is that at the origins of this awakening of parental responsibility, which was to induce them, after the seventeenth century, to space out births, there lay the absolute respect for life preached by the most determined adversaries of all contraceptive practices.

*

Out of the multitude of sexual prescriptions and prohibitions regarding sex that claimed to regulate relations between men and women, even within marriage, married people of the later Middle Ages retained above all the appeal to moderation that medical "authorities" had recommended since classical antiquity to anyone who wanted a healthy and numerous progeny. This did not mean that all marriages were rationally motivated, nor that all passion was banished from "family life." But the ideal of the good marriage that moral and satirical literature tended to impose during the three last centuries of the Middle Ages deplored excessive ardor and intemperate desire, equating them with a gluttony that would destroy the inner equilibrium of the humors. "Use temperately with [your wife] and do not ever let yourself go too far" one Florentine advised one of his sons; otherwise he would ruin his "stomach and kidneys," have only daughters or "sickly" sons, or lead a "tedious, shameful, melancholy, and sad" life.

The proper "use" of wives meant, in fact, that the man must constantly be on guard against their demands. Their bodies, so necessary to the survival of lineages, were ruled by an overly inconstant nature. Poorly governed by women's incomplete reason, the body required that its lord, the husband, use it to satisfy his appetites with prudence and regularity and without abandoning himself to any vertigo of the senses that might diminish his authority.

"Authority" was a key word commanding the male vision of relations between spouses, the only vision to be transmitted to us directly. As God's first creation and his nearest image, and with his more perfect and stronger nature, man should dominate woman. These constantly reiterated themes found their application in the closed field of family life. They justified not only female subordination but the division of tasks that was its corollary. The man had a "natural" authority over his wife. The weakness and inferiority of female nature, the theoretical base underlying a great many treatises from the thirteenth century on, had since classical antiquity imposed a closely circumscribed domain in which women exercised a degree of autonomy.

That domain was of course primarily the house, a space both protected and enclosed, and, within the house, certain even more private places such as the bedchamber, the work areas, and the kitchen, which was sometimes a separate room, in certain regions on the top floor or next to the house. Introducing a new bride into the house always involved certain rites that sanctioned her admission to the household but that also cut her off from the external world. The fragility and the weakness of the woman required protection and surveillance. Her coming and going outside the house must be limited to supervised routes to destinations such as the church, the wash-house, the public bake oven, or the fountain—places that varied with social class, but that were clearly designated. They were also places that aroused curiosity and anxiety in men, since the words exchanged there escaped their vigilant control. This can be seen in texts like the *Evangiles des Quenouilles,* a work brimming over with the perilous wisdom of old wives gossiping together, or like the *Quinze joies de mariage,* which evokes the fascination and disapproval of the husbands before the chatter of women around a woman in childbirth, leaving together on a pilgrimage, and everywhere plotting the ruin of men.

Keeping women inside the house and keeping them busy was the male ideal. This aim permeates the choice of tasks assigned to women. Whereas the husbands—the "bread-winners"—were to amass goods and wealth outside the house, the commonplaces of the medieval literature of domestic economy assign their companions the task of conservation of what the men had stored up and transforming it for family consumption as need arose. The daily management of provisions, the supervision and planning involved in their use, the processes to prepare them for use—all these were activities in which women could display talents credited to them when they showed proof of docility and levelheadedness. A good wife, a sensible, sweet, and temperate woman, knew how to regulate the circulation within the household of the goods that flowed into it from the outside under the direction of the man.

Women who assumed their role fully were essential to the proper functioning of society and guaranteed the harmonious assimilation of the products of male industry. Any excess in their expenditures affected the whole of the body social and the entire exchange network. Thus the sumptuary laws, which assured preservation of the outward signs of social order, were aimed at female extravagance. Vainglory, gluttony, and lust were all sins encouraged by disordered appetites that domestic life governed by women should, to the contrary, regulate and channel.

The *familia* was also an entire set of persons over whom the wife must keep watch and whose rhythms and activities she was to govern. Her husband came first, and he expected to find in the warmth of his home rest and the pleasures of a hot bath, a well-laid table, and a ready bed when he returned, harassed by his tribulations in the outside world. The servants came next, when the family was wealthy enough to employ any: it was the wife's task to direct them and to "punish" them when their behavior threatened to harm the interests of their masters—in short, to see to it that they worked for the honor of the house. Next there were the young children, whose first education was incontestably their mother's responsibility and was furthered more by her example of piety and docility than by her ability to teach them the rudiments of reading. The wife was to assure the peaceful coexistence of all these individuals of differing needs. She was the mistress of domestic order and family peace.

Peace, in fact, was to make the household a reflection of the harmony of the universe—except when female nature, in spite of the rein put on it and all the sermons addressed to women, returned on the sly to perturb what she was supposed to promote. For women were eminently false, flighty, and deceiving, and "all the great dishonors, shames, sins, and expenses are acquired through women; the greatest enmities are acquired through them and the greatest friendships lost." Men's greatest reproach to women, repeated obsessively, was rooted in a sense of eternally being swindled by them. Women's chatter, they complained, filled the calm house, divulging its secrets to the world; aided by their foolish and egocentric prodigality, their quarrelsome spirit dispersed the most solid male reason in a thousand infinitely small worries. All these diatribes came of a profound sentiment of failure that gives the measure of the illusory nature of domestic stability and authority so dear to the men of the age.

The insubordination of women was not only the object of their husbands' censure, however; they were subject to collective disapproval as well. Infractions of the normal order of things and shocking inversions of natural authority invited the community's judgment and symbolic punishment. Beginning in the early fourteenth century, the earliest mentions of boisterous popular rites attest to public curbs on matrimonial choices. Widows who remarried and remarriages in general brought down the fury of youth on couples they judged to be inappropriate or intemperate. Throughout Europe the rite of the *chevauchée de l'âne* punished flagrant reversals of conjugal roles: when the woman dominated her husband, henpecked him, or led him by the nose, the husband, or a neighbor taking his place, was forced to ride through the village seated backward on an ass, holding its tail. Female insubordination threatened the very order of the universe and prompted rites such as these, where redemption took the route of mockery. There was no private sphere in which individuals could resolve their differences without the intrusion of outside censors.

Indocility or duplicity in children did not usually provoke the same sorts of community intervention. That a son should question the power of his father was matter for tragedy, not derision. It would prompt the advice of "friends" and kin, without giving outsiders the right to stick their noses into family affairs that involved problems of inheritance. When the *fabliaux* present difficult relations between generations their moral has a somber ring that contrasts strongly with the bittersweet or bawdy tales of women leading men a merry chase. The father who prematurely distributes his wealth, hence his authority, to his sons is reminded that "One must not trust them, / For sons are pitiless." Another writers states:

> The son remains subject to his father, submissive and humble, as long as the father holds authority [*signoria*] over the house and his property; and when the father has given authority to the son to govern his wealth, he will lord it over the father, will come to hate him, and will think it a thousand years [before] the day that [the father] dies and he will no longer see him standing there.

This picture pertains above all to the ideals and the anxieties of the bourgeois householder. Women were not quite as confined to the house and submissive to their husbands on all levels of the social scale as the husbands and the theoreticians of "saintly domesticity" (*santa masserizia*) might have wished. Peasant women toiled in the fields; artisan-class women worked in their husbands' shops, which on occasion they took over at his death. Even within the seigneurial or burgher household women and girls were never idle, which brings up one important aspect of female work that deserves emphasis.

Educators reveal the purpose of the needlework and lacework that was to occupy all of women's idle hours. They were ways of immobilizing women's bodies and dulling their thoughts; of avoiding reveries dangerous for their own honor and that of the lineage. From their earliest years, women spun, wove, sewed, and embroidered ceaselessly, and the higher their birth and the more honor they were endowed with, the less time they were granted to play, laugh, and dance. Thus even noble girls occupied their hands and their "foolish minds" in the delicate embroidery of chasubles and altar cloths. At least they earned years off Purgatory for their interminable labors. Needlework was justified by the argument that fathers should furnish their daughters with an art that would permit them to live if they fell into poverty. Still, the deeper reason that surfaces in these texts is rather to neutralize unstable and fragile female nature by hemming it in with endless activity. According to Francesco da Barberino, who wrote something like a treatise on the education of women at the beginning of the fourteenth century, the daughter of a "shielded knight or a sworn judge or a sworn doctor or other gentleman whose ancestors and himself are accustomed to maintain honor" must learn to "make or sew or weave purses . . . so that later when she is at home with her husband, she can chase away melancholy, not be idle, and even do some service by this."

Incessant textile activity obviously had an economic function as well, fulfilling the needs of domestic consumption, but it could also be turned toward possible outside earnings. Many poor women tried to balance their meager budgets by what they could earn from "women's work" or from spinners' wages. As more than one taxpayer in fifteenth-century Tuscany says, survival was possible thanks to "the woman's distaff" or "the spinning of [his] girls."

Many women, especially before the crises of the fourteenth century, had more autonomous activities outside their family. For most of them, the need to work was a direct result of their matrimonial state or their loss of family protection. The daughters of poor families entered domestic service, sometimes when they were still children, more often as adolescents, in order to earn enough for their dowries or their trousseaux. Above all, widows, too often the prey of solitude and poverty, made up the better part of the troops of working women. Even in the wealthier classes of medieval society, widowhood threatened women with a rapid decline in social status and a plunge into poverty if they were unable to force their husband's heirs to respect their rights. Even kin were not beneath fleecing the widow and the orphan or leaving her alone and friendless—"Seulette suis sans ami demeurée" Christine de Pisan complains in a famous ballad—the first woman to have lived by her pen, widowed with three children at the age of twenty-five. Medieval romances, following her example, abound in tales of the somber destinies of women alone, surviving in the most precarious situations. They are, incidentally, shown as quite capable of holding their own.

These were women without family, placed outside the "natural" framework that medieval society assigned to females. They were all the more vulnerable, and their reputations were stained from the start. Widows alone, poor women earning their bread by spinning, servant women, recluses living outside a religious community—all were soon suspected of bad conduct and easily accused of prostitution. In the eleventh century, the uprooted women who followed saintly men such as Robert of Arbrissel, the founder of a "mixed" monastery whose direction he entrusted to a woman, and women who joined fourteenth-century flagellants' processions, were recruited from groups of women whose matrimonial status, way of life, and, at times, economic autonomy were enough to designate them as marginal.

*

Societies of the waning Middle Ages found it difficult to conceive of the "feminine condition" independent of the framework of marriage, as we have seen in the discredit of labor outside the household, of overly autonomous manifestations of piety, and of female errancy. Doubtless the couple had acquired a certain autonomy within the kinship group during this period, but female vices and virtues, tasks and comportment, were still perceived in reference to the family founded by the couple. Women remained a mechanism subordinated to the reproduction of the family. Nonetheless, without being denied, that subordination required increasing justification and elucidation—in short, it was disputed and no longer totally taken for granted.

BIBLIOGRAPHY

Burguière, André, Christiane Klapisch-Zuber, Martine Segalen, and Françoise Zonabend, eds. *Histoire de la famille*. Vol. 1, *Mondes lointains, mondes anciens*. Paris: A. Colin, 1986.

De Matteis, Maria Consiglia, ed. *Idee sulla donna nel Medioevo. Fonti e aspetti giuridici, antropologici, religiosi, sociali e letterari della condizione femminile*. Bologna: Patron Editore, 1981.

Duby, Georges. *Le Chevalier, la femme et le prêtre. Le mariage dans la France féodale*. Paris: Hachette, 1981 [*The Knight, the Lady, and the Priest: The Making of Modern Marriage in Medieval France*. Trans. Barbara Bray. New York: Pantheon, 1984].

Flandrin, Jean-Louis. *Un temps pour s'embrasser. Aux origines de la moralité sexuelle occidentale (VIe–Xue siècles)*. Paris: Editions du Seuil, 1983.

Goody, Jack. *The Development of the Family and Marriage in Europe*. Cambridge and New York: Cambridge University Press, 1983.

Herlihy, David. *Medieval Households*. Cambridge: Harvard University Press, 1985.

Nelli, René. *L'Erotique des troubadours*. Toulouse: E. Privat, 1963.

Vetere, Benedetto, and Paolo Renzi, eds. *Profili di donne. Mito, immagine, realtà fra medioevo ed età contemporanea*. Galatina: Congedo Editore, 1986.

SUGGESTED READINGS

Derek Baker, ed., *Medieval Women* (Oxford: Blackwell, 1978).

Heath Dillard, *Daughters of the Reconquest: Women in Castilian Town Society, 1100–1300* (New York: Cambridge University Press, 1984).

Mary Erler and Maryanne Kowaleski, eds., *Women and Power in the Middle Ages* (Athens: University of Georgia Press, 1988).

Christine E. Fell. *Women in Anglo-Saxon England* (Bloomington: Indiana University Press, 1984).

Frances and Joseph Gies, *Marriage and the Family in the Middle Ages* (New York: Harper and Row, 1987).

Penny Schine Gold, *The Lady and the Virgin: Image, Attitude, and Experience in Twelfth-Century France* (Chicago: University of Chicago Press, 1987).

Barbara A. Hanawalt, ed., *Women and Work in Preindustrial Europe* (Bloomington: Indiana University Press, 1986).

Martha C. Howell, *Women, Production, and Patriarchy in Late Medieval Cities* (Chicago: University of Chicago Press, 1986).

Julius Kirshner and Suzanne F. Wemple, eds., *Women of the Medieval World: Essays in Honor of John H. Mundy* (Oxford: Blackwell, 1985).

David Nicholas, *The Domestic Life of a Medieval City: Women, Children, and the Family in Fourteenth-Century Ghent* (Lincoln: University of Nebraska Press, 1985).

Shulamith Shahar, *The Fourth Estate: A History of Women in the Middle Ages* (New York: Methuen, 1983).

Pauline Stafford, *Queens, Concubines, and Dowagers: The King's Wife in the Early Middle Ages* (Athens: University of Georgia Press, 1983).

Susan Mosher Stuard, ed., *Women in Medieval Society* (Philadelphia: University of Pennsylvania Press, 1976).

———, ed., *Women in Medieval History and Historiography* (Philadelphia: University of Pennsylvania Press, 1987).

Suzanne Fonay Wemple, *Women in Frankish Society: Marriage and the Cloister, 500 to 900* (Philadelphia: University of Pennsylvania Press, 1981).

NINE

The Saint

André Vauchez

One of the historian's specific tasks is to point out false continuities set up (or at least implied) when language makes us lose our sense of change by using the same terms to designate realities that differ from one epoch to the next. We need to exercise special caution in the realm of religion—of Catholicism in particular, since the Catholic church has tended to accentuate the permanence of its fundamental beliefs and its institutional framework through the centuries. Some may claim to know what a bishop was in antiquity or a priest in the Middle Ages by referring to those who exercise those functions in the church today. Reasoning by analogy can easily lead to anachronism, however, particularly when identical words lead us to lose sight of changes that in some cases were considerable.

The problem is particularly acute in the case of the saints. The very nature of the documents on which we must rely to study them increases the risks of distortion and platitude inherent in all historical study. Saints' lives and compendia of miracles aim at making the servants of God conform to models corresponding to recognized categories of Christian perfection—martyrs, virgins, confessors of the faith—and, beyond the immediate model, to the figure of Christ. All saints worthy of the title, male and female, attempted during their lifetimes, if not to identify with the person of the Son of God, at least to approach that absolute norm as closely as possible. It is hardly surprising, then, that the saints resemble one another, or that the prodigies attributed to them recall the Gospel miracles, from the multiplication of loaves and fishes to the resurrection of the dead. When our point of departure is a narrative that aims precisely at blurring the individual's traits and transforming his or her lifetime into a fragment of eternity, it is difficult to imagine what might have been the actual existence of such people. Their lives are often reduced to a series of stereotypes. Thus hagiography (and after it, a certain type of historiography) has tended to present the saints not just as exceptional beings but also as repetitious figures whose lives varied only in their spatial and temporal framework, which in itself was defined schematically simply to provide a scenic background to highlight the heroic perfection of the saint.

Toward the end of the nineteenth century, in reaction to these conceptions of sanctity that so emphasized atemporality that they lost sight of the historical dimension, a cultural current that found its chief spokesman in France in Emile Nourry, writing under the pseudonym of P. Saintyves, viewed the Christian saints as successors of the pagan gods. Citing continuity in cultic practices in localities that had already been considered sacred in antiquity (springs, rocks, or woods), Saintyves affirmed that under a varnish of Christianity, Gallo-Roman worship of demigods or genii who embodied forces of nature had continued fairly late into the Middle Ages. Even though there is some apparent confirmation of this thesis, it has the defect, as does the previous view, of removing the saint from history by making his or her cult a simple screen for rites that survived from an earlier age. Defining the cult of the saints in terms of survivals necessarily views it as a form of superstition—which is a hazy concept and one totally inadequate to explain the place of veneration of the servants of God in the religious universe of the Middle Ages. Moreover, under cover of mythology or comparative ethnology, such a view tends to neglect the profound evolution that Christianity brought to relations between humankind and nature. By destroying sacred groves and substituting the cult of the saints for the worship of fountains and springs, the church set out, toward the end of antiquity, on a long process that aimed at nothing less than anthropomorphizing the universe and subjecting the natural world to human control. The saints played an important role in this process. A scientific and objective approach to the problem would necessarily emphasize this fundamental and long-neglected aspect of their works.

The Place of the Saint in Medieval Christianity: The Legacy of Antiquity and of the Early Middle Ages

The Middle Ages did not invent the cult of the saints, even though saints' cults did expand considerably during that period. Failure to take into account the legacy of the earlier centuries risks totally misunderstanding this fundamental aspect of Christianity after the year 1000.

Martyrs, Mediators, and Patron Saints

It all began, in fact, with the cult of the martyrs, who long remained the only saints venerated by Christians, and who continued to enjoy considerable prestige in the church, even after the establishment of other models of sainthood. In spite of certain superficial resemblances, martyrs had nothing in common with the Greek and Roman heroes. In classical antiquity, death marked an impenetrable frontier between humankind and the gods, but in the Christian view it was precisely because the martyrs died as human beings, following the example of Christ and in order to keep faith with Christ's message, that at their death they attained glory in Paradise and eternal life. The saint was a person through whom a contact was established between heaven and earth; the feast day commemorating his or her birth in the presence of God, beyond death, was the Christian feast par excellence as it repeated the salutary gesture of the unique Mediator. Thus the cult of martyrs, far from being incidental to the new religion or a concession to the pagan masses to facilitate their conversion, took root in what was most authentic and original in Christianity as compared with the religions with which it was in competition at the time.

Christianity did not invent everything in the domain of sainthood ex nihilo, however. In late antiquity belief in protective spirits—demons, genii, angels, and so forth—was fairly widespread. Transferring to human beings—the saints—the type of relations that earlier generations had maintained with disembodied spirits, some of the great bishops of the fourth century, men like Paulinus of Nola and Ambrose of Milan, suggested to the faithful and to Christian communities that they take as intercessors the men and women whose heroic faith had earned them the privilege of having God as their personal protector. The taking of patron saints made the cult of martyrs more "democratic" since it was founded on the same notions as clientage relations: the person who asked for protection offered loyalty in exchange for "friendship" and an obligation to provide protection on the part of the more powerful person. In a society threatened with disintegration, in which individuals were haunted by the idea of losing their identity and their freedom, the saints were just what was needed to renew confidence and offer hope for salvation on a daily basis.

Among the more widely debated affirmations of the English historian Peter Brown, concerning the origin of the cult of martyrs, is his hypothesis that it was first organized on a private, familial level and later was taken over by the local church authorities concerned that these proliferating family devotions centering around the tomb might endanger the unity of the Christian community. In reality, archaeological evidence rarely enables us to penetrate beyond the earliest cultic forms, which are always of a liturgical nature. It is true, however, that the bishops played an important part in the diffusion of the cult of martyrs, and that they assigned it a function of enhancing the spirituality of the church when they placed it under their control. This explains both the restoration of the Roman catacombs by Pope Damasus I and the "invention" of the relics of the protomartyrs,

Gervase and Protase, in Milan in 385 and Ambrose's immediate appropriation of them for his cathedral. When a saint became the heavenly *patronus* of a cathedral and a city, he (or she) reinforced the prestige of the bishop, his representative in this world and perhaps the next candidate for sainthood. Moreover, the increasing honors paid to relics on calendar feast days and at translations of relics and saints' bodies gave the urban community an opportunity to display its unity and to integrate marginal groups of peasants or barbarians. Processions created ties between the city and the *suburbia* in which both cemeteries and *martyria*, small sanctuaries containing martyrs' relics, were located. Thanks to this fast-growing liturgy, women (who played a large part in it) came out of their isolation and the poor broke with traditional clientage relations (in crisis from the late fourth century) to place themselves under the protection of a saint and, later, become part of the saint's *familia*. Even the mighty had their share in the cult of martyrs: from the fourth century to the end of the Middle Ages, one of the obligations of those who held power in Christian societies was to build churches to shelter the relics of the servants of God when they were moved from the tomb to a place of honor on the altar.

The Prestige of Asceticism and Fascination with the East

The church in the West, when persecution ended, quite logically shifted from the cult of martyrs to that of the bishops who had organized and maintained that cult, but the East underwent a quite different evolution that later was to have profound repercussions throughout the Christian world. In the post-Constantinian age, new types of saints appeared to take their places beside the martyrs—confessors of the faith like St. Athanasius (d. 371), who made the church at Alexandria the spearhead of an attack on the Arian heresy, and, above all, the ascetic who sought in flight from the world a perfection hard to attain within a society superficially Christianized but which had remained profoundly alien to the spirit of the Gospel. From the fourth century, desert hermits in Egypt, the most famous of whom was St. Anthony (d. 356), the hero of Upper Egypt, and the Syrian stylites perched on their pillars embodied an ideal of sainthood that was to have a brilliant career—that of the man of God (*vir Dei*) who refused power, wealth, money, and urban life, the dominant values of the age, to flee society and lead a solitary life totally dedicated to religion (here, to penance and maceration). It was in the desert and by his resistance to all sorts of temptations that assailed him that the servant of God, as he is presented in the oldest hagiographic texts such as the *Vitae patrum*, acquired the powers that he later exercised for the benefit of humanity. Indeed, in spite of the efforts of these men to conceal their charisma, their self-inflicted privations rapidly made them famous. When they left the world of human culture for the world of nature, they took nourishment almost exclusively from wild plants eaten raw and took no care of their bodies. By going beyond human limits of nutrition, sleep, and even, in the case of the stylites, equilibrium and movement, they appeared to their contemporaries as extraordinary beings. Unlike other marginal figures (whom they resembled in certain ways), however, their constancy in prayer and their intimacy with God not only preserved them from madness but won them great prestige of a supernatural sort in the eyes of their observers—a just recompense for an existence of renunciation.

Eastern conceptions of sainthood were rapidly known and they spread throughout the Roman world. Thanks to Hilary of Poitiers and friends of St. Jerome in Aquitaine, later seconded by John Cassian in Marseilles and the monks of Lérins, in Provence, ascetic influences from Egypt and Syria penetrated into the West during the latter half of the fourth century, where they met with a success reflected in the most important hagiographic work of the period, the *Vita Martini* (Life of St. Martin of Tours, d. 397) written by Sulpicius Severus in the early fifth century. This work, which was to have an enormous influence on medieval hagiography, aimed at presenting Martin as a western St. Anthony. It represents the triumph of the ideal of perfection of Gallo-Roman asceticism conceived, in the words of Paulinus of Nola (*Ep.* 2.12) as a "martyrdom without bloodshed." Like the anchorites of the Egyptian desert, Martin was initiated into the wisdom of asceticism by an "abbot"—in his case, Hilary of Poitiers—and he lived in Ligugé with a group of cenobitic hermits. When he became bishop of Tours in 371, Martin waged an energetic battle against all forms of evil—the Arian heresy, rural paganism, the cult of false martyrs venerated by the local populations—and his missionary works were backed up by the performance of a number of miracles. This is where the *Vita Martini* parts company with its eastern models, however. To the extent that he was both a monk enamored of solitude and an apostle actively involved in evangelization, Martin's life was "mixed." Furthermore, Sulpicius Severus, unlike eastern hagiographers, whose heroes were rarely priests, emphasizes the priestly dimension of his protagonist: the monastery of Marmoutier that Martin founded on the banks of the Loire was a seedbed for bishops. Thus from its beginnings, sainthood in the West was ecclesiastical in nature, distinguishing it from the eastern variety, where, with the exception of a few great prelates, clerics were not considered charismatic.

Saints as Defenders of the People and Founders of Churches

By the end of the fifth century, the places and the persons in which spiritual power resided were not the same in the two parts of the former Roman empire and were evolving in different directions. In the East, the increasing sacred prestige of the emperor, leader of the Christian people, kept pace with that of the hermits and the monks; in the West, submerged by Germanic invasions and divided into several barbarian kingdoms, the bishops, as guardians of the saints' relics and defenders of the cities, became the central figures in the life of the church. Like St. Leo in Rome, St. Anianus (Aignan) in Orléans, or St. Desiderius (Didier) in Cahors, the head of the local church took a prominent role in political, social, and religious affairs during his lifetime, and after death he quite naturally tended to continue to provide a point of reference that enabled the city to demonstrate its unity and collective will to live. The age of the martyrs had ended in the West; the age of hermits in the eastern style had proven itself only a literary fashion, and poor and solitary penitents were soon discouraged by a hierarchical church that no longer conceived of the practice of asceticism outside cenobitic monasticism.

While the saint of later antiquity was an adept of the *vita passiva* who sought perfection by renouncing the world, the West during the early Middle Ages was marked above all by the figures of religious leaders and founders deeply involved in the active life. In this epoch, in fact, the church became the moving force in society, in particular in the cities, where the best bishops stood out for their zeal in defending the city population against the arbitrary powers of the king and his agents. As God's representative in a brutal secular society, the saintly prelate of that age was first and foremost a man of active and effective charity. As defender of the weak, he combated oppression and violations of the law, thus providing city populations with a recourse against arbitrary justice, and he had no qualms about threatening the powerful of this world with divine chastisement. This was translated into concrete form in the establishment of the right of asylum in the churches, places of freedom in which fugitives from justice were placed under the protection of the relics of the servant of God venerated there. This change was aided by the church's increasing pursuit of what would now be called social services—hospices (*xenodochia*) and hospitals, foundling homes, lists or rolls of the poor who received assistance from the local community. The principal area for saintly good works, however, was assistance to prisoners, who were often reduced to slavery. St. Caesarius of Arles and St. Germain of Paris, for example, sold their costly ecclesiastical vessels and church ornaments to ransom captives, and these labors of mercy seem to have contributed to the *fama sanctitatis* that soon surrounded them. The Life of St. Desiderius of Cahors (d. 655) portrays him opening the doors of the prisons for the guilty and the innocent alike, taking it on himself to reintegrate them into society after giving them their liberty, having them baptized if necessary, and distributing them among the churches and cloisters of his diocese. Some missionaries, like St. Amand (d. 675), went so far as to provide for the instruction of liberated slaves so that they could become priests or monks. In the same period abbots and bishops were themselves among the largest owners of *servi*, but contemporaries saw no contradiction in the two attitudes.

Although the saint had become a resource for the disinherited and for victims of justice, with the exception of a few highly political "martyrs" like St. Leger of Autun (d. 678), he did not oppose temporal power. On the contrary, one of the characteristics of the age was the symbiosis between the governing classes, ecclesiastical and secular. The term "hagiocracy" has sometimes been used to designate the period between the late sixth and the late eighth centuries for the high number of saints associated (on occasion, closely associated) with civil power: St. Eloi in France, for example, or Gregory the Great, who took over the defense and administration of Rome when imperial authority failed. His was an exceptional case, however, and north of the Alps the situation was noticeably different. It was not so much that ecclesiastical personnel attained power as it was that the Frankish, Anglo-Saxon, or Germanic aristocracy established its hold over the church, at the same time aiding the church to gain a foothold in rural areas that had thus far escaped its influence, and actively supporting efforts of missionaries like St. Boniface in Thuringia or St. Corbinian of Freising in Bavaria to Christianize still pagan Germanic peoples.

The principal result of this close collaboration between the clergy and the governing circles was, as Karl Bosl has pointed out, a religious legitimization of the aristocracy's preeminence over other people, both free and nonfree. The notion that gained credence at the time, that a saint could only be of noble birth or, conversely, that a noble was more likely to become a saint than other mortals, was not—at least at the start—an ideological superstructure imposed by the dominant classes or the church. It was rooted in the conviction, common to Christianity in the late classical age and German paganism and shared by dominant and dominated alike, that moral and spiritual perfection could not easily be developed outside an illustrious lineage. This explains the close connection—established during this period and later a commonplace in hagiography difficult to challenge—between saintliness, power, and noble blood.

A first consequence of the establishment of the *Adelheilige*—the noble saint—was that persons of obscure social origin were excluded from such posts as bishop or abbot, which at the time provided a royal road to sainthood. Henceforth (and for some time to come) the only way that the humble—the anonymous mass that, from the aristocratic point of view, had neither thought nor freedom—could earn a place of honor on the altar was as a hermit, and eremitism was not widely practiced in Western Europe before the eleventh century. In a society in which poverty and extreme asceticism had been relegated to a marginal role, servants of God were above all founders of churches and monasteries whose memory was conserved by grateful priests and monks in a Life written or a cult instituted in their honor. Noble families often stimulated the monks' zeal by themselves distributing relics of their more illustrious family members. This is what the first Carolingians did, for example, for their ancestor, St. Arnulf, bishop of Metz (d. c.640), or for St. Gertrude of Nivelles (d. 659), the daughter of the Mayor of the Palace, Pepin of Landen, and St. Itta (Ida of Nivelles), the sister of St. Begga. The biographies of these men and women express a new conception of saintliness founded in illustrious birth, the exercise of authority, and the possession of often considerable wealth, all put to the service of the propagation of the Christian faith. The male saints in particular were often endowed with an attractive physical appearance and a great affability in social relations. We are far from the ascetic ideal of the fifth century and even farther from the saints of primitive Christianity.

All in all, the West inherited from the early Middle Ages an entire set of mental representations in the domain of sanctity that were only slowly and only partially questioned during subsequent centuries. For example, saints were preponderantly male (90 percent of the saints of this period were men) and adult, since childhood elicited little interest. Above all, there was a close connection between aristocratic birth and moral and religious perfection.

From a Sanctity of Function to the Imitation of Christ
King-Saints and Angelic Monks (Tenth and Eleventh Centuries)

The first king-saints appeared in this quite special religious context, which was a reflection of an aristocratic society in the making and a close alliance between the church and civil power characteristic of the Carolingian and the post-Carolingian eras. The early Middle Ages had already produced king-saints, however, men like St. Sigismund (d. 523), king of the Burgundians, who had abjured Arianism and founded the abbey of Saint-Maurice d'Agaune in the Valais, or St. Edmund (d. 839), king of East Anglia, killed by the Danes and later considered a martyr for the Christian faith. Aside from these special cases, however, Western sovereigns had shown little interest in the prestige conferred by sanctity as long as they could count on the persistence of a pagan or magic sacrality connected with the function of royal power or with certain of the rulers' attributes, such as the Merovingians' long hair. The new dynasties established in Europe between the eighth and the tenth centuries—Carolingian, Ottonian, Capetian, and so forth—opted to turn instead to the church for legitimacy. To do so, they revived traditions of the Christian empire that had survived in Byzantium, completing them with the rites of anointment and coronation that had been established in Spain for the installation of the Visigoth kings. By their consecration on that day, kings became distinct from the lay aristocracy, moving over to the side of the *oratores* to become something like an "external bishop" to whose acts the church attempted to give direction and moral significance. In England and on the Continent alike, an entire ideology of the *rex justus*, much influenced by the Old Testament, developed around the function of the monarch. The most complete expression of this can be found in the Life of the Capetian king, Robert the Pious (d. 1031) by Helgaud, a monk at Fleury, who skims over the extremely complicated and not very edifying matrimonial life of the sovereign to accentuate the liturgical aspects of the priest-king. Although Helgaud does not claim sainthood for Robert, the king appears in this text as justly renowned for being a special intercessor between humankind and God, who had accorded the king the privilege of curing scrofula by his touch. Thus began the tradition in France of thaumaturgic kings, studied to such good effect by Marc Bloch not too many years ago.

In recently Christianized countries on the periphery of Western Europe during the same period, royal power took on sanctity from the personal sanctification of certain sovereigns. This was particularly apt to happen when the king had died a violent death in tragic circumstances, like St. Wenceslas (d. 929) in Bohemia, killed on the order of his mother and his brother, or St. Olaf in Norway (d. 1030), killed at the battle of Stiklestad. It is extremely difficult to discern how much pagan sacrality and how much church intervention went into the veneration of these two figures. Olaf, for example, was the last descendant of the dynasty of the Ynglings, who claimed divine origin, but he had also achieved the Christianization of Norway. The clergy, in any event, presented him as a martyr and compared him to Christ for his bloody death and the miracles that followed it. He later became his country's patron saint, and at the end of the Middle Ages was considered its *rex perpetuus.* Several similar cases occurred in Sweden and Denmark before the thirteenth century. In Hungary, where the Arpad dynasty retained the sacral prestige that it had held in the pagan era, the church recognized (1083) the sainthood of King Stephen (d. 1038), who converted his people, that of his son, Henry, who became Holy Roman Emperor (d. 1031), and, somewhat later, that of King László (Ladislas; d. 1095). In England the cult of the Anglo-Saxon king, Edward the Confessor (d. 1066), took on a national dimension in the twelfth century when the Plantagenets sought to establish the idea, borrowed from France, of a sacred and thaumaturgic monarchy. Even in the central regions of Christendom, where the saint-king remained the exception, there were attempts—which met with varying degrees of success—to create an aura of sanctity around such princely women as Queen Matilda (d. 968), the wife of Henry I of Germany, in whose honor two successive Lives were written in Saxony in the Ottonian epoch, or Empress Adelaide (d. 999), the widow of Otto I, canonized by Urban II in 1097. Such cults originated when the royal dynasties moved to celebrate their own lineage when they arrived at the height of their power and monks and nuns were eager to show their gratitude toward their benefactors. They were an expression of a society in which the church accepted the task of sanctifying the ancestors of the monarch to defend his legitimacy and, in some cases, to shore up a power threatened by the rising strength within the feudal system of the high aristocracy.

At the same time that this very secular type of sanctity was gaining ground, an ideal developed among the clergy that stressed the monastic vocation and portrayed the cloister as the antechamber to Paradise. These concepts were not new, but they acquired increased credibility when Benedictine monasticism, undergoing a highly active spiritual ferment, initiated a reform of its order. Reform focused on stricter observance of the Rule, particularly in the domain of liturgy, and an exaltation of virginity, considered central to Christian perfection. Monks were saints, collectively, because they prayed and practiced chastity. Their life made them like the angels and contrasted favorably with the less edifying mores of the secular clergy, winning them the sympathy of the faithful. According to Odo of Cluny, the monk was a veritable soldier of Christ (*miles Christi*) who performed the mystery of charity by renouncing private property, violence, and a sexual life; and by his sacrifice he made possible the salvation of a sinful humanity. As an anticipation of the kingdom of God on earth, the monastery was the locus of sanctity par excellence, and it was not by chance that the great Cluniac abbeys sought (as did St. Bernard at a later date) to attract both clergy and laity who displayed outstanding human or religious qualities—to the distress of certain bishops, who saw the best Christians flock to the cloister to flee from a world in which the church badly needed them.

In a spiritual climate strongly influenced by Benedictine cenobitic monasticism, it was of course monastic reformers who attracted the attention of their contemporaries—men like Gérard de Brogne (d. 959), who restored the monastery of that name in the Hainaut, Blessed John of Gorze (d. 974) in Lorrain, and the great abbots of Cluny, St. Odilo (d. 1048) and St. Hugh (d. 1108), under whom the congregation reached its apogee. To give an accurate idea of the influence of monastic saintliness, however, we would need to add several dozen names to those of these great figureheads—names of men and, to a lesser extent, women who gave prominence to an abbey or a priory by the intensity of their spiritual life. We would also need to stress the extraordinary impact of the monastic ideal on all other forms of the Christian life, from the bishop and the priest to the laity, as, for example, on St. Gerald of Aurillac (d. 909), a count from the Auvergne who was portrayed by his biographer, Odo of Cluny, as a monk who had strayed into the secular world.

One of the principal reasons for the extraordinary success of the monastic model in the early feudal age was that it corresponded perfectly to the widely held idea that sanctity was the business of "professionals." Were not the "sons" of St. Benedict unique in their consistently religious life, while the lay faithful and even the clergy practiced their religion only episodically? Did not their prayers and the sacrifice of the Eucharist that they offered for the salvation of souls rise to the throne of God day and night? Thus the masses, feeling disqualified, a priori, in the pursuit of sanctity, shifted to the monks the burden of mediation between heaven and earth without which, all contemporaries agreed, no society could survive.

Following Christ: The Apostolic Life and Evangelical Perfection (Twelfth–Thirteenth Centuries)

From the late eleventh century, however, the traditional Benedictine way of life met with severe criticism, and the most demanding spirits sought other avenues to sanctification, in particular through eremetism, which increased remarkably. This new development was more than a reflection of a need to diversify religious experience, a natural reaction in a society that, after long turning inward on itself, was rapidly expanding demographically, economically, and culturally. On a deeper level, it was the very nature of sanctity that was changing: no longer the result of contemplation of the infinite mystery of a totally "other" and nearly inaccessible God, it was becoming an imitation of Christ—the "visible image of an invisible God"—in whose footsteps one must follow to attain eventual eternal bliss. This shift in the nature of sanctity, which was linked to a rediscovery of the inner life, had profound repercussions for spirituality. Although monasticism was still the main path to perfection in the twelfth century, under the influence of the new climate it attempted to respond better to the religious aspirations of the age. The Cluniacs in particular were reproached with putting such exclusive stress on the liturgical and eschatological aspects of religious life, neglecting work and missionary activities, that they failed to confront the world. Returning, with Cîteaux, to both the letter and the spirit of the Rule of St. Benedict, St. Bernard saw the monk primarily as a penitent who had retired from the world to weep for his sins. It was not simply a matter of renewed austerity after a real or supposed relaxation of Cluniac monasticism: in the spirituality of the new monastic and canonical orders of the early twelfth century, asceticism was only a point of departure in a process—the seven degrees of love—that enabled the monk to progress by stages toward the deification that Bernard of Clairvaux saw as the goal of the spirit's itinerary toward God.

The continuity of monasticism's institutional forms and its ideals must not blind us to the extent of the change that occurred during this period. If saints increased considerably in number in Western

Europe, it was not only because men and women of the twelfth and thirteenth centuries were more enamored of perfection than their predecessors. Earlier, however, there were few saints outside the framework of an *ordo*—essentially, the *ordo monasticus*, which was in itself sanctifying. Another path to sainthood was by the perfect accomplishment of state duties, a way open only to kings, queens, and, more generally, those who wielded power. The new mentality, on the contrary, accentuated the need for the personal involvement of the individual. The Cistercians and the Premonstratensians no longer accepted children or lay brothers in their monasteries, but only "converts"—that is, adults who had of their own will chosen to follow Christ (*sequela Christi*). In this manner, sanctity became above all a personal adventure and an internal necessity, felt in ways that varied with persons and places, but that in all cases responded to the impulses of love.

The repercussions of this new state of mind were considerable. "To follow naked the naked Christ," according to the motto that inspired itinerant preachers like St. John Gualbert (Giovanni Gualberto, d. 1073) in Italy or Robert of Arbrissel in France (d. 1116), meant living in privation and asceticism and giving oneself to the service of the poor and of lepers and to the rehabilitation of prostitutes. The voluntary poor found themselves extolled. Moreover, the church found it convenient to emphasize the maleficent nature of temporal power, and Pope Gregory VII reproached emperors and kings for their unchristian conduct. Although the clergy as a whole was far from seconding Gregory's extreme position, temporal power emerged from the investiture controversy stripped of its sacrality, and henceforth the only sovereigns that the church recognized as saints were those who, like St. Louis (d. 1270), supported its actions as well as providing an example of piety and personal morality. Conversely, the decline of sanctity tied to the saint's function is attested by the fact that the canonization of Charlemagne, decreed in 1166 by the antipope Paschal III, at the urging of Frederick Barbarossa, was never ratified by the Roman church.

The move toward an increasing spiritualization of the notion of sanctity was accentuated by the development of canonization procedures leading to the pope's exclusive right of ultimate decision, a process that was completed by the early thirteenth century. More was involved than simply a victory for centralization of the church in Rome or a problem of church discipline; the Holy See's takeover of the process of canonization was accompanied by powers of verification over the virtues and the miracles of the servants of God, which were subjected to careful examination by the Curia after attestation by persons who had known the candidate for sainthood or had benefited from his or her intercession. Henceforth there were two categories of saints in the West: those whom the pope had approved and recognized as saints and who could therefore be the object of a liturgical cult, and the others, who were restricted to local veneration.

It was precisely the new model of apostolic and evangelical sanctity founded on the ideal of the *sequela Christi* that the Roman church attempted to promote in the thirteenth century, as shown in the canonizations of Francis of Assisi and Dominic, both dedicated to mendicant poverty and the founders, respectively, of the Order of Friars Minor and the Order of Friars Preachers. People of very different sorts (and who varied from one region to another) took up these aspirations. North of the Alps, the strong connection between aristocratic birth, power, and saintliness that had existed from the early Middle Ages continued, and the heavenly and earthly hierarchies coincided nearly perfectly. Admittedly, an increasing number of lay men and women earned a place of honor on the altars during this period, but for the most part they were kings, like St. Louis, empresses, like Cunegund, wife of Henry III, or princesses, like St. Elizabeth of Thuringia (d. 1231), daughter of Andrew II, king of Hungary, or St. Hedwig (d. 1243), duchess of Silesia. Even after the new religious values of humility and poverty promoted by the mendicant orders had fully taken hold, the prejudice in favor of nobility persisted in the north, and the recruitment of new saints remained extremely elitist, to the point that hagiographers attempted to furnish an illustrious origin for their servants of God if their true origins were humble or obscure.

The situation was quite different in Mediterranean lands, especially in Italy, where there were proportionally fewer saints from the governing classes. Saintly bishops—still numerous in France and England in the thirteenth century—disappeared from the group from which southern opinion chose its heroes, the *vox populi* turning instead almost exclusively to men and women who stood out because of the trials they had endured for the love of God and of their neighbor rather than for their illustrious birth or their function. Exceptions apart, violent death and flowing blood were no longer requirements; what counted for a reputation for perfection were above all the privations and sufferings to which the servants of God had voluntarily exposed themselves. Mediterranean saintliness became defined as a way of life and a model of behavior founded on poverty and renunciation. Asceticism now conformed to a model taken from Christ, "who had nowhere to lay his head," the piteous victim of Calvary. St. Francis (d. 1226), the *Poverello* of Assisi who had received the stigmata at La Verna, was certainly the one who went farthest to bring the evangelical message home to this world, to the point of bearing signs of Christ's Passion in his flesh. His life was the fullest expression of the new conception of saintliness that sprang from inner experience and from a love striving to find the face of God in all humankind, particularly in the most bereft.

In Mediterranean lands several quite different categories of saints satisfied the requirements of immediate perception of sainthood through identification with a suffering and compassionate Christ. There were hermits and recluses, errant pilgrims in search of God who died on their way, founders of hospices and hospitals, and benefactors of the poor like St. Homobonus of Cremona (d. 1197), the first lay commoner to be canonized (1199). A number of lay men and women of modest or burgher origins attained local reputations for sainthood during this period. Even in regions north and west of the Alps, where aristocratic models of sanctity remained the overwhelming majority, the quality of the saints' experience had greatly changed since the previous age, as we can see from two saintly princesses, one from the ninth century and the other from the thirteenth. Around 1105, when Turgot, a monk, wrote his Life of St. Margaret, queen of Scotland (d. 1093), he sought to show that she merited veneration by her exemplary conduct as a wife, mother, and sovereign, and he praised her for her good advice to her husband and her children and her generous support of men of the church. Less than a century and a half later, St. Elizabeth (d. 1231), wife of Louis IV, landgrave of Thuringia, became famous for her charity throughout Germany and beyond. If we look closely at their biographies, however, we can see that the two women had little in common. Elizabeth founded no abbeys or churches, only a hospital for the poor. Before she was widowed, she had led the life of a queen in appearance only, attending banquets without eating and gathering up all the leftover food for distribution to the poor. She shocked her entourage by refusing to eat food from domains in which the lord abused his seigneurial power. After her husband's death she wasted no time leaving the family castle of Wartburg, even leaving her own children, in order to live like the paupers and lepers on whom she spent her entire fortune and whom she served with her own hands until her death. Her career is a full illustration of the internalization of sanctity, henceforth founded—differences in social milieu aside—in a shared devotion to the humanity of Christ and on a desire to follow him by imitating him.

The Inspired Word: Mystics, Prophets, and Preachers (Fourteenth–Fifteenth Centuries)

Beginning in the late thirteenth century, the evangelical current that several decades earlier had given rise to the mendicant orders came into conflict with the church, as the revolt of the Spiritual Franciscans against the papacy clearly indicates. The papacy now turned away from an ideal that had become suspect and some themes of which had been taken up by isolated dissidents or heretical movements like that of Fra Dolcino. With the Avignon papacy, the process of the clericalization of the church and its transformation into a power structure intensified still further. In reaction, new forms of sanctity appeared on the fringes of an institution that proved less and less capable of responding to the religious aspirations of the faithful. This was the context in which we need to place the mysticism that arose during the latter half of the thirteenth century in Germany, Flanders, and Italy and spread throughout Christendom around the year 1300; in particular, the rise of a visionary prophecy that steadily gained influence during the series of crises brought on by the Great Schism of 1378 needs to be seen in this context.

Perhaps the most remarkable aspect of this movement was the place that women, particularly lay women, occupied in it. Excluded from the ministry of the Word within the church, women took possession of it by proclaiming divine election. Although they placed themselves under the direction of male confessors or directors of conscience, these women often did not take long to reverse authority roles and turn their confessors into secretaries and spokesmen. The earliest cases of female visionary saints are Margaret of Cortona (d. 1297), Clare of Montefalco (d. 1308), and Angela of Foligno (d. 1309). It is significant that none of these saints was canonized during the Middle Ages, although both during their lifetimes and after their deaths they enjoyed enormous spiritual prestige precisely because they transposed the fundamental institutions of Franciscanism to a new key. In any event, it was during the canonization procedures for St. Clare of Montefalco in Umbria that paramystical phenomena and visions were first taken into consideration by the Roman church and treated to particular examination. When their canonization procedures were unsuccessful, it was perhaps—aside from special circumstances inherent in each case—because these women, who stated that union with God in a loving fusion of wills was possible in this world, aroused the mistrust of the clergy and threatened its role as obligatory intermediaries between humankind and the Beyond. The prophetic aspect of female sanctity intensified during the course of the fourteenth century, as seen in St. Bridget of Sweden (d. 1373), who from 1343 on received and communicated revelations concerning the urgent need to return the papacy to Rome, to reform the church, and to convert the infidel. St. Catherine of Siena (d. 1380) pursued the same objectives with equal passion.

As different as their sensitivity and culture was, these women (and many others, less well known, whose impact was purely local) followed a common path. Rather than addressing the people, they sought to promote reforms from the top down. This explains the socially elitist character of their actions, which took the form of oral or written appeals to popes, sovereigns, and the mighty of this world. In most cases, even though they criticized the inadequacies of existing institutions, they did not challenge their existence itself, but rather attempted to induce the heads of those institutions to play their proper role. They invited the pope to avoid entanglement in political problems and the cares of temporal power; they admonished the king of France to remember his sacred mission and disregard the objections of his unworthy counselors. An evangelism expressed through the inspired word sought to invade the top echelons of the hierarchy, since it no longer found a place in ecclesiastical and social structures. When they turned to the pope and the rulers, these female saints hoped to concentrate the energies of Christendom, weakened by intestine wars, and to elicit a spiritual upsurge that would at last bring on the reform of the church that everyone declared was desirable but viewed as impossible. These celestial messengers held only two weapons to back their demands: the threat of the wrath of God, exasperated by the sins of humankind and the betrayal of the clergy, and the promise of the infinite love and compassion of the sacrificial Lamb who had shed his blood for the salvation of humanity. Although they used these arms with varying degrees of success, there is little doubt that in the Christianity of their age, beset by fragmentation and secularization, these female saints played the extremely important role of witnesses to spiritual values, which earned them considerable prestige.

It was dangerous for the church to permit sanctity to develop on its periphery or, on occasion, when criticism of its inadequacies grew too intense, even to turn against it. Thus in the late fourteenth century and especially in the fifteenth century the more dynamic elements of the clergy reconquered public opinion on the same terrain that the prophets and visionaries had chosen—that of the Word, become crucial in a society in which the masses played a growing role but remained for the most part excluded from the world of reading and writing. The number of great preachers among the saints of the late Middle Ages is striking: there were Vincent Ferrer (d. 1419), Bernardino of Siena (d. 1444), John of Capistrano (Giovanni da Capistrano, d. 1456), James of the Marches (Giacopo delle Marche, d. 1476), and many others, all of whom, incidentally, came from the mendicant orders and were connected with the Observant movement that regenerated both the Franciscan and the Dominican orders after the crises of the fourteenth centuries. Saintly preachers were certainly not a new phenomenon, since in the thirteenth century the church had canonized such holy orators as St. Anthony of Padua, of the Friars Minor, and St. Peter Martyr, of the Order of Friars Preachers. In the fifteenth century, however, the phenomenon was more widespread than ever before.

Throughout Western Europe, with the exception of a few hermits, the only followers of the religious life to arouse mass enthusiasm were preachers who dedicated their lives and their energies to the ministry of the Word. As they moved across Western Europe from Aragon to Brittany and from Italy to Poland and Croatia, these friars were clearly distinguishable from the clergy with whom the faithful were familiar. Moving from city to city and practicing the most extreme poverty, these men nonetheless took the time to become acquainted with their hearers. They often preached a cycle of sermons—throughout Lent, for example—in one place, which gave them a certain familiarity with the problems of that particular city and its inhabitants. Their gatherings, well organized spectacles in which the preachers were both the promoters and the star turns, reminds us more of political meetings or "happenings" than sermons. They generally preached from an open-air platform set up for the occasion, and they were accompanied by confessors invested with the power to absolve sins usually reserved to the jurisdiction of bishops or the pope. On occasion there were also troops of penitents "converted" during the previous session and fulfilling a sort of expiatory pilgrimage through flagellation or the performance of devotions before the orator began to speak.

The preachers generally spoke on the great truths necessary for salvation, usually more from a moral than a dogmatic point of view. Since their aim was to touch and move large audiences, they concentrated on making the faithful aware of sins and urging them to contrition. Preachers demanded tangible signs of the spiritual regeneration they effected, and the mission often ended with an auto-da-fé in which games of chance and female frippery were burned on a pyre. The desire for conversion that inspired these saints went beyond individual morals, however. Conscious of living in a world in which the Christian message had little influence on mores, they sought to introduce the Gospel into the life of society by acting as peacemakers to reconcile feuding families and clans and by attempting to ameliorate the sufferings of the poor and the outcast. Where they preached, hospices were created for the sick and lending institutions (*monts-de-piété, monti della pietà,* etc.) were founded to combat usury. In an attempt to assure stability to the institutions they founded, the servants of God often involved municipal governments, persuading the city councils to approve regulations or communal statutes more in conformity with the Christian ethic and aimed in particular at insolent displays of luxury among the wealthy and the illicit commercial and financial practices of the mercantile bourgeoisie. Thus at the dawn of the modern era, Christian sanctity returned to the tradition of social action and works of charity of the early Middle Ages, a tradition that had been eclipsed for several centuries by the prestige of monastic and spiritual ideals.

An accurate idea of how sanctity was represented in the late Middle Ages demands that we look beyond the men and women who were honored with canonization, for the ecclesiastical hierarchy and the faithful were in serious disagreement on the subject. The papacy tended to reserve the glory of the altar to a restricted number of saints, who were subjected to close scrutiny but did not always meet with popular success. The people, for their part, spontaneously venerated men, women, and even children whose principal merit was to have perished through a violent and undeserved death. Among these "saintly innocents" the "martyrs" supposedly killed by Jews occupied a special place. Particularly numerous in England and Germany, they included such figures as Werner of Bacharach (d. 1287), who was extremely popular in the Rhine valley and the Low Countries in the fourteenth and fifteenth centuries, or Simeon of Trent (d. 1475), whose cult, widespread in the Alps and in northern Italy, deeply divided the clergy. The Roman church generally rejected all forms of sanctity connected with bloodletting, but it also neglected figures with a more central place in popular piety, such as the saintly pilgrim and miracle-worker, whose most famous prototype was St. Roch, invoked against the plague from the mid-fifteenth century. Although churches and chapels were built in honor of St. Roch, his biography remains extremely obscure, and the papacy waited until the seventeenth century to grant him legitimate canonical status, a sign that the people continued to create saints in the late Middle Ages in spite of the increasing control exercised by the clergy.

The Function of the Saints in Medieval Christianity

An Exceptional Corpse

For most people during the Middle Ages, especially before the thirteenth century, a saint was first and foremost an illustrious corpse of someone whose precise history was unknown but who was reputed to have endured persecution and suffering for the love of God during his or her lifetime. This explains the fundamental importance of the saint's body—the only point of contact between the servants of God and the faithful who venerated them—in the development of cults and legends. Indeed, persecutors and, on occasion, the saints themselves attacked their bodies. Dismembered, mutilated by pagans intent on bodily harm, or destroyed by self-inflected asceticism, the body returned to a mysterious integrity after death in a sign of divine election. In the Middle Ages, sanctity was primarily a language of the body, a discourse on "impassible flesh," as Piero Camporesi has put it.

Indeed, in 1387 a synod in Poitiers thought it necessary to take measures against "the simple people who, in imitation of certain infidels, have taken to worshiping the bodies of dead people found intact and of venerating them as if they were saints." Even for the clergy of the time, incorruption of the body in death was a necessary though not a sufficient criterion for attribution of the title "servant of God." In addition to its gift for resisting decomposition and its "good odor," a saint's remains had the marvelous quality (shared with the consecrated Host) of being able to be divided without losing any of its efficacy—that is, of the powers granted by God at the moment of the saint's blessed death. These were the implicit foundations of the cult of relics in the popular mind. Relics were portions of a body that had been sacrificed and fragmented but that, like the body of Christ, nonetheless remained a source of life and a promise of regeneration. The importance of translations and thefts of relics during the Middle

Ages can only be understood in this context. Such transfers and exchanges, which were often accompanied by fraud and even by acts of violence, have long been considered merely picturesque, but their place in the society of the time was central, in that possession of a saintly body—better, of more than one—was a vital necessity for both secular and ecclesiastical collectivities. The saints themselves were conscious of this need, and they often chose to die either in their birthplaces or where they thought that the influence of their mortal remains would be beneficial.

In this way, the Italian hermit, Bl. John Buoni (Giovanni Bono, d. 1249), who had spent most of his life near Cesena, in Romagna, returned to Mantua when he sensed that his end was near, both out of loyalty to his birthplace and to combat the heretics who were solidly entrenched in the city by the posthumous distribution of his relics. In the same spirit, medieval legends teem with instances of a saint's remains putting up a determined resistance to being moved by suddenly taking on great weight. In practice, the only absolute criterion of success or failure in the acquisition of relics lay in whether the move had actually been carried out. Translation or theft could always be justified—whatever the servant of God may have intended—by claiming that the relics' previous owners had left them without honor in an unworthy place. In such cases, carrying them elsewhere was simply a manifestation of piety more to be praised than censured. Even when the papacy (with Innocent III) declared in the thirteenth century that "falsity under the veil of sanctity must not be tolerated" and attempted to establish a minimum of discipline in this domain, the results fell far short of expectations. The faithful were persuaded of their rights and of their piety, refusing to let the light of saints' relics remain under a bushel when they judged them to be insufficiently venerated—a notion vague enough to justify attempts to gain control of relics by any available means.

These notions were all the more tenacious for being rooted in folk culture, the distorted but undeniable echo of which we can find in hagiography, in particular in certain vernacular lives of saints of the twelfth and thirteenth centuries. The servants of God appeared as heroes and heroines immobile in time, gifted from the start with all perfection, and permanently inhabited by divine grace. The years that they spent in society simply permitted them to be recognized as saints by the manifestation of their virtues and their thaumaturgic powers. Tellingly enough, the authors of these texts almost always choose to celebrate the merits of persons remote from them in time and space, emphasizing what was odd or even inhuman in their existence. Responding to the expectations of their public, such writers sought to evoke figures that one had to admire, but that it was out of the question to imitate, particularly since the saints' perfection lay in omission. As presented in this literature, the saint was someone who abstained from everything that other men and women found enjoyable, who practiced chastity and asceticism to a hyperbolic degree and lived in renunciation and bodily denial. On the popular level, the archetype of the saint remained the hermit—the man of privation and renunciation. When they were faced with such unattainable perfection, the masses reacted as consumers, expecting the man of God to pass on to a sinful and suffering humanity the benefits of the grace he had won through his sacrifice. He was seen primarily as an intercessor responsible for protecting those who invoked him. The clergy (at least until the thirteenth century) shared this conviction and wrote lives of saints and books of miracles in the aim of publicizing one sanctuary or another or of confirming the masses in their faith.

An Accessible Salvation

Beginning with the twelfth century—and even with the eleventh century in Italy—a slow but profound change, connected with the cultural and religious transformations taking place in Western Europe, began to affect the representation of sanctity. The vogue of the cult of relics continued until the Reformation, but new forms of devotion also developed honoring men and women who had been granted sainthood by public acclaim for their exemplary lives. People were no longer content to venerate intercessors, illustrious or obscure, who had lived in distant lands and remote times, but instead showed a growing interest (in Mediterranean countries in particular) in more familiar and more recent figures. The saint was no longer just a body endowed with extraordinary privileges, but primarily a living being. Rather than echoing the cult of martyrs that centered on the death of a servant of God, this new conception returned to the tradition of St. Anthony, to the Desert Fathers, and to the penitents who, from Mary Magdalene to Thaïs and Pelagia, had fascinated the Byzantine world and the Eastern Church. In this fashion, it is hardly surprising that among those who were recognized as saints in the West after the year 1000 we find a good number of hermits (such as St. Romuald and St. John Gualbert in Italy) and, more generally, ascetics and converts whose austere life recommended them to the attention of the faithful.

The living saint was recognizable above all for having tamed his own "nature," and in exchange this earned him supernatural power over the elements and the animal kingdom. Thus hermits made springs gush forth near their cells and bare sticks sprout when planted in the ground. They walked through fire unscathed and with a wave of the hand silenced the birds whose song was disturbing religious rites. The underlying anthropological model is free of any moral connotation or idea of exemplarity, and it is common to a number of religions, Islam in particular. Hagiography often makes the connection with Christianity only by comparing the ascetic privations of the servant of God to Christ's suffering. It is less certain that the crowds who thronged to see and touch the saint made the same connection. If the model met with success, it was primarily because it worked: by putting his supernatural power to the service of human beings, notably the least fortunate among them, such as prisoners and the sick, the saint seemed a source of efficacious mediation. The saint exorcised demons and brought the marginal and the outcast back into their groups of origin. Thanks to his prestige and the awe he inspired, the saint halted vendettas, reconciled enemies, and restored concord where hatred and division had reigned.

It would belittle his role, however, to see the hermit saint simply as a clever negotiator who settled quarrels. In reality, his authority came both from the life he led and his detachment from those who solicited his aid. Men of God often sprang from the social and cultural elite, and in all instances they were removed from ordinary humanity. Their asceticism distanced them even farther by making them less "human." When they broke the familial and economic ties that connected them with the world, fleeing the company of women, which might have contributed to tying them down to one specific place, they appeared, in the last analysis, as the only totally free and independent people in a society often paralyzed by internal tensions and contradictions. It was thus logical that society often turned to them as a last recourse in moments of grave difficulty or crisis. As men of faith who had wagered their entire existence on a heavenly bet, their mere presence offered a remedy for anxiety and a response to the need for certitudes of those who turned to them. This is the point at which the religious dimension of sanctity entered into play: the servants of God were expected to devote their accumulated supernatural energies to reestablishing normal relations among human beings and between humans and nature, which the Devil had destroyed. Order in the world, upset by original sin, would be restored by miracle, for at the root of evil there almost always lay an error that the saints' spiritual lucidity enabled them to locate and make clear. When this sin was too deeply seated, they limited themselves to predicting the catastrophes that it would eventually bring on. Thus the man of God was indissociably both thaumaturge and prophet.

Saints, living and dead, provided the faithful with an accessible form of holiness independent of clerical mediation, since all one had to do to benefit from their *virtus* was to seek them out if they were still in this world or visit their tombs after their death. Soon—in any event, from the thirteenth century—it was not even necessary to go to a sanctuary to have one's prayers answered, and a simple invocation, followed by a vow implying a promised offering, was enough to establish a relation between the worshiper and the celestial protector and to assure the saint's intercession. Consulting a living saint, however, as was more and more often the case in Mediterranean lands, risked having the man of God offer more than the healing and protection asked for. The faithful were generally wary of being led too far, as seen in the reaction of one notary who sought out St. Peter Celestine (Peter of Morrone, the future pope Celestine V, d. 1296) in his mountain retreat in the Abruzzi. "Let us occupy ourselves with what we have come for," he answered the hermit, who, knowing that his interlocutor was noted for his dissolute life, had begun to interrogate him about it. In the eyes of the person who had sought out the holy man, the saint was there to cure people, not to convert them. For the saintly hermit, however, the thaumaturgic power that resided in him was a gift of God, not a personal privilege, which meant that he sought to make the granting of favors conditional upon the abandonment of reprehensible behavior. Encounters of the sort led to the development of a pastoral sanctity during the later centuries of the Middle Ages.

Upholders of the Church and Examples for the Faithful

When the Western church became aware that the saints were not merely miracle-workers or the source of relics to ensure the fortunes of a sanctuary but, as St. Thomas put it, "the temples and organs of the Holy Spirit," the honors and the cult rendered them took on a new meaning, not to replace the old ones but in addition to them. One of the most remarkable texts in this connection is the bull of canonization of St. Dominic in 1234. Pope Gregory IX takes the opportunity to review the successive categories of servants of God since the origins of Christianity. He begins with the martyrs "who gave to the Church, innumerably increased, children of all the nations under heaven." As it later happened that "presumption followed soon after the arrival of the multitude and the wickedness of liberty," God enrolled the aid of St. Benedict and his followers to "reestablish through the happy society of a cohabitation full of grace the benefits of life in common that too great numbers had made [people] lose sight of." When primitive Benedictine monasticism eventually exhausted its "virtue," God, "as if to replenish his weary troops," sent the Cistercian and Florensian Orders to restore divine praise to its full purity. They proved insufficient, however, to halt the advance of evil, so that "at the eleventh hour, when day was already fading into night . . . God raised up the spirit of St. Dominic and gave him the strength and the favor of divine predication. The entire sect of the heretics trembled at his sight, while the Church of the faithful shivered with joy." Leaving aside a certain pomposity proper to this sort of pontifical document, this text contains extremely important statements concerning the role of the saints in the life of the church. First, for this pope who had known Francis and Dominic personally, the principal manifestation of Dominic's sanctity lay in the creation of a religious order. Gregory sees the Order of Friars Preachers as a realization in space and time of the charity of St. Dominic. Thus he insists less on the personal virtues of Benedict, Bernard, and Dominic than on the prolific results and historical repercussions of their actions.

This consciousness of the value of sanctity for the spiritual aspects of the church had already existed in Christianity of the classical period, but in the perspective of a particular church under the special protection of a bishop or martyr. In the thirteenth century, it applied to the universal church directed by the Vicar of Christ, who had recently reserved to himself the right of canonization. For the church, the appearance of new saints in its midst was a great comfort, coming at a time when many, claiming it had failed in its mission, chose to follow the teachings of the Cathar "Perfect" or the Waldensian preachers. The papacy did its best to encourage, throughout the West, the cult of new martyrs such as Thomas Becket (d. 1170), the archbishop of Canterbury assassinated in his cathedral by King Henry II's knights, or the Dominican, Peter Martyr, killed near Milan in 1252 as he was carrying out his appointed tasks, as well as the cult of Francis of Assisi (d. 1226), whom his biographer, Thomas of Celano, had called a "new Evangelist." A great many Christians, clergy and laity, saw in Francis's life a sign of the advent of the "new times," an expression that referred both to the immediate present and to the end of history in this world. To his contemporaries the *Poverello* of Assisi (like St. Dominic, for that matter) seemed not so much an upholder of ecclesiastical institutions as a reformer and even more, a reviver of the ancient Christian holiness who, by returning to the message of the Gospels, inaugurated a new and final stage in the history of salvation. Some among the Friars Minor even hailed Francis, who had received the stigmata at La Verna, as a second Christ (*alter Christus*).

More generally, saints were perceived in this period as individuals whose coming, "in the nick of time," was providential for the church. It is no wonder that medieval iconography often illustrated the vision of Pope Innocent III, who saw in a dream a friar (Francis or Dominic, as need dictated) holding up the basilica of Saint John Lateran, threatened with collapse. Hagiography caught up with this new conception of sainthood, albeit slowly. In its more "up-to-date" currents, it now aimed at illustrating the notion that every saint had a historic mission that consisted of grasping contemporary needs from the viewpoint of eternity and dominating them by means of his or her experience of Christ. This was, for example, the ultimate significance of Franciscan poverty, which reacted to the greed and pride of the new world of the city and the mercantile economy by reaffirming the primacy of giving and of renunciation. In the new hagiography of the thirteenth century, the prototypes of which were the Life of the mystical beguine, Bl. Mary of Oignies (d. 1213) by Jacques de Vitry and the first biographies of St. Francis, the life of the servants of God was emphasized far more than their miracles. The idea that saints could be imitated slowly prevailed over the somewhat awestruck admiration that previously characterized relations between the faithful and the heavenly protectors whose intercession they implored. The biographers who offered such texts, first to churchmen and, through them, to the body of the faithful, aimed at giving their readers access to saintliness through conformity (within the limits of the possible) to these models. It was in this same spirit that the earlier companions of St. Francis, having heard that the directors of the Order of the Friars Minor intended to collect accounts of the posthumous miracles attributed to their founder, wrote to the chapter-general in Greccio in 1245 to oppose the project, stating that "miracles do not make sanctity, but manifest it." Even if its full consequences were not immediately seen, this was a remarkable attempt to remove the saints from the realm of magic and place them once again at the heart of the life of the church and of society.

Individual Protectors

These views were far from accessible to all the faithful. For the greater number in final centuries of the Middle Ages, the saints were familiar and helping figures to whom they were connected by affective ties often based on actual or presumed membership in the same professional, ethnic, or political community. From the earliest centuries of the Christian era, in fact, the idea that the servants of God exerted special protection over the place where their relics lay had been widespread. Soon every episcopal city, beginning with Peter and Paul in Rome, had its *sanctus proprius,* the official guardian of its walls and its inhabitants. After the martyrs, it was the bishops who often played the role of defenders of the city and protectors of the poor, since it was natural for the leader of the local church, after his death and by means of his relics, to become a special intercessor.

With the thirteenth century, the desire for a patron saint spread to cities that were not the seat of a diocese, and the smallest town and the humblest confraternity demanded a patron saint of its own. This movement was particularly strong in the Italian communes or regions such as southern Germany, where local particularism and civic patriotism were well developed, but demand was just as high in lands on the periphery of Christendom that had a poorer supply of saints and fewer relics. The author of a Life of St. Nicholas, the bishop of Linköping in Sweden (d. 1391), wrote in 1414:

> Although we cannot solemnize the feasts of all the saints, it is just that every region or even every city or parish venerate its own patron with particular honors. . . . France renders a cult to Denis, England to Thomas, Sweden to Sigfrid. We also, in our diocese of Linköping, we ought to venerate our father Nicholas and make every effort to have him canonized.

Individuals' and groups' frantic search for a patron saint led to two specialized forms of piety, civic cults and dynastic cults. Civic cults occurred above all in regions in which cities enjoyed true political autonomy; dynastic cults appeared in countries of a monarchic tradition, where national unity was already strong. St. Sebald, the patron of Nuremburg, provides a good example of both the nature and the forms of civic religion. Sebald was a hermit of unknown origins who lived in the region of Nuremberg in the mid-eleventh century, at the time of the founding of the city by the emperor Henry III. At Sebald's death, his body was placed in a small chapel in the new town, then transferred to a church, where merchants and craftsmen came to venerate it. At the time he had no cult; Nuremberg was not an episcopal city, simply celebrating the religious feasts of the diocese of Bamberg, of which it was a part. In the thirteenth century, however, as Arno Borst has shown, Sebald gradually came to embody the city's liberty and prosperity, and in 1219 Frederick II recognized the city's privileges. The municipal authorities built a large church in honor of Sebald, consecrated in 1273. St. Sebald's feast day, August 19, was celebrated annually with due ceremony and, after 1256, benefited from an indulgence.

Let there be no mistake, however: popular piety had little to do with these political religious manifestations, tied to an urban patriciate that viewed Sebald as the defender of the grandeur and the independence of the city. This is clear from the earliest rhythmic offices in Latin, composed in his honor around 1280 by clerics in the service of the municipal government, in which the greatest miracle attributed to the saint was the growth of Nuremberg from a small town at the time of his death to one of the most powerful and wealthiest cities of the Germanic world. Later texts made Sebald a noble who had abandoned kin and castles to live a life of poverty and anonymity, or again the son of a king of Denmark who came to the region to die incognito. It was only after 1350, when craftsmen had gained access to the city government, that Sebald became a truly popular saint. As with the cult of St. Ambrose in Milan in the eleventh and twelfth centuries, when the new classes confronted the older governing strata, they placed themselves under the banner of the local patron saint to show their intention of defending the true interests of the city, concealing the novelty of their demands under the cloak of recourse to traditional intercessors. Thus the resurgence of the cult of St. Sebald in the late fourteenth century served to lend legitimacy to the efforts of the rising classes to give access to public affairs to a larger number of citizens. The church dedicated to him was enlarged, and he began to be figured (for the first time) in statues and stained-glass windows. His Life was translated into German, the given name Sebald became common in Nuremberg, and finally, in the early fifteenth century, his effigy was engraved on the city's coins. The only thing he lacked was recognition by the clergy, who seem to have held back until that time, refusing to grant Sebald an official liturgical cult. In 1425, however, the city magistracy obtained the canonization of its hero from Pope Martin V, thus granting him the full honors of sainthood. This was an exceptional outcome, however. The results were not always this successful. In the Italian communes, where people who had lived in the recent past were often the object of civic cults—as in Treviso, for example, with Bl. Henry of Bolzano (d. 1315)—repeated attempts were made to get the Roman church to canonize the new patron saints. The church nearly always refused, but that did not prevent the cities from publicly venerating their municipal protectors when the governing bodies were persuaded that their saints assured the city's prosperity and maintained concord among its citizens.

Similar attitudes existed in the countries where dynastic cults predominated, centering on saints, male and female, whose posthumous destiny was somehow linked to that of the ruling family. Where a strong national consciousness was tied to monarchist sentiment, the patron saint of the royal family tended to become the patron of the nation as a whole. St. Denis, whose remains were venerated in the abbey near Paris that the Capetians had always protected, became the symbol of France, a role in which, curiously, St. Louis never replaced him. The Hundred Years War accelerated the process by intensifying rivalry between states. England saw itself in St. George, Burgundy in St. Andrew, just as Venice had long been identified with St. Mark and his lion. One could cite many other examples. In Scandinavia, the Norwegian national consciousness was built around the cult of St. Olaf, and the Swedish crown managed to popularize the figure of St. Erik, a twelfth-century sovereign traitorously murdered by his rival but whose Christian virtues were not evident (which was why St. Bridget displayed intense hostility to his cult). In this way, saints became something like eponymic national divinities.

There are various ways in which the proliferation of civic and dynastic cults in the late Middle Ages could be evaluated. Even at the time, a certain number of keen minds saw in them a sign of a decline in universal Christianity. Franco Sacchetti, the Florentine humanist writer of the late fourteenth century, denounced the narrow-minded civic pride that guided the choice of new intercessors in his time, fearing, as he said, that "all these new saints would make [him] lose his faith in the old ones." In a similar spirit, a few theologians with a penchant for reform such as Heinrich von Langenstein in Germany or Jean Gerson in France attempted in vain to persuade the Council of Constance (1415) to impose restrictions, and Nicholas of Clémanges wrote a treatise against the introduction of new feast days (*De novis celebritatibus non instituendis*), the title of which speaks for itself. All these men denounced the perversion of their contemporaries who turned away from the great saints of the church—the evangelists, the apostles, and the early martyrs—to scatter their devotions in minor cults often centered on dubious saints.

Looking back on these criticisms (which were not wholly unfounded), we can see that they do not tell the whole story. In the late Middle Ages the cult of the saints was so profoundly integrated into the life of society that it had become an essential part of life, at the risk of sinking to the banal. But was it not precisely the inextricable overlapping of the sacred and the profane—of the political and the religious—in a framework of confraternal and civic religious practice that enabled the cult of the saints to continue to flourish in Italy, France, and the Iberian peninsula for centuries yet to come? North of the Alps the cult of the saints had for the most part kept to more liturgical and more traditional forms, and where it triumphed, the Protestant Reformation had little difficulty in eliminating, by decree, an entire set of beliefs and practices that the urban burgher class of the fifteenth century now saw as mere superstitions encouraged by the clergy in order to maintain their grip on the masses.

Whatever judgment we ultimately make on the place and the function of saints in medieval society, we would do well to remember Robert Hertz's excellent remarks concerning the Alpine pilgrimage of St. Besse in the Val d'Aosta. According to Hertz, the cult rendered the saints through the centuries expressed "the faith that this obscure mountain people had in itself and in its ideal, and its will to survive and to overcome temporary setbacks or the hostility of men and of things." If certain saints of the Middle Ages continued to be venerated and implored—in some cases, to our own day—it is doubtless because successive generations recognized that their predecessors had invested the best of themselves in that devotion and lodged in it their successive conceptions of human perfection.

BIBLIOGRAPHY

Beissel, Stephan. *Die Verehrung der Heilingen und ihrer Reliquien in Deutschland während der zweiten Hälfte des Mittelalters.* Freiburg im Breisgau and St. Louis, Mo: B. Herder, 1892.

Bekker-Nielsen, Hans, et al., eds. *Hagiography and Medieval Literature: A Symposium.* Odense: Odense University Press, 1981.

Boesch-Gajano, Sofia. *Agiografia medievale.* Bologna: Il Mulino, 1976.

Boesch-Gajano, Sofia, and Lucia Sebastiani, eds. *Culto dei santi, istituzioni e classi sociali in età preindustriale.* Rome: L. U. Japadre, 1984.

Bosl, Karl. "Der Adelheilige. Idealtypus and Wirklichkeit, Gesellschaft und Kulture im Merowingerzeitlichen Bayern des VII. und VIII. Jahrhunderts." In

Clemens Bauer, ed. *Speculum historiale. Geschichte im Spiegel von Geschihtsschreibung und Geschichtsdeutung. Johannes Spörl aus Anlass seines sechzigsten Geburtstages dargebrach von Weggenosse, Freunden und Schülern.* Freiburg: K. Alber, 1965, pp. 167–87.

Boureau, Alain. *La Légende Dorée. Le système narratif de Jacques de Voragine (†1298).* Paris: Editions du Cerf, 1984.

Brown, Peter. *The Cult of the Saints: Its Rise and Function in Latin Christianity.* Chicago: University of Chicago Press, 1981.

———. *Society and the Holy in Late Antiquity.* Berkeley: University of California Press, 1982.

Capitani, Ovidio, ed. *Temi e problemi nella mistica femminile trecentesca.* Todi: Centri di Studi sulla spiritualità medievale, 1983.

Cazelles, Brigitte. *Le Corps de sainteté: d'après Jehan Bouche d'Or, Jehan Paulus et quelques Vies des XIIe et XIII siècles.* Geneva: Droz, 1982.

Cerulli, Enrico, and Raffaello Morghen, eds. *Agiografia nell'Occidente cristiano, secoli XIII-XV.* Convegno internazionale Agiografia nell'Occidente cristiano, secoli XIII-XV. Atti dei convegni lincei, 48. Rome: Accademia nazionale dei Lincei, 1980.

Chadwick, Nora K. *The Age of Saints in the Early Celtic Church.* London and New York: Oxford University Press, 1961.

Christian, William A., Jr. *Apparitions in Late Medieval and Renaissance Spain.* Princeton: Princeton University Press, 1981.

Corbet, Patrick. *Les Saints ottoniens: sainteté dynastique, sainteté royale et sainteté féminine autour de l'an Mil.* Sigmaringen: J. Thorbecke, 1986.

Dalarun, Jacques. *L'impossible Sainteté. La vie retrouvée de Robert d'Arbrissel (v. 1045–1116), fondateur de Fontevraud.* Paris: Editions du Cerf, 1985.

Dufourcq, Albert. *La Christianisation des foules. Etude sur la fin du paganisme populaire et sur les origines du culte des saints.* Paris: Bloud, 1903.

Folz, Robert. *Les Saints rois du Moyen Age in Occident, VIe-XIIIe siècles.* Brussels: Société des Bollandistes, 1984.

Gauthier, Marie-Madeleine. *Les Routes de la foi. Reliques et reliquaires de Jérusalem à Compostelle.* Fribourg, Switzerland: Office du livre; Paris: Bibliothèque des Arts, 1983.

Gelis, Jacques. "De la mort à la vie: les 'sanctuaires à répit'." *Ethnologie française* 2 (1981): 211–24.

Gelis, Jacques, and Odile Redon, eds. *Les Miracles miroirs du corps.* Paris: Presses et publications de l'université de Paris VIII–Vincennes à Saint-Denis, 1983.

Golinelli, P. *Culto dei santi e vita cittadina a Reggio Emilia (secc. IX-XII).* Modena: Aedes Muratoriana, 1980.

Goodich, Michael. *Vita Perfecta: The Ideal of Sainthood in the Thirteenth Century.* Stuttgart: A. Hiersemann, 1982.

Graus, František. *Volk, Herrscher und Heilinger im Reich der Merowinger. Studien zur Hagiographie der Merowingerzeit.* Prague: Nakladatelství Čeckoslovenské akademie věd, 1965.

Heinzelmann, Martin. *Translationsberichte und andere Quellen des Reliquienkultes.* Turnhout: Brépols, 1979.

Jones, Charles W. *Saint Nicholas of Myra, Bari, and Manhattan: Biography of a Legend.* Chicago: University of Chicago Press, 1978.

Kedar, Benjamin Z. "Noms de saints et mentalité populaire à Gênes au XIVe siècle." *Le Moyen Age* 73 (1967): 431–36.

Kieckhefer, Richard. *Unquiet Souls: Fourteenth-Century Saints and Their Religious Milieu.* Chicago: University of Chicago Press, 1984.

Leonardi, Claudio, and Enrico Menesto, eds. *Santa Chiara da Montefalco e il suo tempo.* Atti del quarto Convegno di studi storici ecclesiastici organizzato dall'Archidiocesi di Spoleto, Spoleto 28–30 dicembre 1981. Perugia: Regione dell'Umbria and Florence: Nuova Italia, 1985.

Manselli, Raoul. *S. Francesco d'Assisi.* Rome: Bulzoni, 1980.

Orselli, Alba M. *La città altomedievale e il suo santo patrono: (ancora una volta) il "campione" pavese.* Quaderni della Rivista di Storia della Chiesa in Italia 7. Rome: Herder, 1979.

Passarelli, Gaetano. *Il santo patrono nella città medievale: il culto di S. Valentino nella storia di Terni.* Rome: La Goliarda, 1982.

Patlagean, Evelyne, and Pierre Riché, eds. *Hagiographie, cultures et sociétés, IVe–XIIe siècles:* Actes du colloque organisé à Nanterre et à Paris, 2–5 mai 1979. Centre de recherches sur l'Antiquité tardive et le haut Moyen Age, Université de Paris X. Paris: Etudes Augustiniennes: 1981.

Peyer, Hans Conrad. *Stadt und Stadtpatron im mittelalterlichen Italien.* Zurich: Europa Verlag, 1955.

Philippart, G. *Typologie des sources du Moyen Age occidental.* Vols 24–25, *Les Légendiers et autres manuscrits hagiographiques.* Turnhout: Brépols, 1977.

Picasso, Giorgio, ed. *Una santa tutta Romana. Saggi e ricerche nel VI centenario di Francesca Bussi dei Ponziani (1384–1984).* Monte Oliveto Maggiore, 1984.

Poulain, Joseph-Claude. *L'idéal de sainteté dans l'Aquitaine carolingienne, d'après les sources hagiographiques, 750–950.* Quebec: Presses de l'Université Laval, 1975.

———. "Les Saints dans la vie religieuse au Moyen Age." In Benoît Lacroix and Pietro Boglioni, eds. *Les Religions populaires.* Quebec: Presses de l'Université de Laval, 1972.

Rezeau, Pierre. *Les Prières aux saints en France à la fin du Moyen Age.* 2 vols. Geneva: Librairie Droz, 1982–83.

Rusconi, Roberto, ed. *Il movimento religioso femminile in Umbria nei secoli XIII-XIV.* Atti del convegno internazionale di studio sull'ambito delle celebrazioni per l'VIII centenario della nascita di S. Francesco d'Assisi. Città di Castello. 27–28–29 ottobre, 1982. Perugia: Regione dell'Umbria; Scandicci (Florence): Nuova Italia, 1984.

Saintyves, P. [Nourry, Emile]. *Essais de mythologie chrétienne: Les saints successeurs des dieux.* Paris: Nourry, 1907.

Schmitt, Jean-Claude. "La Fabrique des saints." *Annales ESC* 35 (1984): 286–300.

Schmit, Jean-Claude, ed. *Les Saints et les Stars: le texte hagiographique dans la culture populaire: Etudes.* Paris: Beauchesne, 1983.

Siebert, Hermann. *Beiträge zur Vorreformatischen Heiligen- und Reliquienverehrung.* Freiburg im Breisgau: Herder, 1907.

Sigal, Pierre-André. *L'Homme et le miracle dans la France médiévale (XIe-XIIe siècle).* Paris: Editions du Cerf, 1985.

Sorelli, Fernanda. *La santità imitabile: "Leggenda di Maria da Venezia" di Tommaso da Siena.* Deputazione di storia patria per le venezie. Miscellanea di studi e memorie, vol. 23. Venice: Deputazione editrice, 1984.

Sumption, Jonathan. *Pilgrimage: An Image of Mediaeval Religion.* Totowa, N.J.: Rowan and Littlefield, 1976.

Vauchez, André. *Religion et société dans l'Occident médiéval.* Turin: Bottega d'Erasmo, 1980.

———. *La Sainteté en Occident aux derniers siècles du Moyen Age: d'après les procès de canonisation et les documents hagiographiques.* Rome: Ecole française de Rome; Paris: distribution Boccard, 1981.

———. "Santità." In *Encyclopedia Einaudi.* Turin: Einaudi, 1981, 12: 441–53.

Ward, Benedicta. *Miracles and the Medieval Mind: Theory, Record and Event, 1000–1215.* Philadelphia: University of Pennsylvania Press, 1982; rev. ed., Aldershot, ed., London: Scolar Press, 1987.

Weinstein, Donald, and Rudolph M. Bell. *Saints and Society: The Two Worlds of Western Christendom, 1000–1700.* Chicago: University of Chicago Press, 1982.

Wilson, Stephen. *Saints and Their Cults: Studies in Religious Sociology, Folklore and History.* Cambridge and New York: Cambridge University Press, 1983.

SUGGESTED READINGS

Rudolph M. Bell, *Holy Anorexia* (Chicago: University of Chicago Press, 1985).

Caroline Walker Bynum, *Holy Feast and Holy Fast: The Religious Significance of Food for Medieval Women* (Berkeley: University of California Press, 1987).

Sharon F. Elkins, *Holy Women of Twelfth-Century England* (Chapel Hill: University of North Carolina Press, 1988).

Susan J. Ridyard, *The Royal Saints of Anglo-Saxon England: A Study of West Saxon and East Anglian Cults* (Cambridge: Cambridge University Press, 1989).

TEN

The Marginal Man

Bronislaw Geremek

THE MARGINAL MAN DOES NOT APPEAR *EXPLICITE* IN THE DOCUMENTS OF THE MEDIEVAL SOCIAL CONSCIOUSNESS. HE IS MISSING IN WRITINGS that analyze social divisions in the early Middle Ages; he is not present in the works that describe "the levels in this world"; he is absent in the late medieval image of the "dance of death" in which a skeleton lines up figures representing the groups and social categories of the age. Yet he was present in the life of medieval societies as the result of individual or group negation of the dominant order, the accepted norms of cohabitation, and the rules and the laws in force. The marginal inhabited a social world *an sich;* in reality it was one with little internal unity, but society perceived it as different. There was rich diversity in that differentness, in the variety of activities pursued, in categories that, for lack of a better term, we might call professional, and in its varying degrees of separation from established society. We can find marginal figures in medieval literature and in the art of the epoch; religious and moral literature and state, ecclesiastical, and municipal legislation were aimed at them. Absent from the archives of social consciousness, society's outcasts were present in force in judicial and criminal archives.

During the millennium that was the Middle Ages, the structures of social organization, administrative models, and modes of government changed; furthermore, those changes took place at varying rates in the different zones of development of the European continent. As such changes occurred, the phenomenon of marginality took on new forms. Forgoing a detailed presentation of the concrete forms that social marginality took on in medieval Europe in different periods and different areas, I shall hope to delineate here the essential context in which the processes of alienation and exclusion from the various societies took place, attempting also to define the temporal variables that determined the dynamics of the processes of marginalization. What should gradually emerge is a psychological and social portrait of the marginal as a group.

Isidore of Seville examined in his treatise on etymology one of the key concepts of marginality in the Middle Ages, *exsilium,* which he derived from the term *extra solum.* Thus "exile" meant living far from one's own soil or one's own land, beyond the confines of one's homeland. It is clear that this concept contains an element that goes a good bit beyond geographical imagination to define the sociocultural horizon of persons in a traditional society. The natural condition was to live where one was born, where the tombs of one's ancestors provided continuity; it meant living within the context of a community of neighbors united by ties of kinship and proximity. Medieval societies were far from stable spatially. Great waves of migration and the colonization of new lands that from time to time put enormous masses of people into motion, together with the processes of urbanization, led to a demographic imbalance as population flowed continually from rural areas to the city or from the smaller towns to the larger cities. In many cases moving from one place to another was an integral part of a process of socialization or of increasing professional expertise, as in the peregrinations of the knights, journeyman craftsmen, and student clerics and monks. Nonetheless, in the social imagination of people of the Middle Ages, the fact of living in one place, of being rooted lastingly in the same locality and in the same community of persons, had a positive value, since people's sense of order and social security was founded on blood ties and neighborly connections.

The juxtaposition of people of common geographical origin and people from the outside nevertheless operated within a set of very ambivalent ideological implications, since Christian doctrine of the first centuries of the Christian era gave both a positive and a negative value to extraneous elements. In a passage in his *Moralia* commenting on the Book of Job, Gregory the Great considers Satan, the fallen angel, merely "different" ("Quis vero alienus nisi apostata angelus vocatur?"), whereas outsiders displayed a certain malignity. In the same treatise, however, Gregory teaches, following Scripture, that Christians are only wayfarers on this earth (*viator ac peregrinus*), on their way to their true—that is, heavenly—homeland. Patristic literature touches frequently on this theme of the Christian's estrangement from his true homeland, and it was a stimulus to the practice of the ascetic life, an essential part of which was precisely the repudiation of homeland. We can find the same ambivalence in the estimation of outsiders and of diversity in traditional attitudes and customs that assured hospitality and aid to the foreigner but at the same time manifested a basic fear of strangers.

Although the traveler would seem to be the perfect realization of the Christian ideal of the *viator* in this earthly life, an element of alienation, or at least the risk of alienation, was inherent in the concept of the voyage. Travelers who abandoned their own natural milieu and exposed themselves to the perils of the road were sure to have relations with unknown persons and to encounter the insidious perils of nature. Yvain, the knight errant in Chrétien de Troyes's poem, wanders

Par montaingnes et par valees
Et par forez longues et lees
Par leus estranges et sauvages
Et passa mainz felons passages
Et maint peril et maint destroit

(down valley and up mountainside, on into forests deep and wide. He went through many wicked passes . . . treacherous, wild morasses and eerie places . . . until he saw the narrow way. (*Yvain*, vv. 763–67; trans. Cline)

Threats accompanied the knight's adventures but also any voyage that involved leaving one's own territory—that is, a stable, secure place. Tracing a network of roads and using a variety of means to assure protection against eventual dangers was one way to enlarge organized space and to make familiarity with places outside the thickly settled zones more accessible. For the same reasons, hospices of various sorts were constructed and inns and taverns operated along the roads. At the same time, anyone organizing a trip sought to assure the continuation of social ties, thus people set off in the company of relatives, friends, or servants, they joined groups that were traveling together, and merchants organized caravans. The marginality encouraged by travel—long peregrinations in particular—could not be avoided by such means; to the contrary, traveling with a group restricted travel socially. Only those who made being continually "on the move" their way of life, who fled organized social life, or who had been excluded from the community felt the full effect of the processes of marginalization.

Society's outcasts deserve special attention, even in this general description of the world of social marginalization, since such people seem to correspond most fully to the concept of marginality. They were "banned people"—men and women who, by a decision of the community, an article of the law, or a court sentence had been deprived of the right to remain within the confines of a particular territory or had been declared total outlaws. The ban took different forms in Roman law, and it was interpreted in still different ways, as is evident in the compilation of jurisconsults' opinions found in Justinian's *Digesta*. Exile was defined spatially in various ways: it might be expulsion from a particular territory, confinement within a carefully defined area, or being sent to an island (*insulae vinculum*). The latter two forms belong among the "long-term" categories of the penitential tradition; the first form, the prohibition to reside in a certain city or territory, was thought to be the oldest historically. It has quite specific consequences. The denial of "water and fire" (*interdictio aquae et ignis*), which implied loss of the benefits of residence or hospitality (symbolized by slaking one's thirst and warming oneself), did not prevent the person from establishing himself elsewhere and leading a normal life there. Within the area covered by the ban he (or she) was under the threat of death. It is difficult to interpret this penalty, however. It contains the right to impunity *sui generis,* on the condition that the person leaves the place mentioned in the ban, but inherent in it is an element of social exclusion and a privation of all the individual's natural rights. The ambiguity of the institution of banishment based on Roman law may be proof that it involved an ancient tradition that eludes historical research. What needs to be examined is the entire question of the taboo in Mediterranean civilization.

In the "barbarian laws" and the customary law of the early Middle Ages banishment was strictly equivalent to exclusion. It replaced the taking of a person's life, which had been considered compensation for the disturbance of sacral order. Banishment was thus exclusion from the right to peace; it meant stripping people of their natural rights; depriving them of their true condition. The *Lex Salica* (55,2) declares that the banished person *wargus sit,* which meant that he was to be treated like a wolf and chased away from collective human society. To kill him would be legitimate self-defense. Even in this principle of customary law there is an avowal that man, outside social bonds and outside the *patria,* exposed to the risks of a wild environment and subject to the rules of life in the woods and the wilderness, became almost a wolf—a man-wolf, a werewolf. The ogre of the fable corresponds in real life to the asocial man who had transgressed the norms of social life and found himself on the outside.

Canon law applied the penalty of interdict and excommunication, analogous to banishment, to exclude individuals and groups from the church and from the Christian community. The liturgical framework of excommunication and its dramatically stratified verbal structure conferred a dimension of terror to this ecclesiastical sanction. Apart from the fact that the church took to such measures in particular situations (for the most part, to exert pressure when its interests might be endangered), complete alienation was implied in expulsion from the community of the faithful, withholding of the sacraments, and exclusion from the consecrated space of the churches, from all holy places, and from all rites. It was only in the thirteenth century, with Gregory IX, that the distinction between *excommunicatio minor* and *excommunicatio maior* was formulated and that the second implied total exclusion from the Christian community. Christian ethnocentricity relegated people of different religions to the edges of European societies, but they found support in their own religious communities and in their ethnic ties. Excommunication required their isolation—at least in theory, for in practice its effects depended upon the social position of the person or persons involved and was, in like proportion, easily reversed. It cut them off from worldly community relations (any sort of contact with kin was prohibited) and deprived them of hope for eternal salvation.

I am speaking here of banishment and excommunication not in their institutional aspect but as typical processes of marginalization. During the Middle Ages, both punishments underwent considerable evolution, gradually becoming more conventional, hence losing their original power of exclusion. The social morphology of this phenomenon merits further investigation, but what interests us here is the condition of the banned person as someone who lived differently from people who were part of an organized society. Exclusion was not the automatic result of a sentence; it was created *via facti,* by a way of leading one's life, with all the repressive actions deriving from that choice. Chilperic's edict of 574 defined malefactors as bad persons who commit bad deeds, who have no fixed abode, who possess nothing that could be confiscated for their wrongdoings, and who roam the woods. Here the lack of worldly goods has a certain importance, and it should be understood in the more extended sense of an absence of specific sources of revenue (which is what interested the laws of the late Middle Ages). The other two points regard lack of stability. In Charlemagne's capitularies we often encounter mistrust and hostility toward vagabonds and wanderers. Even pilgrims came under this heading, as is clear in the *Admonitio generalis in synodo Aquensi a. 789 edita:* it was better that a person who has committed some grave fault remain in one place, working, serving, and doing penance, rather than travel about dressed as a penitent affirming his desire to cancel his guilt. In later centuries the church sought to provide pilgrims with organizational structures to assure them *stabilitas in peregrinatione,* thus making pilgrimages a part of stable order.

Fostering stability was an understandable phenomenon in this society whose basic structures were formed in the conditions of enormous migrations that made nomadism a widespread life-style. Apart from the changes in the degree of mobility that took place in the course of the Middle Ages, this association of spatial mobility with a sense of threat to the public order remained as a permanent trait. As time went on, these negative associations came to be limited to rather precise social groups—popular groups above all, but surely not to them alone, because an errant knight did not merely evoke admiration, the traveling merchant was treated as a vagabond, and the traveling monks who took to vagabondage were unambiguously condemned in the monastic rules as *gyrovagi* (vagrants).

Clearly, spatial mobility was not in itself equivalent to an asocial life. It could be considered useful when people had to be moved from inhabited territories to undeveloped zones or zones poorly adapted to the needs of human settlement. People had to stop in such places during voyages, pilgrimages, and migrations. In the medieval imagination, forests and wilderness areas played an important role: they aroused fear, and they were the natural negation of social life. Furthermore, the opposition stability/mobility must not be taken too literally, as there were some who lived in wild areas by choice, even though their way of life was considered asocial. Demonic forces were thought to reign in the wilderness, reinforcing the harshness of living apart, but also some who sought eternal salvation by fleeing humankind went there. Sanctity crossed paths with the reign of Evil.

The concept of marginality in the Middle Ages was derived from spatial metaphors and it directly regarded space, perceived as "inside" or "outside," center or periphery, the first term in these pairs always being judged preferable. This image of spatial differentiation was superimposed on social organization, separating out from the "center"—that is, from society organized into family and group solidarities—all sorts of marginal figures—the excluded, criminals and outlaws, protesters, heretics, and dissidents. The same dichotomy operated on the highest scale of the *ecumene,* the human species, or Christendom, where the ranks of the "different" were filled by monsters, savages, pagans, and infidels. Although this vast scale was present in the medieval consciousness and in the literature of the epoch, nonetheless the fundamental meaning of "diversity" was based in local structures and in the realities of daily life. What led to social marginalization was the transgression of juridical and ethical norms, customs and models, or fundamental values. On occasion people who transgressed such norms were also set apart spatially by exile from the city or the territory or confinement in disreputable neighborhoods and city ghettos. It is important to note, however, that this sort of separation was only relative. Basically, contacts between those who obeyed the current moral and social norms and those who disregarded them continued to exist.

Marginal figures have left few traces in historical documentation. They established few relations, inherited no property, acted as the protagonists of no great enterprises that could be passed on to history. When they do appear it is above all in the archives of repression, thus in a reflected image that shows the anxiety and the hatred of organized society as well as its justice. For this reason, the data available regard society itself, and only on a second level the objects of society's repression. Furthermore, our information refers more to legal norms than to persons. For many centuries of the Middle Ages, the best we can do is ask what customary law considered punishable and how social groups executed its orders. Thus everything took place within local societies, which could stigmatize offenders (with branding, for example) but rarely did so. More often they were directly excluded by being banished from the community. No written traces remain of such procedures; custom had no need for documents. Even when written reports on judicial procedures had become a fairly widespread practice and court registers had begun to be used, a good many disputes were resolved by extrajudicial means, leaving no records. From the twelfth century on, the archives of repression made their appearance in medieval Europe, and in the late Middle Ages they became the general rule. They furnish both an overall picture of delinquency in the Middle Ages and existential portraits of marginal individuals.

All of this, however, does not in any way give an impression of rigid separation between praiseworthy and punishable behavior. Quarrels and brawls of all sorts abounded, and violent actions seem to have been characteristic of medieval daily life, particularly in urban areas. In Antwerp during the second half of the fourteenth century there were three times more court cases for various forms of physical violence than for thefts. In Ghent, municipal records for the fourteenth century attest that brawls and physical violence were common in the life of the city, but we should not forget that the same sort of thing happened within the social elite and seems to have been an integral part of the life-style of the younger generation. In the early fifteenth century in Brescia, nearly one-half of the sentences imposed by the city's *podestà* (the chief magistrate) and the *guidice dei malefici* (judge of the criminal court) regarded brawls, wounds, and exchanges of insults, whereas thefts accounted for less than 2 percent of verdicts. Judicial archives tell us less about the situation in rural areas. Although historians manage to arrive at an overall view of the phenomenon of rural crime (Barbara Hanawalt has investigated more than twenty thousand cases of criminal behavior in fourteenth-century England), criminal activity was inherent to social life; it was a sort of collateral activity, even a momentary repudiation, that interrupted a regulated and stabilized way of life. If the connection with price fluctuations is clear, in particular in the case of common crimes such as thefts of food products and small objects (during the famine of 1315–17 the number of crimes in England more than tripled in comparison with the preceding years), one still cannot state that criminal activities were confined to the lower echelons of society. Often, both the plaintiffs and the accused whose names appear in the judicial registers come from the clergy and the noble classes. The English historian R. H. Hilton even states that at the end of the thirteenth century members of noble families appear with such frequency, relative to their numbers, in English judicial records that violation of social order seems almost a customary activity of their class.

Thus the difficulty does not lie in any mistrust of global quantitative concepts referring to a static historical documentation but in the fact that marginality and criminality were of a different essence. Only criminal behavior that involved class demotion and desocialization thrust a person, a family, or a group beyond the limits of society. Observation of these processes requires examination of individual biographies, furnished, of course, by criminal archives, albeit in sketchy form.

The Bedfordshire coroners' rolls note the case of a violent quarrel that took place on 28 April 1272 in Dunton. Some vagabonds freshly arrived in town—two men and two women—first attempted (unsuccessfully) to sell an animal skin, then, also in vain, to obtain hospitality. A fight broke out between the two male vagabonds and one of them dropped dead of knife wounds. One of the women took refuge in the church, claiming right of asylum, and later admitted to the coroner that she had committed a good many thefts and declared that her companions were thieves as well. The murderer, sentenced to be hanged, was defined in the verdict as "a vagabond and a person belonging to no tithing."

We know nothing of the earlier history of this group. I might add, though, that they came from different parts of England, which bolstered the opinion that they were indeed vagabonds. They had managed to live, moving from one place to another, by robbing, begging, hunting when they had the chance, or working sporadically. The group had formed after a chance meeting on the road when they had eaten together in a tavern. After, they had occasionally organized thefts together. More often they acted independently, at times as "married" couples. One of the men, who came from Berwick-upon-Tweed, and one of the women, from Stratford, were referred to as a married couple, perhaps in a "marriage" resulting from their travels. The phraseology of the sentence characterizing the vagabond murderer as of no tithing is telling, as it reveals the important fact that he belonged to no local group and was thus cut off from social ties. This was considered an argument for hanging.

One portrait of a vagabond *sui generis* comes from a Tuscan judicial register for the year 1375. Sandro di Vanni, called Pescione, who came from near Florence, is identified as a robber, a forger, a man of evil reputation, and a vagabond without fixed domicile either in or around Florence or elsewhere. Furthermore, he had been banned from Florence and its surroundings. The list of his offenses includes several dozen court cases, for the most part for thefts of linens and sacks, often involving deceit when he presented himself as a buyer's agent or a collector for charity. Such petty thievery and fraud required continual changes of place, but Pescione operated within a fairly limited area, never leaving Tuscany and selling his goods and spending the winter in Florence or in Pisa.

Judicial records normally furnish a distorted image in that they center attention, obviously, on the unlawful acts that led to the suspect's arrest. Still, on occasion court procedures called for biographical information. The woman who confessed her thefts to the coroner of Bedfordshire in 1272 did so knowing that the laws covering the right of asylum stipulated that a person who confessed to crimes in that manner might avoid punishment for them, the judge pronouncing by which port the banished criminal would leave the kingdom, making his or her way carrying a cross. The *lettres de rémission* in France usually give not only a description of the crime for which the person mentioned in the letter was imprisoned or sentenced, but also a detailed list of wrongdoings committed throughout his or her lifetime. According to the king's law, the letter of remission lost all its value if any offense committed by the person involved did not figure in the list, so it was in the suspect's interest to confess to all crimes committed to that date. The biographical information that comes to light in this manner is sparse: place of birth, the profession of the person's father and his or her own profession; changes of residence. At times court records show malefactors of a clearly asocial profile who come from criminal milieus and whose life was one of unwavering delinquency. More often, however, marginality for these people seems to be instable, accidental, one might say, close to normal life.

The people we find in criminal archives are basically common men and women from the organized working world, set in contexts of family and good neighborly relations, but who broke with those structures at some point, suddenly or gradually. In Paris in 1416 a cleric who had for a while even been a Carmelite monk but had left the monastery was brought to justice, accused of theft and homicide. We know the particulars of his life through the exchange of arguments between ecclesiastical and secular jurisdictions contending for the right to judge him. Of illegitimate birth, he had loved gaming from childhood. After leaving the Carmelites he had enrolled in a military company. He had also worked as a lackey in the court of a noblewoman and, before his arrest, had appeared in the Paris marketplace in "public farces." This, at least, is how this malefactor and vagabond was presented by the king's prosecutor, who argued that the accused did not have the right to the benefits of the *privilegium fori*. The representative of the ecclesiastical jurisdiction affirmed that the cleric had obtained a dispensation from the church because of his illegitimate birth, and had participated in public spectacles for amusement and not for gain. Thus "il n'est buffo ne gouliart ne jongleur ou basteleur" (he was neither a buffoon nor a player nor a juggler nor a tumbler), so the objections to his right to enjoy clerical privilege did not pertain. Arguments aside, there was a fundamental conflict in his curriculum vitae: he was a cleric, a soldier, a vagabond, and an actor. Every now and again he had committed a robbery, and he had ended up in prison on at least four occasions. We can suppose that this "jack of all trades," a medieval precursor of the *picaro*, had had long periods of law-abiding life, at least in the sense that he had earned his living and had had a master over him. Were his violations of the law then only accidental situations that did not define his life in general? Only one thing is certain: organized society, of which the police and the courts were institutionalized expressions and which in turn protected that society, treated him as a vagabond, an unstable individual, and an outcast.

In the case narrated here, we can see that even a noncriminal life led to marginality when it lacked professional stabilization or when the trades that were exercised touched the limits of social acceptance or were considered degrading. The same could be said of a Parisian musician who ended up on the gallows in 1392. When he grew too old to support himself with his trade in Paris, he went from place to place in Normandy, committing petty thefts (stealing tin basins from houses). Here the reason for his marginality was old age, but we can find roots of it in his earlier mode of life, as he had already been imprisoned for theft. Urban delinquency was most commonly due to the presence of a number of workers carrying out a great variety of activities, often outside the purview of the guilds. In the unstable way of life of this sort of people day-work alternated or coexisted with robbery and begging. One day-worker and mason's helper (*homme de labour et varlet à maçon*) sometimes worked in the city, but at other times did seasonal work in the country. His wife remained in Paris, where she sold cheese. Work or no work, this man committed a number of thefts, both in Paris and its suburbs. In some of his undertakings he was helped by a companion, a roast-meat seller by profession, who had been crippled in military service (which explained his nickname, *Court-Bras*) and who later worked as a stevedore. When Court-Bras no longer could find work, he begged, then turned to robbery, operating alone or with an accomplice. In 1390 another day-laborer was imprisoned in Paris for stealing the tools furnished to him. During his interrogation he declared that he had worked for many years as a carter, transporting wine to Bourges, Flanders, Picardy, and Germany. Under torture he admitted to various other thefts, so he mounted the gallows. The judges had no doubts that he was a vagabond. One might say that this was how day workers were treated, since for the most part they were immigrants, which means that they were far from local and familial ties and were excluded from the guilds. Although they were only sporadically accused of crimes, still they were treated with suspicion and considered a burden on society. The few who fell into the clutches of the law were severely punished, even though the lives of this large group of workers, as we have seen, combined honest earnings and crime. This milieu, which was to increase in numbers in the late Middle Ages, continued to occupy an intermediate zone of its own, a liminality between city and country, between work and delinquency, between free vagabondage and corporative stability.

A category of persons who could be defined as "professional delinquents"—persons who more or less permanently based their existence on crime without pursuing any other sort of work—also existed in the Middle Ages. It is difficult to delimit this category with any precision, since on certain levels the confines between delinquency and labor tended to disappear. Labor in these cases was unskilled, unable to satisfy the requirements of artisanal specialization, and lacking corporative organization. Furthermore, even though participation in an organized criminal band could be considered proof of professional delinquency, this sort of life could not be pursued for more than a limited time. In Amiens in 1460, for example, a band of vagabonds was arrested and accused of having committed a number of thefts and robberies during fairs and festivities and of running houses of prostitution. (They were sentenced only to banishment, for insufficient proof of the charges.) We know little about the members of the band: one was a bastard twenty-six years old who came from Lens in the Artois; another, thirty years old, came from near Grammont in Flanders; a third, thirty-two, was a barber from Louvain; a fourth, a laborer from near Tournai (*pyonnier, piqueur et manouvrier*) was twenty-eight; a fifth, sixteen years old, declared himself a serge worker from Valenciennes. Some of these men were defined by their trade, some not. All were foreigners or immigrants in Amiens.

Marginality in the late Middle Ages was greatly accelerated by war, which created possibilities for existence outside the normal life experience of peasants and artisans, first in regularly commanded companies and then in autonomous bands. The difference was not great between normal military service and brigandage, between an army company and a robber band. A letter of remission of the king of France dated 1418 describes the case of one poor wretch between twenty and twenty-two years of age, a carter's helper by profession (*varlet charretier*), who, when he failed to find work, enrolled in the army on the side of the "Burgundians" and against the "Armagnacs." He and some other soldiers were making their way one day from Provins to Meaux, when they met a monk who asked them for directions, showing by his speech that he was a foreigner. They forthwith robbed him. This is certainly typical of the life of soldiers of the time. Another document of this sort speaks of a young blacksmith from Amiens who, after practicing his craft for two years, left in 1415 with some fifteen companions to go to Paris to sign up as soldiers, "as young people have been wont to do in the last two or three years." On their way, however, the band attacked two livestock merchants. On another occasion in 1420 two armed young men were involved in a simple skirmish that ended up in a homicide. The first, a barber by trade, was the illegitimate son of a noble; the other was an ex-vintner who led a brigand's life and gave his name as "Coiner," which might have been a family name or might refer to counterfeiting. The reason for their quarrel is less important than the question of whether the first man could really have been a nobleman if he was a barber. Even more important, war and the military profession were enough to cancel previous professional descriptions. To cite one more example: three soldiers who had fought in various regions of France were unable to find work on their return from Guienne in 1407. Since they were "poor companions without means," they set out for Beauce in search of ready money through robberies.

It is clear that war—specifically the Hundred Years War—led to some general decline in morals. But above all, it gave encouragement to a widespread process of demotion in class status; artisans and merchants, sons of noblemen and farmhands, vagabonds and clerics found in war a taste of the easy life as well as a suspension of social norms and of the rules for distinguishing between social roles. Even when an opportunity for a more stable situation presented itself, the previous experience of such people and their close ties with others of their sort inevitably led them to a marginal sort of life. In 1457 a Dijon saddler and harnessmaker found himself in prison. He had served as a soldier in Lombardy, where his company had fought for the duke of Savoy against Francesco Sforza. On his return to Dijon, he managed to obtain a post in the municipal watch, but it was only a cover for his criminal activities. In Lombardy he had met a Gascon soldier who already had some experience as a counterfeiter, a brigand, and a burglar. The Gascon introduced our Burgundian into the criminal underworld, gaining entry for him into the great band of the Coquillards, which, according to the police report, operated in several regions of France and counted at least sixty members. When the house of this craftsman and member of the city guard was searched, two false florins and five picklocks and burglars' jimmies were found, which at the time were taken as undeniable signs of professional criminality.

In Florence in 1391 a man from the parish of Santa Maria Maggiore was sentenced to be hanged as a robber, a murderer, and a traitor. The verdict enumerates a long series of crimes committed in Florence and its surrounding territory. The man usually operated with an accomplice or an acquaintance, and his offenses were not simple thefts but armed robbery, aggravated assault, brigandage, and kidnapping for ransom. In connection with one of his assaults, committed in Sienese territory this time, we learn that he and his accomplices belonged to a military company. We can state, then, that the phenomenon of "knightly gangsterism," as M. M. Postan has called it, was succeeded by military gangsterism.

War was thus one of the means by which marginality was fostered.

It was a quite special "rite of passage," and the marginal population grew. War also had the opposite effect, however. One might say that it brought a certain social stability to the marginal population, in that once all vagabonds and all those generally considered a burden on society had become soldiers, they found a place within organized society. This process, which I might call "demarginalization," was short-lived, since when the war ended, such people became even more of a danger to social order. The brigand bands in France or in Germanic lands in the fifteenth century were not only a consequence of war but a continuation of war for private purposes.

The professionalization of robbery demonstrates how marginality became consolidated. The thieves who appear on the registers of criminal sentences for the fifteenth century in the city of Wrocław, in Silesia, generally used burglars' jimmies and other tools such as drills, special knives for opening doors and coffers, and hooks for pulling out clothing. In 1469 one malefactor confessed to belonging to a great band of thieves, four members of which ended up on the gallows in Poznań, as did three others at Lublin. The band operated over a vast area, then, since the two cities are more than two hundred miles apart, and Poznań was in Silesia, therefore outside the borders of the kingdom of Poland. In spite of this, however, more professional delinquents operated alone or with an "associate" than in the large bands. The Wrocław register mentions one thief, Marcinko of Opole, who specialized in robbing churches. In one night, with the aid of villagers of his acquaintance, he broke into four different rural churches, but in the fourth he was cornered by the local people and, "with the miraculous aid of the saints, was captured before he could steal anything" ("miraculose sanctis cooperatibus detentus et captus fuit non potens sacras res deportare"). Sentenced to death, he was burned for sacrilege in 1454.

In the Florentine criminal archives we find a detailed description of the career of a Polish delinquent who could be defined as a professional. One Bartolomeo di Giovanni, called Griffone, was a notorious brigand of humble origin and a bad reputation. In 1441 he was in Venice with two companions, robbers of Polish origin. Together they attacked a Greek priest, robbing him of twelve *fiorini,* for which Bartolomeo ended up in a Venetian prison. He later escaped, along with other prisoners. In August of 1444 we find him in Rome, again with two Poles. This time their victim was a canon of Saint John Lanteran, from whom they took four *fiorini.* In the same month they robbed a canon of Santa Maria Maggiore of a silver chalice worth eighteen *fior-*

ini. In October of the same year, Bartolomeo was back in Florence, this time with a Hungarian and another Pole, with whom he robbed a tavernkeeper. Soon after, he and the Pole went to Bologna, where they stole three *ducati*. They were joined by another Hungarian, with whom they left to return to Florence. Along the way they robbed a peasant who was sleeping with them in an inn. In Florence the Pole lodged with the Hungarian in a house that he rented. One day the Pole stole from a German who lived in Florence a letter signed by Francesco Sforza, and he used it as a model to counterfeit a letter for himself, knowing that with it he could circulate freely anywhere, thus facilitating his robberies. He managed to remove the Sforza seal from the original letter with the aid of horse urine, and he placed it on his false document with a little hot wax. He and his Hungarian companion then went to Siena, which was on a main route for pilgrims making their way to Rome. Later he returned to Florence, where he was captured, sentenced, and hanged.

We have no way of knowing how this Pole entered the criminal underworld. His contacts with other Poles and with Hungarians and Italians show that he was already at home in Italian criminal circles, that he knew people who would buy stolen goods, and that he knew where and whom one could rob. It is legitimate to suppose the criminal activities of this Polish vagabond were in some way a collateral result of pilgrimages or migratory labor.

Court records often use such phrases as "of bad fame" or "marked with infamy" when they speak of malefactors or vagabonds. Ill fame resulted from knowledge of previous criminal activities, but at the same time it was an essential argument in judicial proceedings, since it demonstrated that the matter at hand was not an isolated law-breaking act but part of a life-style counter to the norms of social cohabitation. During the Middle Ages, the concept of "infamy" functioned in another context as well. It was associated with the performance of certain occupations that by law and in social consciousness were considered "dishonest" or "unworthy" and that stamped with infamy the people who exercised them (and sometimes their descendants as well). In this case, infamy was a mechanism of social exclusion very similar to the situation in caste societies—that is, to the creation of the pariahs in India or the *eta* in Japan. Or at least it was an analogous civilizational tendency.

In the ideological discourse of the Middle Ages, the problem of value judgments concerning occupations arose in the context of praise of the "three orders" of society (the "division of labor" between those who prayed, those who fought, and those who worked the land), in celebrations of the virtue of rural occupations, and in the condemnation of certain trades. Tertullian, for example, demonstrated that from the moral viewpoint trades like those of artists who painted divine images, astrologers, teachers, and merchants were suspect or even unacceptable to Christian culture. He holds merchants and others in the luxury trades responsible for the spread of wealth. The occupational categories held to be morally blameworthy changed in the works of the Fathers of the church and in theological writings, with usury, prostitution, and the dramatic arts henceforth leading the list. It should be noted that not only were occupations subject to moral evaluation; some were branded as contemptible, thus justifying the widespread exclusion of those who practiced them from Christian society. This is explicit in canon law and clear in municipal practices.

Canon law used the terms *mercimonia inhonesta* or *vilia officia* in connection with a certain number of occupations held to be irreconcilable with membership in a corporate association and in order to deprive a person *via facti* of the enjoyment of clerical privilege. The latter concerned not only priests but many who, once their schooling had ended, had obtained minor orders and could even marry without losing their rights as clergy. Lists of occupations prohibited to the clergy vary in form, and from the great compilations of canon law to the individual synodal statutes they gradually grow shorter. A cleric could not be a jongleur or an actor; he could not pursue activities associated with prostitution or a trade that had anything to do with blood, animal carcasses, waste or rubbish, or usury. The earliest documents even forbade all commerce. Synodal statutes and the articles of customary law often also mention as *personnes diffamez* by reason of their trade innkeepers, wizards and magicians of various sorts (*enchanteurs, sorciers*), and people responsible for city hygienic services (who cleaned the latrines, for example). The "infamy" connected with such trades not only barred the way to an ecclesiastical career but, in some cities, disqualified a candidate for city office.

Statutes regulating the crafts in German cities show ample proof of the concept of a degrading profession affecting a person's descendants. Where guild statutes specified the registration of "worthy birth" as a prerequisite to the acquisition of corporate rights and privileges, they excluded not only persons born out of wedlock or of unfree parentage but also the offspring of persons in certain professional categories. The long list includes executioners, jailers, executioners' assistants and lesser law-enforcement officials, gravediggers, butchers, custodians of public baths, barbers, prostitutes and their protectors, musicians, acrobats or buffoons, canvas weavers, fullers, and shepherds. (In German folklore, the maxim *Schäfer und Schinder, Geschwisterkinder*—shepherd and jailer are like two cousins—is eloquent proof of the persistence of this attitude.) The exclusion of people of "degrading occupations" outlived the Middle Ages, if it is true that even in the seventeenth and eighteenth centuries the laws of the German states felt it necessary to take up the question, and ethnographic studies have demonstrated that even today the problem is not completely dead.

A certain discrepancy existed between the norms—in canon law, municipal law, or juridical custom concerning trades and professions—and the actual social situation, and in time some of the occupations considered dishonorable obtained full rights to dignified social status. The area of operation of such norms, in terms of both time and space, has as yet been little studied. The importance of the phenomenon is nonetheless beyond doubt, and its documentation in canon law had a certain effect in an epoch in which the church provided models for the principal ideological structures and social behavior patterns. The strictures of Roman law concerning "infamy" undoubtedly influenced medieval norms regarding degrading occupations, as did barbarian law concerning persons deprived of rights. Clearly these were deeply rooted traditions touching on the violation of taboo as well as cultural attitudes toward certain professional occupations valued according to criteria of "pure" and "filthy." These traditions and these attitudes imposed marginality on some persons because of the trades they exercised. We need to examine some of these occupations in greater detail.

Professional entertainers figured prominently among the disapproved categories. Roman law regarded those who earned a living as actors as persons without dignity; Germanic customary law treated the *Spielleute* and their associates as *unrecht* through their occupation, by analogy to those who were *unrecht* by birth. In the tradition of the first Christians, *histriones* were treated the same way as prostitutes, and St. Augustine even denies them the sacraments. Actors and musicians were held to spread evil and were considered allies of the Devil. Synods and councils expressed themselves on the subject with clear hostility. As the centuries passed, the terms defining the various artistic activities changed, but the condemnation of players and entertainers remained in force in articles of the law, in theological treatises, and in religious oratory. "Jongleurs" and "histrions" were thrust into the lowest social categories, along with beggars, vagabonds, and cripples. Admittedly, however, greater moral value was gradually attached to the players' art in the ideological context of the thirteenth century.

Thomas Aquinas was persuaded that acrobats, minstrels, actors, and players of all sorts of musical instruments were equally reprehensible. Thomas excludes from his list the *ioculatores* who recounted the lives of the saints and the heroic actions of rulers to the accompaniment of musical instruments: they had a chance of saving their souls. Francis of Assisi went a good deal further, even calling himself "God's fool" (*ioculatore Dei*). Still, condemnation of these occupations remained. In countries of Orthodox Christianity, direct persecution of the players called *skomoroch* followed moral condemnation of them. The climate of moral ambiguity that surrounded the acting profession in early modern societies doubtless derived from this long tradition of condemnation.

Was it true, though, that medieval jongleurs and minstrels were people who existed at the fringes of society? That depended on how they actually lived. Organized corporations of minstrels who performed during city festivities and played at weddings existed within the structures of communal life. In the courts, days passed according to a special rhythm, and professional entertainers were a permanent and often a stable part of court activities. Nonetheless, there continued to be groups of players who, by their nomadic life, resembled vagabonds or were considered equivalent to them. Such occupations often recur in the biographies of the accused criminals discussed above, together with other activities typical of vagabonds. The church's ideological mistrust of a profession that threatened its cultural monopoly, combined with the traditional disrepute attached to these occupations, found justification in the unstable, and therefore asocial, lives of a professional category that had no place in the organized structures of society, in the distribution of social roles, or in the division of labor.

John of Salisbury maintained that jongleurs and prostitutes were generally to be considered monsters with human bodies, and thus should be exterminated. One of the arguments for the condemnation and exclusion of players was their involvement with prostitution and licentious living in general, though the condemnation of prostitution was much more evident than that of players. Even in this case, however, scholasticism to some extent revised its positions, indicating that prostitution had a certain utility. This did not mean that it was any less degrading; only that a basis for its reintegration into organized life, more precisely into urban life, could be created.

Prostitution took many forms in the Middle Ages. It was by no means confined to the city, as judicial archives show it to have been widespread in country areas. Prostitutes were present wherever the rural population met, at markets and fairs, near mills, and in taverns. Prostitutes went from one village to another, accompanying groups of harvesters, workers, or merchants. They were permanent fixtures in the cities, and venal love was one of the products offered on city markets. The municipal authorities permitted "houses of toleration" to remain open, and some cities used city funds to organize their own *postribulum publicum,* leasing it out to a manager. Even the public baths functioned as bordellos. Some cities had ghettos of prostitution—*la rue aux putains* of the French cities.

The moral and religious condemnation that struck prostitutes and their consequent social exclusion were commonly accepted facts. Here again, however, the prostitute's actual way of living was the determining factor, and there was a remarkable heterogeneity among prostitutes, both of category and in their standard of living. Some Venetian and Florentine courtesans lived sumptuously, became famous, and played an important role in the evolution of culture, even to claiming a social prestige beyond the wildest dreams of the pensioners of the city brothels. The city's prostitutes also enjoyed a measure of stability, but a good part of the category was made up of itinerant prostitutes at the mercy of go-betweens and "protectors." Often prostitution was a "second job" for women day workers and, more generally, for plebeian women. A common destiny, a similar way of life, and personal acquaintance linked them to vagabonds and criminals.

Despite the various forms of stabilization associated with them, prostitutes were in fundamental opposition to the reigning social order since they remained outside the family, not having the right to have a family of their own. Even when medieval literature presents a miraculous change in the life of a prostitute, the "happy ending" could only be a trip to heaven for the repentant sinner or her entry into a convent. In one French story of the twelfth century, a prostitute called Richeut decides to have a child, but only as a way to increase her earnings by attributing paternity to a series of gullible men. When the child is born, she participates in the usual religious rites, she makes an offering to the priest, the baby has godparents, and other representatives of her "craft" take part in the baptismal ceremonies. When the son grows up, he takes on the craft of *lescherie*—that is, he becomes a pimp, drawing on his mother's knowledge. The mother, for her part, takes the trouble to introduce him into her circle, but she treats him as an outsider when he shows signs of attempting to outwit her. Connubial ties in the world of prostitution, established by a "promise of love," were a negative reflection of the matrimonial relation, since they sealed the professional bond between the prostitute and her protector. When we encounter a couple or a family connected with this profession, there is usually a loss of caste involved that has led to prostitution as an occasional or stable source of earnings.

On occasion prostitutes were under the rule of a *roi des ribauds*, a *podestà dei ribaldi*, a *podestas meretricium*, or a *roi des filles amoureuses*—functionaries who had little authority outside the world of prostitution. The leaseholders of city brothels—usually communal appointees, on occasion the executioner, thus also of an "ignoble occupation"—had no prestige but were tolerated by both the church and the law. Public opinion and the judicial machinery for repression unanimously condemned anyone who organized prostitution outside "houses of toleration." To be a pimp or protector, an occupation that usually accompanied other activities associated with delinquency, was considered evident proof of an asocial life.

Detailed analysis of the professional activities that led to social exclusion reveals various instances of the violation of taboos. Marginalization nonetheless depended upon economic conditions and upon the sort of life such people led. Credit operations did not lead to marginality, even when they were truly usurious, hence open to moral condemnation. This was true even independently of the evolution of the canonical doctrine of the church, which, through the idea of restitution and the prospect of Purgatory, gave usurers hope of saving their souls and even made a place for them in Christian society. Marginality depended primarily upon position in society. Shepherds worked within the agrarian world—which usually came in for praise during the Middle Ages—and theirs was a seasonal activity universally practiced. Nonetheless, the shepherds' world prompted profound mistrust. Sheepherding required a migratory life; it meant living far from permanent settlements and spending long periods in solitude, and migrations and solitude were two elements in marginality. Furthermore, the shepherd was also a butcher, so he had contact with blood; he acted as a veterinarian and even as a physician for the country people—all of which quite naturally aroused suspicion and fear at the time. Living alone with animals for long periods, far from home and from collective society, the shepherd attracted suspicions of various sorts, among them, of bestiality and sodomy. In Germany shepherds were much scorned; indeed, many among them were simpleminded. It is not known, however, whether this negative attitude, amply documented in Germanic lands, was common throughout medieval Europe.

Problems concerning the body cannot be left out of any consideration of the condemnations, the infamy, and the marginalization connected with certain occupations. Such problems were determinant in the alienating effects of sickness and in the social condition of the ill and the infirm. Charity toward the sick went hand in hand with fear of contagion and with aversion and contempt for the crippled.

Leprosy provides a classic example of the connection between marginalization and contagious disease. The church and public institutions acted together to effect a total separation of lepers from the rest of society. The person struck by that terrible disease underwent a sort of civil death that included a spectacular ceremony—almost a funeral service—to accompany him or her beyond the confines of the inhabited area. In the *Congés* of Arras two leprous troubadours describe their leave-taking of their friends before going to the lepers' hospital. When the gangrene of the sinful soul passed into the body there was hope for eternal salvation, but in this world the leper was obliged to live apart from healthy people, hence separate from society. Still, the leprous enjoyed society's aid: they were provided for copiously enough to arouse envy, and collections were continually taken for them. They had to remain outside inhabited areas, however, they could not touch anything touched by healthy people, and they had to announce their presence by sounding a rattle (as if their horrendous aspect were not enough of a warning). Public opinion observed them fearfully, perhaps also with hatred. They were thought to practice unrestrained sexuality (as seen in the story of Tristan and Isolde), and were suspected of hatching villainous schemes against the society of the healthy. These attitudes extended to the offspring of lepers, who were obliged to live in ghettos and limited to the practice of trades held to be dishonorable or dirty. The marginalization of lepers in medieval society was so evident that in German they were called *Aussätzige*, or *die Üszetzigen*—the excluded. Furthermore, they were excluded forever. When Hartmann von Aue, in his *Der Arme Heinrich*, portrays first the protagonist's loss of caste through divine castigation (considered the cause of leprosy) and then his miraculous cure and consequent return to society, he is presenting a quite unusual case. This simply did not happen in real life. Although they were excluded and forced into a sort of ghetto, lepers nonetheless remained part of the social scene, and every time they appeared among people, in the city or the countryside, it reinforced their differentness.

Leprosy was clearly a quite special illness, but in the Middle Ages we find a certain ambivalence toward sick people in general and an attitude of mixed compassion and marginalization. Much depended on the social status of the sick person. If he (or she) belonged to a wealthy family, he could remain at home and could count on assistance. Even in the case of leprosy, a well-to-do person could avoid social exclusion. Among the lower classes, on the contrary, where existence depended upon physical labor, sickness meant marginalization. The sick were objects of charity. They were beggars, and they had to live on alms and try to find a shelter in an institution. The Christian doctrine of charity accorded cripples and sick persons the right to live by begging. Some writers, Guilelmus de Sancto Amore in the thirteenth century, for example, cited St. Augustine and enlarged on the notion of weakness to authorize extending aid even to those who by their upbringing and because of their traditional social status were not used to doing physical labor but who had fallen onto evil days. Although these *pauperes verecundi* still enjoyed a certain social consideration, the rest of the poor had to force recognition of their right to be aided by a public display of their infirmity, their weakness, or their penury. Infirmity had a socially degrading effect, at least in the sense that sickness was identified with destitution.

If we note that the process of marginalization was based on an exclusion that moved people outside social bonds, on their voluntary abandonment of those bonds, or on their loss of a place in society's division of labor or in the allotment of social roles, it becomes difficult to consider beggars marginal. Beggars were needed because they gave others the opportunity to demonstrate charity. They were organized and established; they respected the norms of social coexistence. An ambivalent attitude toward beggars and poverty ranging from disapproval of their way of life to praise of the virtue of renunciation can be traced as early as the writings of the Fathers of the church. In medieval society acceptance of the beggar's functional role prevailed as long as beggars did not compromise the work ethos or the equilibrium of the labor market. The dramatic social crises that led to seasonal or permanent pauperization prompted a change of attitude with respect to beggars. The change that took place in the doctrine of poverty during the thirteenth century was an expression of precisely the sort of situation that caused a spread of repressive and exclusionary attitudes toward beggars.

Mechanisms for degradation were inherent in the beggars' condition, however. In the last analysis, begging was an occupation that relied on techniques for arousing people's pity. Not only did beggars display their real physical defects; they used subterfuge to simulate infirmity or illness. Tales from Arabian literature of the early Middle Ages paint a picture much like the one presented in fifteenth-century France in the *balades* of Eustache Deschamps, in the Italian *Speculum cerretanorum,* and the German *Liber vagatorum.* The stabilization of beggars affected only a part of this world, and in reality wandering brought better earnings. Trades and professions could mix in an errant life and the vagabond could work, beg, or rob. Confusion in occupations meant marginalization in the Middle Ages.

Groups that remained outside organized society for sociocultural reasons also deserve a place in our panorama of marginality. It is difficult, however, to distinguish cultural from other criteria in the processes of marginalization, although a cultural element was clearly at work in "dishonorable" trades and in the marginalization of lepers. For this reason, I shall use the notion *sensu largo* to include religious and ideological factors. It was the heretics and the infidels—that is, people of a different faith and pagans—who were excluded from the Christian community, hence from the fundamental structures of medieval Europe. The simple fact of not accepting the truths of Christian orthodoxy was sufficient reason for a sense of difference and for exclusion. Other elements contributed to the stereotyped judgments concerning such groups to emphasize their difference: the Saracens of the *Chanson de Roland* were reproached for failing to fulfill their obligations as vassals; the records of the Inquisition and polemical writings charged heretics with deviance from established sexual norms and refusal of authority and social obligations; the Jews were accused of plotting to exterminate Christians, of spreading epidemics, and of practicing usury. Since they had no part in the dominant religion and the dominant culture, these groups were considered a danger to the very bases of social order. Furthermore, more than any other marginal group, they were conscious of their own difference.

I have used various criteria in this description of marginality in an attempt to throw light on the determinant social and cultural processes of separating individuals and groups from society. I have also spoken of phenomena of voluntary marginality resulting from a radical rejection of the dominant system, from a search for internal spiritual perfection, or even from a combination of the two. It is clear that we need to reach beyond these specific social processes to discern sociopsychological processes. For the marginal, these would be an awareness of the differentness of their situation; for society, they would be an internalization of collective norms and of the principles governing the social status quo, realized through condemnation of those who failed to conform to those norms. On the one hand, then, people were to some extent conscious of their own individual destiny, though this was less true of groups; on the other hand, there was the sense of community precisely in relation to those who were different.

Social condition was fixed in medieval culture, and this was one aspect of the semiotic nature of this culture. This was true for the marginal as well. Certain categories stood out clearly: difference in skin color or language set apart ethnic minorities; a certain type of work could function just like external signs of disease or an obvious infirmity. Dress was the most frequent form of "distinction." Vagabonds and felons did not dress substantially differently from others from the lower social strata, but we can suppose that they were defined by the rags they wore and the staff in their hand—the classic image in prints from later centuries. A missing ear denoted a thief. For beggars, rags over a naked body—effective in eliciting alms—were obvious signs of social condition. Jews could be recognized by their dress: in German regions they wore a characteristic pointed hat, but the Fourth Lateran Council of 1215 also introduced the wearing of a distinguishing sign, a practice that became common throughout Christendom and stamped the Jews with infamy. In many countries prostitutes had to conform to strict norms regarding their dress, and they too were often obliged to wear a distinguishing sign. As for heretics, one mark of their penitence might be a cross on their clothing, front and back, and heretics were often sentenced to exposure in public wearing or bearing some defamatory sign such as a mitre, a letter H, and so forth.

These objective signs of marginal condition were thus instruments of infamy, exclusion, or repression more often than they were natural symptoms. We know nothing (or next to nothing) about marginal people's consciousness of their own situation. We can occasionally make an inference about it thanks to some personal note in reported testimony, and occasionally through literary discussion, as in the work of the goliards, Rutebeuf, or Villon.

The infamy of marginal groups was not only exploited instrumentally but actualized in the life of society. Jews were obligated to participate in royal entries in ways that degraded them and, according to later testimony (in Kraków such matters were recorded in the seventeenth century), the tradition continued in a repressive and segregationist manner in Corpus Christi processions. One analysis of collective acts of humiliation and degradation encountered in the context of armed conflicts between Italian cities in the fourteenth century reveals that races between prostitutes or lackeys (*ribaldi, barattieri*) were major aggressive events. Festive contests in which "ignoble" people took part were held in Périgueux as early as 1273; they developed into such institutions as the *palio* of the cities of Italy, which surely go back to the early fourteenth century. Vagabonds and men and women of the underclasses took part in foot races and horse or mule races. Their marginality, which was based on their social condition, had a function, since it reinforced the honor of the community organizing the exhibition and served to humiliate the community that the city considered its enemy.

Naturally, there were essential and, on occasion, capital differences between the various categories that made up the marginal world in the Middle Ages. There were gradations of exclusion and segregation, and demotion in class did not mean the same thing for the knight and for the peasant. Nor did social marginalization always involve exclusion and segregation. Boundaries were rarely as rigid as they were in the case of lepers. All of these categories of persons, however, were characterized by the difference of their way of life, by their not being subjected to established norms and life models, and by their refusal to work or to play the social role assigned to them. The marginal were also united in the aversion, sense of alienation, fear, and, on occasion, hatred, that society displayed toward them.

BIBLIOGRAPHY

Exclus et systèmes d'exclusion dans la littérature et la civilisation médiévales. Actes du colloque organisé par le C.U.E.R.M.A. à Aix-en-Provence, les 4-5-6 mars 1977. Sénéfiance, 5. Aix-en-Provence: Editions CUERMA; distrib. Paris: H. Champion 1978.

Les Marginaux et les exclus dans l'histoire. Cahiers Jussieu, 5. Paris: Union générale d'Editions, 1979.

Allard, Guy H., ed. *Aspects de la marginalié au Moyen Age.* Montreal: L'Aurore; distr. Quebec: La Maison de diffusion, 1975.

Dosio, Giorgetta Bonfiglio. "Criminalità e emarginazione a Brescia nel primo Quattrocento." *Archivio Storico Italiano*, 1978: 113–64.

Geremek, Bronislaw. *Les marginaux parisiens aux XIVe et XVe siècles*. Trans. Daniel Beauvois. Paris: Flammarion, 1976 [*The Margins of Society in Late Medieval Paris*, Trans. Jean Birrell. New York: Cambridge University Press, 1987].

Guglielmi, Nilda. *Marginalidad en la Edad Media*. Buenos Aires: Editorial Universitaria de Buenos Aires, 1986.

Hanawalt, Barbara A. *Crime and Conflict in English Communities, 1300–1348*. Cambridge: Harvard University Press, 1979.

Hartung, Wolfgang. *Die Spielleute eine Randgruppe in der Gesellschaft des Mittelalters*. Wiesbaden: Steiner, 1982.

Jusserand, Jean J. *English Wayfaring Life in the Middle Ages (XIVth Century)*. Trans. Lucy Toulmin Smith. Rev. ed. London: Methuen; New York: Barnes and Noble, 1961.

Ladner, Gerhart B. "Homo Viator: Medieval Ideas on Alienation and Order." *Speculum* 42, 2 (1967): 233–59.

Le Goff, Jacques. "Licit and Illicit Trades in the Medieval West." *Time, Work, and Culture in the Middle Ages*. Trans. Arthur Goldhammer. Chicago: University of Chicago Press, 1980.

Mollat, Michel. *The Poor in the Middle Ages*. Trans. Arthur Goldhammer. New Haven: Yale University Press, 1986.

Pinto, Giuliana. "Un vagabondo, ladro e truffatore nella Toscana della seconda metà del '300." *Ricerche Storiche* 2(1974): 327–45.

Trexler, Richard C. "Correre la terra. Collective Insults in the Late Middle Ages." *Mélanges de l'Ecole Française de Rome, Moyen Age, Temps Modernes* 96(1984): 845–902.

SUGGESTED READINGS

John Boswell, *Christianity, Social Tolerance, and Homosexuality* (Chicago: University of Chicago Press, 1980).

———, *The Kindness of Strangers: The Abandonment of Children in Western Europe from Late Antiquity to the Renaissance* (New York: Pantheon, 1988).

Robert Chazan, *Daggers of Faith: Thirteenth-Century Christian Missionizing and the Jewish Response* (Berkeley: University of California Press, 1989).

Jeremy Cohen, *The Friars and the Jews: The Evolution of Medieval Anti-Judaism* (Ithaca: Cornell University Press, 1982).

Norman Cohn, *The Pursuit of the Millennium.* Rev. ed. (New York: Oxford University Press, 1970).

R. H. Hilton, *Bond Men Made Free: Medieval Peasant Movements and the English Rising of 1381* (New York: Viking Press, 1973).

R. H. Hilton and T. H. Aston, eds., *The English Rising of 1381* (Cambridge: Cambridge University Press, 1984).

Malcolm Lambert, *Medieval Heresy: Popular Movements from Bogomil to Hus* (New York: Holmes and Meier, 1976).

Jacob Marcus, *The Jew in the Medieval World* (New York: Athenaeum, 1972).

Michel Mollat and Philippe Wolff, *The Popular Revolutions of the Late Middle Ages* (London: Allen & Unwin, 1973).

R. I. Moore, *The Formation of a Persecuting Society: Power and Deviance in Western Europe* (Oxford: Blackwell, 1987).

Guido Ruggiero, *Violence in Early Renaissance Venice* (New Brunswick, N.J.: Rutgers University Press, 1980).

Brian Tierney, *Medieval Poor Law: A Sketch of Canonical Theory and Its Application in England* (Berkeley: University of California Press, 1959).

Index